MW00718183

MARCHING INTO DARKNESS

MARCHING INTO DARKNESS

The Wehrmacht and the Holocaust in Belarus

WAITMAN WADE BEORN

Harvard University Press

Cambridge, Massachusetts · London, England

2014

Library of Congress Cataloging-in-Publication Data

Beorn, Waitman Wade, 1977–
Marching into darkness : the Wehrmacht and the Holocaust in Belarus / Waitman
Wade Beorn.
pages   cm
Includes bibliographical references and index.
ISBN 978-0-674-72550-8
1. Jews—Belarus—History—20th century.   2. Holocaust, Jewish
(1939–1945)—Belarus—History.   3. World War, 1939–1945—Atrocities—Belarus.
4. Germany—Armed Forces—History—World War, 1939–1945.
5. Belarus—Social Conditions—20th century.   6. Belarus—History—
German occupation, 1941–1944.   I. Title.
DS135.B38B46 2014
940.53'1809478—dc23   2013014774

Contents

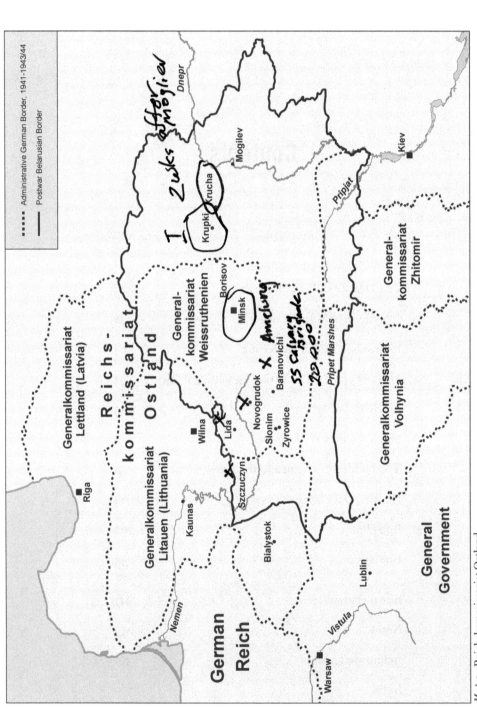

Map 1. Reichskommissariat Ostland

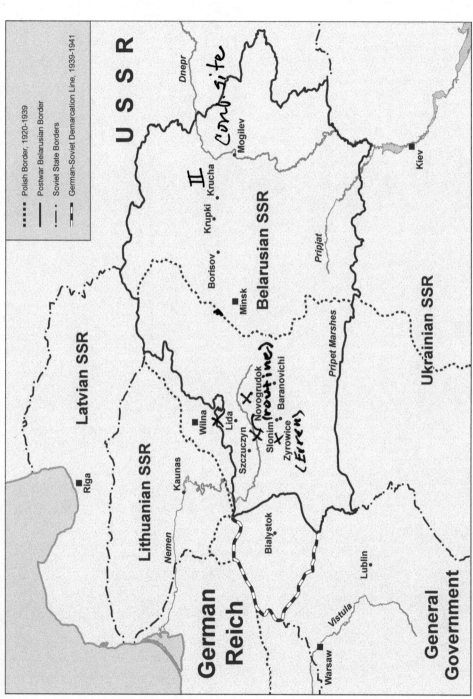

Map 2. Belarusian Soviet Socialist Republic

Introduction

O N A BITTERLY COLD MORNING in November 1941, Lisa and Pola Nussbaum were brought by their mother to the barbed-wire fence surrounding the Slonim ghetto in western Belarus. She told them to squeeze through and hide with a neighbor. Lisa and Pola were just fourteen and nineteen years old, yet they had already escaped death at the hands of the Germans several times. Born in a small Polish town on the German border, the two girls had fled with their family progressively farther east before being trapped in Slonim by the German advance in 1941.[1] Rumors had flown in the ghetto of an impending massacre. Unable to acquire a work permit that might spare her children, Lisa and Pola's mother made the heart-wrenching decision to send her girls away.

Once through the fence, Lisa and Pola took off their yellow Star of David and ran to the house of a Christian neighbor. Upon hearing that the Nazis were preparing a mass shooting, the neighbor forced the girls to leave. Refused refuge in the town, the two girls fled into the harsh Belarusian winter and hid in the nearby woods. In the dark pine forest, they stumbled across the meadow where the Jews of Slonim were being murdered. There, around ten thousand Jewish men, women, and children were forced to sit in groups, guarded by German soldiers. In groups

1

of ten, stripped of their valuables and clothing, they were then shot into three pits. Some tried to fight or run, but few survived the killing.

The girls saw this and fled "from the blood and the screams and the shrieks to the opposite part of the forest to hide." A Polish forest ranger tried to stop them, but they deceived him, saying that they were simply gathering wood for the winter. After having seen the killing site for himself, however, the ranger returned and angrily identified them as escaped Jews. He dragged them back to the road where most of the Slonim Jews were slowly marching to the murder pits and ordered the two girls to get in line. German soldiers were guarding those Jews who could walk, and military trucks carried the elderly and the infirm. But the two girls now knew what lay ahead. Pola grabbed her sister's hand, screamed for them to run, and the two sisters sprinted away from the column across an open field. The surprised ranger threw his ax, wounding Pola in the leg, but the two managed to escape.

Surprisingly, the German soldiers escorting the Jews did not fire at the escapees. The girls ran back to Slonim, where they had to flee from little children who screamed "Jewesses, Jewesses, you took off your yellow stars! The Nazis will kill you! The Nazis will kill you!" The two girls could not find anyone in Slonim who would shelter them. Lisa and her sister finally collapsed from exhaustion in a nearby barn. The barn belonged to a local Christian woman, who discovered them and told the frightened children, "You do not have to tell me where you are coming from. I know. God has brought you to the right house." She fed them, bandaged Pola's wounds, and hid the girls in her sofa as the killing continued.[2]

The next morning a different journey began, this time *toward* the killing site in the Czepilov Forest. German army private Anton N. marched out of Slonim with his squad.[3] These men were tasked with filling in the grave where between eight and ten thousand Jews had been killed the day before. As they marched through a small wood, the squad came upon several Jews who had been wounded during the execution but had escaped. One of them had been shot through the jaw. All were returned to the mass grave and shot by these German soldiers. At the killing site, it was apparent that other Jews had also managed to crawl out of the trenches. As a result, Private N.'s squad leader, Sergeant Martin W., decided to lead the men on a search of nearby communities for escaped Jews.

(Twenty years later, Anton N. found himself sitting in the local police office of the village of Sandebeck deep in the ancient German Teutoberg Forest. He described the results of that patrol to a police detective. "We picked up a man, a woman, and a twelve-year-old boy," he said. "We took them all back to the grave. There, these three were also shot." Of course, Anton claimed that no one from his group actually did the shooting; this was taken care of by a volunteer firing squad. As he and his fellow soldiers shoveled dirt on the mass grave, "it still moved because those Jews who were wounded had not received a killing shot."[4])

The day after the massacre, Lisa and Pola left their hiding place, fearing they had endangered their rescuer. With nowhere else to go, they returned to the ghetto, where they discovered that their mother and aunt had been murdered in the Czepilov Forest with the thousands of others. Lisa's father, Hirsh, and little brother, Busiek, had survived. Lisa and Pola survived in the small ghetto, located on an island in the Szcara River, until the next major massacre, in June 1942. Once again, the girls tried to flee, but Pola was shot to death while attempting to slip under the ghetto fence. Lisa and her future husband, Aron Derman, managed to escape with the assistance of a German army officer. They joined the partisans in the forest.

Unlike millions of others, Lisa, Hirsh, and Busiek survived the Holocaust in the Soviet Union. Lisa moved to the United States, married Derman, and dedicated her life to bearing witness to the Holocaust. She became the president of the Holocaust Memorial Foundation in Skokie, Illinois, and frequently traveled to tell her story of personal loss and survival. On 28 July 2002, at seventy-five years of age, Lisa was giving her testimony at the Illinois Storytelling Festival when she died. In her last words, she urged the audience members to bear witness to her story, saying, "Please remember this story and tell it to others, because I don't know how long I will be here." Then, as the newspaper reported, "she paused, and her chin dropped slowly to her chest."[5]

This book takes up Lisa's story and the story of the tens of thousands of Jews who, like her mother, aunt, and sister Pola, were murdered by the

Germans in Belarus in 1941–1942. Lisa's story is not singular. Similar acts of murder in the Holocaust were repeated again and again across Nazi-occupied Soviet territory between 1941 and 1944. All told, at least 1.5 million Jews were murdered in what Father Patrick Desbois has termed the "Holocaust by Bullets." A figure this large is almost impossible to imagine, the magnitude of the loss difficult to comprehend. Perhaps it is better to begin by considering one person, one family member, one child murdered 1.5 million times in large cities, small towns, and forests across German-occupied Soviet territory.

While the Einsatzgruppen—the Nazis' mobile killing squads specifically tasked with the murder of Jews and others in the East—may have been officially ordered to murder Jews, the German army made itself, in many places, deeply complicit in the Holocaust. Often, historical discussions of the Wehrmacht's role in the Nazi genocidal project have remained vague, subverting very tangible crimes under the bland label of "complicity." In this study, I consider "complicity" to be embodied both by the knowing furtherance of the Nazi genocidal project and/or by an attempt to personally benefit from it. I define the term "Nazi genocidal project" as a much larger Nazi nexus of racial and demographic decimation, extermination, and resettlement, while I understand the Holocaust to be largely the murder of Jews by the regime. This genocide was a central element in the racial and demographic reorganization of Europe, particularly in the East; the magnitude of this suffering and loss should not be seen to be minimized by its inclusion in broader Nazi policy. I will, therefore, attempt to be as clear as possible in delineating the Wehrmacht's role in the Holocaust (the murder of the Jews of Europe) as well as in the Nazi genocidal project (the murder of Soviet POWs, killings of civilian noncombatants, participation in starvation policy, etc.).

Any ill-defined notion of complicity becomes painfully concrete when we look at exactly what that term meant at the local level. German soldiers rounded up Jews, guarded them, marched them to killing sites, and, in some cases, pulled the triggers themselves. They appropriated Jewish property, sometimes sending it home to their own families. Some soldiers engaged in forced sexual relationships with Jews. Yet others evaded participation in such activities and, in a very few cases, actively sought to aid or rescue Jews. Without the aid of the Wehrmacht, the murder of Jews like Lisa's family would have been much more difficult. This is what complicity—and, rarely, its refusal—actually looked like, and it is this multiplicity of experiences that forms the subject of this book.

What did Wehrmacht complicity really look like at ground level? In what ways did units and individual soldiers actually take part in Nazi genocidal policies? How did this participation change over time and with increased familiarity with killing? Why did some soldiers choose to participate (or not to participate) in the ways that they did? In addition, how and why did the Wehrmacht become so involved in the murder of civilians in general and Jews in particular? These are the central questions that remain unanswered, particularly at the local level. By focusing in detail on a series of cases, all of which occurred in the territory of present-day Belarus (then the Soviet Union) in the autumn and winter of 1941–42, this work seeks to provide a more cohesive narrative and analysis of the Wehrmacht's *progressive* complicity over time.

Far from being an aberration, brutal occupation policies on the eastern front revealed the true nature of the Nazi genocidal project. As official plans for the East reflected the truly horrific scale of violence intended by Nazi ideology, it is not surprising that the Wehrmacht was expected to play its part. Despite the popular belief in a "clean Wehrmacht," the frequency and depth to which the army played this role cut to the heart of German identity in connection to the Holocaust; after all, the majority of German rank-and-file soldiers were truly ordinary Germans. Therefore, any accusations of complicity by the Wehrmacht in this area cut deeply and carry much larger implications for the nature of rank-and-file involvement in the Nazi genocidal project. Scholars of the Holocaust have demonstrated that a multitude of organizations, including the German army, played a role in the crimes of the Nazis. They have unearthed agreements and described common aims and mind-sets among the leaders. However, few have been able to present the end result of these more general acceptances of Nazi policy by the army. One scholar lamented that "one seeks in vain a history of the mentality of the Wehrmacht."[6]

In this study, I attempt to explain how German soldiers went from awkward forays into killing to grave robbing to sadistic "Jew games" in

Improvisation → clarification/exhort/execution
routine → internalization

Mogilev = anti-partisan conf

less than six months. I present the development of Wehrmacht complicity through four stages: improvisation; clarification-exhortation-execution; routinization; and internalization. Through five roughly chronological cases throughout Belarus, I trace the evolution of Wehrmacht participation in the Nazi genocidal project. I begin in September 1941, when the 354th Infantry Regiment directly aided in the murder of one thousand Jews in the town of Krupki, near Minsk. The improvised (but effective) manner in which this unit assisted Einsatzkommando 8 characterizes the initial stage of Wehrmacht complicity.[7] Next, I examine a little-studied but critically important anti-partisan conference that took place a week later, at the end of September, in Mogilev—a conference that explicitly connected the murder of Jews with day-to-day operations against partisans. In this chapter, I examine the overt identification of Jews as targets, the incitement to kill Jews in the course of normal operations, and the ensuing execution of these policies, seeking to explain how the German army became more deeply involved in the Holocaust. I show how a Jew-Bolshevik-partisan construct was intentionally used to bring the manpower of the Wehrmacht to bear against Jews in smaller areas that posed logistical problems for the Einsatzgruppen. A direct result of the Mogilev Conference, which articulated this calculus, was the murder of over a hundred Jews in the village of Krucha by the 3rd Company, 691st Infantry Regiment, on October 10. The army carried out this action completely on its own. Yet, given the same order at the same time in the same location, three Wehrmacht units, including the 3rd Company, responded in three distinctly different ways to the requirement to participate in genocide. I also examine the individual and collective decisions that led to the companies' divergent decisions to participate in or refuse to perpetrate the murder of Jews. We then travel to the towns of Slonim and Novogrudok, where, in November and December 1941, two companies of the 727th Infantry Regiment assisted civilian authorities with the ghettoization, expropriation, and murder of ten thousand and five thousand Jews, respectively. These companies exhibit the routinization of complicity within the framework of established relationships with the SS and civil authorities. Finally, the case of the 12th Company in Szczuczyn symbolizes the last stage in this process: internalization of official guidance to murder Jews. While not apparently involved in any "large" massacres, this unit continually murdered Jews in small groups in the course of regular patrols and specialized "Jew hunts," in which its members reported the dead as "partisans," thus demonstrating the continuing influence of the anti-partisan war as subterfuge for genocide. This unit's behavior, then, represents one end result of long-term participation in genocidal policy.

Three important arguments explaining the depth and manner of Wehrmacht involvement in the Holocaust run throughout this book. First, unit cultures and leadership played a vital role in influencing both participation and nonparticipation of German soldiers and units. Units led by particularly brutal men became particularly brutal. At almost every level, army organizational climates in the East encouraged extremism, condoned criminality, and rewarded those who were most radical in their thoughts and actions. In this environment, where all individuals retained some ability to choose, choices leading to ever-deeper involvement in the Nazi genocidal project were privileged and often praised.

Second, almost from the beginning, a Jew-Bolshevik-partisan calculus was used to justify participation within the Wehrmacht in the murder of the Jews. This calculus relied on a greatly exaggerated partisan threat. Nazi authorities deliberately leveraged the manpower and increased territorial reach of the army to alleviate difficulties being encountered by the dedicated killing units in the East such as the Einsatzgruppen. Jews were intentionally conflated with a partisan movement that was largely illusory, and this "connection" was then used to explicitly justify the involvement of the German army in the murder of Soviet Jews. This is not to say that most soldiers truly believed this construction. Rather, the Jew-Bolshevik-partisan calculus provided a convenient cover story, an ideological fig leaf, and a potential psychological shield to obfuscate and obscure increasingly brutal violence. The Wehrmacht integrated this Jew-Bolshevik-partisan calculus well and quickly: in less than a year, German army units were killing Jews independently and reporting the victims as dead partisans.

Lastly, I argue that extended contact with the Nazi genocidal project led to increased and deeper participation in the Holocaust. Not all German army units were placed in a position to become involved in genocide, but a great many of them were predisposed or conditioned to participate, under the right conditions. The specifics of soldiers' behavior on the ground and relationships with Jews and with German civil authorities demonstrate that soldiers typically became *more* complicit over time. Over time, this complicity became more complex and challenges conventional wisdom about the degree to which "ordinary soldiers" took part in Nazi crimes. Increasing involvement of the Wehrmacht in genocide took a variety of forms, from plunder of property to sexual exploitation to escalating brutality. For a small number of soldiers, deepening entanglement in the Nazi genocidal project also revealed opportunities to help or rescue Jews they encountered. As the creator of the groundbreaking 1999 exhibit on the crimes of the Wehrmacht put it, "War is not a machine; it is, instead, a space in which individuals make decisions."[8] This book explores the complexity of the individual decisions made by ordinary Wehrmacht soldiers in the war in the East, decisions that, collectively, resulted in the murder of one and a half million Jewish men, women, and children in this space.

The local context surrounding these events in Belarus played an important role in the nature of Wehrmacht complicity there. Since Belarus had relatively fewer local collaborators for the Nazi regime to rely on, owing to its less well-developed nationalist movement (as compared to the Baltic states and the Ukraine), German forces were often required to take a more leading role in executing Nazi genocidal policy.[9] The relative weakness of organized local participation also heightened the necessity for cooperation between civil, SS, and Wehrmacht groups in carrying out mass murder. In addition, the large numbers of Jews living in this region made the "Final Solution" there of particular significance. Lastly, a nascent Soviet partisan movement in Belarus fed German perceptions of a partisan threat (even if of questionable reality), adding an additional factor in the calculus of Wehrmacht complicity. Indeed, the obsession of the Wehrmacht with the anti-partisan war was in many ways a self-fulfilling prophecy: it not only drove Jews to flee to the forest and to the partisans but also fueled the very excesses that led non-Jewish locals to support the partisans in the first place.

The timing of the killings discussed here in the autumn and winter of 1941–42 is also helpful in focusing this investigation on a period *before* the war in the East became a death spiral for the Wehrmacht. The general tenor of the opening campaigns in the East for the Germans was one of rapid advances and stunning victories. This continued relatively unabated until November, when the Red Army stopped the Germans at the gates of Moscow and the offensive ground to stalemate. With the most brutal and savage fighting yet to come, explanations based upon a "barbarization" of warfare leading to increasing violence by German forces can be at least somewhat discounted. Likewise, the partisan movement in Belarus did not become a real military threat until at least mid-1942. Thus, while this imagined threat played an important role in the mentality of the Wehrmacht and its willingness to engage in atrocities, arguments suggesting genocidal violence as a reaction to a difficult guerrilla war can be set aside for this period. Finally, the participation in the Holocaust of many of the units in this study ends during the military emergencies of 1941–1942, when these units were decimated in conventional combat on the front lines.

Naturally, in an organization such as the Wehrmacht, whose numbers reached over seventeen million, the search for the "holy grail" of historical representativeness can be frustrating. Germans served in different types of units in different locations at different times. Several cases obviously cannot speak for all soldiers in all places. Thus, I will endeavor to explain how these units came to be involved in the ways that they did and how these selected case studies may illuminate the larger phenomenon of Wehrmacht atrocities in other areas. In many cases, this speaks to the *potential* for atrocities by the German army as a whole, given certain situations.

Rather than focusing on generals, divisions, or strategic policy decisions, I will attempt to reconstruct the daily lives and decisions of Wehrmacht units complicit in mass killing. My focus on the lowest levels of the German army is one that has so far been neglected. In order to explain this neglect, I must first briefly explore the myth of the "clean Wehrmacht," which stubbornly asserts that the Wehrmacht participated honorably and apolitically in the Second World War. It is a myth that has already been undermined and pronounced dead—by historians at least, but not the larger public. In many ways, this myopic, popular characterization of the behavior of German soldiers has obstructed an honest portrayal of their role in the larger Nazi genocidal project. Nothing demonstrates the continuing salience of this subject better than the German reaction to the Wehrmacht exhibition in the 1990s.

At 4:40 a.m. on 9 March 1999, a bomb exploded outside an adult training center in Saarbrücken, Germany. While causing extensive damage to the building and shattering the windows in a nearby church, the bomb did little harm to its intended target: an exhibition depicting the participation of the Wehrmacht in the crimes of the Nazis.[10] Yet the anger, shock, and public interest in the traveling exhibit funded by German tobacco magnate and philanthropist Jan Reemstma and organized by the Hamburg Institute for Social Research demonstrated the powerful position that military collaboration in the Holocaust still held (and holds) in the German psyche.

The eruption of public outcry manifested itself in protests and violence from both sides of the political spectrum. A demonstrator from the far-right-wing National Democratic Party (NPD) carried a sign reading, "If all soldiers were criminals and murderers, then I am one of the latter. I do not feel guilty. It was not a humane war."[11] Another visitor represented the opposing view, saying, "The 'innocent Wehrmacht' was always nonsense. . . . People say 'We didn't know.' But there are hundreds of thousands of letters home. There is a lot of self-protection among older people."[12] A conservative historian wrote a volume in response called *Crimes against the Wehrmacht,* in which he documented atrocities committed against German forces by the Red Army, implying that the exhibition suffered from a misplaced emphasis, as if such crimes could efface those of the Wehrmacht.[13] In the four years after it opened, the exhibit traveled to thirty-three Austrian and German cities and hosted over eight hundred thousand visitors.[14] If it highlighted the highly emotionally charged nature of the subject, the exhibition also demonstrated but did not master its historical complexity. In 1999, three historians contested the attribution of several photographs (out of thousands), arguing that they did not depict Wehrmacht complicity; indeed, one *exhibit — 1999 —*

photo mistakenly labeled a local collaborator in the act of killing as a German soldier. This protest led to a suspension of the exhibition as a panel of historians painstakingly examined every photo. The exhibit reopened in 2001, with far fewer photographs, leading to accusations that it was presenting "consensus history" and had "banished the emotions to the footnotes."[15] On balance, the Wehrmacht exhibition raised critical questions that were necessary for German society to ask itself, but had provided no answers. The public presentation generated searing heat but shed little light on the larger issue of the Wehrmacht and the Holocaust.

While the exhibition was successful in raising public awareness, challenging conventional beliefs, and provoking violent emotional responses and debates, its overall historical value was debatable. Questions of representativeness and of internal motivation, of mentality, remained unanswered. In many ways, the format of the first exhibition precluded a methodologically rigorous approach to such questions, for it entailed, by necessity, the "cherry-picking" of particularly egregious or emotive examples of complicity. The exhibit further challenged the academic community through its use of sources. The several errors of attribution regarding photographs, as well as the inclusion of diaries and letters, spawned important questions about what documents should or could be relied on by historians and what these sources are and are not able to tell them. In the end, the *Wehrmacht* exhibition brought the crimes of the German army into public view and caused strong emotional reactions, but its "sound and fury" left many, if not most, of the questions regarding the complicity of the *Wehrmacht* unanswered.[16] Chief among these was the level of participation in—indeed even knowledge of—the Holocaust among German soldiers and how this unfolded over time.

The history of the German army and its relationship with the Nazi regime has followed a somewhat tortuous path since the end of World War II. For much of this period, discussions of the army and the Holocaust evolved in the separate though occasionally convergent spheres of public and academic discourse. For many if not most Germans, individually and collectively, any involvement by the Wehrmacht in the crimes of the Third Reich remained a taboo subject. The massive numbers of

Germans who served in the Wehrmacht at some point between 1939 and 1945 dwarfed those who served in the SS, the only military organization to be officially condemned as criminal at the Nuremberg Trials. Because most Germans knew relatives or close friends who had served or died in the military, there was understandably great reluctance to consider or accept their potential participation in atrocities. The Nuremberg Tribunals did prosecute several high-ranking Wehrmacht officers in a legal proceeding that "turned into a battleground for competing narratives about the conduct and character of the Wehrmacht during the war."[17] Very quickly this personal discomfort about the character of the army, among other things, led to what has become known as the *Mythos der sauberen Wehrmacht* (myth of the clean Wehrmacht). The defendants themselves laid the foundations for this myth, alternating between feigning ignorance and claiming a relativist justification: "the battle in the East had its own character," and "war in Russia had its own methods."[18] According to the "clean Wehrmacht" myth, the German army fought a purely conventional war against the Red Army to protect the homeland. The genocidal crimes and excesses of the Third Reich, while regrettable, were committed by the SS and police apparatuses. The army, if it knew of such atrocities, was deeply disturbed but unable to intervene. The very real violence carried out by the Red Army when it conquered Germany, most notably the systematic mass rapes of German women, further validated the sacrifice and service of veterans by demonstrating the evil that they were combating. While these premises were all historically inaccurate, they were quite effective in insulating the military from sweeping accusations of criminality.

The political exigencies of the immediate postwar era also worked to place any discussion, let alone prosecution, of Wehrmacht crimes often beyond reach. As the Cold War became hotter, America increasingly focused on Germany as a bulwark against the Soviets rather than as the land of the Nazis. One of the effects of this was that "between 1945 and 1953, Allied policy shifted rapidly from enforcing the idea of collective German guilt to differentiation between Germans, then, somewhat more gradually, to appeasement of German indignation at the earlier punishment of war criminals."[19] None other than General of the Army Dwight Eisenhower, distancing himself from earlier more critical comments, declared in 1951 that "the German soldier fought bravely and honorably for his country."[20] One can see this change in sentiments at ground level in the participation of American soldiers in events commemorating German World War II military dead; indeed, the U.S. Army funded the construction of memorials to their erstwhile foes in the 1950s.[21] Thus, the United States "now found itself in two irreconcilable roles: occupier and executor of occupation justice and Germany's would-be ally and 'friend.'"[22] It would choose the latter.

This position served both the larger Cold War need for *Bundeswehr* recruitment and the German public's need to minimize the possible guilt of a large part of the male population. Indeed, in 1953, when asked if they thought "German soldiers could be reproached for their actions in the occupied countries," 55 percent of Germans said no, 21 percent said "in some cases," and only 6 percent answered with an unequivocal yes.[23]

Political expediency in the public sphere merged with a German tendency to focus on the effects of Allied bombing, the experience of POWs and expellees, and the crimes of the Soviet army, rather than addressing issues of complicity during the Third Reich. The POW and refugee issues further served to highlight the role played by the *Wehrmacht* in "saving" Germany from even worse Soviet depredations. This had the secondary effect of both minimizing any recognition of participation by the army in the Holocaust while simultaneously allowing the German people to view themselves as the real victims of the war.[24]

The first published works on the German army after the war were similarly myopic. That should come as no surprise, for the generals themselves often wrote these books. They were sterile, largely self-serving military histories, full of dates, locations, and tactical decisions, but eschewing any mention of the darker side of the Nazi regime and any participation of the army in it.[25] The United States was particularly thankful for these memoirs, given its new interest in defeating the Soviet military. Former generals were brought to the United States to coach American military men on tactics used against the Red Army, in preparation for a future World War III in Europe. The U.S. Army in particular demonstrated (and at times still demonstrates) a peculiar kind of Wehrmacht envy, idolizing German tactical prowess while ignoring the morally bankrupt nature of the organization. Indeed, American public fascination with the Wehrmacht persists to this day, as evidenced in popular culture and the appeal of reenacting World War II from the German side.[26] Even renowned historians were not immune from seeing little complicity between the German army and the Nazis.[27]

However, beginning in the 1960s, a newer generation of scholars began exploring the Holocaust itself more deeply. They started by uncovering the structure of the Nazi state, including the high level of cooperation between the military leadership and regime.[28] This group first discussed, for example, the role of discipline in following orders, the so-called Commissar Order (for the murder of Soviet political officers), and the intentional murder of Soviet prisoners of war.[29] The 1960s also witnessed the spectacle of the Adolf Eichmann trial in Jerusalem and the Auschwitz trial in Frankfurt, which again focused public attention on the Holocaust and its perpetrators. However, both the Eichmann trial and larger German trials focused almost entirely on SS perpetrators and omitted the complicity of Wehrmacht personnel.

Later scholars began building upon the foundations laid for them by historians like Raul Hilberg, exploring the Holocaust in more detail. This new focus on better understanding the events of 1933–1945 also influenced the study of the Wehrmacht as scholars sought to place its behavior in the larger context of the Nazi system. One of the more insightful of these works was the research of Israeli historian Omer Bartov. Focusing directly on the German army on the eastern front, Bartov first recognized and then sought to explain its abnormal brutality.[30] His scholarship laid the groundwork for all others examining the German army and the Holocaust.

In the late 1970s, a hotly contested argument over the very nature of Nazi crimes known as the *Historikerstreit* (historians' debate) shook the historical profession. At the center of the debate was the question of whether the experience of Nazi Germany could be "normalized." Conservative historians sought to relativize Nazi crimes in comparison to those of Stalin and move away from a focus on the Holocaust. Other historians saw in this agenda an attempt to gloss over the past and to revive a new German nationalism. This debate took place at a time when similar issues of nationalism and the role of the military were being raised again in the public sphere. Academic study and public awareness of the Holocaust itself had briefly merged during the famous trials of the early 1960s. They crossed paths again with the debut of the American TV miniseries *Holocaust* in Germany in 1979, which brought the role of ordinary Germans in the crimes of the Nazis into virtually every living room. While the television event may have pushed the Holocaust again to public consciousness, the impetus for trials of Nazi war criminals in Germany was waning, as perhaps the outcome of the trial of Majdanek concentration camp personnel in 1981 indicates. Out of sixteen defendants, only eight were convicted. Their sentences, apart from one life imprisonment, averaged six and a half years in prison. Overseas, however, other nations began taking a greater interest in denaturalizing and prosecuting potential war criminals living within their borders.

Several trials of German war criminals in the SS and Wehrmacht, as well as local collaborators such as John Demjanjuk, have again reminded the public and historians alike that complicity in the Holocaust remains a critical and relevant issue today.[31] Most notable among these is the case of Josef Scheungraber, who, as a Wehrmacht lieutenant, ordered the deaths of at least eleven Italian civilians by locking them in a barn, which was then blown up. The killing was in revenge for a partisan attack upon his soldiers. He was sentenced to life in prison at the age of ninety.[32] Indeed, even as this book goes to press, German authorities are preparing charges against former guards at Auschwitz (reversing a tendency to focus only on higher-level criminals).[33] In Germany, the recent prosecution of these cases is a result, in part, of renewed interest by a younger generation of prosecutors, which is perhaps partially driven by the reaction to the Wehrmacht exhibition of the late 1990s. Yet even today, there is a divide in German households between public and private memory of the Nazi period, as sociologist Harald Welzer demonstrates. While most recognize and condemn the crimes of the Third Reich and may even admit that the Wehrmacht participated, they do not accept that *their* family members could have been involved. Often, within families, stories of the war privilege acts of resistance and disagreement with the regime, rather than admissions of guilt.[34]

The Wehrmacht can hardly claim to have been "clean," not only in the occupied Soviet Union, but also throughout Europe, where many of its crimes have been documented. However, historians are continuing to bring to light new areas of responsibility and modes of complicity. Scholarly studies are also now beginning to focus on the army's actions from a regional perspective, particularly in the context of occupation policy in places like Greece, Serbia, Ukraine, and Belarus.[35] They have also looked at atrocities committed by the German military, including the murder of French black African troops in 1940 and killings carried out by the army during the invasion of Poland in 1939.[36] The latter are particularly significant for this study, as they display the army's proclivity for atrocities in the spirit of Nazi ideology over two years before the invasion of the Soviet Union. A few good low-level studies touch on the behavior of specific units in the East.[37] Others have attempted to address the complexity of the varied experiences of the eastern front through comparison. One of the most recent and useful works is Christian Hartmann's detailed comparison of five different divisions (two infantry, one panzer, one security, and one rear-area command).[38] It is an enormously informative work but, focusing at the division level and on units mainly engaged at the front, is often unable to explore in detail the internal dynamics of killing units.

In the end, the German army's involvement in murder devolved onto individual decisions of officers and soldiers on the ground. Excavating these decisions raises important and fundamental questions: Why did the German army participate to such an extent in Nazi racial policy? How willingly did these soldiers participate? What roles did ideology, the combat environment, leadership, and group dynamics play in the ways and extent of complicity?

The debate over these questions appears far from settled. Scholars have sought explanations for perpetrator behavior in general ever since the crimes of the Nazi state were uncovered. Approaches have varied from ideological to psychological to experiential, from identification of specific characteristics of German culture to connection with universal aspects of human nature. Some explanations are based on systems of belief and others on human conditioning. Those taking the former route have argued that, as a product of Nazi society, the Wehrmacht reflected the high level of racial and ideological indoctrination that the civilian population experienced as well. Perhaps the most influential of these historians is Bartov. His pathbreaking work *Hitler's Army* argued first that the Wehrmacht was Hitler's army, that it was highly indoctrinated and maintained a high level of belief in the Nazi system. Because many units were initially composed of men from the same region, Bartov highlighted the importance of a primary group of military comrades in creating social cohesion. He further contended that ideology replaced the powerful peer influence of primary groups when increasingly barbaric conditions destroyed these social connections early on in the war. He went on to explain that soldiers were allowed (and even encouraged) to commit atrocities as a way to release the tension created by the army's draconian system of discipline. Finally, he concluded that as the situation on the eastern front deteriorated, soldiers clung more and more desperately to the ideologies they were being fed, making them view the war in more and more extreme ways.[39] Bartov's work carefully and judiciously considered ideological issues to be of great importance.

Daniel Goldhagen, however, moved to the most extreme and most untenable end of this spectrum. Eschewing any short-term, situational factors, he argued that a special German "eliminationist" antisemitism was present. Shaped by centuries of German culture rather than years of Nazi indoctrination, soldiers, like all Germans, were eager to kill Jews and simply waiting for the opportunity to do so.[40] It is a position without nuance and one fanatically devoted to an ideological explanation, lacking both the context and the measured tone of Bartov and others.

Some scholars have employed a psychological approach to explain perpetrator behavior in general. One of the first to do so was Theodor Adorno, who attempted to explain inhuman behavior with his conception of the "authoritarian personality," a personality type particularly disposed to complicity in an authoritarian state, given the right conditions.[41] In 1944, U.S. Army sociologists Edward Shils and Morris Janowitz began conducting hundreds of interviews of captured German soldiers, and they focused on the "primary group" as the essential factor behind soldier motivation and combat effectiveness. The two sociologists concluded that "it appears that a soldier's ability to resist [that is, to fight] is a function of the capacity of his immediate primary group . . . to avoid social disintegration. . . . The capacity of the primary group to resist disintegration was dependent on the acceptance of political, ideological, and cultural symbols (all secondary symbols) only to the extent that these secondary symbols became directly associated with primary gratifications."[42] In short, they found that social ties among soldiers were more powerful influences on their behavior as a group than belief systems.

Social-psychological research has revealed that we are often deeply and powerfully influenced by group pressures to conform or live up to culturally constructed roles. Experiments by Stanley Milgram and Philip Zimbardo on deference to authority and role adaptation attempted to explain genocidal behavior in a different way.[43] These studies showed in their subjects a remarkable tendency to accept authority and a disturbing susceptibility to peer pressure. They also demonstrated that social groups and their accompanying peer pressures can develop quickly, with a decisively negative impact on behavior and one's ability to stand up to perceived wrongdoing. Zimbardo's disturbing "Stanford Prison Experiment" illustrated with shocking clarity that individuals quickly adapt to assigned roles, seeking to exhibit the skills and characteristics they believe define those roles. His experiment was so "successful" that it had to be stopped after six days as it became too violent and degrading to the participants. Zimbardo concluded that the social groups in which we find ourselves "define what is right, socially appropriate, or 'in,' and produce adherence to these ideas through such techniques as social rewards, threats of punishment or ostracism, and various other pressures toward conformity."[44]

Zimbardo and Milgram's findings are supported by the theory of cognitive dissonance, which holds that most individuals are distressed by discrepancies between their beliefs and action, and more often alleviate this stress by altering their beliefs. The Nazi policeman who justified his murder of children as a mercy killing because their parents had just been murdered is a powerful example of such behavior in action.[45] Harald Welzer, too, employed this approach in his discussion of a new Nazi "morality of killing."[46] In the end, all this research in social psychology indicates that human beings are profoundly influenced by the social pressures within groups and very often for the worst.

Not surprisingly, these findings also influenced how historians have approached Nazi killers. In his book *Ordinary Men,* Christopher Browning arrived at a conclusion much different from that of Bartov or Goldhagen as to why his reserve policemen participated in atrocities. Drawing on social-science research, Browning argued convincingly that social psychological factors within the context of group dynamics played a pivotal role in motivating middle-aged reserve policemen to commit atrocities and that, at least in these cases, ideology was not the primary motivating factor.[47] The men of Reserve Police Battalion 101 were neither specially indoctrinated troops nor men young enough to have been shaped by Nazi schooling and youth groups. They were middle-aged men, with families, who killed more often because of peer pressure and obligation to duty than out of malice. Finally, they hailed from the industrial, left-leaning city of Hamburg, which was not a hotbed of Nazi activism.

In his study of Reserve Police Battalion 45, Harald Welzer, too, argued for the salience of a social psychological approach. He wrote that "even when we examine ourselves, substantial discrepancies appear between our moral demands and actions; depending on the situation, we are capable of extremely different ways of thinking, acting and speaking."[48] Welzer contended that a new Nazi "morality" governed the behavior of these men. Thomas Kühne went a step further. In his study of comradeship, he maintained first that "the threat of social death, exclusion from the mutual welfare and communication network, was the cement of military group culture."[49] Indeed, he described a "shame culture" that exerted a very real and powerful peer pressure, also incorporating elements of a conception of masculinity that viewed noncompliance as weakness.[50] He then claimed that atrocities themselves served as an initiation into the group. Killing, then, became a collective act of bonding. This last contention perhaps reaches too far, but Kühne's focus on the importance of peer group pressure and masculinity is an important approach in need of further investigation.

Neither ideology nor situation can fully explain perpetrator behavior.

However, the debate between these two explanations dominated much of the earlier scholarship and was constructed in such a binary way that it still casts a shadow on research today. In this study I seek to reframe the debate. I argue instead that understanding how and why individuals engage in criminality on such a massive scale requires untangling the complex interplay of psychological pressures, belief systems, training, leadership, situational pressures, institutional memory, and organizational standards.

Thus, while many of the crimes of the Wehrmacht in their various forms have been laid bare, questions of scope, scale, and motivation remain unanswered. The variety and breadth of these issues demand not only a comprehensive and comparative look at policy and institutional decision making, but also a micro-historical examination of how and why individual units and soldiers participated in these violent policies. The latter investigation of the Wehrmacht in particular has only recently begun to be attempted. Put plainly, what did complicity actually *look* like on the ground?

One of the reasons this line of inquiry remains elusive is that approaches that have worked well for other studies are often less useful at this level. Studies relying on large samples of letters, for example, may be enlightening in telling us about some soldiers' mentalities. However, they often reveal little about participation in atrocities. Even when soldiers write about such things, their letters are often vague and avoid any details about their participation. Without large numbers of letters from the same group of people over time, this source base also cannot show us any progressive change in belief or behavior over time. Indeed, even very recent excellent studies of candid recordings of German soldiers secretly taped describing their attitudes toward and participation in Nazi crimes tell us frustratingly little, as they do not identify with sufficient detail the historical circumstances in which such attitudes were formed.[51] Studies at the regional level looking at policy decisions are valuable, but again often cannot reveal much about individual cases. The propaganda messages created and their distribution can be useful in understanding the indoctrination goals of the regime, but when approaching complex questions of motivation and decision making, the extreme difficulty in measuring the reception of propaganda limits the utility of this approach.

Local studies, by contrast, offer an opportunity to tie policy to behavior in ways that focusing at a higher level do not.

This book weaves together five detailed, connected, unit-level micro-histories of Wehrmacht participation in the Holocaust in Belarus. It reconstructs the internal dynamics of the organizations involved, as well as the details of their behavior. Only by working at this scale with regard to Wehrmacht complicity in genocide can one really begin to weigh the influences of factors such as antisemitism, social-psychological pressures, guidance from above, and situational or positional factors. It is possible to reconstruct this difficult and often obscured past only by relying on diverse forms of historical evidence, all of which have their own strengths and weaknesses. The sources for this work fall into roughly four categories: postwar German testimonies, German wartime military documents, survivor testimony, and fieldwork.

The foundation of this study is approximately four hundred judicial statements given by former soldiers and other Germans after the war. These documents constitute both one of the richest and also most problematic forms of evidence. The Central Office for the Investigation of Nazi Crime was founded in 1958 to act as a central agency for the coordination of all investigations of German citizens involved in Nazi crimes. As such, it also became a repository for records relating to these investigations and trials. Housed perhaps fittingly in a former prison in the small, baroque town of Ludwigsburg outside Stuttgart, this archive contains a wide variety of documents, from legal memoranda to court judgments to interrogation statements. It is the last of these that sheds the most light on the development of complicity by German soldiers. These documents are the records of interrogations and interviews conducted by German police and prosecutors of former members of the Wehrmacht, SS, and Nazi civil administration. The vast majority of these men were, however, called as witnesses rather than as accused.

The challenges of these perpetrator sources are apparent. First, the investigatory environment in which these discussions took place was, by its nature, adversarial. Witnesses were frequently quite aware of the legal risks involved, and certainly careful to avoid implicating themselves.

Second, they were often still concerned with protecting their former comrades; even long after the war, the pressures of group conformity and real or imagined group belonging made many men reluctant to implicate men they served with. Third, investigators did not always ask the questions that might most interest historians, nor did witnesses always volunteer such information. Especially for those accused, but also for witnesses, the nature of the questioning could lead to a great deal of obfuscation, evasion, and outright lying. How does one make sense of such documents? In his discussion of Eichmann's various postwar accounts, Browning provides us with four insightful tests to help determine the relative truth contained in these types of testimony. They are:

1. The Self Interest Test: When a witness makes statements against his self-interest or where telling the truth is in his self interest.
2. The Vividness Test: When the witness describes events with "an unusual attention to details of visual memory."
3. The Possibility Test: When a witness' claims "are not contradicted or proven impossible."
4. The Probability Test: When the accounts "coincide with or fit a pattern of events suggested or established by other documentation."[52]

This methodology allows historians to evaluate these sources critically for veracity and bias. When properly read, therefore, these often seemingly contradictory and self-serving testimonies can yield much valuable information, especially when read against other types of sources.

First, these witnesses provide a wealth of information that is of no legal significance but is very useful in understanding both the nature of the units and the nature of their crimes. As these discussions carried little judicial risk, they also did not receive the same level of careful self-censorship that other subjects may have. These men tell us much about what these killings looked like to those on the ground and how soldiers participated. They also reveal much about the inner workings of their units, describing the leadership, norms of behavior, day-to-day activities, and so on. Second, the very manner in which witnesses and the accused attempt to explain or evade answering can be instructive. Language, even after the fact, can be a valuable way of interpreting how these men understood their participation in these atrocities. For example, what is *not* said can often also be a valuable piece of information. In these sources, silence, or what is silenced, can speak volumes. Finally, despite all these possible reasons for dissembling, many witnesses *do* provide detailed accounts, even of potentially incriminating activities.

Alone, however, these documents still present a skewed view of the Holocaust, reflecting both a perpetrator bias and the judicial environment. They can be evasive, vague, and tend to avoid extensive discussions of antisemitism or particular brutality. Contemporary military documents, therefore, provide one corrective. Military maps, orders, and memoranda are not tainted by postwar reflection or judicial concern. These records are snapshots of contemporary policy and actions. They can show us where units were and, in some cases, who was being killed. Military documents also can elucidate what policies and guidance were being disseminated to the troops. These elements add an important contextual and organizational background that tempers the often-apologetic nature of judicial statements.

Military documents, of course, also provide only one perspective on events—in this case, the perpetrator's. These documents are far from perfect sources. Like the judicial testimonies, military records come with their own biases and silences. While specific about some things, they can often be infuriatingly vague about others, particularly the nature of killings and Jewish policy. Further, as a result of the fortunes of war, the documents surviving in archives often come from the higher levels of the military and thus do not always tell us what the lower-level units were doing. Finally, military documents function under their own internal logic and contain specific language that can be misinterpreted unless carefully read. One must understand this institutional format to properly understand such evidence.

Ultimately, we must never forget that the story we are telling is the story of the Jewish victims, those millions of individuals who died, suffered, or, against all odds, survived the Nazi attempt to exterminate them. Whenever possible, I have tried to integrate the voices of Jewish victims into this narrative. The most powerful source is survivor testimonies, such as that of Lisa Derman, recounted at the beginning of this book. Survivor testimonies provide the vital Jewish perspective. They provide the stories of the family members, friends, and neighbors who did not survive, and they bear witness to the crimes committed against them. In this way, survivor testimony provides a powerful and necessary counterbalance to perpetrator testimony. These testimonies also correct the tendency of judicial statements to minimize mention of cruelty and antisemitism. They also add details and contexts that lay beyond the scope of legal investigation. These survivor testimonies come in many forms, such as legal witness statements, written memoirs, taped oral histories, and Yizkor or community memory books.

All survivor testimony springs from different circumstances, which influence how such testimony is best used. Legal statements given to German prosecutors by survivors are, like the interrogations of the accused, narrowly focused on points of law and the facts of the case and thus often lack a larger human context. However, for those witnesses interviewed relatively more recently after the war, their testimony is less likely to be affected by the effects of memory and collective storytelling, as much later video testimony might be. Written survivor memoirs have all the benefits and limitations of any form of memoir writing and are also affected by author self-censorship, backward-looking analysis, and faulty remembering. Taped oral histories such as those found in the Fortunoff or Shoah Archive collections are very valuable in their great length and the ability of the interviewer to interact with the witness. Of course, the historian cannot himself interact with the subject and is thus limited to relying on the variable skills of the interviewer, who may or may not be asking the most useful questions. Survivors of many Jewish communities also compiled Yizkor or memory books to memorialize both the life and the death of their hometowns. While these documents are certainly of an amateur nature, any tendency by historians to overlook them as a valuable source would be shortsighted. They often provide details about the people in these communities that are absent from legal investigations and at times even corroborate statements made in these investigations. Obviously, these testimonies cannot fill the very physical void left by the absence of the victims themselves. However, at the smallest level, they enable a Jewish voice to be at least partially present in the narrative of the Holocaust.

The final method I have used to uncover the history of these massacres is field research visits to the sites of murder themselves. On an abstract level, these trips represented a sort of methodological pilgrimage, one driven by the conviction that in order to tell this story, I must visit, and pay respect, to the victims. On a concrete level, these visits included oral interviews with those mainly non-Jewish inhabitants still alive who witnessed the killings. These conversations mainly took place with residents who, now elderly, were children or young adults at the time of the massacres. These individuals recounted to me the things they saw as well as their memories of their Jewish neighbors. Their memories add perspectives that cannot be gained from an archive.

Lastly, on the most basic level, the geography and topography of the killing sites are themselves used as historical sources. Walking the ground and visiting the villages where the Wehrmacht killed adds a sense of space and place that textual sources simply cannot provide. Often, such visits can corroborate or refute earlier written testimony. These kinds of site surveys are most commonly done by military and environmental historians and geographers, but Holocaust historians could benefit greatly from similarly spatially sensitive approaches. In these areas of Europe, the landscape itself is a source and should be examined as such. When taken together and read against one another, these varied sources offer us the opportunity to explore for the first time the actual participation of German soldiers in the Holocaust on the ground in Belarus.

The stories of the victim and perpetrator are inextricably connected. They cannot be easily disentangled, nor should they be. In telling the unknown story of those German soldiers who individually both murdered and aided Jews, one also tells the unknown story of the individual lives that were extinguished in the "Holocaust by Bullets." This study focuses on those German soldiers on the frontiers of human cruelty, while never losing sight of the Jewish victims of that cruelty. The mass killing of Jews in the occupied Soviet Union and the participation of the German army in those killings have remained in the shadows of history for too long. Theologian Paul Tillich once said that "morality is not a subject; it is a life put to test in dozens of moments."[55]

This book seeks to illuminate some of those moments. Understanding how German soldiers could become active participants in the Holocaust in Belarus means understanding our own capacity for incredible cruelty. In this way, the complicity of the Wehrmacht in the Nazi genocidal project on the eastern front speaks to the historically central role of militaries in all genocides, from the American West to Sudan. Yet we must not lose sight of the fact that we cannot understand participation in genocide without looking at the ground level and exploring how ideology, experience, organizational norms, and situational factors combined to create genocidal moments.

CHAPTER ONE

The Deadliest Place on Earth

PERHAPS NO PLACE in the former occupied Soviet territories deserves historical attention more than the present-day country of Belarus, which suffered a demographic disaster during World War II from which it is still recovering. It was most assuredly, as Tim Snyder notes, "the deadliest place on earth between 1941 and 1944."[1] Yet the experience of the Belarusians under Nazi rule has been by and large absent from the West's widely popularized images of the Holocaust, such as Anne Frank and Auschwitz. Indeed, the Holocaust in Belarus can in many ways be defined by its local and personal nature. The majority of its victims met their deaths in or around the towns in which they had lived their whole lives, without ever having seen an extermination center like Auschwitz or Treblinka.

This other Holocaust remained remote for the Western public not just as a function of its physical distance. First, many of the Holocaust survivors who made it to the United States, for example, had passed through the concentration camp system. They were collected in displaced-persons camps in Germany before being allowed to emigrate. Thus, this group had a Holocaust experience defined in large part by the camp experience. Second, the almost immediate commencement of the Cold War made the West most reluctant to recognize the very real Soviet suffering under Nazi rule, as the Soviet Union had become the new enemy. Lastly, for a variety of reasons, the Soviet government itself was not interested in distinguishing any specifically Jewish victims from the rest of the victims of the "fascist occupiers." This is particularly tragic, as up to one-third of all Jews who died in the Holocaust were under Soviet rule in 1940.[2] Yet, from the Soviet perspective, where over twenty million Soviets had perished during the war, Jewish suffering was, numerically, just a small part of an immense loss.

This Soviet reluctance to officially commemorate Jewish suffering can be explained in several ways. There was first the ideological problem presented by Marxism, which could not recognize specifically Jewish suffering without recognizing nationality and ethnicity as legitimate social classes; this was deeply problematic for a political system based on the belief that only economic class divided peoples. There were other, less intellectual factors behind the marginalization of the Holocaust in the Soviet Union. After the war, the Soviet government and not least Stalin himself became increasingly antisemitic. Stalin, who had created a Jewish anti-fascist committee during the war, had the same group imprisoned or murdered after it.[3] A lingering antisemitism had lasting effects, as can be seen in the suppression of the *Black Book* of Soviet Jewry, which chronicled the Holocaust and the less-than-respectful treatment of the Babi Yar massacre site where over thirty thousand Jews had been murdered; it was first turned into lake and has now been paved over. Thus, both international and domestic politics have marginalized the massive suffering of Jews in the Soviet Union as an aspect of our understanding of the Holocaust.

This is particularly unfortunate, as the scale of the human tragedy for all Belarusians resulting directing from Nazi policy was extraordinary. Seven hundred thousand Soviet prisoners of war were murdered or deliberately starved. Between 500,000 and 550,000 Jewish men, women, and children were murdered, as well as over 400,000 other civilians. In addition, 340,000 individuals were deported to the Reich as slave labor.[4] It is estimated that one in three Belarusians died during World War II. The experience of Margarita Kosenkova is probably typical. Before she began describing the murder of the Jews in her hometown, she told her own family story of World War II in the East. Her father and brother were burned to death in a barn by the Germans. Her mother perished in a Nazi concentration camp in Belarus. One of her brothers died at the front as a Red Army soldier. She survived in the forests with her aunt after fleeing her native village.[5] Because the true horror of the Nazi genocidal project was visible in all its incarnations in Belarus, this land is fertile ground for investigating the Wehrmacht's role in that endeavor.

Part of the reason for the scale of destruction in Belarus can be found in its history. Belarus is truly—as sociologist Andrew Savchenko noted—a "perpetual borderland."[6] Indeed, no Belarusian state as such even existed before the twentieth century. It is a generally flat country, heavily forested, with large marshy areas to the south. The rivers Dnieper and Berezina have been highways through the region from Roman times, as was the Pripyat River to the south, connecting the Dnieper to the Vistula and thus to Poland. The Vikings traveled an arduous combination of these rivers to trade with the Byzantine Empire. With major population centers in Minsk, Gomel, Mogilev, Vitebsk, Brest, and Grodno, Belarus is now home to around ten million people.

For over a thousand years, the region formed part of other nations and empires, beginning with the Grand Duchy of Lithuania, which expanded to include all of modern-day Belarus in the mid-thirteenth century. Belarus remained part of the Grand Duchy for five hundred years before becoming part of the Russian Empire in the eighteenth century. The important Magdeburg Statutes granted self-rule to certain Belarusian cities, establishing them as centers of commerce, beginning in the fourteenth century. This fostered contact with western Europe, which in turn "ensured a fertile reception in Belarus of Renaissance and humanist ideas and values" and led to a "historical exposure to diverse intellectual currents . . . and traditional religious tolerance [which are] a major source of cultural difference between Belarus and its eastern neighbor, Russia."[7] The 1897 census, which lists nine separate nationalities (Belarusians, Jews, Russians, Poles, Ukrainians, Lithuanians,

Latvians, Germans, and Tatars), indicates the multiethnic and multilinguistic nature of the area.[8]

Jews began arriving in large numbers from western Europe in the fourteenth century, many as a result of the increasingly numerous expulsions there. Skill in trades and finance was valued by the rulers of the region, and some Jews enjoyed considerable freedoms. Most Jews were poorer merchants, traders, and craftsmen, limited in their economic opportunities, forbidden to own land, and excluded from certain guilds. Here, as elsewhere in eastern Europe, much of Jewish life centered on the shtetl. Jews lived together in towns and villages, where they often formed the majority of the population; they traded with and provided services to non-Jewish peasants. Often they worked as traveling peddlers or pawnbrokers. Those better off served as middlemen between the farmers and larger markets, buying livestock and grain wholesale, or as tax farmers and estate managers for the nobility. For most in the shtetl, it was a hard life, with a slim margin. This is not to say that all was misery and poverty. These small communities had lively religious and cultural lives that at least somewhat compensated for the hardships of daily life. In towns and cities, where they often formed a large percentage or even a majority of the urban population, Jews lived in a Jewish street or quarter. This geographic and occupational concentration persisted until World War II.

By 1795, Belarus had become part of the Russian Empire in the wake of three great-power partitions of Poland. In the context of a struggle between Russia and its subject peoples in the region, the empire put down several nationalist uprisings in the nineteenth century. Particularly in western Belarus, which was mostly ethnically Polish, the tsars attempted to repress Belarusian national consciousness and to "Russianize" these areas. For Jews, annexation into the Russian Empire meant forced concentration in the Pale of Settlement, an area that stretched from Lithuania to the Crimea and included much of Belarus. According to the 1897 census, over 97 percent of Russian Jews lived inside the Pale.[9] It was possible to legally escape the Pale under the tsars, but this opportunity was generally limited to the wealthier and more educated, a trend that worked to keep the remaining population poor and disadvantaged.

Still, Jewish settlements in Belarus, while more isolated and more traditional than those in the West, were nonetheless vibrant and diverse communities. They were marked, for example, by a commitment to education (Jews in Belarus had a literacy rate of 94 percent in 1939).[10] This was due in large part to the high number and quality of Yiddish schools. Like Jewish communities elsewhere, the shtetls contained a variety of charitable organizations *(tzedekahs)*, from loan organizations to aid for the elderly, which supported the members of the Jewish community in a nation that had marginalized them. Throughout the Pale, Jews strove to maintain the separate yet parallel administrative structures that formed a sort of self-government.

Belarus (or more accurately the parts of Poland and Russia it would later encompass) was also an important part of Jewish religious life. This area of eastern Europe saw the explosive expansion of Hasidism in the eighteenth century. This more charismatic version of Judaism that centered on important religious prophets and mysticism was a vital element in daily life, as ever-increasing numbers of eastern European Jews began practicing this more unifying and accessible form. Of course, the development of Hasidism was not without strife. More conservative Jews centered in Lithuania and known as the Mitnagadim ("those who oppose") rejected this unscholarly and more ecstatic approach, advocating instead a rigorous, intellectual approach to Judaic texts. Throughout the eighteenth and nineteenth century, these two branches of Judaism and an accompanying religiosity were well represented throughout Belarus. This vibrant religious life was reflected geographically with famous yeshivas for Torah study in many towns, such as Minsk, Bobruisk, Slonim, Lida, Novogrudok, and Baranovichi, and many Hasidic dynasties appearing throughout the region.[11]

Under the tsars, Jews suffered periodically from both governmental oppression in the form of formal anti-Jewish laws and informal pogroms. The Chmielnicki massacres of Jews, which took place in Ukraine during an uprising of Cossacks against Polish rule, held a particularly prominent place in eastern European Jewish memory. Deadly pogroms such as those following the assassination of Alexander II in 1881, a tsar who had cautiously approached reform, were not infrequent. Indeed, these violent outbursts spurred much of the immigration of eastern European

Jews to the United States during the last decades of the nineteenth century and up until World War I. However, systematically sustained mass violence was the exception rather than the rule. The bizarre combination of Jewish autonomy and ancient hatreds can be seen in the town of Slonim, where Jews were elected to a majority in the town council in 1921 in spite of the fact that a week earlier blood libel charges had been brought against a local Jew, who had subsequently been beaten and imprisoned.[12]

During the First World War, the Germans occupied practically all of Belarus until 1918. They confronted there a complex ethnic, religious, and linguistic landscape. As historian Vejas Liulevicius writes, "the terms of national identity [in the East] seemed unfamiliar and dangerously unstable to the newcomers."[13] The German military administration struggled to sort out the diverse groups in the East. It also sought to bring *Kultur* (German culture and civilization) to the region in the form of education, economic improvements, and cultural events. Though certainly paternalistic and often heavy-handed, the German occupation during World War I was an ambivalent one, which resulted in some very real improvements. For example, in Borisov near Minsk, electric lighting arrived for the first time with the German occupation troops.[14] While latent German antisemitism occasionally presented itself, the occupation was not on the whole hostile to Jews; for example, cultural authorities in Ober Ost, the massive German military administration, took pains to protect Jewish "sacred objects" and artifacts, such as precious seventeenth- and eighteenth-century wooden synagogues.[15] The character of this occupation would color the expectations and reactions of Jews and non-Jews alike to the arrival of the Nazis, often leading them to expect a more lenient experience, similar to what they remembered from the First World War.

The Bolshevik Revolution and post–World War I battles with Poland resulted in the division of Belarus between the Soviet Union and Poland at the Treaty of Riga in 1921. This left a small, largely powerless Belarusian Soviet Socialist Republic, which had been formed in 1919, while the remainder of Belarusian territory was incorporated completely into Poland without any recognition of its own particular demographic composition or historical background. This partition had significant impacts for both Jews and non-Jews. Indeed, this was a tale of two polities. By 1926, the Belarusian Soviet Socialist Republic (BSSR) had more than doubled in size to 48,500 square miles (125,000 sq km) and quintupled in population to almost five million. This territory came from the inclusion of Belarusian "ethnographic areas" that had remained within the Russian republic. Some 82 percent of Belarusians lived in rural areas, and 91 percent were peasants.[16]

The Bolshevik New Economic Policy began to slowly change this, increasing industrialization, commerce, and urbanization. Education also improved. In addition, in the 1920s and 1930s, emigration of younger Jews from the more traditional shtetls to the cities increased. However, to a large extent, these shtetls "preserved [their] unique character right up to the outbreak of the war with Nazi Germany."[17] A 1924 decree established equal language rights for Russian, Belarusian, Yiddish, and Polish.[18] Hebrew was outlawed as a bourgeois language, and Hebrew schools and language education were repressed. Still, Yiddish enjoyed a resurgence, as the Soviets viewed it as a proletarian language.

The Bolshevik Revolution proved to be a mixed blessing. The USSR's need for "literate cadres provided numerous economic opportunities," and the state "assigned the Jews the status of a national minority, with all the advantages attached to it in the Soviet system of ethnic politics."[19] The Soviet Union officially outlawed antisemitism, and while Lenin opposed any concept of Jewish nationality, Jews rose to high positions in Soviet leadership, though in doing so they would not have identified themselves as Jews. As one historian has noted, "Soviet communism promised equality but demanded secularization."[20] Jews were overrepresented in administrative posts throughout Belarus, but the attraction of Jews to socialist and communist ideology is not surprising, given that they were excluded from nationalist, Christian, and conservative parties; therefore, socialism and communism were the only options that at least purported to offer equality and freedom from antisemitism.[21] However, Jews also suffered along with their neighbors from the purges and terror of the Stalinist era. Soviet authorities under the NKVD continually shot Belarusians, both Jews and non-Jews, in the Kurapaty Forest near Minsk from 1937 to 1941. An estimated 250,000 were killed.[22] The Stalinist purges that focused in particular on older Communists with residual memory of and loyalty to Lenin and Trotsky also decimated the first generation of Jewish Communists and replaced them with new recruits and supporters of Stalin, who were less often Jewish. Jews became thus both less conspicuous and less numerous among the Stalinist leadership than earlier.

For the area of Belarus incorporated into Poland, however, the next eighteen years were markedly different. The political scene in the new Poland was dominated by two ideological positions. The Endeks, led by Roman Dmowski, sought a "united, monocultural, and monoreligious Polish state," while Józef Piłsudski and his supporters represented, ostensibly, a more tolerant, more liberal vision.[23] However, the conservative Polish government under Piłsudski was not interested in any real Belarusian political consciousness. As he wrote in 1920, "I am in favor of some significant concessions to the Belarusians in the field of their cultural development but I do not wish to make any political concessions favoring a Belarusian fiction."[24] Piłsudski's successors were even more nationalistic and conservative, so that in the end, not even these concessions were made, and for the former Belarusian areas in Poland, the reality was increased oppression and further attempts at Polonization.

For Polish Jews, the period after World War I offered the prospect of increased equality. Poland reluctantly signed the Minorities Treaty, which theoretically granted legal and political protection to Jews and other ethnic minorities. While the period saw a flowering of Jewish political activity, given Polish reticence to recognize national minorities, this activity resulted in little true change. If Piłsudski restrained the most antisemitic, right-wing groups, he also did not offer Jews autonomy or a significant change to their political power. When he died in 1935, however, "Jews sincerely mourned [him] . . . as the lesser evil, as a man much to be preferred to his National Democratic [Endek] and fascist-leaning opponents."[25] They were right to feel so, for in 1935, Piłsudski's successors refused to recognize protections for minorities. All political parties officially sanctioned antisemitism, with the exception of the Polish Socialist Party, whose power was certainly not increasing. Official antisemitic actions, though not reaching the level of mass violence, included attempts to limit ritual slaughter, the exclusion of Jews from membership in civil organizations, and the segregation of Jewish students in Polish universities.[26] Jews were viewed as "an alien, hostile and unwanted element in Poland," and in the town of Jedwabne in eastern Poland (later to be the site of an infamous pogrom), half of the Jewish-owned shops were "liquidated" between 1932 and 1939.[27]

On 17 September 1939, Stalin invaded eastern Poland, fulfilling his prior agreement with Hitler. For many Belarusians familiar with Poland's repressive nationalist policies, Soviet occupation promised some relief. The two years of Soviet governance proved to be repressive as well, though for some less so than previous Polish rule. For Jews in these regions, the arrival of Soviet power brought with it the hope that conditions would improve, compared to earlier discrimination they had experienced under Polish oppression. Above all, of the two alternatives, they preferred occupation by the Red Army rather than the German army. Many refugees fleeing the Nazis also arrived in western Belarus. This, too, explains the often-warm welcome that the Red Army received, especially from Jews. In some towns, the only Communists remaining were Jews, and the Soviets turned to these locals for help administering the newly occupied territories. In Slonim, for example, the new head of the police installed by the Soviets was a former Communist named Haim Homsky, presumably a Jew.[28] Yet, for many, Soviet "liberation" was not a happy experience: about three hundred thousand people were deported by Soviet authorities before the German invasion in 1941.[29]

For Jews in both eastern Poland and Belarus, the experience of Soviet rule was, on the whole, a painful one. The nationalization of businesses, redistribution of land, and execution of purges is reflected in much survivor testimony, and many survivors speak of an almost constant state of fear that they would be deported to Siberia. A 1944 study cautiously estimated that 1.25 million Polish citizens (in what would become western Belarus) had been moved into the Russian interior. While those drafted into the Red Army, seeking jobs, or voluntarily leaving were included in this estimate, some 900,000 were forcibly deported as prisoners or "special settlers."[30]

While the eastern Poles and Belarusians were not gently handled by the Soviets, their treatment was both objectively and subjectively less violent than that endured by the residents of Ukraine and the Baltic states. These areas suffered far harsher Soviet repression, due mainly to both their well-developed national consciousness and the accompanying nationalist organizations, which the Soviets rightly saw as clear threats to their rule. Past experiences under the Soviets (and the perceived role of Jews in them) would play a more decisive role in the form that Nazi occupation took in those areas.[31] Because they had a less developed sense of national identity, the Belarusians were less traumatized than their neighbors to the north and south. Moreover, it was in the hopes of a restoration or realization of nationhood through their German occupiers that many locals in the Baltic states and the Ukraine came to collaborate. A comparative lack of a national sentiment reduced the scale of collaboration in Belarus. As Henry Abramson adroitly indicates,

"History . . . is better understood as the unfolding of events based on perceptions rather than as the linear progression of facts."[32] The misperception that Jews were behind the comparatively greater suffering in the Baltic and the Ukraine had a more powerful impact on later treatment of Jews in those areas than it did in Belarus.

Partially because of a lack of these more polarizing nationalist influences, relations between Jews and non-Jews could be at times comparatively better in Belarus, decreasing the appeal of Nazi antisemitic propaganda. Indeed, in some instances this led to notable support and rescue of Jews. Barbara Epstein noted in her study of the Minsk ghetto that "if the Germans assumed unanimous local support, they turned out to have been wrong."[33] Moreover, "the large numbers of Jews and Byelorussians who engaged in resistance from outside the organized underground also played a crucial role, creating a solidarity between Jews and non-Jews."[34]

The city of Minsk might admittedly be a special case, but the reticence of locals to collaborate contributed to the increasing manpower problem for the killers, to the extent that units of Lithuanian and Latvian collaborators were often brought in to fill the roles that local auxiliaries performed in the Baltic and Ukraine. This is not, of course, to suggest that there were no Belarusians ready and willing to collaborate with their German occupiers. Without the complicity of local officials, local police, and militias, the Holocaust in Belarus would have been much more difficult to carry out.[35]

Jewish Belarusians themselves viewed the German invasion with trepidation, while their non-Jewish neighbors adopted a cautiously optimistic wait-and-see attitude. After all, what could be worse than Comrade Stalin? They would soon discover the answer, as a massive German army crossed the Soviet border on 22 June 1941 into this long-contested region, forever changing all their lives.

CHAPTER TWO

A Weapon of Mass Destruction

Bolshevism is the mortal enemy of the National Socialist German people. . . . This war demands ruthless and aggressive measures against Bolshevik agitators, partisans, saboteurs, and Jews and tireless elimination of any active or passive resistance.

"Guidelines for the Behavior the Troops in Russia,"
29 May 1941

THE GERMAN ARMY'S HISTORY of treating civilians harshly extended at least back to the Franco-Prussian War of 1870–1871, Germany's colonial experience, and certainly the First World War. Isabel Hull, in her study of the institutional and doctrinal development of the Imperial German Army, describes an organizational culture of violence, extremity, and excess that helps explain the behavior of the Wehrmacht in the Soviet Union.[1] Some of this organizational history was first written during Franco-Prussian War and during the German army's execution of genocide against the Herero and Nama between 1904 and 1907 in what is now Namibia. She outlines four basic assumptions that guided German military thinking from the late nineteenth century through World War II. First, war was "existential," without limits, and tended toward the extreme. Second, the military was obsessed with the establishment of complete order in occupied areas. Third, this unrealistic demand for order created a predilection for extreme violence against civilians when this order was disrupted (as it inevitably would be). Lastly, all of the above pathologies combined with a general German tendency to reject any binding notion of the international law of war.[2] Our examination of the behavior of the Wehrmacht in the Soviet Union will explore the repercussions these tendencies had as they became canonized in the institution.

Additionally, high-ranking military officials had historically played a leading role in the governance and foreign policy of Prussia and then Germany. During the period of *Kaiserreich*, the military had a very free hand with the kaiser, who helped limit interference by the civilian government to intermittent reviews of budgetary matters. The constitution itself "thwarted policy coordination," not least by removing the "political, legal, economic, diplomatic, and social considerations a civilian chancellor and a cabinet ought to have brought to military thinking."[3] Earlier in its history, German civilian government thinking, though not liberal or progressive, tended to be relatively more moderate than that of the military; this became a cultural norm to which the army became accustomed.

Indeed, during the murderous German colonial escapades in German Southwest Africa, large swaths of the public had eventually opposed German military actions. The colonial governor there, Theodor von Leutwein (who would subsequently be replaced), argued that the native rebellion was a "natural response" and that "one can no longer say that the whites have shown themselves to be the morally superior race."[4] The German chancellor, Bernhard von Bülow, also advocated for less extreme colonial policy, albeit for economic reasons.[5] He argued that increasingly murderous German military plans would "demolish [Germany's] reputation among the civilized nations," which was, as Isabel Hull notes, quite strong language for the imperial government.[6] Neither Leutwein nor Bülow was particularly concerned with native human rights. However, they did oppose the dominant military perspective (as did a very few army officers). Civilian authority then advocated different (and often less lethal) treatment of natives that admittedly included racial subjugation, valorization as "noble savages," and "partial assimilation."[7] Though not entirely successful by any measure, the civil imperial government did manage to brake and mitigate German military policies that were becoming ever more genocidal.

By the Nazi period, this dynamic would be reversed. While the German army had earlier been trained to defend itself from civilian interference in its exercise of excessive violence, it was ironically unprepared to deal with a situation where the civilian government itself drove the military toward the extreme. Hitler's government would ask the military to embrace rather than abandon more murderous policies. Preexisting institutional mind-sets would contribute to a much more brutal force, which would build on a history of violence toward civilians dating back to the Franco-Prussian War, where an actual civilian irregular force had caused great fear in the army.

Atrocities committed by German soldiers in World War I also prefigured the violent behavior that would come later in the Soviet Union. In that war, the German army distinguished itself from the other combatant nations in its violence against civilians in response to an almost completely mythical civilian opposition. John Horne and Alan Kramer note three dimensions leading to the myth of the *franc-tireur* or partisan in this war and to the resulting violence inflicted upon the local French and Belgian civilian populations that resulted in sixty-five hundred civilian deaths.[8] They argue that "first, a set of fictional representations of the enemy crystallized in the first few days of the war . . . portraying the enemy as the exact opposite of the German soldier and the qualities he embodied." The "circumstances of the invasion" imposed by the Schlieffen plan and the "exhaustion and nervousness of troops in a hostile land" were the second dimension. Lastly, "the defining feature of the *franc-tireur* fear of 1914 was its capacity to convince large numbers of people that something which was an illusion was actually happening."[9] German behavior toward civilians in general and Jews in particular in the Second World War demonstrates that a very similar dynamic was in operation in the Soviet Union in the fall of 1941, ultimately on a far larger scale and over a far longer period of time. Finally, as Omer Bartov points out, one must take into account the tradition of draconian discipline in the German army: "The strict obedience demanded from the troops, and the draconian punishments meted to offenders, doubtlessly played a major role in maintaining unit cohesion under the most adverse combat conditions."[10] This discipline and cohesion combined with a mythic association of Jews, Bolsheviks, and partisans as contributing factors to participation in atrocities.

One must, however, be careful not to draw too straight a line from colonial or imperial German military practices to the army's behavior in Operation Barbarossa, Hitler's invasion of the Soviet Union. Certainly, the Wehrmacht was different from these earlier organizations. It was larger, increasingly less professional, and more highly ideologically influenced. It also fought under the banner of an openly racist regime and in arguably more desperate conditions. Yet one cannot discount the important influence of institutional memory and culture on the decision making of the army, at both high and low levels. Militaries, like other large bureaucratic organizations, tend to be conservative, resistant to change, and prone to retaining practices and mindsets from previous eras. They are even more likely to behave this way as, given their specialized tasks and expert knowledge, they are less susceptible to intervention by civilian authorities. However, as we have seen, the German army actually became *more* vulnerable to interference by the Nazi civilian government. Rather than mitigating military aggression, the new government's intentions resonated with an endemic proclivity for violence. The German army that entered the Soviet Union did so with a set of baseline practices and default responses to dealing with civilians that already veered toward excess.

Understanding the overlapping areas of interest between the Nazi leadership and the Wehrmacht requires situating its civil-military relations in the chaos of post–World War I Germany. The military collapse in 1918 was a crushing defeat, both physically and emotionally, for the German army. It was catastrophic not only in its material effects but also in its lingering emotional and intellectual impacts on German military culture and organization. Principally, the loss of World War I created three loci of discomfort in the German military leadership. The first was the loss of prestige suffered by military decision makers. Throughout German history, military leaders had directly advised the kaiser on both foreign and military affairs. The army had been a force to be reckoned with and a proud symbol of German national power. After the abdication of Wilhelm II and the bankrupt advice that had gotten Germany into the war, the military felt keenly its loss of sovereignty in this government and overall prestige. One of the most obvious symbols of this loss was, of course, the Versailles Treaty, which sought to permanently neuter all German armed forces.

Connected to this loss of influence was the very real physical loss of a military German empire in eastern Europe. While the war on the western front was predominantly a conventional military endeavor, in the East, the imperial army under the command of Erich Ludendorff had created what was very nearly an autonomous military empire in which the army controlled all aspects of life for the occupied population.[12] Ironically, the Germans had realized their dream of eastern empire that Hitler would long for, only to lose it at the end of World War I. For a staunchly anticommunist and conservative officer corps especially, the loss of this *Lebensraum*, imagined vital "living space" in the East, was particularly painful.

Lastly, the "stab-in-the-back" myth *(Dolchtosslegende)* served as a unifying explanation for the German defeat in the war and for the accompanying losses mentioned above. Under this formulation, advanced by right-wing groups and by Ludendorff himself, the German army had been brought down not by force of arms, but instead had been betrayed at its moment of victory by a combination of Jews, Socialists, democrats, and liberals who had sabotaged the war effort at home. The manner of the war's end did not help to counteract this myth. While the military (and the kaiser) had been responsible for directing all aspects of the war, a more representative civilian government was only brought in at the end to supervise the surrender and the humiliation that followed, though it had had little to do with the defeat. The first post–World War I German government with a true chance of creating democracy was thus left holding the bag for those who had brought the country to its knees in the first place. The end of the First World War left Germany with millions of military men who were conservative, anticommunist, anti-Jewish, antidemocratic, rabidly nationalistic, and angry. This generalization does not apply to everyone equally, particularly the rank and file, but it holds for much of the officer corps and especially the upper leadership.

Perhaps a liberalized and reformed German military could have occurred in a relatively stable state. However, postwar Germany was anything but. It found itself very quickly thrown into a chaotic battle between paramilitary groups of the Left and the Right. The massive numbers of men in uniform under military control stood as a powerful force for whomever they chose to support. To this end, the quartermaster general of the army, Wilhelm Groener, approached the new chancellor of the fledgling republic, Friedrich Ebert, on 9 November 1918 offering military support for the government in exchange for guarantees of government noninterference in army affairs and freedom from revolutionary (and democratic) reforms. Indeed, when the Reichstag deliberated a series of radical reforms to the military, General Groener threatened to withdraw military support from the government in the face of increasing violence from the communist Spartacists and the right-wing *Freikorps*. The civilian government was forced to abandon these reforms and to rely on the old military institutions for its support and legitimacy.

This uneasy partnership soon proved to be an unequal one. Given its strong nationalist and anticommunist leanings, the army enthusiastically crushed socialist and communist groups while mostly ignoring right-wing extremist groups. Occasionally, it even actively enlisted in these endeavors the technically extralegal *Freikorps,* violent conservative militias operating outside the law. Indeed, during the Kapp-Lüttwitz putsch of 1920, elements of the military resisted demobilization and joined *Freikorps* units in an attempt to take over the government. However, when the civilians turned to the army to suppress the revolt, they were rebuffed. Perhaps the ultimate expression of this betrayal was famously summed up in Hans von Seeckt's statement that "troops do not fire on troops. . . . When *Reichswehr* fires on *Reichswehr,* then all comradeship within the officer corps has vanished."[13] His open recognition of the *Freikorps* as comrades was a telling indication of the allegiance of the army. Only a general strike called by socialist leaders eventually brought the coup to an end. It therefore became clear that the civilian leadership could not rely on the military to support a constitutional government yet also could not bend that military to its will. Instead of honoring the Ebert-Groener agreement, the military—steadfast in its commitment to the stab-in-the-back legend, having at least partially recovered its nerve from the recent military debacle, and capitalizing on widespread resentment against the Versailles Treaty—refused any true loyalty to the Weimar Republic.[14]

In 1921, a new German army, the Reichswehr, was created. This force was to be a reformed military suitable only for national defense. Though smaller, this new army very much resembled the old. In keeping with the Ebert-Groener Pact, the law that created a provisional Reichswehr, though putatively requiring it be "built on a democratic basis," in fact dictated that its leadership be drawn from the ranks of the imperial officer corps and *Freikorps* veterans.[15] In effect, therefore, the same conservative elite remained in power. Throughout the Weimar period, the military remained a deeply suspicious and antidemocratic organization, but one concerned with honor and stability. Thus, when Hitler attempted his own putsch in 1923, military forces in Bavaria stood behind the Bavarian government and supported the right-wing but less radical Gustav von Kahr, civilian state commissioner of Bavaria. Conservative order trumped revolutionary change, even change from the right.

In the internecine bureaucratic maneuvering that characterized the end of the Weimar Republic, military leaders remained an ever-present force. They supported only civilians they believed they could control or who would at least not interfere in the world of military decision making. When Hitler became chancellor in 1933, the army again remained neutral and probably agreed with Vice Chancellor Franz von Papen's contention that he could be controlled.

Even so, Hitler had to actively work to win the army's support for his party, though he had certainly gained a following, particularly among the younger demographic but also among some in the general officer ranks. General Ludwig Beck, chief of the General Staff from 1933 to 1938, wrote a friend in 1933 welcoming the Nazi "political transformation."[16] However, Ernst Röhm, the leader of the paramilitary arm of the party, the SA (Sturmabteilung), a group of rough-and-tumble street brawlers who had helped Hitler come to power, increasingly sought to erode the military's unique role in the German government. Indeed, he envisioned a new people's army under the leadership of his SA. The possibility of a rival military organization did not sit well at all with the leadership of the Reichswehr. In order to solidify future military support, Hitler purged his SA in June 1934 during the "Night of the Long Knives," confirming the primacy of the army in the Nazi state and securing its support. The military also succeeded in eliminating any threat to its supremacy, except from Hitler himself. A month after the "Night of the Long Knives," all servicemen swore an oath of allegiance to Hitler himself, rather than to the constitution.

In March 1935, the military reintroduced conscription and began to grow again. Hitler also undertook a project of rearmament that was certainly viewed favorably by many, both within the military and without. Yet as his aggressive foreign policy aims became increasingly clear, some military leaders balked and wished to limit Hitler's power. Over the protests of his military advisers, Hitler carried out the remilitarization of the Rhineland in 1936 and the annexation of Austria in 1938 while repudiating the Versailles Treaty. As he turned to Czechoslovakia, his senior advisers hesitated again. Hitler, benefiting from SS chief Heinrich Himmler and Luftwaffe head Hermann Göring's own quest for more power, was presented with an opportunity to remove these reluctant army men. Key generals Werner von Blomberg and Werner von Fritsch found themselves discredited and driven from public life as Hitler gradually sought to recenter military control in his hands alone. General Ludwig Beck, the chief of the General Staff and a onetime supporter of Hitler, resigned in protest. However, at Hitler's request, he did so in secret, which largely eliminated any value Beck's protest might have had. With the appointment of the pliable Wilhelm Keitel as the chief of the OKW (Oberkommando der Wehrmacht, or High Command of the Armed Forces), Hitler had effectively made himself both the titular and the actual head of the German forces, a move that would have serious implications as war loomed in 1939.

If German military leadership eagerly embraced rearmament and had mixed emotions about Hitler's foreign policy, what was their attitude toward his racial ideologies? The evidence indicates that the army was at least passively supportive. The old German military establishment was no stranger to antisemitism. Jewish officers, while permitted, faced a glass ceiling that prohibited them from advancement to higher ranks. Given the conservative and aristocratic background of its leadership, it is not surprising the German military was reluctant to fully realize the

Jewish emancipation begun in the nineteenth century. Perhaps one of
the clearest examples of such institutional antisemitism was the infamous "Jew census," which the Imperial High Command commissioned
in 1916 ostensibly to "prove" that Jews were underrepresented in the war
effort. In order to further support the stab-in-the-back theory, a manipulated version of the results was released to antisemitic publications after
the war. A more systematic study in the 1920s, however, demonstrated
that this census represented "the greatest statistical monstrosity of
which an administration had ever been responsible."[17] Indeed, it actually showed that Jewish Germans fighting for their fatherland were statistically *overrepresented*. Regardless, the army reflected its continuing
willingness to discriminate against Jews by bringing its policies in line
with Nazi objectives after Hitler's rise to power. For example, it duly applied the Law for the Restoration of the Civil Service to its ranks as well,
removing Jewish service members and requiring proof of Aryan hered-
ity for its members.[18] Though its antisemitism often remained "polite,"
the German army was becoming increasingly more racially "aware" and
more predisposed to supporting extreme policies, even as it prepared
to go to war.

The first real combat for the Wehrmacht was the campaign against Poland beginning on September 1, 1939. While it was not so much a test of
the Wehrmacht's combat prowess, the Polish campaign *was* an experiment in how deeply the military would become involved in the Nazi
genocidal project. Poland would be the first nation to fully experience
the first iteration of the traveling execution squads called the Einsatzgruppen, a phenomenon the army would encounter in all its bloody
details. While the scale of violence may not have been immediately apparent, army leadership could have had "no illusions about the general
criminal character of the coming actions of the Einsatzgruppen."[19]

As early as July, General-Quartermaster Eduard Wagner had coordinated with Reinhard Heydrich, head of the Reich Security main office
and "architect" of the Final Solution, to arrange liaisons between the Ic
(intelligence) sections of Wehrmacht units and the Einsatzgruppen. The
five Einsatzgruppen would be responsible for "combating all enemy ele-

ments in enemy territory behind the fighting troops."[20] The higher leadership of the Wehrmacht quickly divined the meaning of this typically Nazi euphemism. Keitel, chief of the OKW, informed his head of military intelligence, Admiral Wilhelm Canaris, on 12 September that "the matter [of the execution of Polish elites] had already been decided by the Führer; the commander of the Army had been informed that if the Wehrmacht refused to be involved, it had to accept the pressure of the SS and the Gestapo. Therefore, in each military district, civilian commanders would be appointed who would carry the responsibility for ethnic extermination [added in pencil: political cleansing]."[21] After the annexation of western Poland in October 1939, Hitler told the supreme commander of the Wehrmacht (OKW), Field Marshal Keitel, that the occupation of Poland would allow them to "purify the Reich territory also of Jews and Polacks."[22] That army units knew of the employment of the Einsatzgruppen can be seen, for example, in orders such as that concerning logistics for the Eighth Army Corps in August 1939: "It can be assumed that only weak police forces will be available in enemy territory [therefore] Sipo *Einsatzgruppen* will be employed in rear areas fighting all anti-German elements. The Quartermaster of the Eighth Army will oversee the deployment of *Einsatzgruppe* III."[23] Knowledge of the intent of the Einsatzgruppen did not, however, initially translate to a good understanding of how this was to play out between the army and SS on the ground.

The military, particularly at the lower levels, was (at least initially) shocked at the scale of the violence. The discomfort felt by some leaders and soldiers is evident in several written orders and complaints. An order issued in July 1940 by an army commander stated: "I wish to emphasize the necessity of ensuring that all soldiers of the Army and, in particular, the officers refrain from any criticism of the struggle being waged with the population in the General Government, for example, the treatment of the Polish minorities, the Jews, and Church matters." This order suggests that some soldiers and officers in Hitler's Wehrmacht were not pleased with the actions of the SS in Poland. Certainly if such criticism was not widespread enough, an order would not have been necessary to end it. In February 1940, General Wilhelm Ulex, in command of the southern sector, wrote to his own superior that "the acts of violence by the police forces, which have increased recently, demonstrate a quite incredible lack of human and moral feeling, so that it can be called sheer brutalization."[24] General Ulex further recognized that "it seems as if the superiors privately approve of this activity and do not wish to intervene."[25] His fellow general officer, Johannes Blaskowitz, went even further, calling for the SS and police officials to be arrested and tried by military authorities.[26] These protests would quickly end the military careers of both men.

In fact, a policy of nonintervention better describes the evolution of the army's collaboration with these first Einsatzgruppen in Poland. As Dieter Pohl rightly states, "Among the generals themselves the repudiation of mass killing was not very widespread. At the most, discontent was directed against crimes that were not remotely justified by 'military necessity' [even by the military's own expansive understanding of that concept] . . . or were accompanied by excessive cruelty."[27] The army's actions in Poland represented a "prelude" to the war of annihilation through both participation in the extensive killing of civilians and especially in the massive violence against suspected *Freischärlers* or partisans that was already occurring in 1939.[28] In Poland, with the coming of Nazi civil government, the army was relieved to wash its hands of Nazi racial policy—which became the clear purview of the SS and Gestapo—in preparation for the war against France. Indeed, the initially awkward interactions between the army and SS killing squads would inform the planning for future cooperation in the Soviet Union as Nazi authorities would seek to prevent such friction during Operation Barbarossa.

The French campaign beginning in May 1940 and fought against a less racially denigrated opponent on territory not targeted as future German Lebensraum, was not generally characterized by mass violence against civilians, either from a security or racial standpoint. It was a more conventional, far less racialized war than the one fought in Poland. There certainly were atrocities, such as the 1940 Vinkt massacre in Belgium, where at least eighty-six civilians were executed by the German army.[29] However, no Einsatzgruppen were sent into France seeking to conduct mass executions, as in Poland. This is not to say that no racially motivated killings took place. In contrast to Poland, when such killings occurred in France they were conducted almost solely by the Wehrmacht. Rafael Scheck's innovative research on the fates of French colonial troops captured by the German army demonstrates a disturbing continuity of racism. He shows that between fifteen hundred and three thousand black African soldiers fighting for the French were summarily executed by the Wehrmacht during the invasion of France, because they were black.[30]

Though some generals had initially disagreed with the recklessness of the führer's invasion plan, one of the most important repercussions of the French campaign was an almost universal "recognition" of Hitler's strategic brilliance in the face of military misgivings; indeed, many generals "no longer wished to remember their previous skeptical criticisms."[31] This vindication of Hitler and the accompanying boost to his ego would contribute to an increasing lack of general military dissent.

The war with the Soviet Union, in contrast, would be fundamentally different (and even more violent) than the Third Reich's previous campaigns. It was to be a "war of annihilation," a clash of cultures in which only one ideology, Nazi or Bolshevik, and one race, German or Slav, could triumph. As Karel Berkhoff writes in his study of the systematic murder of Russian POWs, the "'Russian' . . . had been irreversibly 'infected' with Bolshevism, the vicious ideology and political party created by 'Jewry.'"[32] There could be no cure for this "infection" other than annihilation. Race and politics were thus irreversibly combined, and the coming conflict with the Soviet Union was seen to be inevitable. As Hitler himself had written eighteen years earlier in *Mein Kampf,* "Germany will either be a world power or will not be at all."[33] Nothing more fully epitomized this all-or-nothing mentality than the invasion of the Soviet Union and the German plans for its colonization and the accompanying decimation of its populations. Nazi behavior in the East represented the purest form of the genocidal project upon which the regime was embarked. Indeed, occupation policies in western Europe were exceptional for their comparative sensitivity. Put another way, the conquest of the East followed the ideal Nazi model, a model not practical in the West.

The roots of the yearning for land in the East extended back into a distant and predominantly imaginary German past.[34] The desire for an eastern empire had several components. One was nostalgia for a return to a romantic era when Teutonic knights ruled fiefdoms there. The leading Nazi agricultural theorist, Walter Darré, repeatedly and fondly recalled an agrarian world in the East where Germans could "return to their heritage, 'an authentic nobility in the Old Teutonic sense.'"[35] Another was a desire for additional territory (Lebensraum), which, for Germans, historically and logically lay in the underdeveloped and racially inferior lands to the East, as Germany had no chance or desire for overseas colonies; the loss of the few German colonies outside of Europe after World War I was particularly traumatic in this regard. The Nazi publication *Reich Agriculture* stated that "the land is the life basis of the people."[36] In the Nazi worldview, Slavic peoples who could not efficiently farm the land did not deserve to own it. Ben Kiernan notes the disturbing parallels between the Nazi plans for expansion in the East and earlier settler genocides: Hitler compared the partisan war to the struggle against the "Red Indians," called the inhabitants of the Soviet Union "aboriginals," and justified German violence via a comparison with the conquistador Cortés.[37] A recent study of German colonial genocide rightly concludes that "Hitler's 1941 statement that he would treat the Slavs 'like a colonial people' has lost its resonance, but for the Führer it was a phrase full of meaning, a shorthand readily understood by a generation of Nazis who were boys when the Kaiser sent his armies to Africa to destroy native rebels who had placed themselves in the path of Germany's racial destiny."[38] Imperial policies and even personalities from the German genocide in Southwest Africa suggest important continuities between the mass killings of the Second and Third Reichs.

Finally, in more modern times, an intense fear and hatred of the Bolshevik menace in the Soviet Union led to a desire for both buffer territory and the total destruction of this enemy. Bolshevism was "alien to this Nazi view of race, soil, family, and history."[39] Bolshevism was more than a political ideology; it was a disease that merged with a belief in a Jewish domination of the Slavic race and could not be easily cured except by total destruction. For those who had experienced the unsettling political turmoil of the Weimar period and those who had the most to lose from the social and economic reorganizations proposed by communism, the Bolshevik threat appeared quite real and quite terrifying.

[handwritten: 600 yrs/ large space Eastern Empire]

Hitler himself had already expressed many of these themes clearly in *Mein Kampf*. Harking back to prior mythic Germanic glory, he proclaimed, "We take up at the halting place of six hundred years ago."[40] On the necessity of space, he wrote, "Only a sufficiently extensive area on this globe guarantees a nation freedom of existence."[41] Regarding the Jewish connection to Bolshevism, Hitler stated, "The struggle against Jewish bolshevization of the world requires a clear attitude toward Soviet Russia. You cannot drive out the Devil with Beelzebub."[42] Even if Hitler's more rabid antisemitic beliefs were not always shared by the military, these concepts held great sway. The structure of the Holocaust evolved over time, but for Hitler and many of his supporters, a yearning for an Eastern empire was present from the start.

Operation Barbarossa operationalized these ideological concepts into very real plans for a decimation of the occupied East, an "apocalyptic project of ethnic engineering."[43] In the first place, Hitler was committed to avoiding any significant negative social impact of the war on the home front through economic deprivation or severe rationing, as had happened in World War I. To that end, the military was expected to feed and supply itself generally from the land it conquered. Food for the military was to come at the expense of local residents, who were simply to starve. This was but one element of what became known as the "Hunger Plan," which quite openly recognized that "without a doubt umpteen millions of people will starve when we extract all our necessities from the land."[44] Accompanying the Hunger Plan was the brutal *Grüne Mappe* (Green File) economic plan. Together, these documents outlined the planned systematic starvation, deportation, expropriation, and depopulation of the occupied East in preparation for the Germanic settlers that Himmler imagined would occupy the region. Some Nazi administrators circulated the number of thirty million as the likely death toll.[45] The vast majority of these projected deaths were to be non-Jewish Slavs. Yet as the numbers of Jews under German control increased almost exponentially with the occupation of the Soviet Union, the Final Solution naturally also became part of this destructive dynamic in the East. The military, which would be wielding a great deal of power, at least initially, would be expected to play its part in all these policies.

[handwritten margin notes: no hardship at home; cost to locals; Hunger Plan; Green File; starvation; deport; exprop; depopulate; 30m.]

To highlight this fact, the Army High Command disseminated three important documents *before* the invasion of the Soviet Union. These had been written at the instigation of Hitler himself beginning in the spring of 1941. The first was a 13 May 1941 Führer Decree, which suspended prosecution of German soldiers for most criminal actions in the East. It clearly stated, "Punishable offenses committed against enemy civilians do not, until further notice, come any more under the jurisdiction of the courts-martial and the summary courts-martial." This decree removed enemy civilians from protection of military law, giving German soldiers legal impunity in their treatment of civilians. A later clause authorized "punitive measures" against villages on the authority of battalion commanders.[46] Any prosecution of crimes was to be considered only if "necessary for the maintenance of discipline or the security of the troops."[47] These would be the same crimes that *would* (or could) be prosecuted elsewhere in Nazi-occupied Europe. Legal punishment was reserved for the good of the army, not the population. Thus, German soldiers were not only given the freedom to do as they pleased, but they were also encouraged to be violent, if not downright criminal. The decree even provided a justification for this violence, blaming "the break-down in 1918, the time of suffering of the German people after that, and the numerous blood sacrifices" of the Nazi movement on "Bolshevist influence" and instructing the troops to defend themselves "ruthlessly against any threat by the enemy civil population."[48] The effect of these orders was to release German soldiers from the constraints of "civilized" warfare and to both rationalize and promote brutal behavior toward civilians and "enemies."

In the second document, the "Guidelines for the Behavior of the Troops," issued down to company level prior to 21 June, soldiers were informed that "Bolshevism is the mortal enemy of the German people" and that "this war demands ruthless and aggressive action against Bolshevik agitators, snipers, saboteurs, and Jews and tireless elimination of any active or passive resistance."[49] Political agitating, sniping, and sabotage are all behaviors, yet being Jewish was, in the Nazi worldview, an immutable racial category. Jews were thus explicitly targeted as racial enemies to be eliminated by the military regardless of their behavior. The order went on to note that the "Asiatic soldiers of the Red Army are

Commissar Order

obtuse, unpredictable, underhanded, and unfeeling," again painting the war in the East with a racial palette.[50]

A third directive, the so-called Commissar Order *(Kommissarbefehl),* instructed the troops that the uniformed political commissars who accompanied the Red Army were to be shot out of hand by frontline troops, and if encountered in the rear areas were to be turned directly over to the Einsatzgruppen for similar treatment. Hitler's pronouncement that the Communist is *"kein Kamerad"* (no comrade) was immediately accepted by those crafting the order. The order in one stroke both explicitly authorized an abandonment of the laws of war and encouraged closer cooperation with the organization responsible for the "Holocaust by bullets" in the Soviet Union, the SD (Sicherheitsdienst, or Security Service). The Commissar Order stated that "political representatives and commissars are to be eliminated" and that "the decision rests with an officer of disciplinary power whether that person is to be eliminated. Identification as political functionary is sufficient proof."[51] This blanket execution order directly contradicted all previous laws of armed conflict (to which Germany was a party) and sent a powerful message to all in the military that they would not be bound by such codes. Through its vague language, it also left the door open for a dangerously broad interpretation of "enemies."

A personal message from Hitler to the troops on the eve of the invasion further reinforced the antisemitic message from the "Guidelines." "Alone for over two decades," the führer claimed, "the Jewish-Bolshevik rulers from Moscow have sought to set fire to not only Germany but all of Europe. It was not Germany but the Jewish-Bolshevik rulers in Moscow that have steadfastly sought to force their domination not only spiritually but above all physically upon ours and other European peoples."[52] Hitler thus painted the war against the Soviet Union as a defensive one forced upon Germany by a Jewish-Bolshevik government in the USSR. These, then, were the explicit messages and justifications that German soldiers carried with them into the Soviet Union.

In addition, bureaucratic groundwork had already been laid for cooperation between the Einsatzgruppen of the SD and the Wehrmacht. This relationship was to be far better defined than it had been in Poland. On 13 March 1941, OKW Keitel informed the military in the "Guidelines" that the Reichsführer SS had received from Hitler the "authorization to carry out special tasks" in the army rear areas.[53] General-Quartermaster Wagner served as the army's representative to the SS and SD in ironing out the details of this relationship in discussions over the proposed use of the Einsatzgruppen. After a month of talks, Wagner and Heydrich reached an agreement in the form of a draft memorandum circulated on 26 March 1941.[54] Wagner then met with Kurt Daluege, head of the German Order Police, and Heydrich and Himmler on 16 April to further iron out relationships between the police and army.[55] The final version of the agreement was disseminated to the army on 28 April under the signature of General Walther von Brauchitsch, the commander of the army. In it, Wehrmacht units were tasked with "march, quartering, and supply" support of the Einsatzgruppen and were told that the "combating of enemies of the state and Reich" was the general responsibility of Army Group Rear area commanders.[56]

Lower-level orders echoed this agreement, as in a directive of 15 June 1941 in which the 28th Infantry Division, assigned to Army Group Center (Rear), or rückwärtige Heeresgebiet Mitte (rHGM), informed its units in Belarus that "the Reichsführer SS is carrying out special tasks in the rear areas with his own organs and under his own responsibility. In the rear army areas, only a small group of Security Police and the SD (Sonderkommandos) is to be used to carry out certain tasks specified at the outset of operations. . . . Sonderkommandos of the Security Police and SD work together with the Army Ic."[57] The rHGM itself stated clearly in an order dated 24 June 1941 that the Einsatzkommandos were "subordinate to the commander [of Army Group Center Rear] concerning march, supply, and accommodation."[58] Though Wagner said in a meeting in May 1941 that OKH had refused "real support of all these units [presumably meaning in actual operations] and the execution of political tasks," the true nature of this relationship between the army and the Einsatzgruppen would quickly encompass far more than logistical support.[59] The existence and the mission of the Einsatzgruppen were certainly no secrets to the army, which would take the first steps toward mass killing with its own prisoners.

The relative ease with which the Wehrmacht presided over the mass murder of Soviet POWs under its care gives a good indication of the potential for brutality that this organization already possessed even before the war in the Soviet Union began. The intentional absence of any preparations for the care and housing of massive numbers of Soviet POWs ominously foreshadowed their predictable mass deaths in German hands. Though the army envisioned a series of giant encirclements that would by necessity result in massive numbers of prisoners, the man responsible for planning for the welfare of prisoners of war, General-Quartermaster Wagner, made no adequate plans for POW camps to accommodate them.[60] Prisoners were to be held with minimal supplies in open-air enclosures. While postwar apologists would claim that the army was overwhelmed by the sheer numbers of captured Russians and was unable to properly care for them, the truth is that they were intentionally neglected. An OKW order from 8 September 1941 stated that the "bolshevist soldier" had "lost all claim to treatment as an honorable opponent in accordance with the Geneva Convention."[61] A telling indicator of this intentional neglect of POWs is a directive from the 4th Army Corps on 9 June 1941 *before the invasion* that clearly stated that "prisoners of war are to be fed with the most primitive rations (for example horse flesh). High quality and scarce food and luxury foods may not be given out to them."[62] A detailed historical survey also found that, from the beginning, the daily caloric intake of Soviet POWs was not sufficient to sustain life.[63] The military also fully cooperated with the "selection" of its prisoners for execution by the SS and Einsatzgruppen. It knowingly sought out Jews among captured Red Army soldiers and allowed them to be murdered. As Christian Streit points out, "The military leadership of the OKW through its willing cooperation in the creation of a hierarchy of POWs placed itself in a situation in which active collaboration with Nazi extermination policy was a logical result."[64]

While the official military standpoint toward POWs was one of apathy and enmity, those at the ground level sometimes saw things differently. One German lieutenant, Konrad Jarausch, in charge of a kitchen in a large POW camp, described the conditions there in letters home. While he viewed the locals as "primitive," he described with concern the twelve thousand POWs who had arrived after a twenty-five-mile (40 km) forced march. Some were shot charging the field kitchen, while others "rolled around in the mud, howling from their hunger pains."[65]

Jarausch's extensive correspondence reveals a man struggling to align his moral compass, military duty, and prejudiced views of Slavs. It also shows that German army units involved in POW policy could absorb an unhealthy dose of genocidal experience before ever encountering tasks related to the Holocaust.

Yet, one cannot separate the war from the Holocaust. In the East, soldiers and Nazi executioners literally traveled together from the beginning. As the less numerous armored units advanced rapidly, the slower-moving infantry formations followed behind, mopping up immense pockets of thousands of encircled Soviet soldiers. Accompanying the faster-moving formations were the approximately three thousand men of the Einsatzgruppen, Himmler's mobile killing squads. Each group operated in an Army Group rear area, with Einsatzgruppe A behind Army Group North, B behind Center, and C and D behind South. Tasked with the elimination of "enemies," including Jews and Communist functionaries, the leaders of these had been highly indoctrinated and specially trained at SS training centers prior to the invasion, and the men had been informed of their mission in the East. To support their tasks, they were also equipped with wheeled vehicles to facilitate their rapid deployment. They were followed by units of Order Police, Waffen-SS, and Einsatzgruppen zbV ("for special assignment") to assist them in the killing process. Higher SS and Police Leaders (HSSPF), such as Erich von dem Bach-Zelewski in rHGM, were responsible for coordinating operations between the SD/SS and Wehrmacht and, later, for carrying out anti-partisan operations.

In Belarus, Operation Barbarossa would usher in a period of the most intense suffering the region had seen in its history. German troops, part of the over one hundred Wehrmacht divisions committed, crossed the 1939 Polish frontier and advanced quickly, covering over two hundred miles (320 km) and reaching Minsk in two weeks. By 22 August, most of the region containing 30 percent of the Soviet Union's Jews had been occupied.[66] Huge pockets of hundreds of thousands of Red Army soldiers had been surrounded and captured. Even so, thousands more bypassed Soviet soldiers escaped Nazi encirclements, some attempting to return to Soviet lines, a few continuing to fight in the German rear, and some merely returning to civilian life. The much-lauded partisan bands of

1943 did not exist in 1941, as Stalinist planners and the man himself had steadfastly refused to entertain the possibility of Soviet land under foreign occupation and thus had made no preparations for guerrilla warfare.

The planned cooperation between the Einsatzgruppen of the SD and the Wehrmacht in Belarus took shape early on. In late August, the Einsatzgruppen could already speak of "pleasant cooperation with the army authorities."[67] In contrast to the Polish campaign, the SS/SD and the Wehrmacht developed a more functional working relationship. This was thanks in no small part to the combination of sanctioned brutality toward civilians, official antisemitism, and organizational cooperation with the SD, along with the Jew-Bolshevik-partisan calculus, which permeated the environment in which the campaign would progress.[68]

Why it worked

Wehrmacht units in Belarus had already signaled their support for the Nazi racial policy by establishing Jews as a different and inferior category of civilians. Jews, for example, were the first to be identified and used for forced labor. In July 1941, the 350th Infantry Regiment "evacuated" the male Jewish populations of the Bialowiezer Forest, which was to become Göring's private hunting preserve.[69] The division order then specified that "all Jewish men [were] to be placed in a camp and to be concentrated into work details."[70] A rHGM order concerning pay of road repair crews specified that Jews "*may* only be compensated in the form of food."[71] The 221st Security Division (also stationed in Army Group Center Rear) ordered that Jews be rounded up and forced to gather straw and clean houses in preparation for a Wehrmacht unit's arrival.[72]

The 403rd Security Division's intelligence section further observed that "not all soldiers have the proper attitude toward the Jews. They do not approach the Jewish laborers with the desirable ruthlessness and the distance that should be self-evident for National Socialist soldiers. Emphasis must be given to intervene against this thoughtlessness."[73] Such a statement demonstrates both that some military authorities conceived of a "proper" attitude of brutality to be taken with Jews and, at least in this division, were intent on imposing it. It also suggests that some soldiers were not brutal or antisemitic enough for the army's taste. This initial use of Jews for forced labor, at least by these units, seems to have preceded an official decree from the civil administration in the East forcing all

Jews from eighteen to sixty years of age to report for labor.[74] Even in the first months of the war in Belarus, Wehrmacht units were also already killing Jews; twenty were killed in Lida, seventy-three in Baranovichi, and thirty in Slonim.[75]

Participation in the Holocaust evolved over time. However, the Wehrmacht was immediately and, for the most part, completely in agreement with the execution of the Commissar Order and POW policy. In his thorough study of the *Kommissarbefehl*, Felix Römer painstakingly recreates both the creation of the order and its execution.[76] He shows that some units took it more seriously than others, but most complied. Yet the numbers are damning. More than 100,000 serving political officers in the Red Army were lost during the war, according to Soviet statistics; 57,608 were killed as a result of military action, and an amazing 47,126 were "missing."[77] The vast majority of these missing were likely executed in accordance with the *Kommissarbefehl*. The victimization of POWs did not end with commissars. Anti-Jewish policy was carried out in the POW camps as well. An operations order issued on 17 July to the SD operating in POW camps instructed that "all Jews" found among the captured soldiers were to be executed.[78]

There is evidence that some leaders objected to the order and that its enforcement across units was not uniform; however, on the whole, commissars had a short life expectancy in German captivity (if they even made it there). As Jörn Hasenclever notes, even those refusing to execute the order did not always do it out of moral reasons but were often more concerned with the pragmatic effect it would have on the combat ahead of them; enemy soldiers fight less tenaciously when they are not convinced of certain death upon capture.[79]

The POW policy was met by some with shock and concern, particularly those like Jarausch who, as professionals, took seriously their task of providing for prisoners, as well as those who simply saw the policy as inhumane.[80] Most Soviet POWs found themselves in *Dulags* (*Durchgangslagers,* or transit camps), which consisted of little more than open fields surrounded by barbed wire and sentry posts. The men were underfed, exposed to the elements, and in need of medical attention. Indeed, the army itself radicalized its own policy, ordering that "mainly" Russian medical personnel and "only" Russian medical supplies were to be used to treat wounded prisoners.[81] The mortality rates were enormous. Of the 5.7 million Red Army soldiers taken prisoner during the war, 57.9 percent did not survive the war.[82] Two-thirds of the three million prisoners captured in 1941 did not live out the year. More Soviet soldiers died *daily* in the hands of the Wehrmacht than American or British prisoners did in the entire war. By contrast, of German POWs in Western captivity, less than 1 percent died; even the brutal treatment of German POWs by the Soviets resulted in a death rate of "only" 35.8 percent.[83] Only toward the end of 1941, when the disastrous POW policy had already had devastating effects, did the Nazis realize the growing labor shortage and the potential utility of Red Army POWs as slave labor. However, from the beginning, non-Russian ethnicities were often released to join German auxiliary forces.[84] The army itself soon realized that it would need to release more POWs to help bring in the harvest. A few officers even suggested that mistreating POWs made defeating the Soviets more difficult. While issues of military utility led to a change in POW treatment, such factors had little if any effect on Wehrmacht anti-Jewish policy.

As the army became more stationary in Soviet towns, it also became more directly involved in promulgating Nazi antisemitic policy. Because military administration was the first form of German government across the occupied East, it also first initiated restrictions against Jews. Local military commanders instituted the wearing of the Star of David, curfews for Jews, and various other regulations. They also created ghettos, sometimes on their own initiative. On 19 August 1941, the Army High Command, for example, specifically ordered the creation of ghettos in towns with large Jewish populations, provided it was "necessary and possible given the local situation and assistance at hand."[85] The army also became quickly involved in the expropriation of property and forced labor of Jews under its jurisdiction.[86]

As the front stabilized east of Mogilev, Belarus was partitioned again in September 1941, this time between military and civilian authority. An area of almost 87,00 square miles (225,000 sq km) with over 9.8 million inhabitants, roughly west of Borisov to the border of the General Government, became the "White Russian" region (Weissruthenien) of Reichskommissariat Ostland (RKO) under the control of Heinrich Lohse.[87]

The area east of Borisov to the beginnings of army unit rear areas remained under the control of rHGM, a corps-level unit commanded by infantry general Max von Schenckendorff.

As these rear-area units began settling into their jurisdictions, the *issue* of the "partisan threat" became more and more pressing, even if the *reality* of the threat itself did not. Stalin himself aided in this to some degree. On 3 July, he addressed the Soviet people via radio. "The enemy," he said, "must be hunted down and exterminated, and all his plans foiled."[88] This mostly empty threat angered Hitler and perhaps prompted his statement of 16 July that "the Russians have now ordered partisan warfare behind our front. This partisan war again has some advantage for us; it enables us to eradicate everyone who opposes us." Regarding the security situation in the East, Hitler went on to advocate "shooting anyone who even looks askance at us."[89] Interestingly, Kaiser Wilhelm II had used similar language in exhorting German soldiers headed to brutally put down the Boxer Rebellion in China: "There will be no mercy; prisoners will not be taken," he said, so that "a Chinese will never dare even to look askance at a German."[90] Hitler's exhortation to more brutal behavior was then echoed and refined by Field Marshal Keitel, head of the armed forces. On 12 September Keitel published a memorandum whose subject was "Jews in the newly Occupied Soviet Territories." He informed the troops that "the fight against Bolshevism necessitates indiscriminate and energetic accomplishment of this task, especially also against the Jews, the main carriers of Bolshevism," again reinforcing a drive toward increasing antisemitic violence.[91] Another order three days later proclaimed that the proper ratio of Communists to be executed per German soldier killed by partisans was to be between fifty-to-one and one-hundred-to-one.[92]

High-level exhortations and directives found their expression in low-level orders and policies prior to September 1941 as well. In July, units in rHGM were instructed that captured partisans (in civilian clothes) were to be treated as *Freischärlers* and summarily executed; in addition, civilians who in any way supported these partisans were to be treated similarly.[93] The rHGM ordered that all former Soviet soldiers found west of the Berezina River were to be summarily executed if they had not turned themselves in by 15 August.[94] A further demonstration of the early escalation of violence can be seen in orders that female Soviet soldiers were to be shot out of hand. In the early days of the war, however, the German army's contact with "partisans" consisted mainly of identifying and capturing bypassed Soviet troops. Though not presenting a general military threat, these bands could be locally dangerous and may have helped to fuel rumor and overreaction. They were certainly not the partisans of 1943–1944. The inflated fear of partisan activity, eerily reminiscent of the summer of 1914 in Belgium, would have disastrous consequences for the Jews of the Soviet Union.

Developing along a parallel path that soon intersected with the Wehrmacht's area of responsibility was the escalation of Nazi genocidal policy in general and the evolution of the Holocaust in particular. As mentioned earlier, the Einsatzgruppen killing squads followed along behind frontline army units, executing "enemies of the state." This broad category included commissars, Communist functionaries, and intelligentsia. At least initially, there was no order to exterminate all Jews in the Soviet Union.[95] Heydrich's 2 July order specified only "Jews in the service of the party or the government."[96] Soon Jewish POWs were also included, and in some places virtually all male Jews of military age were targeted.

In the summer of 1941, however, the targeting of Jews continued to expand until it encompassed the systematic killing of all Jews regardless of age or sex (or actual government or Communist affiliation). As a specific order from Hitler or Himmler to this effect has yet to be discovered, historians can only track this shift through the actions of various killing units on the ground. It is most likely that this change in policy was passed through a verbal order from Himmler and his top subordinates.[97] Christopher Browning was one of the first to trace this issue also from a manpower perspective, showing that the reassignment of Police Battalions to "frontline" killing duty in late July signaled a move toward the extermination of all Jews.[98] Waffen-SS units in Belarus began conducting a more expansive form of killing in late July. The SS Cavalry Brigade under Hermann Fegelein reached Baranovichi on 27 July 1941. After a meeting there with Erich von dem Bach-Zelewski, the Higher SS and

Police Leader, and with Himmler's representative Kurt Knoblauch, Fegelein ordered his men to "handle all Jews [with the exception of skilled workers, doctors, and such] as plunderers"—that is to kill them.[99] Soon, this killing extended to woman and children as well. Himmler had ordered on 31 July that "all Jews must be shot. Drive the female Jews into the swamps."[100] Gustav Lombard, commander of the 1st Regiment, had then informed his troops that "in future not one male Jew is to remain alive, not one family in the villages."[101] The 2nd SS Cavalry Regiment reported in the same period, "We drove women and children into the marshes, but this did not yield the desired result, as the marshes were not deep enough to drown them. In most places, the water was not more than three feet deep."[102] One of the features of this targeting shift was that it appeared at different places in different times, reaching its apex in the killing of thirty-three thousand Jews at Babi Yar near Kiev at the end of September 1941, a massacre partially instigated at the behest of the Wehrmacht and one that represented the largest single mass shooting of Jews in the war.

At the same time, important decisions regarding the Final Solution in Europe were also being made. Reinhard Heydrich had already been authorized by Göring on 31 July 1941 to begin preparing plans for a comprehensive mass murder of European Jews beyond that taking place in the Soviet Union. Yet this plan had not crystallized. Regarding European Jews, Hitler, in a meeting on 19 August, would only promise Propaganda Minister Joseph Goebbels to begin deportations of German (and, thus, European Jews) "immediately after the end of the campaign."[103] However, Hitler had been personally receiving the reports of the Einsatzgruppen beginning on August 1.[104] By mid-September, he had changed his mind regarding the onset of deportations. On 18 September, Himmler recorded that "the Führer wishes that the Old Reich and Protectorate be emptied and freed of Jews from west to east as quickly as possible."[105] The first deportations from Germany to the East began on October 15 as German Jews began to be sent to ghettos in Poland and the Soviet Union.[106] Construction of the Belzec extermination center also began in October 1941, as did planning for other extermination centers. Thus we can see a parallel radicalization of both overall genocidal planning and its execution in the Soviet Union.

The reactions of both Belarusian Jews and non-Jews to the initial stages of German occupation were hesitant. The prospect of liberation from the repressive Stalinist regime was appealing to many. Indeed, one measure of the violence and brutality of the Nazi regime is that very quickly many Soviet citizens would long for the return of Stalin. Some Jews managed to flee further east, but most were quickly trapped by the speed of the German advance. While some news of German antisemitic actions in Poland had reached Belarus, most Jews knew very little of current German behavior, much less of plans for the future, and were unwilling to abandon property and family on what they considered unfounded rumors. When the war struck, many Jews fled to the countryside to escape the immediate effects of combat upon their cities. Finding themselves quickly far behind the lines without any resources, they soon returned to what was left of their homes. The summer and fall of 1941, then, found large populations of Jews trapped by the German advance. Many of them resided in smaller towns, and were still waiting for their first encounter with the conqueror.

CHAPTER THREE

5.t.
1941

GA
1st
mass
murder

Improvised Murder in Krupki

I only know that the people waiting began to scream and cry as the
first shots were heard. There was downright panic. A few people
including men, women, and children tried to escape. However, the
fugitives were caught again and beaten with clubs. It was a terrible
sight. People who didn't immediately jump in the pit were shoved
and kicked in. Even mothers with their children at their breast
were not spared this fate. The Action lasted until around 5 pm.
Twilight had already arrived.

Former German soldier Erich S., 14 April 1965

ON AN OVERCAST THURSDAY AFTERNOON in September 1941, the
Jews of Krupki in central Belarus wound their way out of town,
across the Minsk-Moscow highway.[1] Army trucks followed slowly behind,
carrying the elderly and the infirm. SS killers from Einsatzkommando
(EK) 8 awaited their arrival about one and a half miles away, as storm
clouds gathered overhead. German army soldiers guarded this column
as it marched. Here and there, they beat the Jews with rifle butts when
they did not move fast enough.[2] Somewhere in this group walked a female opera singer from Minsk. Among the soldiers guarding this column was twenty-year-old private, Walter K. As he marched, he noticed a
small child whose pants had fallen down around his ankles. Though his
mother tried to help him keep up, the child was in danger of being
trampled by those behind. Walter K. pulled the mother and child out of
line and allowed her to pull up his pants. He remembered twenty-five
years later that this incident caused him "great distress," as he was al-

ready married and had two children of his own.[3] He returned the mother
and child to the column, and they were soon shot in an open pit. In this
way, the entire Jewish community of Krupki (one thousand people and
over half the town) disappeared.[4]

In Krupki, we see a killing emblematic of the German army's first encounters with mass murder, one of the many small Holocausts that took
place across the East before the industrialized mass murder of the extermination centers. The 354th Infantry Regiment improvised in its first
encounter with murder; that is, the leadership operated without a set
procedure. Beyond vague guidelines mandating logistical support, these
men had no agreed-upon procedures for supporting an Einsatzgruppen
killing. Yet, even in this early stage, the Wehrmacht involved itself in all
aspects of killing and had a surprising number of close interactions with
the Jewish population itself. The Krupki killing offers the opportunity
to *detail* the actual complicity of one unit on the ground and to investigate how it became so deeply involved in executing racial policies.

Krupki remains a small town today. Some sixty-nine miles (111 km)
northeast of Minsk on the main highway to the regional capital of Mogilev, the town is situated on a gentle rise, surrounded by fields on three
sides and forests to the north. Small, brightly colored houses line the
streets leading from the formerly Jewish quarter to the nondescript main
square. Behind a red and white fence made of scraps from a metalwork-
ing factory lies a vacant lot where Krupki's synagogue once stood. Nothing has been built on the spot, but its position near a central square at-
tests to the historical importance of the Jews in the town. A few hundred
yards away is the house of a nineteenth-century nobleman situated in a
shady park. This house and a nearby building served as the German
headquarters in 1941.

Krupki's Jewish community was first recorded in the 1700s. In 1939,
approximately 870 Jews lived there, representing 25 percent of the total
population of 3,455.[5] According to Yad Vashem, approximately 40 percent of the Jewish population consisted of craftsmen and laborers.[6] The
majority lived on Lenin and Sovetskaya Streets.[7] One resident of a nearby
village recalled that some Jews would often travel from village to village

selling their wares: "There were no stores in the village, and so they traveled from one village to another, on horses, with carts. In their carts they had all kinds of things and household items that people needed, from matches and needles to clothes, headscarves, shirts, dishes, children's toys, all kinds of whistles . . . and they did not sell it for money—peasants had no money—but exchanged them for food items, berries, dried mushrooms." She also intimated that she thought the Jews cheated the peasants in these trades.[8] As was the case throughout Belarus, most Jews resided in towns, making a living trading with the villagers from the countryside. Soviet collective farms occupied the open fields north of Krupki, with small villages consisting of houses along a short a stretch of road. Beyond some moderate growth, the town seems little changed from the midsummer of 1941 when the 3rd Battalion of the 354th Infantry Regiment arrived.

The 354th was formed in August 1939 as part of the 213th Infantry Division, with the 1st and 2nd Battalions coming from reservists in Upper Alsace and the 3rd Battalion from Bunzlau in modern-day Poland (though this part of Silesia remained part of Germany after World War I). The unit itself is interesting in that it was drawn from two border regions, one east and one west. It is likely that the geographic distribution (and the ages) of the soldiers meant that some were less exposed to Nazi ideology. On the other hand, such border regions, particularly Silesia, were steeped in a long history of competing nationalisms and ethnic identities that could lead to a more intense feeling of German identity. Scholars have documented such geographical influences on ideology in other instances. Michael Mann noted, for example, the overrepresentation of Germans from borderlands in the extremist *Freikorps*.[9] A similar disproportionate membership in the SS has been seen, for example, in those of Austrian origins. Others have suggested that antisemitism, anticommunism, and German nationalism could be more culturally significant in German border regions and annexed territories.[10] Finally, Ben Shepherd has also observed increased proclivities for violence based on geographic origin, at least among general officers, in his study of Wehrmacht divisions in Serbia.[11]

The men consisted mainly of blue-collar laborers, while the officers were a mixture of lower-middle-class officials, professionals, and reserve officers. The average age of the regiment's soldiers, which was around thirty-six in 1941, reflected its second-rate quality, as the better-quality units received younger and fitter men.[12] Officers and NCOs averaged thirty-six and thirty-four, respectively.[13] In short, there was nothing exceptional about these men from a training or demographic perspective, save their borderland origins.

From September 1939 to May 1940, the 213th Division provided occupation troops in Poland, which must have seemed like a bit of a homecoming for some soldiers in the 354th like thirty-nine-year-old Friedrich F., who was born in Lodz.[14] In December 1940, the 354th Regiment was reorganized into battalions of four companies each. The 4th, 8th, and 12th Companies became machine gun units, each with one heavy mortar platoon. The infantrymen were then placed on leave from July 1940 to February 1941.[15] In March 1941, the regiment was remobilized and transferred to the 286th Security Division, which would be tasked with rear area security in rHGM. The 354th would form the division's main combat power, its "Response Force." Training guidelines for security divisions published in March 1941 stated that "the Response Troops are the strong combat reserves of the commander. They will be held available for the commander at key points on supply routes and will be employed offensively against enemy forces that threaten the supply routes."[16] This was perhaps self-evident, as the remainder of the division's fighting troops were composed of even less martial *Landesschützen* reservists. Along with the rest of the 286th Security Division, the 354th Infantry Regiment left its staging areas in Parczew, Poland, north of Lublin, shortly before the invasion of the Soviet Union and moved along Highway 1 toward Brest, Kobryn, and Sluzk.[17]

After helping secure the Bialystok pocket against breakout attempts, Major Johannes Waldow's 3rd Battalion arrived in Minsk at the beginning of July. Waldow was a forty-eight-year-old veteran of World War I, who in that war had seen action in Poland, Romania, and France. In the interwar period, he worked as a schoolteacher until his activation in August 1939.[18] There is no evidence that he was either particularly brutal or particularly antisemitic. He was remembered by his soldiers as "correct," "decent," "conscientious," "respected," and "beloved."[19]

From 6 to 17 July, the battalion guarded the massive POW enclosure just outside of Minsk, probably the Drozdy camp.[20] In Drozdy, the battalion first encountered the harsh realities of Nazi policy and the "war of annihilation" in the Soviet Union. It was also the site of the unit's first participation in those crimes.[21] Drozdy held over one hundred thousand Soviet POWs in an open area, surrounded by barbed wire and bounded on one side by a stream, which with a particularly cruel irony lay outside the wire.[22] A quartermaster officer in the 4th Panzer Army wrote that the conditions in the camp were "untenable" and that prisoners were "completely exposed to the searing heat." Moreover, as transports of prisoners to the rear (which had only been allowed in open railway cars) had been discontinued by the 4th Panzer Army because of "hygienic reasons" (the uncleanliness of the cars), the numbers of prisoners continued to rise on a daily basis.[23] A lieutenant in the 354th Infantry Regiment remembered that "the conditions in the camp were indescribable" and that "there were rumors that the prisoners had eaten each other."[24] As part of their guard duty, soldiers often killed prisoners, either when the starving men rushed the field kitchens or when they crossed into off-limits areas. A soldier on battalion staff recalled that a prisoner found in possession of a nail or a straight razor had been brought to Waldow, who remarked that there were already enough POWs and ordered his execution. When the man broke down crying and could no longer finish digging his own grave, 354th soldiers shot him in the vicinity of the battalion headquarters.[25]

The men of the 3rd Battalion witnessed more than these abuses. Drozdy was, in many ways, an introduction to the genocidal policy in which they would become more and more complicit. The camp had been divided into sections for commissars and for Jews, containing both Red Army soldiers and civilians from Minsk.[26] The commanding general of the 4th Panzer Army had ordered the internments and the execution of ten thousand inmates (most of them Jewish), which followed.[27] A Jewish survivor from Minsk remembered that all military-age men from the city were briefly interned there until the Jews were separated out and the rest released.[28] The Jews remaining were permitted water only twice a day.[29] Soldiers from the 354th witnessed the SS and SD conduct frequent selections among these prisoners. In one of these, all Jewish professionals were asked to step forward in order to register for jobs. Instead, they were taken out and shot.[30] Men from the 3rd Battalion also witnessed these killings and visited the open graves. Knowledge of the shootings and of the role of the Einsatzgruppen in them was widespread.[31] Former soldier Bruno Menzel stated in 2007 that "every morning the kommissars among the prisoners were pulled out and shot." When asked who these men were, he replied, "Kommissars were Jews. . . . The kommissars were mainly Jews." Menzel also admitted bringing home photos.[32] An Einsatzgruppen experience report from 4 September 1941 stated, for example, that 733 "inferior elements" had been culled from POW camps and liquidated in Minsk.[33] A diary from a 3rd Battalion soldier, Richard Heidenreich, states that the unit itself shot Jews in the camp. This diary entry appears in a Soviet book published after the war, and despite its problematic origin is likely accurate.[34] Bruno Menzel previously admitted in 1961 that shootings were carried out "mostly by soldiers from our battalion," though he denied this in a 2007 television interview. In that interview with German television, Menzel helpfully explained why the Jews were shot, remarking that "Hitler was quite antisemitic."[35] The brutalizing impact of the Drozdy camp may best be seen in a report from a Nazi official on 10 July 1941, which noted that "the limited guard force, which bears the burden of guarding, without being replaced for days on end, turns to the prisoners in the only possible language, and that is the language of weapons, and they do this mercilessly."[36] Thus we can see Waldow's men already becoming progressively more violent and experienced with the execution of Nazi genocidal policy.

Around 28 July, the 3rd Battalion arrived in the vicinity of Krupki.[37] There it was tasked with securing Highway 2 and the railroads between the towns of Borisov and Bobr, a distance of some thirty miles (48 km).[38] The 11th Company appears to have been stationed outside of town and not involved in the subsequent killing, but the 10th and 12th Companies were quartered in and around Krupki. The battalion used the town as an operating base for patrols into the surrounding countryside, combating sporadic partisan attacks on the road and railways and rounding up bypassed Red Army troops. At least one German soldier, however, testified that these patrols often had as their target Jews as well.[39] On 19 September, the 3rd Battalion reported on an operation in which it had worked alongside Police Battalion 317, a notorious killing unit that frequently worked with the Einsatzgruppen. Waldow's men captured 164 people, of whom 16 were "shot as snipers [*Freischärler*] or while attempting to escape after capture."[40] It is significant that the 354th appears to have already been working alongside a unit tasked with killing Jews, though the exact nature of this prior cooperation remains unclear. The formulaic phrase "shot while attempting to escape" was, however, often used to mask outright executions.

In addition, Waldow's men also made forays into the then still murky world of anti-partisan war. Particularly active in these efforts was *Oberfeldwebel* Schrade, platoon leader of 2nd Platoon, 12th Company. Schrade submitted an experience report on anti-partisan patrolling in October 1941 that was so well received at the highest levels that it was forwarded to all units in rHGM. Among the recommendations was that "women and children be ruthlessly prohibited from leaving the village" and also that "because the Russian fears the club more than the gun, beatings are the most effective method." He added, "recently, women have been found in [partisan] camps. In almost every case, these were Jewish women whose task was to determine whether villages were free of the enemy. It is also women who do not appear Jewish."[41] The latter comment seems to come from a basic assumption that Jews were allied with the partisans. Schrade also recommended that anti-partisan patrols be conducted by soldiers disguised as civilians (which stood in clear violation of the laws of war and was a tactic about which the Germans themselves complained when used against them by the partisans).[42] A member of his platoon recalled that they outfitted themselves from clothing belonging to the murdered Jews of the nearby village of Kholoponichi; the soldiers picked their clothing from huge piles stored in the local synagogue that the mayor referred to as "Jewish rags."[43] There is, therefore, substantial evidence that the 3rd Battalion was already involved in some anti-Jewish measures on its own initiative before the visit of Teilkommando (Subsection) Schönemann of Einsatzkommando 8 in September 1941. The arrival of these SS men would drastically expand the nature of the 354th's forays into genocide.

Werner Schönemann, commander of this killing subunit, was a thirty-year-old Berliner and Gestapo officer.[44] During his second semester of law school at the University of Berlin, he was ordered to Pretzsch, where the Einsatzgruppen were assembling.[45] There, he joined EK 8, whose explicit task was the murder of the Jews of central Belarus. Schönemann was an intelligent yet crude man who bragged of his sexual exploits and who sent an eleven-year-old "Aryan-looking" Belarusian girl home to live with his parents in Berlin.[46] In his work during this bizarre break from his studies, he was cold, single-minded, and without compromise. He often began shootings himself, jumping into the pits and firing the first shot "to set an example and to show that he did not shirk his duty."[47] He was not a sadist in that he did not behave in an excessively brutal manner beyond that required and did not apparently torture his victims; it is, of course, an indication of the warped Nazi worldview that shooting men, women, and children in pits was not considered brutal. Though disciplined and conscientious, Schönemann still appeared uncomfortable with his task of mass murder and required that the killings take place very quickly and efficiently.[48] He seemed glad when killings were over, and was "on edge" and "hardly approachable" afterward.[49] Upon his return to Berlin in October 1941, he attempted suicide twice by slitting his wrists.[50] These suicide attempts might well indicate his emotional state after prolonged participation in murder, but any distress he felt did not diminish his utility as a leader of murderers.

It was this enigmatic yet effective killer who arrived at Waldow's headquarters in Krupki a few days before the planned massacre, to make arrangements for support from the Wehrmacht. Understanding the nature of the negotiations and Schönemann's reception at battalion headquarters is the first step in both re-creating and explaining the unit's participation in the Krupki massacre. The historical evidence, in fact, indicates that this was not the first time Waldow had worked with Schönemann. A memorandum from the Einsatzkommando leader reported on 5 August that because of reports of partisan attacks, Schönemann had made contact with the 286th Security Division, represented by a Major Waldow of the 3rd Battalion.[51] The 3rd Battalion also reported to the 286th Division on a "large action" carried out by Police Battalion 317 (the notorious killing unit mentioned above) west of Lepel on 29 August.[52] The nature of their earlier meeting and collaboration remains unclear, but multiple testimonies by soldiers in the battalion headquarters help to re-create the scene when the two met again in Krupki in September 1941.

Waldow and his adjutant, Lieutenant Speth, met Schönemann and another SS officer in the orderly room. The group then went into Waldow's office. Schönemann apparently informed the major of the planned killing of the Jews of Krupki and requested two companies for support.[53] Waldow himself testified that Schönemann revealed he was there to kill the Jews but that his group of only about twenty men was far too small to carry out the operation on its own. Waldow said he would not participate in any shootings, to which Schönemann replied that he would not have to supply shooters but merely provide security for the operation.[54] Schönemann also requested additional ammunition, which Waldow claimed to have refused. On his way out, Schönemann allegedly turned to the adjutant and said, "We have to carry out this unhappy task, shooting all the way to the Urals. As you can imagine, it's not pretty and one can bear it only with alcohol."[55] It is, perhaps, important to note here the tendency of many accounts of first encounters with mass killing to be apologetic and to allege reluctance and regret. The dilemma for the historian, of course, is to attempt to determine which cases of these responses are legitimate and which are fabricated. That the interviewee is testifying about a third party lends this account more credence, as does the fact that Schönemann here is still not professing moral resistance to his job, only that it is disagreeable.

Major Waldow, apparently still uncomfortable with this looming task, called regimental headquarters for clarification and perhaps to avoid participation. The regimental commander of the 354th, Colonel Sigfried von Rekowski, was not available, but Waldow spoke to his regimental adjutant, Captain Wilhelm Meyer-Schöller.[56] Waldow asked whether he should participate, to which Meyer-Schöller replied, *"Jawohl!"* (Definitely!).[57] Lieutenant Speth provided a credible explanation for this decision, noting that "there was an order that Army units should support the SS."[58]

After the departure of the SS, preparations in the 3rd Battalion began in earnest. Waldow held a meeting with the company commanders during which he informed them of the coming shooting and allegedly added that the individual soldier "was not to come into contact with Jewish civilians" or to "enter the wood where the killings would occur."[59] Sometime after this meeting, the commanders of the 10th and 12th Companies met with their platoon leaders and passed on the order.

Likely the next day, Lieutenant Nick, a platoon leader in 12th Company, ordered Corporal Franz M. to saddle two horses, and the two rode wordlessly out of town. After about half an hour, they arrived in a swampy open area near the Starozhevitsa River and the tiny workers' village of Lebedevo. After inspecting an existing trench two meters deep, where peat had been harvested earlier by the locals, the lieutenant remounted, and the two rode back.[60] He then turned to Franz and asked him to estimate the distance to the site, which he guessed was about eight hundred meters (half a mile).[61] Lieutenant Nick had just selected the Krupki execution site. Clearly, Schönemann had entrusted his new Wehrmacht partners with far more responsibility in preparing for the massacre than they cared to admit after the war. Choosing a murder site far exceeded any originally planned cooperation between the army and the SD.

Early on the morning of 18 September 1941, the soldiers of the 10th and 12th Companies assembled. They were told of the task ahead of them or had already been told the night before (as in the case of Lieutenant Kerker's 4th Platoon, 12th Company). "Men," Kerker had allegedly announced, "we have a serious task ahead of us tomorrow. Whoever doesn't trust himself to handle a sensitive and serious assignment does not need to be ashamed and can back out."[62] According to a soldier in headquarters, the Jews of Krupki had also been notified by the mayor the night before that they were going to be resettled in the morning.[63]

At first light, soldiers tasked with conducting the outer *Absperrung* or cordon took their positions outside Krupki. They were told that no Jew was to be allowed to leave the village and that any who tried were to be shot.[64] Though no one admitted personally shooting, several soldiers remembered hearing isolated shots all morning. Paul W. recalled a fellow soldier telling a Jewish man driving his cattle out of town to turn around.[65] The first sergeant of 12th Company, Hans H., heard from his men later that "young Jewish women ran to the sentries begging for their lives and pleading that they were too young to be simply shot."[66]

After the cordon had been established, at around seven that morning, Schönemann's Teilkommando of killers arrived in the small market square. Schönemann spoke briefly with a Wehrmacht officer and then said, "Let's get started."[67] As the mayor of Krupki rang a bell, the roundup of the Jewish inhabitants began.[68] Lieutenant Nick and a group of fifteen to twenty volunteers reported to the SD men and began pulling Jews from their houses.[69] Slowly, the market square filled with people. They arrived in family groups with their belongings. They had been told to take only money and valuables, lock their houses, and surrender their keys to the mayor.[70] German soldiers guarded the Jews in the square. Once the approximately one thousand Jews of Krupki were assembled, an SS man or possibly the mayor stood on a platform and read out a list of names to be accounted for.[71] Some witnesses also recall the involvement of local Belarusian police. This registration lasted until the afternoon, when the Jews were formed into columns to be marched out of town.[72] The elderly and infirm were instead roughly thrown onto waiting trucks and wagons supplied by the Wehrmacht.

In the late morning or early afternoon, the Jews began marching out of town along Sovetskaya Street, escorted by German soldiers. During the forty-five-minute journey, SS men *and* soldiers drove them on with rifle butts when they did not move fast enough. As they neared the execution site selected by Lieutenant Nick, soldier Bruno H. recalled that "someone told them [the Jews] they could throw away their things as they were going to be shot anyway. Some did this and the people became very agitated. Someone else then said that they had to take their things with them anyway."[73] The execution trenches lay in a field near several collective farms, bordered to the east by a swampy area and a forest. As the Jews arrived here, they quickly understood what was to happen. As one soldier recalled, "many started to scream and cry. The SS-men beat them until order was restored."[74] Margarita Kosenkova was a child in 1941 and lived in the village of Lebedevo, near the killing site. She remembered that the "procession was peaceful but once they reached the pit they started to scream. There was an awful scream that they could hear in Lebedevo."[75] Walter K., who had escorted the toddler and his mother to the killing site, observed a "panicked state among them, but the guards kept the Jews together."[76]

However, the 3rd Battalion's work was not yet complete. Wehrmacht soldiers were also responsible for guarding the execution site along with local police, while the SS shot. The Einsatzgruppen men selected groups of ten from the mass of Jews forced to sit or kneel in a meadow approximately twenty-five feet away, in full view of the killing operation, according to one survivor.[77] Erich S., in the *Absperrung,* watched as the Jews approached the grave. He saw an SS man shouting, "Undress and give up your jewelry."[78] The Jews then removed their shoes and outer coats, throwing them onto a pile near the trench, and were forced to deposit their jewelry and watches in a nearby box.[79] For a time, it seems that boards were placed across the pit, from which the victims were shot.[80] S. continued, "Finally, most of them were pushed into the pit because they were afraid to go on their own."[81] The brutality of the scene was so great that even the usually dispassionate postwar German court noted in 1969 that the Jews "spent the time which separated them from death in agonizing fear and despair without any opportunity to escape their fate."[82]

Soldiers surrounding the graves watched as men, women, and children were forced to enter the pit, lie down on the bodies of those already shot, and then were themselves shot by a squad of SS men standing above.[83] The SS men, who were drinking as they worked, would hold babies up by their legs and shoot them.[84] A local Belarusian bystander, Petr Bulakh, observed the killings. He was twelve at the time and was so shocked by what he saw that he spoke with a stutter for the rest of his life.[85] After the war, Schönemann explained the process in a bizarre attempt at appearing more humane. "I ordered," he said, "that each time, the next group would lay their heads on the backs of the previously shot people so that they wouldn't touch the gunshot wounds [of the dead]. I must say frankly that I tried, under the circumstances, to find the relatively best method of shooting."[86]

Men of the 354th, probably from 12th Company, set up machine guns around the site to secure it. One witnessed several Jews stand up and attempt to run away, but they were beaten with clubs.[87] One who did escape was Maria Shpunt. She first tried unsuccessfully to convince the Germans that she and her baby were not Jewish. Apparently, she fell into the pit alive after the rest of her group was shot. When the shooters went to get the next group of victims, she crawled out and ran into the brush. Though the Germans (likely from the 3rd Battalion) shot at her, she managed to escape.[88] Observing all of this from a small rise were officers from the battalion, including the commander, Waldow, his adjutant Speth, and the 10th Company commander. From a perch in a nearby oak tree, a local girl named Klara Buryi watched along with them.[89]

While the involvement of soldiers in most of the operation is well documented, one area remains only dimly illuminated: participation in actual killing. Yet, even in this early encounter it is apparent that they killed Jews in several instances. First, it is likely that the battalion killed Jews attempting to escape both the town and the shooting site; it also appears that some of its soldiers participated in the pit shooting alongside Schönemann's SS men. Determining the nature of this participation in the actual killing is difficult, as very few former soldiers are willing to discuss such behavior. What is clear from the documents is that some men *did* shoot.

Testimony points to two ways in which Waldow's soldiers ended up shooting. The first comes from Richard Heidenreich's diary. In it, he claimed that he himself had volunteered for a special task after his lieutenant asked for "fifteen men with strong nerves." He accurately described the execution site and the rainy weather, which was also independently described by others present, including SS men. Finally, he wrote that this group of volunteers also shot Jews in the execution ditch.[90] Some soldier testimony supports this possibility. Herbert C. of 12th Company testified that he was certain that "shootings were carried out by the 2nd Platoon led by Master Sergeant Schrade." Moreover, he continued, he had seen photographs taken by a sergeant in the company in which Schrade was seen pointing a pistol at a group of ten Jews kneeling before a ditch.[91] One soldier testified during his initial questioning that Schrade had indeed sought "fifteen men with strong nerves" the night before (though in later questioning, he said only that Schrade had sought volunteers; in any case, he did not admit participating in any shooting).[92] Perhaps, while not intending to provide the bulk of killers, Waldow had agreed to provide a "reserve" squad of men. This would explain the fifteen-man squad mentioned by Heidenreich and others, which was identified the night before. Then, when time or ammunition dictated, this group was added to the pool of available shooters. There is no conclusive evidence in postwar testimonies to support this; however, it is also the last thing to which most men would have admitted. It remains unclear whether this premeditated arrangement took place. Certainly it is also possible that some spontaneously volunteered. The statement of one soldier provides evidence of this voluntarism: he testified that a fellow company member "freely told me after the shootings that he himself had shot several Jews at the grave. I did not have the impression that he did this unwillingly."[93] There is evidence from elsewhere in the East that SS shooters would often allow others to participate. A Luftwaffe lieutenant colonel secretly recorded in captivity stated frankly that at one killing "the SS issued an invitation to go and shoot Jews. All the troops went along with rifles . . . and shot them up. Each man could pick the one he wanted."[94] He was not referring to the Krupki killing, but such testimony certainly presents a counter-image to that of SS men threatening Wehrmacht soldiers with their own execution for failure to participate, a description frequently given of the SS by soldiers.

Another possible scenario and one also strongly supported by the evidence is that those soldiers tasked with guarding the execution site were then included in the shooting as the action progressed. It appears that, perhaps as a result of Waldow's refusal to supply the Teilkommando with ammunition, Schönemann's men were running short of bullets, and Wehrmacht soldiers were then asked or ordered to assist with their rifles.[95] Another reason that the men of the 3rd Battalion were included may have been to accelerate the operation. Schönemann stated that "it went incredibly fast, in order to avoid any delay, in the interest of both sides, the victims as well as those participating in the execution."[96] Certainly he did not have the victims' interests in mind, but he was, as noted previously, uncomfortable during these operations and wanted them to go as rapidly as possible. In addition, the weather was deteriorating.[97] Storm clouds were swirling, and it had begun to rain. A member of the SS Teilkommando testified that "clouds appeared and a thunderstorm approached. Schönemann therefore had things proceed very quickly."[98] Perhaps the men of the 354th helped speed things along.

Former German officers from Waldow's battalion also confirmed that soldiers had participated in the Krupki killings. The battalion surgeon, Dr. Konrad G., reported that he and a platoon leader in 12th Company informed the battalion adjutant, Lieutenant Speth, that 3rd Battalion soldiers were shooting Jews, to which Speth allegedly became angry and replied that "the participation of Wehrmacht soldiers in the shooting had not been ordered."[99] In the final analysis, Wehrmacht soldiers in Krupki did take a direct hand in the work of the Einsatzgruppen, either according to plan or in an improvised, ad hoc manner. The chilling testimony of one SS Teilkommando member highlights the amateurish nature of the killing. "As we were just about ready to leave," he testified, "a Russian came running after us. He apparently had the task of covering the grave. He said something in Russian that was translated, and one of us was sent back. I myself had a look around and saw a three-year-old child sitting on the pile of bodies crying. The child was shot by the man who had been sent back."[100] A local witness also remembered the killing of a child who had survived the first shooting.[101] Around five in the afternoon, after the last Jew had been shot, Schönemann collected the victims' confiscated valuables and drove away along with his men.

Local Belarusians also participated in elements of the Krupki killing. Local citizens filled in the grave and covered it with lime.[102] Seventy men from the town fulfilled this task under the watchful eye of the local police chief and the mayor, a man named Makaravich.[103] As the killing process in Belarus became more routine, non-Jewish Belarusians would become more and more involved.[104] Both at the killing site and in Krupki, the non-Jewish inhabitants also looted the possessions left behind by the Jews.[105] One Belarusian eyewitness recalled that there was a "fair" organized in the town where "everything was sold off, furniture, clothes."[106] The reaction of the local non-Jewish inhabitants of Krupki is difficult to gauge. The testimony of this eyewitness, however, presents the complex juxtaposition of sympathy and latent antisemitism that may have been present among many. When interviewed in 2011, she remembered local support for the Jews: "Everyone treated [the Jews] with great sympathy." Yet she also described the Jews as "guileful/wily" and as people who when trading with local peasants always took advantage for their own financial gain. She also noted pointedly that there were those who "made their 'fortunes' because there was no fairness, no 'neatness' in [the expropriation of Jewish property]." On the other hand, she recalled Krupki Jews being hidden by local Belarusians who disguised them as family members.[107]

After the killing, the soldiers who had been tasked with guarding the execution site marched back to Krupki, whose Jewish community had just ceased to exist. As the local men were covering the grave, they discovered twenty-one-year-old Sofia Shalaumova still alive. She had fallen into the trench unhurt and survived. She asked the laborer, whom she knew as an acquaintance, not to bury her alive, and he allowed her to escape.[108] Local civilians remembered that individual Jews caught in the area after the shooting were also shot.[109] Margarita Kosenkova visited the site soon after the killings with a group of other children from her village. "The ground was moving," she said, "and blood was coming out of the ground. For two years after, there was blood there."[110]

Schönemann reported the killing to EK 8, and a month later the following summary appeared in the operational report of Einsatzgruppe B to Heinrich Himmler: "Two larger actions were carried out by the unit [EK 8] in Krupka and Sholopenitsche [*sic*]. In the first town 912 Jews were liquidated and in the second 822. With this, the Krupka region can be seen as *Judenfrei*."[111] The killings in Kholoponichi, which resulted in an additional 822 victims, had been supported by two platoons from the 10th Company.[112] A report from the 354th Regiment on the next day did not mention Krupki, nor did any other report from either the 3rd Battalion or the regiment.[113] The whole incident either had passed without notice or was intentionally not reported in writing. The commander of the 354th Infantry Regiment perpetuated this lapse in memory after the war, testifying that "I am hearing today for the first time that, in the fall of 1941, the Jewish population of Krupki was rounded up and escorted, with the assistance of the 3rd Battalion, to an execution site where they were then shot."[114]

The events in Krupki resulted from both Nazi genocidal policy at the highest level and its negotiation and implementation at the lowest. Representing the bulk of the division's combat power, the 354th Infantry Regiment was assigned the most important task of protecting the vital logistical rail and road links behind Army Group Center, which accounts for how it arrived in Krupki. How, then, did the 3rd Battalion become so deeply involved in executing the racial policies of the Third Reich on the ground?

The answer lies at many levels. One must begin with the Army High Command, which had agreed before the invasion to support the killing units. A November 1941 order from another division in rHGM laid out the areas of responsibility of the various security organizations, including the SD (Einsatzgruppen). It identified as keywords for the SD "Politically suspect civilians, Bolsheviks, Jews, and Gypsies" and under SD missions listed "Solution to the Jewish Question" and "the Gypsy Question."[115] In addition, the well-known "Criminal Orders" set an unmistakably murderous example for German soldiers in the East, and the tasks and purpose of the Einsatzgruppen proved a mystery to no one.

The Jew-Bolshevik-partisan calculus also played a vital role in disguising Wehrmacht participation in genocide. Coupled with the Hitler order of 13 May 1941, which suspended prosecution of Wehrmacht soldiers for any crimes committed against civilians in the Soviet Union, high-level orders not only condoned but in fact encouraged brutal action against civilians in general and Jews in particular. In this calculus, all Jews were pro-Bolshevik, all Bolsheviks were partisans, and hence all Jews were partisans (that is, not all partisans and Bolsheviks were Jews, but all Jews were Bolsheviks and partisans or sympathizers). The rHGM informed its units that "cooperation with the SD and GFP is to be made even closer in all actions by the divisions and their subordinate staffs. . . . Requests for local operation of individual squads of SD Einsatzkommandos are to be submitted to the commander."[116] Thus, the relationship between the army and the death squads was to become even more intimate. The support provided to the Einsatzgruppen also appears at the division level. In its summary for the period from September to December 1941, the intelligence section of the 286th Security Division (the 354th's parent unit) appeared happy to report that "constant contact was maintained with the Security Service, specifically the Einsatzgruppe of *Gruppenführer* Neumann, the Einsatzkommando 8 of *Sturmbannführer* Dr. Bratfisch [*sic*], and in particular with *Untersturmführer* Reschke's Orscha-based squad [note: Orscha is 60 miles (97 km) east of Krupki]."[117] This statement hints at much more than merely a logistical relationship.

In addition to supporting the mobile killing squads, Wehrmacht organizational culture and that of Army Group Center Rear also propagated the message that Jews were a group distinct from the general civilian population, inferior and expendable. Jews were already targeted this way in the "Guidelines for the Behavior of the Troops." On 18 July, another security division in rHGM ordered "hostages (particularly Jews)" to be rounded up in reprisal for an attack on a German sentry and a messenger.[118] The 354th Infantry Regiment itself reported on 7 September that it had participated, in conjunction with a signal battalion, in the killing of the entire Jewish population of Tschereja in reprisal for an attack on German troops.[119]

Finally, all these factors coalesced under the aegis of an anti-partisan war, though a largely ethereal one. The Jewish population was "militarized"—that is, Jews were transformed into combatants (as partisans or partisan supporters) and thereby speciously deemed legitimate targets for military action. In Krupki, this must have been purely rhetorical, as it was evident to all that those being killed were not partisans. This type of broad targeting also occurred in the 3rd Battalion. In the 354th Regiment's area of operations, little *real* anti-partisan war was occurring. Personnel records indicate that, in the period from 22 June to 30 September, only seventeen men were killed and thirty-two wounded in the entire division of seventy-five hundred.[120] It is likely, therefore, that the unit was involved in the far less dangerous task of rounding up bypassed Red Army soldiers, Communists, and, perhaps, Jews. One soldier remembered, "We often carried out so-called raids, mostly at night. The resident Jews would be rounded up and assembled in the town. After they were assembled, a site would be chosen in the surrounding woods and they would be shot. Sometimes non-Jews would be taken along to dig the graves and they took the Jews' possessions with them."[121] That was not combat; it was murder. Major Waldow's selection as a speaker and trainer at a corps-level anti-partisan conference in Mogilev a week after the Krupki massacre is evidence that the actions of his battalion were in no way condemned by his superiors, but on the contrary were viewed as an accomplishment that qualified him for a special assignment.

Why did Major Waldow agree to allow his battalion to participate to such a degree? It is possible that he was reluctant to provide his soldiers as firing squads, at least in the initial meeting. He did call his regimental headquarters for clarification on whether he should assist Schönemann. It is unclear whether this was a result of his objection to *any* participation, or merely his desire to have the action approved by his superiors. One should not, however, assume that his objections were based on any moral grounds. No evidence exists explaining his reluctance, except that he found the whole thing distasteful. He stated during questioning that "my concern was to avoid members of the battalion coming into immediate contact with the Jewish inhabitants of Krupki or the SD."[122] Such concerns that the killing of women and children was a dirty job and not the mission of the regular army were common but did not necessarily represent disagreement with the policy itself. In any case, these reservations did not prevent him from fully assisting Teilkommando Schönemann, down to choosing the execution site for them. Moreover, given the postwar legal situation, it would have made good sense for him to play up his moral objections, even if these were fabricated. Yet, Waldow did not make any such claims. Finally, there is evidence that Krupki was not the first time he had worked with Einsatzkommando 8, as we have seen. In the final analysis, Waldow and his men provided vital support, without which the ten to twenty men of the Teilkommando could never have carried out such a large action. Indeed, it would have been impossible for the approximately three thousand men of the Einsatzgruppen to murder 1.5 million Jews in the Soviet Union without support from other organizations.

As we have seen, the majority of Wehrmacht soldiers participating in the Krupki "action" were not volunteers but also did not evade participation. How then did they approach this experience, and what does their experience and that of the victims tell us about such killings? We may start with their knowledge of the intent of the operation. Did these men realize that their actions were directly responsible for the murder of a thousand human beings?

Naturally, most soldiers purported to have had no idea that they were participating in mass murder, claiming that they thought the Jews were to be deported to labor camps. This must be, for the most part, a postwar construction. Waldow and the company commanders certainly knew that the Jews were to be shot. It is almost certain that they passed this information on to their soldiers. In any case, a sufficient number of soldiers confessed knowledge of the real goal to cast serious doubt on any claims of ignorance. For example, Erich J. described a conversation with a fellow soldier on the day of the shooting. "The stated reason for the registration was only a pretext," he admitted; "from the way the conversation went it was clear to me that the Jews would be shot."[123] Another soldier, recalling executions of Jews the unit had already witnessed in Minsk, said it was obvious these Jews were to be "liquidated" too.[124] Finally, Sergeant Paul D. related: "Supposedly we knew that these Jews were to be resettled. However, all Wehrmacht members, including me, would have known that these people were going to their deaths."[125]

At least one former soldier testified to having opted out of participation. Private First Class Martin S. requested to be relieved from guarding the execution site. After the war he explained his behavior, saying, "I didn't want to witness this. I was married then and had four children. I remember clearly that I thought of my family and felt that the imminent events were wrong. I simply couldn't witness the shooting of these people. I went then to Lieutenant M. and told him he should release me from any further escorting of Jews to the shooting site. I know I told him I couldn't watch it because I had four children at home. M. told me I could go and do guard duty."[126] Why, then, out of 130 former officers and soldiers questioned after the war, did only Martin S. request a different assignment?[127] There are likely several explanations.

First, many soldiers saw no way out or perhaps did not realize the full meaning of their participation until they were committed. Corporal Paul L.'s statement is typical: "In this moment, it was clear to me that the Jews I was escorting would be shot and I had no further task. I would have not been able to change anything."[128] Another said, "I didn't dare do or say anything because I was only a simple soldier and couldn't have changed anything."[129] Many refer to their station as "simple soldiers." Second, as Omer Bartov has shown, these soldiers did operate under a system of draconian military discipline. Though this was *not* a combat environment where failure to obey could result in death, such a system was certainly a factor in the men's decision making. For example, Bruno H.

stated, "When I am told that at the latest I must have known at the execution site that the civilians were to be shot and that it had nothing to do with war, this is true. I didn't have the courage at the time to do anything against it or to refuse the order because I certainly had to count on being shot myself."[130] For many if not all German soldiers, obedience was seen as an important military virtue.[131] Such statements certainly result in part from the postwar situation of the witness and the ubiquitous "obedience to orders" excuse, but there is also likely an element of truth in them. The men of the 3rd Battalion were not experienced in these sorts of mass killings and perhaps had not discovered the methods of evasion and refusal that other soldiers would later use. Many men were also perhaps overcome by the speed and extremity of events and unable to react (should they have desired to do so).

Still, some men clearly refused to admit their understanding of the situation at the time. During his 2007 interview, Bruno Menzel attempted to deflect questions about his participation and his knowledge of the purpose of the action in Krupki. Though he claimed his platoon leader offered the men a chance to back out, he denied any knowledge that the action was to kill Jews. Menzel further states that his duty position in the grenade launcher platoon precluded him from participating in encircling the town. He also frequently refers to the necessity of obeying orders and the threat to his life if he disobeyed, though he states twice that he was given the opportunity to not participate in this "difficult task."[132]

Some men describe a fear that the SS or army would shoot them for refusing to participate. This is almost certainly a self-serving falsehood. These soldiers would not have feared being shot by the SS or even by the army, though many claimed so after the war. German units (of any ilk) simply did not shoot each other out of hand, especially when the offender was not even a member of the same branch. While it was probably clear to most that soldiers would not be shot on the spot, the specter of other types of punishment was undoubtedly present. It must be recognized, however, that military culture functions by necessity under increased disciplinary pressure, and for some this pressure may have been enough to mute any evasion, especially as, unlike in later situations, those opposed to such participation had not yet discovered successful ways to evade. However, it is important to point out that no historian, or German defense attorney, for that matter, has been able to document an instance of a German being executed for failure to participate in executions such as these. Such extreme measures were unnecessary, as sufficient numbers of killers could always be found.

Lastly, the division of labor provided some psychological protection for these men. The tactics involved almost mirrored those employed against partisans in terms of surrounding towns and identifying suspicious persons. This "tactical muscle memory" may have allowed some soldiers to tell themselves that this operation was no different from previous operations of which they had been a part. Except for those who may have actually been shooting, soldiers could claim (both to themselves at the time and after the war) that they had not *actually* participated in the shooting. As one man stated after the war, "We merely had to carry out the *Absperrung*. At this time, we didn't know what was actually going on."[133] It stretches the bounds of reason to suppose that many soldiers would not have known what they were enabling. However, such separation of tasks likely allowed some of them to believe or convince themselves that they were not assisting murder.

This dichotomy is particularly clear in the following statement from a soldier employed in the outer cordon encircling Krupki: "We soldiers were merely employed in the *Absperrung*. . . . We had nothing to do with the killings."[134] Participants attempted to consciously divorce their actions from the whole, to intentionally avoid acknowledging that their behavior was directly connected with the final killing step. Lieutenant Nick, who had chosen the execution site, reported that "those in the *Absperrung* were so depressed that evening that they wouldn't eat anything." Men who do not feel disgust or guilt at their actions rarely become depressed after the act. Nick went on to describe how he explained the murder to his men: "I had to really persuade them that they had to eat. I added, 'Eat, men. Don't worry about it because there are many atrocities in war. We are not responsible for it.'"[135] This "explanation" appears to have had some purchase. Former corporal L. told police, "I could not have changed anything. In answer to your question, I must say that as a result I found myself in no moral conflict. . . . I am therefore not aware of being guilty of anything."[136] One is forced to wonder here whether he is speaking more to himself than to his interrogators. One researcher who studied Holocaust perpetrators noticed that "some of the perpetrators could recall one vignette of their wrongdoing, which they would 'replay' all the time in their 'inner video,' feeling remorse about or being guilty for what they had done. This activity gave them a certain assurance that they were human beings . . . after all. With the help of this memory, they could 'forget' or repress all the other atrocities they had been involved in."[137] Perhaps this explains some of the psychological responses of German soldiers to their participation in mass murder.

However, if some soldiers were reluctant participants swept up in the operation, others were very willing. We have already seen that volunteers were sought and found for the more distasteful duty of rounding up the Jews from their houses and possibly for shooting. There were soldiers in the unit whose antisemitism made these killings welcome. Private Reinhold L. recalled that one soldier had aimed his rifle at a Jewish girl "for fun" a few days before the execution.[138] Certainly men such as this were not uncommon, but the German testimonies do not contain many references to them. Witnesses do describe two junior leaders who stood out as *Draufgänger* or "go-getters" of two different varieties and who likely had their counterparts among the other noncommissioned officers and men.

The first was Master Sergeant Schrade, who led the 2nd Platoon in 12th Company. He was described by one soldier as "an arrogant person" *(Windhund)* who "didn't have any time for his people."[139] He often led "partisan hunts" and "always had 'his' people who went with him."[140] Schrade used volunteers for these missions, which he conducted often in civilian clothes. As mentioned, he published a treatise on small-unit anti-partisan tactics that was disseminated throughout rHGM. Clearly, he was an active and avid fighter. But what of his participation in anti-Jewish actions? Heidenreich was in Schrade's platoon, and another 2nd Platoon soldier supported his contention that it was indeed Schrade who had sought the fifteen men with "strong nerves." He was also placed at the execution site by several witnesses. He appears as a dedicated soldier and an ambitious leader who may have been involved in anti-Jewish shootings during his partisan patrols and during the execution. In any

case, Schrade ranks high as a potential suspect in the commission of
Wehrmacht atrocities against Jews.[141]

Another platoon leader in 12th Company was noted for his extremity
as well. While Master Sergeant Schrade appears as a diehard and zealous soldier, Lieutenant Hermann Nick is remembered more as a brutal
and fanatical man. He was "unpopular with all the soldiers because of
his ruthless behavior. He tormented those who gave him any opportunity."[142] One of his soldiers recalled that during an anti-partisan operation, Nick had approximately twenty to thirty men pulled from their
houses and shot on the spot, allegedly because shots had been fired from
the village the day prior.[143] Sometime after the Krupki shooting, he tortured a local mayor for information regarding partisans by first repeatedly hanging him from a balcony and then forcing him into a freezing
lake until he talked.[144] On a different operation, the lieutenant allegedly
burned down a house with a woman in it who was suspected of shelter-
ing partisans. He and his men watched as the house burned to the
ground with the woman inside, at the window.[145] Finally, one soldier reported that he had personally seen Nick shoot five or six children who
peeled potatoes in the company kitchen for extra food.[146] It is probably
no coincidence that it was Nick who found the execution site and who
was one of those responsible for the *Absperrung* there.

Unlike the Einsatzgruppen unit that swooped into town, conducted
its killings, and left, the 3rd Battalion had been present in Krupki for
over a month before the killings. This meant that the unit experienced
significant contact with the civilian population, including the Jews, despite the best of Major Waldow's intentions. The speed of the German
advance, arriving only six days after the invasion, ensured that most of
the town's Jews were trapped under German occupation. A ghetto had
already been established in July for approximately a thousand Jews, but
likely was not closed or guarded.[147]

Like Wehrmacht units elsewhere, the 3rd Battalion used Jews as forced
labor for various tasks. One lieutenant recalled that they were used for
repair work.[148] However, most soldiers particularly remembered the Jewish girls who were "employed" as maids or janitors in the headquarters
or barracks. Perhaps women were viewed as less dangerous than men and
were chosen for such tasks, or perhaps there was simply a shortage of

Jewish men. In any case, daily contact with these Jewish women must have bred familiarity, for it is almost exclusively these women who represented the victims in the minds of the perpetrators.[149]

A clerk in the 10th Company related the following encounter. On the morning of the execution, he looked on as a twenty-year-old Jewish girl stepped outside to empty the trash. A Soviet civilian appeared and gruffly spoke to the girl. The clerk concluded, "the girl was very frightened and returned to Krupka [*sic*]. I thought to myself that this girl would now certainly be shot."[150] Yet the clerk apparently did nothing to prevent this. A private on battalion staff recalled watching two twenty-year-old girls who cleaned for them leaving the village to be shot.[151] He, too, did nothing. This level of inaction suggests at least some level of recognition (and/or acceptance) that Jews lived and died according to a different set of rules than Germans.

For Major Waldow, close contact with Jews had at least some personal impact. His battalion ordnance officer, Lieutenant Werner K., told investigators that Major Waldow lived in the house of a Jewish pharmacist.[152] Waldow's orderly testified that the major had tried to persuade the man to escape because he would be shot the next day. However, the man apparently refused and was likely killed along with the rest.[153] This incident, if true, adds some depth to our understanding of Waldow himself. He appears to have been a man with reservations about killing Jews, willing to warn those with whom he had personal contact, but, as an officer, prepared to fully cooperate with the killing when it was asked of him.

Familiarity did not always breed empathy, however. It also bred contempt. As mentioned earlier, one soldier pointed his rifle at a Jewish girl apparently in an attempt to frighten her. According to the witness, the girl told this soldier, "Go ahead and shoot! Whether today or tomorrow, doesn't matter to me."[154] The witness concluded from this that she knew of the impending execution. Two weeks after the killing, a soldier in 9th Company wrote in his diary: "The local Russian police brought us bacon which the Jews had set aside. These Jews were shot. There the mayor had them annihilated."[155] Belarusian witness Nadezhda Dranitsa recalled that German soldiers "treated all the Jews as if they were some lepers."[156]

Perhaps the most intriguing and puzzling of the interactions these men had with their victims concerns a Jewish opera singer from Minsk.

This woman was shot along with the others but appears to have been well known among the 3rd Battalion soldiers. When speaking with an eyewitness of the executions, Sergeant Erwin K. asked whether all the Jews had been shot, "even the pretty women." The other soldier replied, "Yes, all shot. Also, the singer from Minsk."[157] Another soldier, asking about the fate of the cleaning women, was told that a girl from the theater, who was "pretty as a picture," was also shot.[158] It is even more unexpected that two SS members of the Teilkommando also remembered that this opera singer had been among those murdered.[159]

What is the significance of this woman in the memory of the perpetrators? Who was she? Why was she so well known (and so well remembered)? Unfortunately, her story raises more questions than it answers. It is likely that she fled Minsk, perhaps because she had relatives in Krupki. It is possible that she was even forced to perform for the soldiers there. In any case, it remains doubtful that the Germans became aware of her only on the day of the shooting. Moreover, how did the SS find out about her? Did the soldiers tell them? If so, under what circumstances?

It could be that women in general figure so highly in soldiers' memories because they highlighted most clearly the extreme nature of this action. Murdering pretty women was perhaps the most shocking element of this new kind of mission. Other servicemen elsewhere in the occupied East made similar comments while in captivity, such as the conversation between two U-boat crewmen who witnessed a mass murder in Lithuania. They had an extended conversation about a "marvelous," "smartly dressed," "pretty Jewess" from Germany who was shot.[160] In any case, this singer from Minsk reminds us both of the individual lives and stories that came to an end in Krupki, and that to these men, their victims were not necessarily faceless or nameless but were killed all the same.

In the fall of 1943, an SS lieutenant in Minsk named Müller began preparing cards listing locations of mass graves in occupied Belarus.[161] These lists were then handed over to Sonderkommando 1005, a unit whose special task was eradicating the evidence of Nazi crimes before the Red Army recaptured the territory. In Krupki as elsewhere, Soviet

prisoners were forced to dig up corpses and burn them. Vladimir Baranchik from Krupki recalled in December 1945 that "German thugs
burned the bodies of killed Jews before retreating. Burnings were carried out with the involvement of arrested Soviet citizens who were
brought from prison in Borisov. They were also burnt afterwards. I can't
give you the exact number of bodies burnt, but the number of Jews was
about 2,000."[162] Margarita Kosenkova remembered that the "smell was
terrible and the villagers saw [the burning operation] from the roofs of
their houses."[163] The Red Army entered the town on 28 June 1944.[164] As
elsewhere in the Soviet Union, they uncovered the crimes of the "fascist
occupiers," including the murder of the Jews of Krupki.

The Krupki killing site is little changed today, a large meadow on the
edge of an evergreen forest sloping gently down to a marsh alongside the
Starozhevitsa River. It lies off a gravel road running north of the town
and across the highway, likely the same road that the Jews were forced
down in 1941. Still visible are the remnants of the peat pits and excava-
tions. In 1969, a memorial was constructed at the site, funded by relatives of the murdered.[165] However, because the Soviet authorities would
not allow any mention of Jews, the inscription reads only "Buried here
are 1,975 peaceful Soviet citizens, brutally murdered by the German
Fascist occupiers, September 18, 1941." The particularly Jewish suffering during the Holocaust was to be systematically erased from Soviet
memory under the slogan "Do Not Divide the Dead."[166] A few trees have
been planted around the monument. It is a humble memorial, but the
grass is kept trimmed, as is the meadow where the Jews awaited their
deaths. Nadezhda remembered that her fellow teachers at the small school
in Krupki after the war, who were both Jewish, would visit the site every
September in memory of their murdered family members.[167] The rural
landscape of much of Belarus is dotted with small, simple stone monu-
ments and metal fences surrounding graves. Belarusians throughout the
region seem to quietly remember their Jewish neighbors by maintaining
execution sites and even Jewish cemeteries.

The Krupki killing gives us a window into another Holocaust. The
sterile numbers in the Einsatzgruppen reports return to real places and

Krupki became blueprint
Waldow to
Mogilev
conf.

re-form into real lives destroyed. It also corrects a prevalent depiction of these killings as routine and without incident. On the contrary, we see that horrible scenes of misery, brutality, and sadism occurred on an intimately personal level. The victims did not go quietly to the pits, resigned to their fates; they cried, they screamed, they pleaded, they tried to escape. And the German army was there—guarding, escorting, and also shooting.

Here, in Krupki, one sees the end product of the high-level staff coordination and promises of support and cooperation between the Einsatzgruppen and the Wehrmacht. This was not just an agreement on paper, but one that on the ground resulted in German soldiers loading sick people onto trucks to be killed, guarding them in their last moments, and, in some cases, killing innocent men, women, and children themselves. Wehrmacht collusion in the Holocaust has often been described as haphazard rather than systematic, and of secondary rather than of primary importance. Yet Krupki shows how important this participation actually was and how coordinated it became, even in the early stages. Regardless of how the soldiers viewed their part, the army was essential in the murder of this community and provided the manpower, the force, and the intimidation that allowed a small group of SS shooters to kill one thousand people. Moreover, as this and other cases show, the soldiers of the German army did not remain aloof but instead pulled triggers themselves.

There was an afterlife to the Krupki massacre. Just one week after the massacre, Major Waldow traveled to the regional capital of Mogilev to participate in a conference on the anti-partisan war in the rHGM. He brought with him the lessons of his collusion with the Einsatzgruppen. Along with other officers, he would share these experiences as the Wehrmacht codified its role in the anti-Jewish policy and deliberately began to target Jews. In this way, the lessons learned by Major Waldow became part of the blueprint for future Wehrmacht collusion in the Holocaust.

CHAPTER FOUR

Mogilev and the Deliberate
Targeting of Jews

It was said that the Jews of this town were to be liquidated. Because they did things with the partisans. Who said this first, I can't say. It spread by word of mouth.

Sergeant Leopold W., 3rd Company, 691st Infantry Regiment

ON OCTOBER 10, 1941, the soldiers of the 3rd Company, 691st Infantry Regiment, were uneasy. The task ahead of them was something new: they were to kill the entire Jewish population of Krucha, a village in central Belarus.[1] A few hours later, Private Wilhelm Magel stood with another soldier in front of four Jewish women and an old man with a long white beard. The company first sergeant, Emil Zimber, ordered the Jews to face away from the shooters, but they refused. Zimber gave the order to fire anyway, but Magel and his colleague, a former divinity student, balked, intentionally missing their targets. They requested to be relieved from the execution detail and were reassigned to guard the remaining Jews waiting in the village square.[2] This German army unit, without assistance from other organizations, then murdered at least 150 Jewish men, women, and children as a direct result of an anti-partisan conference that had taken place over a week earlier at the headquarters of Army Group Center (Rear) in Mogilev.[3] Two officers from the 1st Bat-

92

talion (of which 3rd Company was a part) had returned from this conference with the message "where there is a Jew, there is a partisan." A week later, the battalion commander, Major Alfred Commichau, ordered the murder of all Jews in his area of control.

The Mogilev Conference offers us the rare opportunity to investigate the relationship between the anti-partisan war and the Wehrmacht's participation in the Holocaust on the ground. This little-studied conference represents an important turning point in the Wehrmacht's participation in the Holocaust, at least in Belarus. The evidence strongly suggests that, at least in rHGM, the anti-partisan war was used as a vehicle by which to enlist greater support from the Wehrmacht in executing Nazi genocidal policy. Jews were added to an approved list of enemies to be systematically eliminated. This chapter will examine how the Mogilev Conference accomplished this expansion of Wehrmacht responsibility into genocide and present evidence of increased complicity in the murder of Jews throughout rHGM and Belarus in the weeks and months following the conference.

As explained earlier, the Wehrmacht's role in the Holocaust developed both in the course of a military campaign and also in the context of long-term cultural and organizational inputs such as latent antisemitism, military discipline, and institutional violence. The intent here is not to discount these long-term contextual factors, but to investigate how the anti-partisan war and the Jew-Bolshevik-partisan construct were used to more fully incorporate the Wehrmacht in genocide.[4] Though many historians have noted a connection between the anti-partisan war and the Holocaust, what is less clear is how this argument was instrumentalized at the unit level—that is, how it influenced behavior on the ground. The nature of the partisan threat was, in fact, intentionally mobilized to provide useful ideological, psychological, and tactical expedients with which to bring the substantial manpower of the Wehrmacht to bear against the Jews. The Mogilev Conference, which has not received much treatment historically, is a very significant event in this regard.[5] It is evidence of an intentional effort to include the Wehrmacht in the Holocaust at its most basic level.

The town of Mogilev is a provincial capital, located on the Dnieper River in eastern Belarus, over 120 miles from Minsk. Founded in the thirteenth century, it functioned mainly as a center for commerce between Russia and western Europe.[6] The Germans entered the largely destroyed city on 26 July after almost a month of stiff Soviet resistance. On 7 September, the staff of rHGM set up its headquarters in the city.[7] The Wehrmacht had quickly moved through this wooded and swampy region, advancing over 280 miles from Warsaw to Minsk in less than two weeks. While the armored spearhead rushed forward, infantry units followed more slowly behind to reduce the huge pockets of encircled Red Army units. However, given the sheer number of soldiers involved, large groups of dispersed or bypassed Red Army soldiers remained at large in the countryside.[8]

While most of these groups were leaderless and probably seeking either to return to Soviet lines or to their civilian lives, some armed groups carried out minor attacks on German infrastructure and units. Large numbers of agile, vicious, well-armed, and well-organized guerrillas harrying German troops in the snows of Russia were yet to come; this popular image of the partisan movement was still two years away in 1941. The overall impact of the partisans in German rear areas is still under debate; only now can much of the triumphalist Soviet historiography of the partisan effort be more evenly evaluated. Certainly, as time passed, the partisan movement had an increasingly greater effect on the German war effort, tying down troops, destroying communications, and interrupting logistics efforts. Though Russia had a history of effective guerrilla units such as the Cossacks, Stalin's prewar refusal to countenance any thought of combat behind the lines left the Soviet Union woefully unprepared for the occupation of its territory. An indication of the relative threat posed by insurgents can be seen in that only fifteen German regular or security divisions were employed in the rear areas out of more than one hundred divisions fighting the Red Army.[9] Even by October 1943, of 2.6 million men on the eastern front, only 100,000 were concerned with security behind the lines.[10] One historian argues that the "fragmented and largely unpopular partisan movement posed no major threat to the German occupation" through the end of 1941.[11] In the summer and fall of that year, partisan organization and combat ability remained "rudimentary at best" as the rapid advance of German forces occupied large amounts of territory, leaving little time for insurgents to organize.[12] The effect was that, in vast areas of occupied Soviet territory, hundreds of miles behind the front lines, resistance was at first left to spontaneous and scattered groups of NKVD, die-hard Communists, so-called "destruction battalions," and dispersed Red Army soldiers willing to carry on a fifth-column war in the enemy rear. Indeed, at this point in the campaign, one can reasonably argue, as Hannes Heer does, for an "antipartisan war without partisans."[13]

While the actual partisan threat in rHGM remained low in the summer and fall of 1941, both the Wehrmacht paranoia about it and the use of the civilian "danger" as a cover for more direct genocidal policies increased. In July 1941, for example, rHGM already warned of "partisan detachments" and ordered that any civilians supporting them be treated as *Freischärlers*—that is, summarily executed.[14] Army headquarters (OKH) also set the tone for this paranoia by informing rHGM on 25 July that the "unconditional security of German soldiers must be the key in any action and in all measures to be taken."[15] However, German casualty figures do not support the existence of a lethal partisan movement. The rHGM reported a total of 1,993 German soldiers killed in the period between June 1941 and March 1942, which equates to 200 soldiers a month.[16] The 286th Security Division in the same area recorded a total of 18 killed between June and December of 1941, out of an average strength of 5,700.[17] Yet from August through December, the same division reported 598 enemy combatants killed in action and 8,131 prisoners taken. This works out to roughly 30 partisans killed for every German, and one German killed for every 451 prisoners taken. These casualties hardly indicate a vibrant and dangerous insurgency.[18] Ratios such as these would be extraordinary for actual combat, let alone for fighting against an elusive enemy like the partisans. This begs the question: Who were the Germans fighting? The answer must be by and large noncombatants. Along with bypassed soldiers and "suspect" civilians, unarmed civilian Jews were killed as well.

Implicit in the killing in the summer and fall of 1941, especially on Soviet territory, was the Jew-Bolshevik-partisan calculus already mentioned. In this formulation, all Jews were Bolsheviks, all Bolsheviks were partisans (or at the very least supporters of partisans), and thus, all Jews were also partisans or partisan supporters. This formula is important in explaining the murder of Jews under the guise of the anti-partisan war.

The Jew-Bolshevik conflation was a well-worn trope of Nazi propaganda before World War II. However, its extension to partisans was something newer. Ironically, the same construction had been used by many Russians themselves during the Russian civil war to justify violence against Jews.[19]

Emphasizing the Communist and "enemy" nature of Jews likely helped activate in the Wehrmacht greater support for genocidal policy based on latent anticommunist feeling and the appearance of a legitimate military threat. In effect, this construction, along with the criminal orders, "militarized" the Jewish population of the Soviet Union and allowed them to be "legitimately" targeted by the army. The units represented at the Mogilev Conference had already been conflating Jews and partisans and had already killed both at times throughout rHGM. General Schenckendorff, the commander of rHGM, was himself fully aware that the majority of killings reported to him as partisans and "plunderers" were primarily Jews.[20] This prior experience constituted an important prehistory to Mogilev, for many of the key commanders previously involved in killing Jews would participate in the conference.

The regional characteristics of Belarus, or the Belarusian Soviet Socialist Republic, as it was called at the time, are critical to both the nature of the Mogilev Conference and the events that followed. In many ways, this region was fundamentally different from the regions occupied by the Germans to the north and south—the Baltic states and the Ukraine. As we have seen, unlike the Baltic and the Ukraine, Belarus had little deep-seated nationalist fervor. Indeed, it saw none of the spontaneous pogroms that occurred in other regions of the Soviet Union.[21] This was partly because it had comparatively weaker national movements willing to support the Nazis for promises of, or even just wishful thinking about, eventual sovereignty.

On September 16, rHGM requested that officers who "as a result of their performance and experience in the battle against partisans can provide a valuable experience report" participate in a three-day "exchange of experiences."[22] General Max von Schenckendorff, the commander of this rear area, personally welcomed these officers to Mogilev.

An analysis of the participants yields some telling clues about the nature of this conference. Sixty-one officers from various units in rHGM traveled to Mogilev. Wehrmacht personnel represented an overwhelming

Mogilev Conference Participants
Displayed by Rank (61 total attendees)

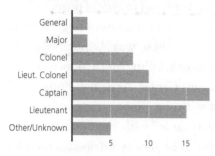

Graph 1. The majority of participants in the Mogilev "Anti-partisan" Conference were officers who had been directly involved in leading soldiers at the lower levels of command.

82 percent of the participants and came mostly from the three major divisions in rHGM (221st, 286th, and 403rd Security Divisions), as well as rHGM staff. One representative of the Army High Command (OKH) attended. Also notable is that 38 percent of the officers attending were commanders at the battalion or company level.[23] Over half the army officers were captains or lieutenants. Thus, the attendees were heavily Wehrmacht and largely junior officers and low-level commanders; significantly, they were those usually responsible for executing policy rather than making it. In this context, we see another example of the complex interaction between center and periphery in Nazi policies, with local actors contributing directly to the evolution of higher-level policy while simultaneously being influenced by directives from above.

Some of these attendees had already distinguished themselves as particularly violent or complicit with genocidal policy. Major Waldow, of the 354th Infantry Regiment, provides a prime example, his battalion having directly supported Einsatzkommando 8 in the murder of one thousand Jews in the town of Krupki less than a week earlier. A captain from the 350th Infantry Regiment was also present; his regiment had already assisted in the removal of Jews from the Bialowiezer Forest to create a private game preserve for Hermann Göring. Another officer in this regiment had earlier counseled that "the Jewish Question must be more radically solved. I recommend the collection of all the Jews living in the countryside in guarded detention and work camps. Suspect elements must be eliminated."[24] Indeed, Michael Wildt's description of the high-level officers in the SS as "flexible, mobile, eager, able to fulfill their job everywhere" could be applied to these men with a high degree of accuracy.[25]

In conclusion, the Wehrmacht officers attending had likely been chosen *for* their extreme and brutal records and certainly not *in spite* of them.

The non-army attendees are also critical in understanding the tenor of the Mogilev Conference. First among these was Arthur Nebe, the commander of Einsatzgruppe B, the mobile killing unit assigned to murder the Jews overtaken by Army Group Center. Nebe had "promptly" volunteered for service in the East with the Einsatzgruppen in an attempt to advance his career and "curry favor" with Heydrich.[26] He had also arranged for one hundred people to be shot as a demonstration for Himmler on 15 August 1941, and in September had experimented with dynamite and exhaust gas as killing methods on mentally disabled people.[27] By the end of the year, over 190,000 Jews had been murdered in Belarus, most of them by units under Nebe's command.[28] The presence of an Einsatzgruppen commander indicates that the conference's focus would not remain a purely military one.

Nebe was joined in Mogilev by the Higher SS and Police Leader (HSSPF) for Army Group Center, SS *Obergruppenführer* Erich von dem Bach-Zelewski. Philip Blood describes the man as obsessed with restoring family honor after the disgraceful death of his uncle and most of his unit at the hands of Hehe tribesmen in colonial German East Africa. He was a man who "behaved like the champion of all the Nazi rhetoric and dogma that punctuated the SS cult. His frequent meetings with the head of the SS would bear out this close relationship. He was a driven man motivated to exterminate Jews and Communists in the name of *Lebensraum*."[29] After some early criticism for not being sufficiently radical, Bach-Zelewski strove to be more extreme and won the patronage of Himmler himself.[30] Interestingly, the brutal nature of his work took a psychological toll on him, and Bach-Zelewski had a breakdown in the winter of 1941–42.[31] In any case, by September 1941 he had already proven himself a great supporter of anti-Jewish actions: his meeting with the head of the Order Police in August had been a "prelude" to a mass murder of Jews in Minsk.[32] It is not surprising then that he would go on to become the chief of anti-partisan warfare and preside over the wholesale slaughter of civilians and Jews during massive sweeps and the creation of "dead zones" in Belarus; Bach-Zelewski would later direct the large "anti-partisan" operations such as Hamburg and Bamberg in the summer of 1942, which would murder thousands. These systematic campaigns of killing would add significantly to the already massive death toll in Belarus.

Men like the commander of the SS Cavalry Brigade, Hermann Fegelein, and the commander of its Cavalry Regiment 1, Gustav Lombard, rounded out this cast of experienced killers. Interestingly, the other SS cavalry regimental commander, Franz Magill, was not invited to participate. He was, perhaps, viewed as the less extreme officer, having mainly restricted himself to killing Jewish men.[33] The SS Cavalry Brigade began killing Jews in early August in the Pripet Marshes and would kill over twenty thousand by the end of that month.[34] Along with the police battalions, it also presided over the turn toward killing all Soviet Jews regardless of age or sex. Christopher Browning has convincingly argued that, at the end of July or beginning of August 1941, Himmler verbally notified subordinates that now all Jews, regardless of age or sex, would be targeted for execution.[35] Shortly after, Jewish women and children who had been previously spared found themselves now included in mass killings. Himmler had ordered on 1 August that "all Jews must be shot. Drive the female Jews into the swamps."[36] Lombard had then informed his troops that "in future not one male Jew is to remain alive, not one family in the villages."[37] The Second SS Cavalry Regiment reported in the same period, "We drove women and children into the marshes, but this did not yield the desired result, as the marshes were not deep enough to drown them. In most places, the water was not more than three feet deep."[38] The commander of Police Regiment Center, Lieutenant Colonel Max Montua, and the commanders of Police Battalions 307 and 316 also attended; these units, too, had already conducted numerous mass killings of Jews in Bialystok, Brest-Litovsk, and elsewhere.[39]

Both the professional killers who had already been dealing with the "Jewish question" and Wehrmacht officers—some with proven track records of violence and complicity—arrived in the regional capital of Mogilev on the morning of 24 September 1941.[40] General Max von Schenckendorff encouraged them to participate in a "frank discussion because the war against the partisans is completely new to all of us."[41] He informed them from the outset that "townspeople will be used [by the partisans] as guides, scouts, and informants. Particularly the elderly, women, and adolescents, because they are least suspicious, will be utilized for reconnaissance."[42] The commanding general thus convened the conference by immediately placing women, children, and the elderly, in play as enemy combatants.

Fifteen-minute presentations of lessons learned in the anti-partisan war by various high-level commanders, including SS Cavalry Brigade commander Fegelein, Lieutenant Colonel Montua of Police Regiment Center, and Colonel von Rekowski of the 354th Infantry Regiment, occupied the first morning.[43] At 11:30, Einsatzgruppe commander Arthur Nebe gave a presentation covering three areas: first, cooperation between the troops and the SD during anti-partisan operations; second, the selection and employment of local collaborators; third, and most ominously, the Jewish question, with particular consideration toward the anti-partisan movement.[44] While we do not know what exactly was said here, it is likely that this was the moment where the importance of the killing of Jews, and the growing participation of the Wehrmacht in this endeavor, were stressed. After all, Nebe had already reported in July that "a solution of the Jewish Question during the war seems impossible in this area [Belarus] because of the tremendous number of Jews."[45] Certainly, he is referring here to the insufficient numbers of Einsatzgruppen killers available and must have been interested in leveraging the manpower of the Wehrmacht in solving this problem.

This manpower problem originated from a convergence of several factors. First, the decision to kill all Jews regardless of age or sex naturally increased the number of Jews to be shot to such an extent that the Einsatzgruppen and SS foresaw problems in accomplishing this mission, as Nebe indicated. Second, Hitler's decision to allow deportations of Jews from Europe to the East before any death camps had been constructed meant that room would have to be made for the deportees. This would entail killing operations directed at the main ghetto cities, one of which was Minsk. These actions would, in turn, occupy much of the SS/SD killing apparatus, leaving little for other areas. Third, with the advance deeper into the Soviet Union beyond what had been the Pale of Settlement, Jews were more geographically dispersed, making operations against them more manpower intensive. Christian Gerlach argues that an early October killing of women and children in Mogilev marked the "start signal" for the general murder of Jews in rHGM.[46] Yet, as we have seen, this massacre had already begun. However, Gerlach is correct in marking an important surge of police battalion activity in killing, particularly in the countryside, which is further evidence of an expansion in targeting.

Nebe was followed after lunch on the first day by Bach-Zelewski, who spoke on "The Capture of Kommissars and Partisans in 'Scouring-Actions.'"[47] The HSSPF had already been particularly active in such operations with the SS Cavalry Brigade in the Pripet Marshes. In the afternoon, the officers observed an exercise conducted by Police Regiment Center, which demonstrated the occupation of a village by surrounding it, and also the dissemination of leaflets. In the evening after dinner, the participants adjourned for a concert of Russian music in the headquarters building.[48]

The next morning, the exchange of experiences continued, with SS Cavalry Regiment 1 commander Gustav Lombard leading off. Then, various company-grade officers gave short classes or led sand table exercises on a variety of tactical situations, such as the entry of a battalion into an unsecured area, securing a stretch of highway, and reacting to the murder of a mayor by the partisans.[49] In the afternoon, the officers observed another actual operation conducted by 7th Company of Police Battalion 322. The German unit surrounded and searched the town of Knjaschitschi, approximately 11 miles (18 km) northwest of Minsk. A summary written afterward states: "Suspicious strangers to the village [*Ortsfremde*] and a few Jews were discovered. (32 executions)."[50] Supporting the police was a sixteen-man detachment from the SD.[51] The war diary of Police Battalion 322 provides more telling detail: "Strangers to the village, in particular partisans, could not be found. Instead, the investigation of the population revealed 13 Jewish men, 27 Jewish women, and 11 Jewish children. Of these 13 men and 19 women were executed with the help of the SD."[52] In Knjaschitschi, the conference participants were provided with an actual demonstration in which the murder of Jews was carried out as a default targeting option in the anti-partisan war. The message was clear: Jews were always to be killed, regardless of the presence of partisans or evidence of their connection with the enemy. Indeed, in this model operation Jews were explicitly identified as not being partisans and were killed regardless.

At dawn on the final morning, the participants observed another actual operation, executed this time by Security Regiment 2. According to the operations order, the goal was to "practically experience not only the registration of a town but also the seizure of partisans, commissars, and communists and the investigation of the local population."[53] It should be noted here that, again, Wehrmacht command elements planned and organized a live exercise to model for participants to observe what an ideal operation against "partisans" (or Jews) should look like. The order contained descriptions of the individuals targeted, who appeared to be mainly former Communist functionaries, though four individuals were suspect because they apparently spent large amounts of time in the forest.[54] After the suspects were rounded up, the participants were to observe the interrogation of these suspect civilians and a subsequent "instruction" of the population.[55] It is unclear exactly what was meant by "instruction." This could have been some kind of political education or even the killing of suspects. Upon completion of this operation, the participants left to return to their units.

The final product of this conference was a sixteen-page executive summary of the lessons learned, under the signature of General Schenckendorff. This document began with a brief history of partisan warfare and discussed mostly organization, equipment, and tactics of the partisans, as well as recommended techniques for combating them. Much of it was devoted to the nuts and bolts of conducting various forms of anti-partisan operations. Other recommendations, however, advocated more extreme measures. Readers were advised that the elderly, women, and children were used for enemy reconnaissance.[56] Moreover, streets were to be kept free of "wanderers," who were to be handed over to the GFP (Geheime Feldpolizei, or military secret field police), SD, or civilian labor camps. The guideline was to have "streets free of any Russian."[57] Individuals not native to a village, for whom the mayor was not willing to vouch, were also to be turned over to the GFP, SD, or nearest transfer camp, with death being almost certain.[58] The most chilling statement introduced the section on fighting the partisans. "The enemy must be completely annihilated," it declared. "The constant decision between life and death for partisans and suspicious persons is difficult even for the hardest soldier. It must be done. He acts correctly who fights ruthlessly and mercilessly with complete disregard for any personal surge of emotion."[59] A statement like this seems to implicitly recognize a need to explain the necessity of annihilating the enemy; however, one must ask why soldiers would need such additional urging if their enemy was actually trying to kill them? Perhaps they needed such reinforcement precisely because those "partisans and suspicious persons" being targeted did not fit the threatening image of a military enemy. This document was distributed to the company level in all units in rHGM, which meant that its lessons both became approved policy and reached units that had not had representatives in Mogilev. Even more telling, it appears that this same document was retransmitted to the police battalions in November 1941.[60] It is certainly intriguing that, in this case, police units were being instructed in brutality by the army. Moreover, the conference led directly to participation by the Wehrmacht in the murder of Jews. Even a conservative German court that was reluctant to convict former Wehrmacht members found that "the training in Mogilev was described outwardly as an anti-partisan training but in reality it served to promote the annihilation of the Jews for racial reasons."[61]

The executive summary of the Mogilev Conference did not specifically mention Jews. What, then, was the impact of the conference on the Wehrmacht's participation in genocidal policy? Could literal identification of Jews have been unnecessary, as they were assumed to be targets? It certainly seems that a desired goal and visible result of the conference was to more fully incorporate the army in killings of Jews, in conjunction with an increasing brutality toward civilians in general. What evidence supports this? First, it is no great leap to assume that Nebe's presentation regarding the "Jewish question" and the partisan war contained exhortations for the killing of Jews both during and outside of anti-partisan operations. He was, after all, presiding at the time over the murder of hundreds of thousands of Jews in Belarus. Indeed, the very composition of those attending strongly suggests that the inclusion of Jews as targets was an experience to be shared and emphasized. These men were practitioners, not theorists, after all. Second, the demonstration operations carried out reinforced messages from the conference: Jews were clearly both targeted and executed in the operation carried out by Police Battalion 322. In this action, the murder of Jews present in the village obviously became a default position when other "suspects" could not be found. Finally, throughout the conference (and in meetings afterward at corps level) greater cooperation with the SD was encouraged. In several subsequent operations, this cooperation entailed Wehrmacht support of the Einsatzgruppen in mass killing.

The most damning evidence appeared a little over two weeks after the conference. In the small town of Krucha, soldiers of the 3rd Company, 691st Infantry Regiment, rounded up and executed all the Jews in their area. The order to do so originated from their battalion commander. The battalion adjutant, a Lieutenant Grosskopp, had just returned from the Mogilev Conference bearing the message that "where the Partisan is, there is the Jew. Where the Jew is, there is the Partisan."[62] The commander of the 1st Company, Josef Sibille, who refused to carry out this order, wrote after the war to the prosecuting attorney, testifying to this connection in the 3rd Company case. He recalled that an anti-partisan conference had taken place in Mogilev and further contended that "the main subject was Jews and partisans." He believed that the conference and the battalion order to kill all the Jews in the area in early October were connected.[63] Indeed, the evidence for this connection is made all the more convincing by the appearance of a captain from the 691st and at least six other officers from the 339th Infantry Division on the list of attendees at the conference.[64]

The battalion commander, Major Alfred Commichau, upon receiving the message from Mogilev, ordered his battalion to carry out mass shootings of all Jewish men, women, and children in his area of operations. This is significant because it is a rare documented case of the German army independently carrying out Nazi genocidal policy. Here, an army unit did not merely assist other killing units but instead carried out all aspects of the mass murder on its own, and by all accounts as a direct result of the Mogilev Conference. The German court itself found that the Nazi leadership instigated the extermination of the Jewish population "under the cover of partisan fighting."[65]

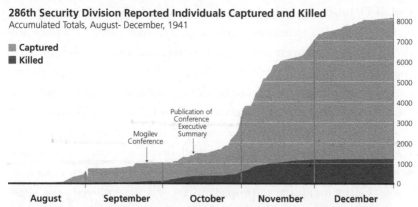

Graph 2. Numbers of individuals reported killed or captured by the 286th Security Division from August to December 1941 reveal a clear increase following the Mogilev Conference. These numbers were derived using only those statistics reported to the division (and surviving in the archives).

Graph 3. Like its parent division, the 354th Infantry Regiment also experienced a marked increase in killing following the Mogilev Conference. Note: the 354th did not report the Krupki massacre nor include it in their numbers here.

A survey of operations reports across rHGM provides some suggestive quantitative evidence for a deadlier turn in "anti-partisan" operations. We can see the stark increase in individuals reported killed and captured by the 286th Security Division beginning in October. The 354th Infantry Regiment represented the main combat force in this division and had three attendees at the conference. It, too, exhibited a lethal turn after Mogilev. The 1st Company of the 354th reported at the end of October that it had shot three Jewish families and two young women of Jewish appearance it termed *Flintenweiber*, or female soldiers, though they were shot trying to flee, and there is no indication they were armed.[66] Given typical Nazi euphemistic language, the racial identity of many Wehrmacht victims remained intentionally unclear. Categories such as partisan, partisan helper *(Partisanenhelfer)*, suspect civilian *(verdächtige Zivilisten)*, stranger to village *(Ortsfremde)*, wanderer *(Wanderer)*, and civilians without identification *(Zivilisten ohne Ausweis)* could easily be applied to both Jews and non-Jews. German military propagandists also employed the Jew-Bolshevik-partisan calculus in their messages to the Belarusian populace; one leaflet (likely from 1941) warned them "Don't forget. These elements [partisans] are no danger for the German Army and never accomplish anything. The Jewish bandits and partisans, however, are a serious threat to you!"[67]

The numbers of killed and captured for the last three months of 1941 demonstrate a marked increase in violence against civilians; partisan activity had not risen to the same extent, and German casualties still do not indicate any real combat. In the October reports from the 350th Infantry Regiment (which also had attendees at Mogilev), every Jew mentioned was formulaically noted as "shot while trying to escape."[68] Captain Balitzki, the attendee at Mogilev from the 350th Infantry Regiment, wrote on 14 October that "it is unacceptable that officers have to shoot while the men watch. The majority of the men are too soft. This is a sign that they have never or only poorly been instructed about the meaning of the 'Partisan War.'"[69] This officer, a conference speaker, apparently found that some of his men had not yet absorbed its lessons, though he and his fellow officers were attempting to model this brutal behavior for them. This is also a telling indicator of who the people being shot were; most soldiers would not have needed to be instructed to shoot at enemy guerrillas who were attacking them. It is also worth noting that the numbers of those captured skyrocketed as well. This merely delayed their deaths, as these people were handed over to the SD or transfer camps *(Dulags)*, with typically lethal results. These were, in short, not benign transactions.

Greater collaboration between the SD and the Wehrmacht also became more evident after the conference. Indeed, Himmler "placed great emphasis on maintaining a cooperative relationship" with the army and had already on 2 August encouraged his leadership to "maintain the 'greatest amity' with" the Wehrmacht.[70] Increased cooperation manifested itself after the Mogilev conference in two ways: greater utilization of SD detachments in interrogations of suspect civilians and vetting of local auxiliaries, and more active support—far beyond mere logistical support—of those SD units directly involved in anti-Jewish measures. Three days after the conference, rHGM instructed its units that "cooperation is to be still more closely organized between the divisions and the SD and GFP. . . . Requests for local [*ortsfesten*] operations by individual troops of the Einsatzkommandos of the SD are to be submitted to the commander."[71] "Cooperation with the SD" was also on the September 30 agenda for the rHGM staff meeting with its subordinate division staffs as a lesson from the conference.[72] In its summary for the period from September to December 1941, the intelligence section of the 286th Security Division appeared eager to report that "constant contact was maintained with the Security Service, specifically the Einsatzgruppe of *Gruppenführer* Neumann, the Einsatzkommando 8 of *Sturmbannführer* Dr. Bratfisch [*sic*], and in particular with *Untersturmführer* Reschke's Orscha-based squad."[73]

In November, the 339th Infantry Division (which contained the 691st Infantry Regiment in Krucha) published a guide to the duties and responsibilities of the security forces. Under the SD, it listed the following as "keywords": "politically suspect civilians, Bolsheviks, Jews, and Gypsies." Among the SD responsibilities, the army enumerated "Solution of the Jewish Problem" and the "Gypsy Question." Finally, the memo instructed that "the troops must shoot Jews and Gypsies only if they are proven to be partisans or their supporters. In all other cases, they are to be handed over to the SD."[74] Thus, we can see both a clear knowledge of the mission of the SD and an emphasis on improved cooperation and coordination with it, as well as the fig leaf of military necessity. Cooperation between the army and the Einsatzgruppen appeared in its purest form in the 707th Infantry Division to the west, in the Reichskommissariat Ostland (RKO). Following a clearly defined division of labor, this unit explicitly targeted Jews in the countryside, freeing the SD to focus on cities. The division commander, General Gustav von Bechtolsheim, published orders in November 1941 that clearly stated that "where larger or smaller groups of Jews are encountered in the countryside, they may either be executed [by the units themselves] or consolidated in ghettos in designated places where they will then be given over to the civil administration, that is, the SD."[75]

The preponderance of the evidence surrounding the Mogilev Conference and the lethal turn in Wehrmacht "security" operations that followed demonstrate that these three days were an important galvanizing moment in deepening the complicity of the German army in the Holocaust in Belarus. The conference instructed the Wehrmacht to intentionally target Jews in its anti-partisan operations. This verbal transmission of guidance regarding Jewish policy was not without precedent, as we have seen already regarding Jewish policy. On July 8 in Bialystok, Himmler himself met with Bach-Zelewski, General von Schenckendorff, Colonel Montua of Police Regiment Center, and the commanders of Police Battalions 322 and 316. That same night the police began killing Jews there.[76] Given the attendees at the conference, the nature of the presentations, and the actions that followed, it appears that such a discussion also occurred in Mogilev.

Given the prior history of the German army regarding treatment of civilians and the already well-established belief that the Jews were behind Bolshevism, the anti-partisan war was the perfect vehicle for harnessing the combat power of the army to help solve the "Jewish problem." The commander of the German army, Field Marshal von Brauchitsch, published "Guidelines for the Fighting of Partisans" to the entire army one month after the Mogilev Conference. In it, he copied *word for word* the closing text of Schenckendorff's summary: "The constant decision between life and death for partisans and suspicious persons is difficult even for the hardest soldier. It must be done. He acts correctly who fights ruthlessly and mercilessly with complete disregard for any personal surge of emotion."[77] Yet, we have evidence for an even more ringing endorsement than this one. On 18 December 1941, the man responsible for the Final Solution in Europe, SS chief Heinrich Himmler, met with Hitler.

Afterward, Himmler wrote in his appointment book: "Jewish question / to be exterminated as partisans."[78]

How and why did the German army become so deeply involved in enacting Nazi genocidal policy? The fabricated partisan connection should not be underestimated, for it played into a current of extreme brutality toward and paranoia of civilian irregular movements that ran deep within German military organizational memory, beginning with the Franco-Prussian War in 1871, when masses of armed French civilians had caused significant discomfort behind the lines. Isabel Hull describes the effects of this experience on the German army, noting a particular tendency to hold "the unrealistic expectation of perfect order . . . which turned enemy civilians into criminals subject to harsh military law. In short, 'order' encouraged reprisals when it inevitably failed."[79] A tendency to both "see" and react violently to imagined civilian resistance had, after all, already reared its head in the First World War.[80] For many individual soldiers, the environment itself constituted a menacing presence. Hitler himself expressed frustration at the difficulty of the Soviet environment in one of his "table talks," saying one cannot "fight a battle in the forest."[81] He is likely speaking here of both the difficulty of fighting an insurgency and the harsh terrain in the East. More research should be done in this area, but it seems certain that the oppressive environment soldiers encountered, from vast flatlands to dense forests, from searing sun to frigid snow, affected their overall mindset and sense of unease in the Soviet Union. Letters from German soldiers across the eastern front contain evidence of this. "The land here is bleak and desolate," wrote one man.[82] A former philosophy student turned soldier felt that he had been "thrown into this violently chaotic endless gray expanse of the East, that men have hardly touched."[83] The land seemed at times to be an enemy as well, isolating the men in a strange, frightening, and seemingly endless territory. Such discomfort certainly made soldiers more susceptible to any actions that they could perceive as improving their chances for survival, however specious the justification. The environmental isolation also increased the power of group dynamics and social pressure inside these units whose members had nowhere to turn but to each other. Environmental factors could enhance a feeling of constant danger (real or imagined) and likely contributed to increased levels of violence.

There were also compelling arguments for the army's participation in the Nazi genocidal project at higher institutional levels. From the perspective of those like Nebe and Bach-Zelewski, additional manpower was necessary in the fall of 1941 to accomplish the murder of the expanded number of targeted Jews resulting from the inclusion of women and children. Including Jews under the umbrella of the anti-partisan war eased and enhanced the participation of the army in the Holocaust. Indeed, the SS/SD lacked the ability to systematically search for Jews in small villages in the countryside. By killing Jews in the course of its normal anti-partisan patrolling in these areas, the Wehrmacht could relieve the Einsatzgruppen of this challenge.

While the Wehrmacht was not in opposition to the execution of the Final Solution in the East, it was sometimes reluctant to dirty its own hands with it. Incorporating Jews into an already hyperaggressive anti-civilian policy eased this transition and paved the way for greater complicity by the army, up to and including killing. Raul Hilberg explained some of this complicity, writing that "the generals had eased themselves into this pose of cooperation through the pretense that the Jewish population was a group of Bolshevist diehards who instigated, encouraged, and abetted the partisan war behind the German lines."[84]

Not everyone bought this argument. An inspector in the Army Economic and Armament Office in the Ukraine, for example, reported to his boss in December 1941 that "there is no proof that Jewry as a whole or even to a greater part was implicated in acts of sabotage."[85] For both officers and soldiers who may have been reluctant to kill women and children, explicitly connecting all Jews with a developing anti-partisan movement may have both partially allayed these concerns and lessened inhibitions by placing anti-Jewish actions (and any resistance to them) in the context of "legitimate" combat operations.

Testimony from former soldiers of 3rd Company supports this conflation of anti-partisan operations and Jew killing. One soldier claimed "it was generally known that Jews made up the lion's share of the partisans and that the partisans were constantly supported by the Jews in the villages, particularly the women."[86] Another noted that "at the time of the shooting, many attacks by the partisans had taken place and that the battalion had suffered losses." He continued, "The members of the company were of the opinion that the Jewish shooting was a reprisal and preventative measure as a result of partisan attacks. . . . Any harmless civilian could be a partisan. There were observations of Jews supplying the partisans."[87] However, again, there is little indication that the unit had taken any serious casualties. From September to December 1941, the 339th Division reported only twenty killed and thirty-seven wounded.[88] While at some level these statements certainly reflect the postwar environment and attempts at self-exculpation, they also likely echo justifications that the soldiers found convenient to believe in 1941. Of course, one must recognize that such a self-serving justification would certainly break down when one was killing women, children, and the elderly; few men could realistically view such people as partisans. Regardless, remarks such as those above parrot similar ideas from the Mogilev Conference.

Antisemitism among the officers and men perhaps reinforced this conflation of Jews and enemy combatants. This prejudice could come from a variety of sources. Certainly some men carried anti-Jewish feelings from home.[89] The official sanction of discriminatory measures and then outright collaboration in mass killing by the army inevitably allowed those with racist predilections to act on them and normalized anti-Jewish brutality within an organizational climate that already prescribed excessive brutality against civilians as a matter of course. Instances of Wehrmacht participation in killing throughout Belarus repeatedly featured officers and men who stood out in the memories of their comrades as particularly virulent antisemites, convinced Nazis, or simply as brutal men.[90] A soldier in 3rd Company remembered, for example, one sergeant who was "radically opposed to partisans and Jews."[91] Racist soldiers and officers were often tasked or volunteered to carry out Jewish killings, thus minimizing the necessity of compulsory participation by those less inclined and the potential disruption of morale.

Finally, the tactics of participation allowed soldiers to compartmentalize and minimize any psychological trauma associated with the murder of people who did not fit the conventional image of the enemy.

Consider the techniques involved in capturing partisans in "small operations" that were demonstrated at Mogilev and disseminated to the units in rHGM. Villages were to be surrounded in the last hour of darkness or shortly before dawn. Assault troops were then to enter the village and assemble the population and the mayor. Those who were not native to the village or who supported the partisans were to be identified and handed over to the SD, GFP, or nearest transfer camp.[92] If Jews were by definition partisan supporters, the import of these instructions was clear. Jews were to be rounded up as targets of these operations and handed over to the SD for almost certain execution. In operations where the Wehrmacht assisted in the murder of Jews, these were the same tactics used to identify and round up the victims. Thus, it could be possible to maintain the illusion of a "normal" operation—to a point. The use of this operational framework had a secondary effect: it could help minimize the psychological discomfort inherent in these actions, which was one of the reasons the Wehrmacht had attempted to limit or avoid direct participation in mass killing.

The mobilization of intentionally vague and euphemistic language in both reporting those killed and describing those targeted also assisted in this process. Terms such as "stranger to village," "wanderer," "suspect civilian," "partisan helper," and "civilian without identification" highlight the inexact and elastic nature of these categories. Moreover, consider the equally fluid "evidence" used to prove collusion with the enemy, compared with the very real circumstances of Jews at the time. German persecution of Jews inevitably induced behaviors among the victims that were then cited as evidence of enemy activity, which then justified the necessity of extermination. Women, children, and the elderly were characterized as particularly suspect as partisan supporters; in many areas, Jewish men had either been killed or had fled, leaving a majority of women, children, and the elderly. Behavior such as running or hiding was treated as highly suspect, if not outright incriminating, and Jews naturally often attempted to flee and hide from the Germans, particularly in the forest. Similarly, civilians without identification were immediately suspect, and Jews did not receive identification cards from German authorities (with the exception of work permits, which also clearly identified them as Jews). Thus, if they were caught outside their

villages, they would likely have forged identification or have no identification at all. Finally, the SD was to be employed in ferreting out suspected Communists and partisans as well as finding and killing Jews.
The cumulative effect of these similarities was that Jews were easily
merged into categories that resulted in an automatic death sentence.

This "tactical muscle memory" from other actual anti-partisan actions
created for some at least a semblance of familiarity and an illusion of legitimate military operations. A similar emotional refuge could be found
in the spatially compartmentalized nature of these operations: sentry
duty during the encirclement, searching houses, escorting victims, and
cordoning off the execution site. Every action save actual shooting offered soldiers the opportunity to tell themselves they were not really
participating in murder. This is of great importance, because many soldiers recognized at the time that these killings did not constitute real
conventional combat. Private Magel from the 691st shooting admitted
that "we also knew that the Jews hadn't done anything and that the
shooting represented an injustice, at least as far as it concerned women
and children."[93] It is also interesting to note here that Magel appears to
have believed that male Jews still deserved to be shot. Because what they
were doing resembled a legitimate operation, these men could tell themselves that they were participating in acceptable military behavior.
Surely this is postwar self-exculpation, but it also likely demonstrates a
conscious (if not always successful) distancing from the act itself that
was also evident in 1941. The psychological toll of these kinds of mass
killings was not something recognized only after the fact but was a
concern of key leaders at the time. As early as 11 July 1941, Colonel Max
Montua (commander of Police Regiment Center and a speaker at the Mogilev Conference) enjoined his subordinate commanders to "provide for
the spiritual care" of those participating in killing and ordered that "the
impressions of the day are to be blotted out."[94] Given such concerns
(which were also likely held by the Wehrmacht) regarding the psychological impact on their personnel of face-to-face killing, the utility of exploiting the similarity between anti-partisan and anti-Jewish operations
was not lost on army leadership.

The Mogilev Conference and the events surrounding it offer one compelling explanation for the complicity of army decision makers at the

regional (and local) levels. It seems that the military leaders involved were willing to accept specious security considerations that categorized all Jews as supporters of the Bolsheviks and thus partisan accomplices. This justification dovetailed nicely with ongoing Wehrmacht violence against Communists and Red Army soldiers. However, one cannot overlook the very real possibility that at Mogilev these leaders were informed of their role in the overall Nazi genocidal project and that many of them needed no further justification as camouflage for their actions.

The Mogilev Conference does not perhaps prove beyond a shadow of a doubt that the Wehrmacht was specifically ordered to increase its complicity in the Holocaust, but few decisions regarding the evolution of the Final Solution are easy to identify. The conference and the events that followed provide a convincing convergence of evidence highlighting the Mogilev Conference as a watershed moment in the German army's participation in the Holocaust, at least in Belarus. The prior records of the conference participants, the messages and "demonstration" operations observed, as well as the subsequent sharp increase in divisional "body counts" and in anti-Jewish killings, all point to the significance of this event.

The conference by itself should be seen as a lens that focused a variety of existing mindsets and situational factors to mobilize the support of the army for genocidal actions. Extant antisemitism and anti-Bolshevik fervor combined with a history of paranoia and excessive brutality toward civilians. Hitler himself had remarked in a meeting on 16 July 1941 that "the partisan war has its advantages: it gives us the opportunity to exterminate those who oppose us."[95] In Mogilev, men like General Schenckendorff, Nebe, and Bach-Zelewski intentionally blurred the line between the "Jewish question" and conventional war. They instructed (and learned from) lower-level officers, men at the sharp end of the spear, at least some of whom had been selected intentionally for their past record of brutality and/or extreme beliefs. These men of action then brought this message back to their units, resulting in an observable change in behavior of the Wehrmacht in Belarus.

In order to better understand the larger context of the Mogilev Conference, the Serbian experience provides a valuable comparison. In the Balkans in the fall of 1941, the Wehrmacht faced a very real insurgency and a dangerous guerrilla movement that inflicted real casualties. Here, too, the German military viewed the local population through a racial lens and adopted the most extreme measures to subdue them.[96] Military-age male Jews and Gypsies were routinely executed in reprisal for German casualties, though they rarely actively supported the Communist partisans or were partisans themselves. On 23 September 1941 (the day before the Mogilev Conference began), Wehrmacht troops launched a "punitive expedition" in Serbia, executing 1,127 "suspected communists" and interning over 20,000 men.[97] After this operation, the key divisional commander—who was not as brutal as the commanding general in Serbia, Franz Böhme, demanded—was demoted for being "too slack."[98] In Serbia, the system rewarded officers professionally for interpreting orders more violently. A recent detailed study of the Wehrmacht in the Balkans by Ben Shepherd concluded that there, as in the Soviet Union, "too many German commanders, weaned on the long-standing practices of the military establishment to which they belonged, were excessively enamored of brutal reprisals."[99]

In addition, Shepherd emphasizes the influence of "Social Darwinism and its anti-Slavic and antisemitic corollaries," at least on the decisions of general officers.[100] Being located at the epicenter of the early Holocaust in the East amplified these ideological perspectives at lower levels for soldiers in the Soviet Union. As Christopher Browning notes, "If the policies of the Wehrmacht [in Serbia] did not yet constitute the 'Final Solution' . . . the killing of adult male Jews and 'Gypsies' simply because of their ethnic identity was quite simply genocide."[101] The tribunal in the Hostage Trial at Nuremberg agreed, concluding emphatically that "pre-existing international law has declared these acts . . . unlawful."[102]

Thus, Serbia provides another important background for the Mogilev Conference. We can see in another theater the Wehrmacht tendency to incorporate racial thinking in its attitudes toward local populations. The army also demonstrated its ready acceptance of Jews and other "racially inferior" groups as legitimate targets for execution. In addition, German commanders were already being recognized positively for their extreme brutality. Mogilev, then, represents both a continuation of these trends and a departure: no longer were only male Jews targeted, and no longer were these killings associated with a legitimate counterinsurgency as supposed reprisals. Though the anti-partisan war had an important rhetorical purpose, the Wehrmacht was now harnessed directly to the Nazi genocidal project in killings at which even commanders in Serbia might have balked.[103]

It is a sad tribute to the effectiveness of the intentional conflation of Jew, Bolshevik, and partisan that the instrumentalization of this concept on the ground has not been more deeply explored. The view that the anti-partisan war was a simple counterinsurgency action is one perpetuated by the killers themselves. Phillip Blood rightly describes this process as "how the fallacy of antipartisan warfare expunged the record of *Bandenbekämpfung*."[104] The use of this term, which meant "bandit fighting," rather than the earlier *Partisanenbekämpfung*, which denoted a more conventional war against guerrillas, deliberately obscured a wide range of atrocities justified by the former with the cold military precision of the latter. This linguistic gymnastics was not without precedent both in the German army and elsewhere. In Southwest Africa (Namibia) in the early twentieth century, German military forces justified their genocidal attacks on the Nama people by calling them "born thieves and robbers, nothing more."[105] During the American occupation of Haiti (1915–1934), U.S. Marines received an official order instructing that they refer to Haitian guerrillas as "bandits."[106] The Nuremberg Tribunals did not uncritically accept the term as one synonymous with a "clean" anti-partisan war, however. During the High Command Trial, the tribunal categorically dismissed any legality of German reprisal killings, stating that "the safeguards and preconditions required . . . were not even attempted to be met or even suggested as necessary." Referring to the Hostage Case, it termed the killings in the Balkans where "hostages" were overwhelmingly Jews to be "merely terror murders."[107] While the court recognized the theoretical legality of reprisals and hostage killings after a lengthy list of requirements had been met, it noted that such a case of the correct use of reprisal could not be found during the war and roundly condemned the German army for its actions.

It is, perhaps, more correct that the police battalions saw that "the destruction of the Jews could be semantically disguised as *Bandenkampf* and later after the war used with initial success as an exculpatory myth for the perpetrators."[108] This was not a successful legal strategy at the

Nuremberg hearings but may have had more traction in later trials and certainly in the constructed memory of veterans. It appears that the Wehrmacht benefited from a similar mythmaking strategy. Indeed, after the war, many soldiers doggedly stuck to the story that the Jews killed were really partisans. However, victimization of Jews was not due to frustration, casualties, or a loss of control in the style of the My Lai massacre, but resulted from a conscious, deeper incorporation of the Wehrmacht in Nazi genocidal policy.[109]

About a year after the Mogilev Conference, the following statements appeared in a Wehrmacht operations order and the subsequent after-action report for a large anti-partisan operation creatively named "Dreieck-Viereck" (Triangle-Square).

> Because throughout the "Triangle" region enemy mines are to be expected, "Minesweeper 42s" (members of Jewish labor battalions or captured bandits with hoes and rollers) are to be available in sufficient quantities. Units are to equip themselves with cords to use as leashes with which to control the Jews or bandits.
>
> —Operations order for anti-partisan Operation Dreieck-Viereck,
> 11 September 1942[110]

> 2nd Battalion, 727th Infantry Regiment which was employed as the lead battalion, broke the enemy resistance in a quick attack, in spite of the fact that the advance proceeded slowly due to heavy mining. 4 "Minesweeper 42s" were blown up into the air, thereby sparing any losses of our own troops.
>
> —After-action report, Operation Dreieck-Viereck,
> 19 October 1942[111]

Here, the German army was describing, in official communications, the use of both Jewish and non-Jewish civilians as human minesweepers and applauding their deaths in preventing friendly casualties. Such a development speaks to the impact of the messages from Mogilev and the rapidity with which military violence in conjunction with anti-Jewish policy escalated.

The Holocaust and the anti-partisan war have long remained separated in the historiography, with anti-Jewish actions inhabiting the history of Nazi genocide and the anti-partisan war the military history of
the war on the eastern front. This is a false division. As Edward Westermann concludes, the "fact that the Jewish population of the Soviet Union
became a major target of the anti-partisan campaign is indisputable."[112]
Indeed, we can now speak of a war of annihilation from the bottom up,
as a "method of fighting and occupation in which all citizens of the Soviet Union, regardless of whether they were soldiers or civilians, had
become fair game."[113] The Mogilev Conference shows that the war behind the lines and the Holocaust were never separate, but intentionally
connected in an effort to more efficiently include the combat power of
the Wehrmacht in Hitler's genocidal projects in the East.

CHAPTER FIVE

An Evil Seed Is Sown

How each experienced the event was not spoken about openly, however, rumors about it were always going around amongst the men. It was clear from their demeanor that most expressed a rejection of the measure. I do wish to emphasize that the population of the village seemed very satisfied with the measure.

Former German soldier Karl V., 22 September 1953

So I acted only out of a sense of duty. I myself can't even say whether I actually hit a Jew with my one shot. I didn't relate this incident to gloat only to bring home to my wife how terrible the war was.

Former German soldier Wilhelm Magel, 24 June 1951

I N MAY 1951, a forty-three-year-old carpenter named Wilhelm Magel brought the mayor of Steinbach, Germany, and a policeman to his second-story apartment. Magel was unlucky in love. He was on his second marriage, and that relationship was not long for this world. Poor Wilhelm was separated from his second wife, Elisabeth, and lived with his older son in the apartment above her in what must have been a very awkward living situation. Elisabeth had the annoying habit of keeping all the good clothes for their daughter who lived with her, while only giving raggedy clothes to their son upstairs because he lived with his father. Wilhelm's frequent confrontations with his wife about her hoarding often resulted in knock-down fights. On this Thursday, Wilhelm was bringing the mayor and a police officer with him to witness his wife's mistreatment of him and their son. Not surprisingly, an argument ensued. As Magel, the mayor, and the police officer left, Elisabeth leaned out the window with, in his words, a "smirk on her face" and screamed at him, "You murderer, you dirty murderer, what else do you want?" Incensed, Magel yelled back, "Watch out, you lying bitch! Shut the window!"[1] With Magel's daughter and many of the neighbors looking on, the three men beat a hasty retreat from the furious housewife. Magel then filed a libel charge against his wife for attempting to sully his good name. In the process of the ensuing investigation, the former army private admitted participating in a killing in the Soviet Union. He remained somehow surprised when he was asked to explain his involvement in the mass shooting of around 150 Jewish men, women, and children that had taken place ten years earlier in a tiny village in what is now Belarus. This killing had been carried out by the 3rd Company, 691st Regiment, 339th Infantry Division, in Krucha on 10 October 1941.

The 339th Infantry Division had formed in Thuringia in central Germany in December 1940, with the 691st Infantry Regiment being created out of a fortress infantry regiment.[2] The division chose the nickname "Kyffhäuser" Division, after a mountain range in Thuringia, and the unit patch featured the turn-of-the-century Kyffhäuser monument.[3] In an ironic twist, this monument sits atop the mountain where, according to legend, Frederick Barbarossa sleeps, waiting to be awakened in Germany's hour of need. Instead, the 339th awoke as Nazi Germany became an increasingly genocidal state. From May to August 1941, the division performed occupation duty in the Loire Valley in France.[4] By 7 September, however, the 339th found itself just north of Minsk, moving to take over the duties of a security division in rHGM, which it did officially on 19 September.[5] It must have been quite the transition.

By 9 October, the 1st Battalion, 691st Regiment, had occupied the small town of Krugloye, in what had once been the 354th Infantry Regiment's sector.[6] The 3rd Company, commanded by Captain Friedrich Nöll, was stationed in Krucha, just eighteen miles (29 km) from Krupki. Nöll's company was the only German unit in the town and was quartered in the local schoolhouse.[7] The 1926 census registered a Jewish population of 297 (52.4 percent of the total).[8] In 1941, according to one German soldier, at least 150 Jews lived there, out of a total population of around 500.[9] Third Company soldiers remembered that the Jews lived together in a particular part of town, but there does not appear to have been a closed ghetto; indeed, it appears that the 691st had resettled all Jews of Krucha on Kozlina Street, creating an "open ghetto."[10]

Around 6 or 7 October, the company messenger, Sergeant B., walked into the headquarters bearing a verbal order from the 1st Battalion commander, Major Alfred Commichau, instructing the 3rd Company to kill all the Jews in its area. It seems that upon receipt of this order there was a discussion among the company leadership about what to do. The commander, Captain Nöll, First Sergeant Emil Zimber, and, likely, the platoon leaders gathered in the company office. Another soldier present testified that, from the discussion, he "gathered that ties existed between the partisans and the Jewish population and that the Jews had supported the partisans. The discussion centered upon how the order should be interpreted, namely whether the Jews should be shot."[11] According to Nöll, this order caused him "great confusion and agitation."[12] He stated that, after meeting with Zimber and the platoon leaders, he intended to ignore the order. However, shortly thereafter a second written order arrived stating: "To 3rd Company, 691st Infantry Regiment: Jews in [Krucha] are to be shot." This order was signed by the battalion commander, Major Commichau.[13]

Nöll decided to proceed. One of the platoon leaders stated that Nöll first asked for volunteers to carry out the killing, but none stepped forward.[14] Company tailor Adam V. had his workshop in the same building as the headquarters and recalled hearing a "loud argument" from the office regarding the order to shoot the Jews. He heard Captain Nöll saying that he had until the next day to report to Major Commichau that the order had been carried out, but because he did not want to do it himself, he would have to assign this mission to someone else.[15] That someone else appears to have been his later codefendant Zimber. Nöll claimed after the war that Zimber "in his capacity as First Sergeant took over the assembly and disposition of the company."[16] Zimber did not refute this claim but vehemently denied that he had volunteered to carry out the shooting order.[17]

Regardless of whether he volunteered or not, Zimber *did* take over the organization and execution of the killings in Krucha and exercised considerable initiative. Soldier Wilhelm Magel described what happened next. His 1st Platoon had just returned around noon on 10 October from an overnight operation. After the soldiers had cleaned their weapons and eaten, they were resting when they received the order to assemble without helmets and gear, only field caps, rifles, and ammunition belts. The instruction not to wear helmets clearly indicates that no combat was expected and, thus, that this was in no way an anti-partisan operation, as many soldiers claimed later. When the men had formed up, First Sergeant Zimber read out the order that all the Jews in the village were to be shot. Magel remembered that there was apparent "indignation" among the soldiers. Zimber reacted to this by saying, "We can't change anything. Orders are orders." He then divided the men into separate *kommandos:* shooting, guarding, evacuation, and cordon.[18] Local police would also assist.

The evacuation *kommando* then moved to the Jewish quarter and began rounding up Jews. One soldier remembered that the Jews of Krucha "who in the beginning did not know what was going on came voluntarily out of their houses."[19] In the end, at least 114 Jews had been assembled in the small square, where they were guarded by German soldiers.[20] Once the roundup was complete, another *kommando* began leading groups of about thirty to an execution site in the forest, approximately a quarter mile (400 m) south of the village itself.[21]

A member of the *Absperrung* described the operation at the shooting site. "The Jews," he remembered, "were taken from us in groups of four to five and led about 200 [meters] away where they disappeared into a depression."[22] This depression was allegedly an excavation for a planned munitions bunker that the Jews had been forced to dig.[23] Here Zimber was in full command of the executions, and it was here that he had chosen to position himself. Two German soldiers were paired off with each Jew, and then Zimber gave the order to fire. Perhaps attempting to maintain some semblance of military procedure, he had the victims face their executioners in the manner of a formal military firing squad. Some remembered that he also walked among the victims, shooting those still alive.[24] Because the executions took place so near the village, those Jews not yet killed heard the shots and screams from the forest and "cried out for they had concluded what stood before them."[25] One woman asked a soldier before she was shot, "Is this German culture?"[26]

After all the Jews had been shot, the soldiers returned to their quarters. Local civilians and police were also present. One soldier recalled hearing that the killing "ended horribly," with villagers "eagerly" beating to death those Jews who were not already dead.[27] These civilians also were tasked with covering the grave but had left arms and other body parts protruding from the ground. Once this task was complete, they were "allowed to plunder the homes of the murdered Jews."[28]

In contrast to the Krupki killings, the responses of the soldiers in the Krucha action are well documented. It is important to note that, while statements of regret and disagreement are common in postwar testimonies, the detail and variety in the 3rd Company case are exceptional and thus lend a greater degree of credibility to the statements. Perhaps owing to its intimate nature, the action appears to have caused intense emotional reactions among the men. "A certain unease was noticeable in the company the whole day," a former soldier observed.[29] Another remembered that he "could read on the faces of my comrades that they detested this method of dealing with the Jews."[30] The company clerk presented an even more differentiated analysis of the company's reactions. "Overall," he testified, "I had the impression that the larger part of the company carried out the order with reluctance and felt its rationale to be poor. However, there were also people who found the order, while brutal, necessary with regard to the experience with the partisans."[31] Taking a different position, one soldier recalled that "the shooting was derided amongst the men because it had been people who had not fought and were only being shot because of their race."[32] The experience was both collective and deeply personal. Willi S. explained, "We were all so shocked that as we sat down together that evening, hardly anything was said about the incident. In particular, no one related what he personally had done."[33] Indeed, it seems that this event was not a topic of conversation for most. "Not much was said in soldier circles about the execution," a private recalled. "The events rushed ahead so that one had no time to indulge his own thoughts."[34] If the killings were not discussed at the time, there is evidence that many soldiers in similar situations shared their experiences when home on leave. A high-level government directive from October 1942 noted that rumors of "'very sharp measures' against Jews in the east were widespread, especially because of the talk of soldiers home on leave."[35]

One soldier who had been in the shooting detail told a comrade that he would never forget what he saw.[36] Another told a friend that it "affected him so much that he couldn't eat."[37] Wilhelm Magel, who had refused further shooting at the pits, wrote his brother that evening that "this had been the most terrible day of my life and that it was said that an evil seed had been sown."[38] Many who had been in proximity to the shooting were "completely shaken and very close to a nervous breakdown."[39]

The men of 3rd Company demonstrated a variety of emotional reactions to this killing. Clearly most men felt some form of shock. By all accounts, this type of operation was not something that they had been exposed to before, certainly not in the Loire Valley. The men were upset, uneasy, and disgusted. However, the reasons for these reactions were often unclear. Some soldiers thought that this was not a job for the army or that the Jews were not legitimate targets. For others engaged more intimately in killing, the violent scenes and physical revulsion were traumatic enough. There also seems to have been a sense of shame and denial for some who did not wish to speak about or recognize what they had participated in. It is not apologetic to recognize the stress and emotional trauma the killings caused. Moreover, these emotional reactions do not by themselves signal disagreement with the policy in principle or an increased tendency to resist or evade participation. They do, however, at the very least indicate that, at this point in time, these men were neither zealous killers nor numb to the gravity of what they were doing. "If I was asked today," one former soldier stated, "what my comrades said about the execution, I can only say that everyone back then said that they would never do something like that again."[40] Correcting for a postwar tendency to protest too much, these testimonies tell us that at least a sizable number of soldiers found killing women and children distasteful, even when presented with the highly dubious Jew-Bolshevik-partisan calculus. On the other hand, for most of the men these reactions did not lead to any meaningful action such as refusal. This is at least equally as insightful, for it shows an organizational culture that was prepared to accept the unpleasant necessity of murdering defenseless civilians.

This case does contain two examples of men who made the decision not to participate in the first place. One of them surfaced in the postwar trial. Wilhelm Magel had been selected by First Sergeant Zimber as part of the shooting detail. Wilhelm found himself walking next to a sergeant who was also a theology PhD. They discussed "how they could get out of the situation as quickly as possible."[41] At the shooting site, Magel was paired off with the theologian, and a soldier brought five Jews to stand in front of the ten-man firing squad. While a local policeman yelled at the Jews to face away from the soldiers, the theologian asked Zimber if they could be relieved from this detail. He replied that as soon as the next two soldiers arrived to relieve them, they could return to guarding the Jews in the square. Zimber then gave the order to aim and fire. Magel fired as ordered, though he claimed that he closed his eyes and did not aim, and that "his" Jew had not been hit. At Zimber's order, the local policeman shot this remaining Jew, and Magel and the theologian were released from shooting. They then returned to Krucha for guard duty in the square.

It will perhaps forever remain unclear whether or not Magel actually did miss his target. However, both reporting of the trial and corroboration of his emotional reaction at least lend credence to this version of events.[42] He told his brother of this occurrence while lying wounded in a hospital in 1942, and also his wife after the war. Another soldier supported Magel's claim of being released from shooting. Magel was certainly disturbed by the action and did write about it that evening in a letter home.[43] Another man also refused to shoot. Sergeant Leopold W. stated that Zimber had told him the night before the execution that he would be in the shooting detail. W. replied that "this wasn't my thing and there were enough people who would do this voluntarily." Zimber reassigned him to guard duty.[44]

Leopold W. and Magel's version of events raises several crucial points. First, clearly there was an opportunity to withdraw from the shooting without any negative consequences. Second, if this opportunity was apparent at least to W., Magel, and the theologian, then it would presumably have been apparent to others as well. This, then, raises another question. Given the general unease and discontent with this operation, why didn't more soldiers ask not to participate? Of course, it is possible that others did opt out and that their stories did not make it into the record. However, it seems more likely that most did not. One significant factor in the men's reaction of traumatized compliance may have been the paralyzing effect of the newness of the operation. This was a unit recently on light duty in France and not yet accustomed to the brutalities of the eastern front. Indeed, the use of two soldiers for each victim speaks of a traditional military firing squad, not the more economical one bullet, one victim technique of killers experienced in mass executions.

Before one lends excessive weight to evidence of refusal or to the pressures to participate, however, it is important to consider the question of complicity from another perspective. While there is evidence in this event (and the others) that individuals refused to kill, there is almost no evidence of anyone refusing to participate in the operation as a whole. These soldiers were sometimes reticent to actually commit the act of killing, but according to the records available, none of them renounced participation in the operation at large. Even Magel and the theologian who were reassigned to the guarding detail found this role bearable, if not acceptable. After all, Magel does not claim to have requested exemption from the entire operation (even though this would have been in his legal best interest, whether true or not). The end result of even refusals such as Magel's was still the same as even individuals with some objections to the killing materially participated in it just the same.

However, one man chose to refuse, not just for himself but for his entire unit. This most remarkable example of a refusal to participate in killing comes not from this company, but from the 1st Company of the same battalion, commanded by forty-seven-year-old Josef Sibille. Sibille refused the order outright. In fact, what makes the 3rd Company case unique is that three companies of the same unit in the same area were simultaneously presented with the same order to kill Jews, and yet this order resulted in three different outcomes. The 2nd Company, under First Lieutenant Hermann Kuhls, age thirty-three, who was both a party and SS member and considered to be "radical and anti-religious" and an outspoken antisemite, complied immediately and eagerly with the order, executing the Jews in his jurisdiction.[45] The officers of 3rd Company hesitated but eventually complied, but Sibille (also a Nazi Party member) refused.

There is frustratingly little information about why this commander took this action. He briefly explained himself in a letter written to the senior prosecutor in February 1953. In it, he states that on 6 or 7 October he received a telephone call from the battalion commander, Major Commichau, in which he was ordered to kill all the Jews in his area. Sibille testified at the Nöll/Zimber trial that Commichau told him "as long as the Jews are not eliminated, we will not have any peace from the partisans. The Jewish action in your area must therefore be completed in the end."[46] Sibille connected this order directly with the Mogilev Conference, writing, "In the fall of 1941 around the end of September, a training course was held in the city of Mogilev. As far as I remember, the Regimental commander and an officer from each battalion took part. From my battalion, I/691 the adjutant, Lieutenant Grosskopp was sent. . . . The subject of the training was primarily: Jews and Partisans."[47] He further related that the order to kill Jews caused him "anxious hours and a sleepless night" until he made his decision. After repeated urgent phone calls from the battalion commander, Sibille informed Commichau that "my company would not shoot any Jews." He explained that he could not "expect decent German soldiers to dirty their hands with such things."[48] Major Commichau then asked Sibille when he would "be hard for once," to which the lieutenant replied, "in this case, never." Commichau then said, "Enough. You have three days to carry out this order." Again, Sibille refused, saying he would never carry it out and that he would not besmirch his honor or that of his company.[49]

There appear to have been no real consequences to Sibille's disobedience. He wrote that "as a result of my behavior, I later heard that I had been judged as too soft."[50] Beyond these insults, Sibille did not suffer any punishment. First Lieutenant Sibille saw Major Commichau five days later, and Commichau did not mention the incident at all.[51] Sibille considered himself vindicated by a later army order forbidding the participation of the Wehrmacht in Jewish shootings. This was, however, a misinterpretation of army policy forbidding soldiers to participate without orders. As the Mogilev Conference indicates, the army was certainly willing to do so when the anti-partisan rationale was marshaled.

Beyond his honor argument, we know very little about Sibille's motivations. Were his objections based solely on some form of honor and professionalism, or was that a standard cover for a deeper moral objection?[52] There is some evidence from his family to support both explanations. As a World War I veteran who had fought on the western front, Sibille could have found the conduct of World War II in the East disagreeable if not unlawful. According to his granddaughter, he was also a religious man who refused to allow his two sons to attend Hitler Youth gatherings because they conflicted with church. He only acquiesced after he received career pressure from Nazis in the school where he taught.[53] Sibille's membership in the Nazi Party seems therefore less instructive in this context. What is undeniable is that First Lieutenant Sibille refused openly and repeatedly to carry out an order to kill and that he suffered no repercussions for this behavior. If Sibille and Kuhls represent the extremes of response, then Nöll and Zimber likely represent the norm (and the reactions of the majority of soldiers and officers in similar positions). Therefore, understanding their response is vital. Given the hesitation and debate, how did they come to the decision to obey rather than choosing Sibille's path?

When examining any organization's participation in mass murder, one must begin with the leaders themselves, for it is improbable that 3rd Company soldiers would have killed had *their* commander, like Sibille, refused. Captain Friedrich Nöll was forty-four and, like Major Waldow and Lieutenant Sibille, a schoolteacher. He had served in World War I on both the western and eastern fronts and ended the war as a lieutenant, joining the reserves in 1919. His nephew recalled that he tolerated no "back talk" from the children and was very strict even in his own family.[54] Captain Nöll appears in a wartime photo every bit the stern schoolteacher, wearing wire-rimmed glasses, with a leather map case on his belt and binoculars at his neck.

Nöll joined the Nazi veterans' organization but not until 1938. His Nazi credentials were not insignificant; he became a Nazi Party member on 1 May 1933, very shortly after Hitler's rise to power. Nöll also joined the SA relatively quickly, being a member from July 1933 until January 1937. He also joined the Nationalsozialistischen Volkswohlfahrt, a Nazi charity group, in 1934. His participation in the Nazi Lehrerbund (Teacher League) beginning in 1933 is not particularly damning but does give an indication of Nöll's further integration into the Nazi state, as he along with most other teachers positioned himself with the official Nazi professional organization. His membership in the Reichskolonialbund (Reich Colonial League) also suggests that he was supportive of German imperial aims.[55]

Characterizations of him by his soldiers are mixed. One soldier judged him to be "respected and beloved due to his correct and fair attitude."[56] Another, however, described him as "ruthlessly strict and bureaucratically minded," an officer who "had only his favorites but was otherwise not well liked by us."[57] One noted that, "like many schoolteachers who became officers, he was excessively correct, one could say exaggeratedly so, and considered all orders to be carried out with pedantic accuracy."[58] Nöll does not come across as a particularly strong leader. He "mostly remained in his quarters" while sending squads out on antipartisan operations.[59] Indeed, Nöll himself claimed that on the day of the shooting he stayed in the company office.[60] Subsequently, as a battalion commander, he apparently was accused of cowardice before the enemy and only escaped execution when the Russians overran the German position.[61]

Nöll, a weak and indecisive man, felt perhaps that he personally should not participate, but instead of refusing also on behalf of his men, he chose to delegate the unpleasant assignment to his subordinate. During his trial, Nöll stated that one of the reasons for his failure to protest the order was that he did not want his actions to be "interpreted badly" by others.[62] He did not want to appear weak or disloyal . . . and because of this he allowed at least 150 people to be murdered. He further attempted, under oath, to minimize his responsibility as a decision maker regarding Commichau's order: "As a company commander, I didn't need to know the details. It was enough that the Major knew them."[63] Certainly this was a desperate attempt at self-exculpation but also reflected Nöll's unwillingness to take any ownership of his actions. Even after the war, Nöll continued to describe his actions in a vague and evasive manner. He told a German magazine in 1969, "That was really something. You know, there we were stumbling around and one didn't know what was going on behind the next hill."[64]

In many ways, First Sergeant Emil Zimber was the perfect complement to Nöll. Zimber was born in Switzerland but moved to Freiburg, Germany, at the age of seven after his parents divorced. In 1934, he joined the state police in Freiburg. Zimber entered the Wehrmacht in 1937 as a noncommissioned officer with a twelve-year commitment.[65] He claimed after the war to have not been a member of any Nazi organization, which seems to be stretching the truth more than a little. A neighbor testified to authorities after the war that Zimber was "an outspoken Nazi and militarist who was always talking about the final victory and miracle weapons in the bomb shelter."[66] By the time 3rd Company arrived in Kovno, he was the first sergeant, the highest-ranking enlisted man in the company. His soldiers, however, did not hold him in high regard. Adam V. was Zimber's orderly and knew him well. "He was very timid," V. remembered. "I also don't believe he was a good soldier at the front. From my perspective, he lacked courage. He had, however, a good appearance."[67] Company clerk Hans W. confirmed this opinion, and his characterization bears repeating in its entirety.

> If I remember correctly, he was a career soldier. When I first met him, he was still a sergeant. His single ambition was to become a First Sergeant, which he finally had achieved. He was very ambitious. From outward appearance he came across as extremely tough and brusque. One could tell that he took great pains to give this impression to the outside world. In reality, however, he was of weak disposition. As a result, he sometimes hazed us. For example, when minor infractions occurred within the company, he was anxious to cover them up so that they wouldn't come back on him as First Sergeant. This had the effect that he would avenge offenses that he couldn't officially punish through petty treatment, extra duty, etc. The weakness of his character explains how he could quickly be-

come enraged but in a few minutes be reconciled and calmed by a few appropriate words.[68]

Zimber's character is vital to understanding how the Krucha shooting took place. He was an ambitious career soldier but a small, petty man, concerned about keeping up appearances. His personality also cast serious doubt on his claims of great reluctance in organizing the action. It seems clear that when Nöll could not passively evade following the order, he delegated it to Zimber and withdrew from the situation. Zimber, ambitious but also intent on hiding his weakness, then took charge of the operation to such a degree that his orderly who had followed him to the execution site observed him "walking through the bodies when the shooting was over."[69] Actions such as these, as well as choosing to personally lead the shooting operation (rather than one of the other less intimate details) and giving the fire commands, do not support merely carrying out orders, as Zimber later protested. He claimed that he thought the killing to be a mess or a disgrace *(Schweinerei)* at the time. However, the judge in his trial referred to a letter Zimber had written in reference to his prosecution that wondered why people were "seizing on these old war stories."[70] However, perhaps Zimber *was* telling the truth when he lamented, "If Captain Nöll would have found the courage, his subordinates would all have been relieved. He has burdened all our consciences."[71]

The discussion of the Krucha killing must also be viewed in the context of the organizational culture of the unit. Why were these orders given? The first stop after the Mogilev Conference must be Major Alfred Commichau. Commichau, the son of a factory owner, had been born in Bialystok (modern-day Poland) in 1896 and entered service in World War I as a private in August 1914, was twice wounded during that war, and earned the Iron Cross (second class).[72] He was apparently financially well off, as he spent his interwar time as an agricultural official at a manor in the Spreewald on the Polish border. It is interesting to note that this estate was worked between 1933 and 1945 by forced labor from the nearby women's prison in Cottbus.[73] It is conceivable that Commichau himself managed this labor on the property. In any case, he seems to have been eager to rejoin the army when the war broke out, having written authorities asking to be recalled to active service.[74] His background, particularly as someone born as an ethnic German in Poland, may have played an important role in his disposition toward the murder of the Jews in his area.

Those soldiers who testified about him remembered him as a good superior. There was no mention of antisemitism. However, it seems clear that Commichau's orders were tolerated if not approved by his superior, despite the regimental commander's protestations that "Jewish shootings were neither ordered nor carried out in my regiment."[75] Indeed, the commander, Colonel Erich Müller, had the temerity to claim that he had reprimanded Commichau and had him transferred from the regiment. Even then he couched this "punishment" as telling Commichau that he had "gone too far" in a "reprisal measure."[76] However, if Commichau was to have been transferred for bad behavior, why was he still in the regiment five months later, and why did Müller himself rate him in February 1942 as an officer of "impeccable character" who demonstrated "agility and vigor in the leadership of his battalion"?[77] The answer is that Commichau's actions were neither deemed objectionable nor condemned at the time, and that Müller's postwar account is a transparent fabrication, possibly aimed at deflecting attention from an organizational participation in genocide in which he was also complicit if not responsible. Documentary evidence indicates that the 691st Infantry Regiment was no stranger to operations directed against Jews. In a report filed on 14 November 1941, Einsatzgruppe B reported, "According to a report from the 691st Infantry Regiment, the Jews in Asmonj [sic] are providing relief in every way possible to the partisans in the vicinity. On 9 October 1941 81 Jews were shot during the occupation of the town because they had violated the directives of the occupation authorities."[78]

Indeed, this murderous climate in the 691st also reflected the larger divisional stance toward participation in the Holocaust. In a 15 November memo to rHGM, the 339th division commander, General Hewelcke, noted that the employment of *Ordnungsdienst* units "led to unpleasant incidents during the execution of the Jews of Borissow [sic]. Local actions should only be carried out with simultaneous coordination with the troops. Instructions of the SD for the *Ordnungsdienst* may only be given through *Orts* [Town]-, *Standort-* [Site], or Section command-ers."[79] Far from distancing the Wehrmacht from anti-Jewish actions, this communication directed that the two be more closely integrated. In the same memo, General Hewelcke suggested that some of the possessions taken from the murdered Jews of Borisov be handed over to the local ci-vilian populations. The November operational summary from the 339th Infantry Division contained even more telling evidence of an organiza-tional anti-Jewish stance. It noted, "in places where a cleaning up of Jews by the SD has not yet taken place, a greater reticence of the population can be detected. In such areas, pacification actions only rarely lead to full success because the approach of the troops is betrayed in time."[80] The lessons of the Mogilev Conference could hardly be more clearly ar-ticulated than in this entry: Jews were the enemy or, at the very least, supported the enemy, and their removal made things easier and safer for the Wehrmacht.

For the men, the situation was at least in some ways similar to that in Krupki. They were unaccustomed to such actions and, by extension, were as unpracticed in methods of evasion as they were in the techniques of mass executions. However, the nature of the environment also un-doubtedly intensified some important social-psychological pressures. First, 3rd Company was isolated, alone in the village, ten miles from its headquarters. The unit was also still in the process of adapting to the nature of the war in the East, having only two months before been in France. While the threat from partisans was low, patrolling the hostile environment of Belarus with its dark forests and swamps must have cre-ated a degree of apprehension. Here the anti-partisan justification was explicitly used to play upon these fears and to justify killing Jews. Fi-nally, the same compartmentalizing division of labor was used as in Krupki, with the crucial exception being that there were no SS units present to carry out the actual killing. Third Company carried out the Krucha execution more or less completely on its own, with limited as-sistance from local police. However, while these pressures perhaps made evasion or refusal harder for individual soldiers, it was clearly not impos-sible, as the Magel and W. examples demonstrate. Moreover, it is possi-ble that First Lieutenant Sibille interpreted these same conditions of isolation as giving him the space to ignore the order, knowing that his commander could not easily check up on him or personally confront him.

The Krucha killing is highly instructive in a variety of ways. First, it conclusively illustrates dissemination of the Jewish-Bolshevik-partisan calculus as formulated in Mogilev, from the highest level to the lowest. It is a rare example of a *direct causal link* between such exhortations to increased violence against Jews as partisans and actual killing actions. Second, the case of 3rd Company demonstrates the intense emotional impact of these killings on soldiers, the factors leading to their participation in spite of these responses, but also the real opportunities at both the soldier and officer level to *avoid* involvement without adverse consequences. Moreover, we see the importance of leadership at the ground level in determining whether units would participate or not participate. In other words, the draconian discipline of the Wehrmacht worked both ways. Any Wehrmacht proclivity for extreme obedience meant that soldiers ordered not to kill presumably would not. Finally, the progression from the Mogilev Conference to the Krucha action to the November reports from the 339th Division demonstrates, at least for this unit, a movement from ad hoc complicity in genocide to a more regimented, habitual form. The increasing velocity of the Wehrmacht's bloody downward spiral can be seen when we consider that in less than a month, army units in Belarus had gone from somewhat hesitant collaborators to clumsy but brutal killers.

Figure 1. Officers of the 3rd Battalion, 354th Infantry Regiment. *From left to right:* Lieutenant Nick, Battalion Adjutant Lieutenant Speth, Battalion Commander Johannes Waldow, Lieutenant Liehr, Lieutenant Kerker. (Landesarchiv NRW—Abteilung Westfalen, Q 234, Nr. 3541)

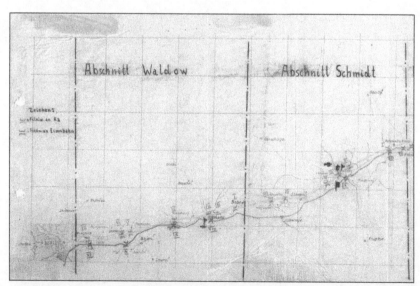

Figure 2. Hand-drawn map of Highway R2 and rail lines from Borisov to Orscha, July 1941. Note the "Waldow Sector" assigned to the 3rd Battalion, 354th Infantry, and the headquarters stationed in Krupki. (Bundesarchiv-Militärarchiv)

Figure 3. Members of 12th Company, 354th Infantry Regiment, returning from an anti-partisan patrol dressed in civilian clothes, 1941. Some soldiers testified that these civilian clothes came from murdered Jews. Original caption: "Berger and two men on reconnaissance patrol." (Courtesy of Wolf-Hagen Berger)

Figure 4. The Krupki killing site, photographed in 2009, where one thousand Jews were murdered on 18 September 1941. The 3rd Battalion, 354th Infantry Regiment, participated in this killing. (Photo by author)

Figure 5. Alfred Commichau, 1940. Commichau commanded the 1st Battalion, 691st Infantry Regiment, 339th Infantry Division. After receiving guidance from the Mogilev Conference, he ordered his three company commanders, including Nöll and Sibille, to murder all the Jews in their area of operations. (Bundesarchiv-Militärarchiv)

Figure 6. Friedrich Nöll, 1946. Nöll commanded the 3rd Company, 691st Infantry Regiment, 339th Infantry Division, which murdered at least 150 Jews in the town of Krucha on 10 October 1941 as a direct result of the Mogilev Conference. (HStA Darmstadt H-3 Nr. 36533)

Figure 7. Emil Zimber, 1953. As the highest-ranking enlisted man in the 3rd Company, Zimber took command of the Krucha killing operation, including stationing himself with the shooters. (HStA Darmstadt H-13 Nr. 535)

Figure 8. Members of the 3rd Company, 691st Infantry Regiment, 339th Infantry Division, on anti-partisan operations, 1941. Original caption: "Partisans (Bandits) were marched away." (HStA Darmstadt H-13 Nr. 529)

Figure 9. Josef Sibille, after the war. Sibille commanded the 1st Company, 691st Infantry Regiment, 339th Infantry Division. He steadfastly refused the order to murder the Jews under his control and suffered no consequences. (Courtesy of Richard and Christiane Sibille)

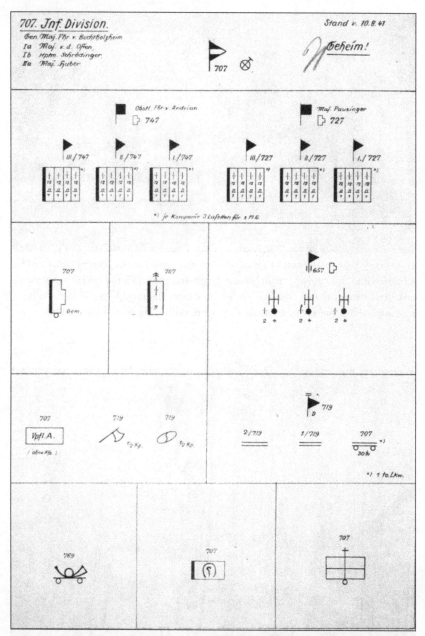

Figure 10. Organizational chart of the 707th Infantry Division, 8 October 1941. This unit was deeply complicit in carrying out the Holocaust in Belarus. (Bundesarchiv-Militärarchiv)

Figure 11. The monastery at Zyrowice, near Slonim, 2009. First Lieutenant Glück and his men from the 6th Company, 727th Infantry Regiment, 707th Infantry Division, rounded up and murdered, on their own initiative, around twelve hundred Jews. Former soldiers remembered this monastery in connection with the killing action. (Photo by author)

Figure 12. The Great Synagogue in Slonim, before 1939. Jews made up the majority of the population of the town. There were around twenty-five thousand in Slonim and the surrounding area in 1941. (United States Holocaust Memorial Museum, courtesy of Tomasz Wisniewski)

Figure 13. The market square in Slonim, before 1939. In Belarus, Jews often worked as peddlers, craftsmen, merchants, and middlemen between rural non-Jewish peasants and larger, urban markets. (United States Holocaust Memorial Museum, courtesy of Tomasz Wisniewski)

Figure 14. The Slonim Jewish orphanage, before the war. The orphanage's children were murdered on 14 November 1941 with between eight thousand and ten thousand other Jews of Slonim. (Kalman Lichtenstein, *Pinkas Slonim* [Tel-Aviv: Irgun ole Slonim be-Yisrael, 1961])

Figure 15. The Nussbaum family in 1938. *Left to right:* Lisa Derman's sister Pola, father Hirsh, brother Busiek, mother Gita, and Lisa. Lisa's mother was murdered in the *Aktion* on 14 November 1941. Her sister, Pola, was shot trying to to crawl under the ghetto fence to escape the second *Aktion* in June 1942. Lisa, Busiek, and Hirsh survived the war with partisans in the forest. (Image taken from the interview of Lisa Derman provided by the USC Shoah Foundation—the Institute for Visual History and Education, http://sfi.usc.edu/)

Figure 16. Killing site in the Czepilov Forest, photographed in 2009, where between eight thousand and ten thousand Jews from Slonim were murdered on 14 November 1941. The 6th Company in Slonim participated in all aspects of this *Aktion*. (Photo by author)

Figure 17. The Novogrudok killing site in the Skridlevo Forest, photographed in 2009, where five thousand Jews were murdered on 14 December 1941. The 7th Company, 727th Infantry Regiment, 707th Infantry Division, participated in this killing. (Photo by author)

Figure 18. The Stolowicki family, 1939. *Left to right:* Michael (who changed his name to Stoll after the war), sister Bella, father Leon, and sister Ann. The Stolowicki family was aided by German soldier Joachim Lochbihler in the Pupko brewery, which helped them survive. Michael worked as an electrician in the brewery. His mother, Sara, was killed in Majdanek in 1942, but Michael, his father, and sister Bella escaped from the train and survived the war. His other sister Ann hid in the brewery and escaped to the forest. She also survived the war. (Image taken from the interview of Michael Stoll provided by the USC Shoah Foundation—the Institute for Visual History and Education, http://sfi.usc.edu/)

Figure 19. Josef Kiefer, 1940. Kiefer commanded the 12th Company, 727th Infantry Regiment, 707th Infantry Division, in Szczuczyn. This unit conducted frequent "Jew hunts" and participated in sadistic "Jew games" in the ghetto there in the winter of 1941–42. (Bundesarchiv-Militärarchiv)

CHAPTER SIX

Making Genocide Routine Slonim

I had been given a silver cigarette case by a Jew as a gift that had a tsarist eagle engraved on it. I took it to a Jewish jeweler to have it made into a locket for my wife. The jeweler asked to see my hand. I showed it to him. He then said something to his wife that I didn't understand. I asked him what he had said. He had said to his wife, "He wasn't there." Upon my further questioning, he said, "at the digging of the mass graves meant for the Jews."

Franz L., 20 March 1961

ON THE EVENING of 14 November 1941, Franz L. climbed out of a truck on the outskirts of the town of Slonim. Only a series of campfires built by the soldiers broke the darkness. Franz was met by his sergeant, Hans R. "Franz," he said, "it would be better if we just put a bullet in our heads now." Together they walked to the edge of one of three mass graves, where Sergeant R. explained that several thousand Jewish men, women, and children had been forced to strip naked and were shot. By the flickering firelight, Franz saw thousands of naked bodies and several containers of alcohol near the grave. Piles of clothes divided by age and sex lay nearby. As Sergeant R. spoke, tears ran down his cheeks.[1] Soldier Karl M. also guarded the Slonim execution site and remembered that the scene was "terrible and ghastly to see. The air stank of blood and sweat." Suddenly, he heard a child's voice cry out several times for "Mama." The voice, it seemed to him, "sounded buried, crying out from the depths." Then all was quiet.[2] At dawn, after spending an icy night keeping watch over the murdered Jews of Slonim, the soldiers of the 6th Company, 727th Infantry Regiment, returned to their barracks.

The actions of this company in Slonim (and of other 727th soldiers in surrounding areas) are emblematic of an escalation in Wehrmacht collusion in the Holocaust. German soldiers no longer merely assisted in killings in towns in which they found themselves while advancing. The units in the following cases lived side by side with the Nazi administration and its Jewish victims for extended periods and found themselves involved in far more than just killing. The behavior of German army units in Slonim and Novogrudok demonstrates the depth of this cooperation, in particular how the army negotiated its role in the Nazi genocidal project and the extent to which that role became routinized.

The 707th Infantry Division was born on 2 May 1941 in Bavaria. It had two infantry regiments: the 747th and the 727th, coming from the Munich area.[3] The division was intended to function as a second-line occupation unit, and the average age of thirty reflected this. At the same time, however, it was made up of a large number of elite mountain troops from the 1st Gebirgsdivision and had, perhaps, been destined for action in the Balkans. Indeed, its future commander had been getting a "refresher" in troop leading on the staff of the 99th Gebirgsjägerregiment in Serbia in April 1941.[4] He certainly would have fit in there.

This officer, fifty-two-year-old Major General Gustav Freiherr von Mauchenheim genannt Bechtolsheim, was a Bavarian with a gaunt, skeletal face whose father had also been a general.[5] As in Krupki and Krucha, leadership was vitally important at all levels. Bechtolsheim began by setting the tone at the division level. He had fought in World War I from beginning to end, serving as an infantryman. He was wounded at Verdun and then again in Macedonia, and had seen extensive action, fighting on the western, eastern, Serbian/Macedonian, and Italian fronts.[6] After World War I, Bechtolsheim served in various positions in the Reichswehr, the army of the Weimar Republic.

He was also a dedicated Nazi. An evaluation report in 1939 credited him with "a high sense of responsibility and a positive attitude toward the National Socialist state."[7] In 1943, he was evaluated as someone "embodying the major ideas of National Socialism" who "understands to communicate the national socialist body of thought to others."[8] Part of this worldview was a rabid antisemitism. As a fervent racist and Nazi, Bechtolsheim was a driving force behind the behavior of his division, as his directives indicate.

If the general of the 707th was a great Nazi, he was certainly not a great general. He seemed well suited to killing civilians but less able to lead when it counted. His last evaluation as a division commander rated him as "average," criticized him for lacking the "quick decision-making ability and necessary force to drive things forward" at the front, and ended by recommending his immediate relief.[9]

The 707th Division arrived on the eastern front in August 1941 with the 2nd Battalion, 727th Infantry Regiment, reaching the Baranovichi region on the 14th.[10] A number of companies of the 727th were stationed in the area: the 6th Company in Slonim, the 7th Company in Novogrudok, the 8th in Baranovichi and Stolpce, the 12th in Szczuczyn, and the 10th and 11th Companies in the vicinity of Lida. Most of these units would be deeply involved in the murder of Jews in the Soviet Union.[11] By mid-October, the division had sufficient experience with the Nazi genocidal project that its operations officer would order the murder of the Jews of Smolevichi by Reserve Police Battalion 11.[12] One scholar credits the 707th Division with the eventual murder of up to nineteen thousand Jews.[13]

On 1 September, the region of Belarus roughly from Borisov west to the former German-Soviet border became part of the civilian-controlled Reichskommissariat Ostland (RKO). This division marked the boundary between continued military and newly established civilian administrative control, with everything to the east remaining part of rHGM. The RKO fell under the control of the Ministry for the Occupied Territories led by Alfred Rosenberg, a Baltic German and one of the Nazi Party's chief racial theorists. While Rosenberg envisioned four *Reichskommissariats*, the circumstances of the war allowed for the creation of only two: Ostland (which included the Baltic states and Belarus) and Ukraine.

The RKO was under the command of Heinrich Lohse, a forty-five-year-old politician and pudgy functionary who also served as the *Oberpräsident* of German Schleswig-Holstein. Though he claimed to be guided by a dedication to "construction and culture," in reality he was "neither a significant personality nor a dynamic leader."[14] At times, though, his more economic approach to Jewish policy conflicted with the more annihilationist bent of the SS. Within the RKO, Lohse presided over four administrative units called *Generalbezirken*.

Of these, we are most concerned with the Generalbezirk Weissruthenien (White Russia) governed by Wilhelm Kube, a fifty-four-year-old Prussian bureaucrat. For the Nazi administration, White Russia (formerly eastern Poland and modern-day Belarus) was not nearly as important as the Baltic states or the Ukraine, lacking as it did the same potential for active collaboration and the same economic resources. Perhaps this explains Kube's appointment. He had been removed in 1936 from his position as president of Brandenburg owing to corruption. Hitler, however, felt "sympathetic toward him and fingered him for a position in the occupation administration in the East."[15] Kube saw this job as a new start and sought to "optimize the economic exploitation of the region through cooperation with the population."[16] While subscribing to the Nazi goal of exterminating Jews, he was disturbed by the deportation of German Jews to Minsk. He hoped that these "human beings from our cultural sphere" would at least be killed in a "humane way."[17] He objected to German Jews being killed in the same brutal manner as "lesser" eastern Jews. Kube's attitude toward the Jews was pragmatic but certainly not beneficent. He stated in July 1942, for example, that he would "prefer to eliminate the Jews in *Generalbezirk Weissruthenien* once and for all as soon as the Jews are no longer needed by the Wehrmacht for economic reasons."[18] Kube would be assassinated in 1943 by means of a bomb placed under his bed by a partisan. The final civilian administrator of interest, Kube's immediate subordinate was Gerhard Erren, *Gebietskommissar* (a regional administrator) for the Slonim region.

Slonim

The 6th Company had occupied Slonim in western Belarus by 21 August.[19] Slonim is a very old town, first mentioned in medieval chronicles around 1040, and was most often part of Poland. As the town rests in a valley along the Sczara River, its name likely derives from a Slavic word for valley or lowland.[20] Aharon Shapiro, a former resident, recalled that "the river is an important part of everything. Bathing in the summer, ice skating in the winter, swimming and canoeing in the summer. . . . The river was an important part of our childhood."[21] In 1941, an island in that same river would become a Jewish ghetto. A Jewish community was recorded in Slonim in 1551.[22] This community formed a large part of the town itself. In 1897, Jews accounted for 10,588 of the town's 15,893 inhabitants.[23] This already high percentage greatly increased after 1939 as Jewish refugees from Warsaw, Lodz, and other cities under Nazi occupation flooded into the area around Slonim. According to Gerhard Erren, in 1941 there were around twenty-five thousand Jews in the surrounding area, with sixteen thousand in the town itself. Other estimates run as high as twenty thousand.[24] Historically, Slonim had a vibrant Jewish life, with at least seven synagogues, the largest of which, built in 1642, remains today in a semi-ruined state. Slonim was also the center of an important Hasidic dynasty founded by Rabbi Abraham Weinberg. Down a small alley from the main synagogue was the old marketplace, where Jewish merchants would gather to sell their wares.

The river provided the foundation for a relatively brisk economy centered on breweries, tanneries, and brick factories; the monopoly for brewing in Slonim, in fact, had been held by Jews since 1558.[25] One historian noted that even though the town developed into an industrial locale near the railroad junction of Baranovichi, it became even more a "Jewish shtetl."[26] Relationships between Jews and non-Jews appear to have been cordial, if not close. One survivor recalled that, though there were frequent antisemitic articles in the newspaper, there were no "outbreaks of hate."[27] When the Soviets arrived in 1939, dividing up Poland with the Nazis as a result of the Molotov-Ribbentrop Pact, Slonim's Jewish inhabitants, like many Jews in Poland, probably shared Luba Abramovich's feelings: "We were pleased to see them, we were worried that the Germans were coming and we were delighted when the Russians arrived."[28]

German troops did come to Slonim, however, on 24 June 1941, likely elements of the 47th Panzer Corps.[29] The wearing of the yellow star was instituted quickly, and Jews were soon ordered to move to the First of May Street.[30] Killings began almost immediately. Several Einsatzgruppen units visited the town because of its important (and convenient) location along the R2 main logistical route. Elements of Einsatzkommando

8 were stationed in Slonim on 3 July.[31] On 17 July, the 252nd Infantry Division reported that "police roundups" had netted a large number of "communists and unsafe elements."[32] This was likely the first major action in the town, carried out by Einsatzkommando 8, in which two thousand men of Slonim were driven to the old market, where they were humiliated and forced to dance and sing Jewish songs.[33] Luba Abramovich's husband, Lazar, was murdered in this action.[34] Police Regiment Mitte reported the killing to Berlin: "During yesterday's 'cleansing action' [*Sauberungsaktion*] 1,153 Jewish plunderers were killed by Police Regiment Center"; Police Battalion 316 was likely the killing unit.[35] On August 12, Einsatzgruppe B reported killing fifty-two "followers of Bolshevism" and "looters" in Slonim.[36] These actions characterized what Raul Hilberg referred to as the "First Wave" of Einsatzgruppen killings, which were somewhat limited, focused on intelligentsia and prominent residents, and for the most part did not include women and children, as these victim groups were not yet officially targeted.[37]

The commander of the 6th Company, First Lieutenant Fritz Glück, set up an *Ortskommandantur* (local military headquarters) to administer the town upon his arrival. Several men of the company were permanently employed in this administrative office, while others served in dual capacities. Glück himself was a Nazi Party member and rabid antisemite. A 6th Company soldier described him as a "Jew-hater" who "drank lots of schnapps and was often drunk."[38] Others recalled him drinking during the day and painted him as a "fanatic National Socialist."[39] His top NCO in the Ortskommandantur remembered he was a wearer of the prestigious "Blood Order" medal, awarded to distinguished party members who had participated in the Munich Beer Hall Putsch on 9 November 1923 and later extended to include those imprisoned or wounded in the service of the party. Fewer than six thousand were ever awarded, making it an indication of early if not deep commitment to the Nazi cause.[40] One of his men summed him up simply as "mostly drunk."[41] Allegedly, an intoxicated Glück had once dragged two Jews out of a house and shot them. Franz L. recalled that "not a day went by that he didn't stagger around the *kaserne* courtyard in a very drunken state, firing wildly with his pistol." This violent and aggressive officer reportedly ranted at two of his soldiers who had balked at carrying out a hanging of "partisans" he had ordered. "Are you crazy?" he was said to have fumed. These victims were later left to hang in the central square for three days next to a sign that read: "So gets every Partisan!"[42]

This man and his soldiers governed Slonim until the civilian administration became fully operational. German military authorities had already mandated the wearing of the yellow star for Jews by 12 July.[43] During his tenure, Glück carried out at least one killing operation entirely on his own authority. One early morning sometime before mid-November 1941, Glück mobilized at least one platoon (likely the 3rd) and read them an order whereby the Jews in the region were to be liquidated.[44] In a postwar letter alerting the German authorities, former soldier Robert R. said that this order to kill the Jews had been justified by alleged Jewish support of the partisans, which he termed "an out-and-out lie."[45]

Glück and the 3rd Platoon Lieutenant H. then marched the men to the small town of Zyrowice. Four miles (6.4 km) south of Slonim, Zyrowice is distinguished by a beautiful and massive Eastern Catholic monastery. In the shadow of its bright blue dome and green metal roofs, some of the soldiers of 6th Company searched homes for Jews.[46] Others surrounded the town in a cordon. Glück and Lieutenant H. stood on the square as the Jews were assembled. Private Otto S. testified "that during the roundup of the Jews force naturally had to be used."[47] Once the roundup was complete, the Jews were loaded onto trucks. Soldiers rode along to make sure no Jews jumped out on the way to the killing site.[48]

The trucks drove about two and a half miles north of the town into a forest, where they met a detachment of Lithuanian soldiers.[49] Apparently, a test shooting had been carried out a few days earlier to ascertain whether the locals could hear shooting from the killing site.[50] Glück ordered his men to dig a grave, which they did. It appears that the Lithuanians did the bulk of the shooting, making marks on their rifles for each Jew killed."[51] It is probable that some 6th Company soldiers also joined in voluntarily. Gebietskommissar Erren's interpreter and driver, Alfred Metzner, was present and took part in the killing throughout the day, by his own admission. "I participated the entire time," he said. "The only time I paused was when my rifle was empty and I had to reload. It's impossible for me to say how many Jews I murdered during this three to

Zyrowice—
self-initiated
decentralized

Glück / Erren

Zyrowice
coordinated
complex
comprehensive
organized

meeting
assigned
roles

①

Marching into Darkness

four hour period."[52] As his driver was present, it is quite possible that Erren himself was present at the Zyrowice shooting. As in other executions, the Jews were forced to strip and hand over valuables. A day or so after the killing, German army driver Franz L. retrieved two truckloads of clothing from the shooting site. He estimated the number of dead at two to three hundred.[53] In reality, twelve to fourteen hundred Jews had been murdered.[54]

The Zyrowice action represents both a relatively decentralized and self-initiated action and also the depth to which Glück was committed to the murder of Jews. He undertook it on his own authority, using mostly his own soldiers. Indeed, many men remembered that the Lithuanian unit was under Glück's control as well. Also, his choice of one or two platoons suggests that he had already identified junior leaders and soldiers ready and willing to participate in these types of killings, a tactic we have already seen. The use of the Jew-Bolshevik-partisan calculus as a pretense for the murders is also consistent with the messages from the Mogilev Conference two months earlier. After a meeting of all the players (including Glück) following the Zyrowice killing, Gerhard Erren was described as having been "satisfied" with the action.[55]

Like the Zyrowice killing, the much larger November action in the Czepilov Forest provides a sharp contrast with Krupki and Krucha; it represents Wehrmacht participation in mass murder as a highly coordinated, more complex, comprehensive, and organized operation in conjunction with local civilian authorities. This was something fundamentally different. Sometime before 14 November, a meeting took place between the Gebietskommissar Gerhard Erren, First Lieutenant Glück, SS Unterstürmführer Waldemar Amelung, and Hauptwachtmeister Krein, a platoon leader from the 3rd Company of Reserve Police Battalion 69, which was also stationed in Slonim.[56] Amelung headed up the SD office in nearby Baranovichi. Likely also present was the leadership of the German police in Slonim.[57] The outcome of this meeting appears to have been a relatively detailed plan of action, in which the 6th Company would play vital roles.

First, soldiers of the company dug the graves themselves, an uncommon mode of participation for the Wehrmacht. A few weeks before the shooting, the men marched into the Czepilov Forest, several kilometers south of Slonim, on the road to Baranovichi. Here trucks met them with shovels. The men then dug three or four trenches, approximately one hundred meters long, three meters wide, and three meters deep, with a few sloping entrances.[58] The work took two to three days but was "not hard due to the sandy ground."[59] At least one Jewish survivor stated that sixty Jews were also taken to dig graves and did not return.[60] One soldier claimed that the men thought these were to be antitank ditches. However, it is unlikely that anyone truly believed this; at the time Slonim was over 435 miles (700 km) behind the front, and antitank ditches do not require sloped entrances for people to enter.

The men of the company assembled in the early morning hours of 14 November. It was bitterly cold—according to one survivor, twenty degrees below zero.[61] The company would follow what had become a common procedure. Regardless of postwar statements to the contrary, most men would have known what was about to happen. The day before, German authorities had put in place a curfew confining Slonim's Jews to their houses. This curfew separated Slonim survivor Luba Abramovich from her parents and child, as she was unable to return home from a friend's house; she would never see her family again.[62]

Before the killing operation began that morning, First Lieutenant Glück appeared at the barracks along with an SS officer. Several soldiers recall Glück telling the men that a large *Aktion* against the Jews of Slonim would take place.[63] "We knew then," stated one, "that the Jews would be shot."[64] The company cook, Alexander L., recalled the SS officer informing the company "the Führer has ordered the extermination of the Jews. Because the SS will be occupied with the execution, our company would have to take over the cordon. The shootings would be carried out by a Lithuanian company that already had experience in this area. However, soldiers from the company could also volunteer for this duty." L. was then ordered to fall out and prepare coffee and breakfast by 2 a.m.[65] Several other soldiers also remembered this call for volunteers.[66] According to at least two witnesses, 6th Company men *did* volunteer to participate in shooting.[67]

The operation began shortly thereafter and followed what was now a familiar process. Some soldiers established the outer cordon of Slonim. Unlike Krupki or Krucha, Slonim was a large, populous town, and many

Jews would attempt to flee. This time, the surrounding guard force of soldiers checked for specially issued IDs. Some Jews did try escaping the cordon but were turned around and sent back to town. One Jewish resident of Slonim, Zvi Szeptynski, remembered that he was stopped on his way to work by police and Wehrmacht soldiers and told to return to his house and remain there for the rest of the day, for he had a work permit exempting him from selection.[68] A 6th Company private recalled a Jew who approached him and offered in "perfect German" to give him 50,000 reichsmarks to be allowed to pass. The soldier turned the man back, he later claimed, because he was being observed by his squad and platoon leader.[69]

In the town itself, other soldiers, along with police, Lithuanians, and SS, rounded up the Jews and guarded them in the marketplace. One Jewish chronicler names the Belarussian mayor, Alexander Kisli, as a participant.[70] Though Wehrmacht members avoided mentioning their part in this stage, Luba Abramovich, hiding in a loft overlooking the square, recalled "German soldiers chasing people and beating them, throwing children to the ground. These people were screaming."[71] During the roundup, yellow worker identity cards issued by the Gebietskommissar were of vital importance. Only those holding these so-called "life cards" were spared. Dietrich Hick, head of Jewish affairs for the region, had submitted a list of names, which Erren had personally revised before approving. Luba Abramovich's family must not have been on that list, for when she finally was able to return home, she remembered: "[I] ran to the house, where my parents were with the child. I came and I saw that the door is open, the windows are broken, and nobody is there. So I fainted. . . . I didn't want to live."[72]

All those not on Erren's version of the list had been marked for death. This led to tragic scenes. Eighteen-year-old Rachel Klenicki stood in a crowd with her uncle and cousin as German soldiers sorted out those with work cards. She described what happened next. "When my uncle became aware of what was going to happen," she remembered, "he leapt into the Sczara River. His daughter jumped in after him, and both drowned."[73] German soldiers also witnessed scenes such as these firsthand and must have understood the nature of their actions, if only through the reactions of the Jews.

Erren, Hick, First Lieutenant Glück, and countless soldiers from the Ortskommandantur stood in the marketplace observing the selection process. Erren himself carried a whip, with which he struck the Jews.[74] The marketplace served as the scene of countless horrors. Nachum Alpert survived the ordeal and reported that his cousin, Chemke, refused to be separated from his family, though he had a work permit. After first being forced off the truck carrying his loved ones, Chemke climbed on again and was allowed to accompany them to their deaths.[75] The elderly and infirm were roughly shoved onto trucks, dressed only in night-gowns. One survivor watched from an attic window as the Jews were driven through the streets to the main square, with babies being "smashed against the sidewalk" and others shot.[76] Sixth Company soldiers participated in the roundup and were present throughout.[77]

As in previous cases, the soldiers escorted the Jews to the killing site. Some rode in trucks with them, while others walked beside the long columns moving out of town in the direction of Baranovichi. Accompanying them was a company of Lithuanian "volunteers."[78] In the Czepilov Forest, soldiers unloaded the Jews from the trucks and forced them, along with those arriving on foot, to sit within sight and earshot of the execution pits. Cook Alexander L. delivered food to the killing site several times. As he passed a column of women and girls, several women pleaded with him, "Mr. German soldier, save my life! I will give you money and gold."[79] But L. kept driving.

What was now a standardized routine at the execution pits followed. The participation of soldiers was neither distant nor uninvolved. Indeed, they themselves demonstrated brutality and a willingness to kill those trying to escape. The Jews were forced to sit and wait their turn while others were shot in groups of ten. They were required to take off any valuable clothing and place gold, money, and jewelry in a box. Sixth Company soldiers surrounded the execution site and guarded the waiting Jews. Even at this late stage in the operation, it was necessary to guard against escape. One sergeant admitted that he and a comrade shot at two escaping Jews (though they both naturally claimed not to have aimed at them).[80] Further violence occurred at the trenches. According to one soldier, the Jews were "roughly pushed out of the trucks and driven to the pits. They were beaten with rifle butts and there were heartbreaking scenes between the men and the victims."[81] These behaviors strongly suggest that the men exceeded the minimum requirements of the operation and approached their tasks with a certain dedication.

The shootings themselves appear to have been carried out primarily by the SS and a Lithuanian unit attached to the 6th Company, though, again, German soldiers killed as well. We know that First Lieutenant Glück was on the scene, because a private testified he had delivered several bottles of schnapps to him there around eleven o'clock.[82] SS Untersturmführer Amelung was in full command of the shooting, but Wehrmacht men also shot the Jews of Slonim. A former soldier stated unequivocally after the war that "there were also company members in the shooting *kommando*, who had voluntarily responded to First Lieutenant Glück's request. No one was ordered."[83] Soldiers of the company "held up Jewish infants in the air and shot them with pistols."[84] The men drank to the point of inebriation, and shot alongside the Lithuanian and SS soldiers. As one soldier described the macabre scene, it was a "real massacre. The shooting was somewhat haphazard [and] the shooting *kommandos* were very drunk."[85] Erren's interpreter, who has already demonstrated his openness in discussing his participation in murder, noted that "volunteer soldiers and railway workers from the train station in Slonim participated in this execution when they realized that there was something to be gained."[86]

Some Jews were not killed outright and screamed out from the pit. During this gruesome labor, some soldiers who were shooting "felt ill" and were given more schnapps.[87] The killing of between eight and ten thousand people continued until the late afternoon, so late in fact that the graves could not be covered that night but instead lay open, with the murdered Jews and some survivors exposed to the open air.

However, the 6th Company's mission was not yet over. The men then spent the night at the execution site to prevent unhurt or wounded Jews from escaping. Fires were lit to warm the men not circling around the graves. One soldier cried out in fright when a Jew crawled out of the grave near him.[88] A Jewish resident of Slonim related a similar story.

Esther Fuchsman (herself a nurse) . . . and her younger sister, half-naked in the cold, had been standing at the edge of the ditch. A bullet had gone through her hand and into her sister's head. Both of them fell into the ditch. Still in possession of her faculties, she had struggled to keep her head high enough to breathe, but her moving body out of sight of guards. Her sister had died instantly. . . . Meanwhile, the astounded guards who reported for duty at the ditches, found traces of blood going from the graves to the woods and concluded that during the night some of the corpses had escaped.[89]

Despite the guards' presence, a few Jews like Esther managed to escape. One survivor's testimony described such an escape:

My cousin Hanna Eilender from Suwalki was at the 14 November 1941 shooting. She was among the few—perhaps 60—who were considered already shot, but in reality not dead. A few were completely untouched. My cousin had not been hit. She lay under a few bodies and worked her way out of the grave later in the night. She told me as soon as she returned to the ghetto that Lithuanian auxiliaries had been left behind at the grave, who were completely drunk. In this way, a few others also were able to escape. My cousin Hanna Eilender was still alive when I left the Slonim ghetto. I have not heard anything of her whereabouts since.[90]

Patrols during the night and the next morning resulted in the recapture of some of the escapees. Private N. was part of the detail that marched out of Slonim the next morning to cover the grave. They found "a few wounded Jews, one of whom had been shot through the jaw." German soldiers then returned these survivors to the grave site and killed them there. At this point, N. relates that there they learned that many Jews had managed to flee. His squad leader, Sergeant W, then led the men on a patrol of the surrounding areas, searching for escaped Jews. N. remembered that he and his squad captured a woman, a man, and a twelve-year-old boy and returned them to the grave site, where they were shot again.[91] The 6th Company conducted other more wide-ranging patrols, searching for Jews who had escaped from the pit. This search led back to Slonim, where wounded survivors were dragged out of the hospital where they had sought treatment, and were shot by German civil officials and police.[92] These post-execution patrols stand out as incredibly powerful indications that these soldiers took their role in the murder of the Jews very seriously. Indeed, it would have been easy to avoid this kind of killing, which was individual, decentralized, and far from supervisory eyes. Why did these men continue on a very personal hunt for already wounded victims, when they could easily have reported finding nothing? Behaviors like these force us to seriously consider the possibility that these men approved of their task enough to faithfully carry it out even when no one was looking.

Gerhard Erren, the Gebietskommissar in Slonim, would report in January 1942 that "Slonim was very overpopulated upon my arrival, the housing situation catastrophic. The Jewish *Aktion* of [14 November] provided a tangible relief. . . . This *Aktion* carried out by the SD freed me of unnecessary eaters and the 7,000 Jews remaining in the town are completely engaged in the labor process. They work willingly under constant fear of death."[93] He would later recognize the 6th Company, 727th Infantry, specifically for the pivotal role it played in facilitating and carrying out this massacre and for the help these men provided in the rounding up, guarding, and shooting of the Jewish victims.

Eyewitness accounts of the Slonim massacre would make it all the way to Warsaw, where the famous historian of the ghetto, Emanuel Ringelblum, would record ninety-two hundred Jews being murdered (though he appears to have misdated the killing as occurring on October 15). This information would also be publicized in the Warsaw ghetto via the underground newspapers.[94] Ringelblum lamented privately in his diary that forty rural Jews "consented to be led to slaughter, though they knew what had happened in Vilna, *Slonim,* Chelmno, and other places."[95] Perhaps Luba Abramovich herself best summed up the human tragedy of November 14 when she said, "After this action, I never saw my mother, father, brother, my aunt and her child, my mother's brother and his wife and child, nor my child."[96]

A month later in Novogrudok, the 7th Company of the 727th Infantry Regiment, commanded by forty-eight-year-old Captain Johann Artmann, assisted in another murder of a Jewish community, which resulted in the death of approximately five thousand Jews there.[97] It was probably SS Unterstürmführer Waldemar Amelung who again arrived from nearby Baranovichi to preside over the killing.[98] He likely then met with Lieutenant Martin from the 7th Company and with Wilhelm Traub, an SS man on loan to the civil authorities and serving as the Gebietskommissar in Novogrudok.[99] The participation of this army unit mirrored that of the 6th in Slonim and is further evidence of an emerging standard operating procedure for involvement in this phase of the Final Solution. On 7 December, the night before the executions, 7th Company soldiers assisted in the roundup and imprisonment of the victims in several buildings in the local judicial complex. They stood guard outside, and cooks from the company were even responsible for feeding the Jews during their confinement. One cook recalled that the Jews were only fed kraut and potatoes once a day.[100] The next day, the men of the company escorted the Jews of Novogrudok out of town to a densely forested area known as Skridlevo. One soldier saw Wehrmacht trucks loaded with Jews heading to the execution site.[101] Also in the column were all the girls of the local Jewish orphanage, dressed in their best clothes.[102]

As in Slonim, soldiers guarded the execution site and witnessed similar scenes of terror and misery. One exceptional scene was described by Private First Class Anton H., a medic assigned to the soldiers surrounding the shooting. As a medic, he was able to wander around the site at will. He watched as one Jewish man attacked a policeman with a knife, wounding him in the face. The man was then "handcuffed, thrown into the snow, and beaten to death. He was beaten between the legs, on his genitals. When he was dead, he was dragged to the grave and thrown in."[103] He also observed one of the killers who shot infants and kicked them into the grave, saying, "You are going to Abraham."[104] Again, the employment of Wehrmacht personnel reflected what had come to be a routine division of labor.

German soldiers participated in the actual shooting in Novogrudok as well. The traveling 7th Company blacksmith reported that a sergeant and a private had actively participated in the shooting and then bragged about it to him.[105] Another remembered that one soldier, a Private Kasberger, was "brutal" and "ruthless" and along with several other soldiers had volunteered to participate in shooting Jews.[106] Lieutenant Martin, the 1st Platoon leader, was particularly active in this and other Jewish shootings. One of his platoon members described him as a "fanatic" and remarked in what must have been a gross understatement that "the Jews did not suit him."[107] By ghettoizing, guarding, and shooting Jews, the 7th Company (like the 6th) assisted the Einsatzgruppen and their Lithuanian auxiliaries in completing the murder of five thousand Jews in two days. Major Schmitz, the battalion commander responsible for both 6th and 7th Companies, had nicknamed Novogrudok the "El Dorado of Jews," which was certainly an indication of his disdain for its Jewish inhabitants.[108] In both cases, the Wehrmacht appears more adept and more comfortable with an expanded role in the Nazi genocidal project. Familiarity with the Holocaust led to a dangerous normalization and desensitization. Indeed, soon soldiers would be seeking out other ways in which they could personally benefit from murder.

CHAPTER SEVEN

The Golden Pheasant and the Brewer

He already had in those early days another girlfriend, a young Jewish girl whose name I can't remember. Regina was this girl's friend and often visited her. His first girlfriend always lived with him and Regina occupied herself with the housework. His first girlfriend was liquidated during the 14 November 1941 *Aktion* right in front of [his] eyes.

Slonim survivor Abraham Orlinski, 14 July 1964

Basically, I said that I would fake a Wehrmacht operation and that no one would come inside. Actually, I myself went out at night with my helmet and my rifle and stationed myself in front of the locked door.

Former German soldier Joachim L., 5 July 1965

UNLIKE THE GERMAN units in Krupki and Krucha, the 6th and 7th Companies occupied Slonim and Novogrudok for a relatively long time, approximately seven months. This lengthy occupation led in many ways to much deeper, much more routine, and much more complex modes of complicity in the Nazi genocidal plan. As Slonim and Novogrudok were deep in the Generalbezirk Weissruthenien of the RKO, these towns fell under the jurisdiction of Nazi civilian authorities. This situation placed the Wehrmacht units stationed there in a triangular relationship with both the civilian authorities and the SS/SD. Officially, Wehrmacht authorities were responsible for security issues and for managing any critical logistical operations that impacted the military. However, the

Wehrmacht became, in reality, a major player in all policies of occupation and did not confine itself to simple security concerns.

Instead, it soon became involved in all manner of interactions that far exceeded its military mandate. One such area was the disposition of Jewish property. Another was sexual exploitation, as the long occupation also led to some bizarre personal relationships between Jews and the German soldiers. Finally, normalization of complicity in these towns allowed a small minority of soldiers who wished to aid and perhaps even rescue Jews the opportunity to do so. These personal relationships between occupier and occupied, especially Jews, are rarely seen in scholarship yet are very important in exploring the complexities of the Holocaust at ground level.

An examination of 727th Infantry Regiment units, mainly the 6th Company in Slonim but also the 7th Company in Novogrudok, yields detailed evidence of the nature of the occupation in the East that is instructive for two reasons. First, it offers rare documentary evidence of situations that both survivors and former soldiers were loath to talk about, particularly regarding theft and personal relationships. Indeed, testimony from both victim and perpetrator mutually corroborates these situations. Second, these interactions complicate accepted characterizations of soldier mentalities. Specifically, they call for a reexamination of the attitude of the ordinary soldier to the genocidal project in which he was engaged. In the course of postwar investigations, most soldiers claimed that their involvement in killing resulted from a superior's orders and that they participated only to the minimal extent that they were required. While this is itself a tendentious argument, examining German soldiers' relationships to Jewish property and to Jews themselves offers what may be clearer insights into attitudes toward participation in the Holocaust. If some element of duress induced soldiers to participate in the killing process, no such pressures existed to handle Jewish goods or engage in personal (and sexual) relations with Jews. These men *chose* to actively take part in these aspects of the Holocaust.

Long-term official working relationships that developed between the Wehrmacht, the SS, and local Nazi civil authorities enabled the increasingly deeper complicity in genocide that appears in Slonim and Novogrudok. The development of these relationships thus warrants a brief investigation. The first real structures of military occupation established by the army in the newly conquered eastern territories took roughly three forms: direct rule by the local military commander, control by the local commander via an ad hoc Ortskommandantur (OK) comprised of personnel from his unit, or control by an actual numbered Ortskommandantur unit deployed for the express purpose of governance. In larger towns and cities, a Feldkommandantur (FK) would be erected, to which the OKs would report. These initial military governments were responsible first and foremost for the security of the local area and of logistical routes but quickly found themselves engaged in economic and racial matters as well. These commanders wore two faces, purportedly looking out for the interests of the native inhabitants in their area while also "participating in the massive terrorization the population."[1] On 1 September, the area of Belarus west of Minsk came under civilian control as Generalbezirk Weissruthenien of the Reichskommissariat Ostland, administered by Heinrich Lohse. The addition of a third power center along with the military authorities and the SS created a dynamic in this region different from the previous cases. This tripartite relationship added additional power struggles, along with competing interests and personalities that affected the nature but not the final outcome of Nazi extermination policy.

First Lieutenant Glück had been in control of Slonim for several weeks by the time the Gebietskommissar, Gerhard Erren, arrived at the beginning of September 1941. Erren was representative of the so-called "golden pheasants" (*Goldfasanen*)—preening Nazi officials so named for their brown uniforms, medals, and strutting, arrogant behavior. Erren was a teacher of history, geography, and biology at a *Reichswasserschutz* academy and later a *Freikorps* fighter.[2] In 1936, he began his training at an NS-Ordenburg school for future Nazi elites, where he later became an instructor. He participated in the French campaign in 1940 and was appointed a Gebietskommissar for the Slonim region in August 1941.[3] Gerda R., who served as his only secretary in September, described him as "downright schoolmasterly and petty."[4]

Erren was also an outspoken antisemite who had once remarked after personally killing a Jew working on his headquarters building, "When one has done it once, it is as easy as jumping over a piece of straw."[5] After

Führer Decree

June 25 1941

the Zyrowice killings, his driver and interpreter, Metzner, recalled a conversation with Erren in which he praised Metzner's "industriousness" and expressed his satisfaction with the outcome of this action.[6] A man named Polenz, a member of the civil administration in Slonim, who killed himself before standing trial in 1961, eclectically described Erren in his suicide note as "intelligent, a very good speaker, musical, unfortunately without morals, extremely refined, and without a doubt an alcoholic."[7]

Erren was assisted by Dietrich Hick, his *Referent* (or special assistant) for Jewish affairs. One survivor recalled that Hick had a large dog that he had named "Jew." He liked to walk into the ghetto and shout "Jew!" When a Jewish inhabitant appeared, thinking he had been called, Hick would beat him mercilessly and walk away.[8] Another Jewish inhabitant of Slonim termed him simply a "fanatic" and a "psychiatric case."[9] Also assigned to the civilian authorities were two branches of the Order Police (Ordnungspolizei, or Orpo): a gendarme detachment commanded by Lothar Schulz and a local urban police post (of the Schutzpolizei, or Schupo) under Lieutenant Walter Bonke. The leader of the SS/SD station responsible for Slonim was SS Untersturmführer Amelung, based out of nearby Baranovichi, though there seems to have been a small office in Slonim as well.[10]

Like many power dynamics in the Third Reich, the officially defined relationship between the military and the civilian authorities in *Reichskommissariats* remained somewhat ambiguous and contentious. For example, a Führer Decree dated 25 June 1941 detailed the duties of the Wehrmacht in civilian administered areas: in addition to security concerns, the army was expected to "support the Reichskommissars in their political and administrative tasks and represent them to the military, particularly regarding the exploitation of the land for the provision of the fighting troops. Given a risk of delay, the Military Commander has the right, also in civilian areas, to order measures that are necessary for the execution of military tasks. The Military Commander can temporarily delegate this right to the local commander."[11] Clearly, in areas of logistics, reprisals, and even participation in racial policy, this decree allowed the army authority in the Generalbezirk that overlapped with and on occasion even superseded that of the civilian administrators. "Political tasks" almost always involved anti-Jewish policy and killing. This could cause friction when the interests of the civilian authorities and those of the military differed, particularly regarding logistical issues. A memo from the military commander in Reichskommissariat Ostland gives an indication of the prevalence of this tension. Apparently, German soldiers had not been showing proper respect to civilian authorities, for General Walter Braemer wrote that "in view of the close connection and cooperation between German soldiers and German administrative organs, moreover, in uniform, it is forbidden that they pass one another without taking notice. . . . Every German has the duty to outwardly document the unity of the Germans. . . . It is a rule of politeness and comradeship, not to wait long, but to greet."[12] It is apparent from documents such as these and testimony of soldiers that often some level of irritation or tension existed between the military and the civil authorities. However, when the military commander was a man like Bechtolsheim, ambiguity over what was considered "military necessity" also allowed for brutal initiative taking in the escalation of policy. Subordinate leaders could justify participation in activities against Jews for exactly this reason, a tactic fully in keeping with the lessons of the Mogilev Conference.

In Slonim, civil and military authorities were bound together from the beginning. Glück had established an Ortskommandantur upon arrival in mid-August 1941. Though company members later claimed that their mission had been limited to security (read: anti-partisan operations), this is largely a postwar fabrication. The men of the unit were actually engaged mainly in guarding and operating key commercial and factory sites in and around Slonim, among other things a tannery, sawmill, warehouse for appropriated goods, an oil depot, and a munitions dump. While the handover of authority to the civilian administration officially occurred on 1 September, the Gebietskommissariat in Slonim was in no position then to actually begin governing. When Erren moved into his headquarters, a large stone building on Zamkowa Street, he had only three subordinates, including his driver. The early days of civilian administration were thus plagued by shortages of equipment and personnel. Erren noted in a report that he had to send representatives back to Germany to get supplies and equipment. Two of his key officials

arrived four weeks late, and one returned to Germany two days later
because of illness.[13] By the end of October, however, Erren had received
more personnel and equipment, including several female German civilian secretaries, and could finally begin to administer his new realm. His
attempts to exert his authority encroached upon liberties that the military administration had now become accustomed to exercising. By September 1941, Erren had ordered the creation of four small ghettos in the
town of Slonim, including a separate ghetto on an island in the Sczara
River, reserved for those with work permits.[14] As Erren lacked adequate
personnel and resources, First Lieutenant Glück probably provided the
manpower for this operation.

Many soldiers after the war commented upon the strained relations
between the Wehrmacht and the civilian administration, particularly
during the long transition. There appears to have been reluctance on the
part of the army to hand over the logistical operations it controlled to the
Gebietskommissariat and the civil administrators, who "carried themselves as little kings."[15] Erren himself testified to the initial tensions between the military and the civilian authorities. "The Wehrmacht," he
said, "completely refused in the beginning to hand over administrative
authority and it took a while before we were completely in operation."[16]
The military perhaps correctly feared that the political authorities would
be less efficient and more corrupt, resulting in poorer logistical support.
Certainly, given the Gebietskommissariat's dearth of personnel and
equipment, Erren and his office frequently requested or demanded support from the military. Indeed, one soldier reported that Erren, upon his
arrival, demanded that the company's soldiers vacate a building so that
his staff could live there. This allegedly so enraged Glück that he deployed a light antitank gun in front of the building in order to "dissuade"
them.[17] In these areas, perhaps, the relationship between the two was, as
one soldier described, "tense."[18] While sensationalistic reports that
Glück had placed the Gebietskommissariat under house arrest or deployed artillery are likely exaggerations of the friction between the military and civilians, the records clearly point to tension between the military and civilian authorities.[19] This squabbling should not, however, be
mistaken for principled opposition to Nazi policy.

It is not, perhaps, surprising that differences would arise between the military men and the civilian officials. After all, these Nazi bureaucrats did not represent the best that Germany had to offer. Often, they were posted to the East as a form of organizational exile, or they volunteered, believing that it was the only place they could redeem otherwise stalled careers; they were not all-stars. They quickly acquired the nickname *Ostnieten* (eastern nobodies or failures). The commander of Einsatzkommando 2, Eduard Strauch, called them "'blockheads and ass-lickers, whose careers for the most part had depended on that of the Gauleiter."[20] A Nazi press officer described them in detail in a private memo: "Now in the expanses of the East, with pretentious uniforms, titles, salaries, daily allowances and rations . . . [is] a type who decks himself out with revolver and whip or whatever he feels will lend him a natural mastery, superior bearing and genuine manliness. The idle and worthless type of . . . bureaucrat . . . the eternally hungry 'Organizer' with a swarm of like-minded Eastern hyenas, his whole multitudinous clique, recognizable by the two big 'Ws'—women and wine . . . people who enjoy Eastern luxury in food, lodgings and transport all the more the more modest their original circumstances."[21] It is understandable that professional soldiers would take an instant dislike to these kinds of political hangers-on and carpetbaggers.

However, if bureaucratic and personal disagreements were commonplace, they did not extend to Jewish policy in Slonim. In a letter to Erren dated 4 December 1941, First Lieutenant Glück writes "according to a Regimental order from 29 November 1941, the countryside is to be cleared of all Jews. Jews in villages of less than 1,000 inhabitants are to be ghettoized in the nearest towns and forbidden to return to the countryside." Glück addressed Erren directly: "I am not personally in the position, due to a lack of transport to carry out this order. I request from you written response regarding this issue."[22] Erren's reply, that same day, is instructive. After expressing similar logistical difficulties on his end, he wrote to Glück, "You have supported me up till now in my political and racial tasks in an extremely praiseworthy fashion. I would not have been able to accomplish it with my weak police forces alone. I must therefore ask . . . that you seek to work with your higher headquarters so that you can continue to support the German mission in the East by making your forces available."[23] While Glück and Erren both bemoaned their lack of resources and attempted to avoid overextending their own limited manpower in moving mid-size Jewish populations into the Slonim ghetto, the civilian administration and military authorities agreed on Jewish policy in principle and had for a significant time. The exchange between Erren and Glück shows that the frequent protestations from Glück (and others) regarding poor relations with the civil authorities did not extend to the "Jewish question." Moreover, this letter is documentary evidence that the 727th Infantry Regiment was *directly* involved in rounding up Jews. Finally, this communication falls nicely in line with General Bechtolsheim's order at the end of November, directing that his soldiers kill Jews in the countryside, freeing up the SS and police to kill Jews who had been collected in ghettos.[24]

In Novogrudok, military interactions with the civil authorities were a bit more complicated. Relations between the army and the "golden pheasants" were "cool," and the 7th Company commander, Captain Artmann, was "not amenable to the wishes of the Gebietskommissar," about which he remained "stubborn."[25] As in Slonim, there were initial frictions regarding the handover of "different tasks," in which Artmann "held back."[26] Unlike Glück, however, Artmann does not appear to have been overly energetic in leading his company against the Jews of Novogrudok. His soldiers described him as "a good-natured fellow," as "friendly toward the Jews," "no Jew-hater, in fact, the opposite."[27] Moreover, the 7th Company cook recalled that as they left Novogrudok, Artmann rode with him in the field kitchen on the train to Bobruisk, and during the journey told him that the killings in Novogrudok "had nothing to do with the war" and that he could "hardly bear it." It appeared that "the whole Jewish persecution cut very close to him."[28] However, one Jewish survivor of Novogrudok, Jack Kagan, remembered Artmann much differently. Kagan recalled that Artmann personally shot Kagan's neighbor during a work detail.[29] Such eyewitness testimony demonstrates why we cannot take soldier statements completely at face value. Artmann may not have been a fanatic, but he had his moments of brutality. In addition, as he seemed to be well liked, his men may have been trying to paint him in the best of lights. The 6th Company case does indicate, however, that former soldiers were often not hesitant to characterize their officers as racist or fanatical.

While the depth of Artmann's regret can be debated, he does not appear to have been an eager or aggressive commander. One of his men had the impression that he would "rather be at home."[30] Another depicted him as a man who would "rather be 100 meters behind than in front."[31] There is no evidence that he led any actions on his own initiative in the manner of Glück. However, if Artmann was not proactive either in killing Jews on his own or in collaborating with the civil authorities, his second in command, Lieutenant Martin, was. Martin commanded the 1st Platoon, the "elite platoon," as one soldier called it.[32] Martin was a "fanatic" who had once remarked "there was nothing better or that gave greater pride than being in the party."[33] He was described as more "energetic" than Artmann and as an "arrogant" man who "did not have a particularly affectionate relationship with the company."[34] Perhaps this is also reflected in the willingness of former soldiers to testify against him and to pin the blame on him.

Martin appears to have been more independent and active than Artmann, who was "hardly around" when the men trained or conducted patrols. One soldier noted that he had "never seen Artmann on an antipartisan operation and only saw him perhaps once a week."[35] Martin was a man for whom "nothing could be done quick enough," while Artmann was "calmer and more easygoing."[36] The two officers also did not get along personally. Beyond their different styles of leadership, the two were allegedly "in conflict" over a woman who worked in the Gebietskommissariat.[37]

As a go-getter, Martin appeared to have exercised a disproportionate amount of control over the operations of the company. One soldier from his platoon stated, "At least 50 percent of the company was of the opinion that Artmann was the commander in name only and that Martin did the essential organizing and held the company together."[38] Captain Artmann himself admitted that because he was busy with other tasks as Ortskommandant, Martin "was more concerned with the company."[39] "Martin was not," another platoon member testified, "the kind of man who preferred to do only what he had been ordered to do."[40] Artmann's orderly had the impression that Martin and another platoon leader "overrode" the commander.[41] Further, the company first sergeant noted that Martin "always wanted to take the helm of the company himself, even though he was only a platoon leader."[42] It appears that Martin often *did* take over company leadership, especially when it came to currying favor with the civil authorities.

This streak of independence and ambition increases in importance because Lieutenant Martin, unlike Captain Artmann, maintained a close personal relationship with the Nazi administrators. He was "often with the 'Golden Pheasants,'" one man recalled. He would attend parties, smoking and drinking, and often did not return to his quarters at night.[43] He often hunted with members of the Gebietskommissariat as well.[44] Several soldiers also confirm that he was dating a secretary from the civil administration. One man joked that, while on sentry duty, the men would often see him head after duty hours toward the administration buildings and the men would say, "there he goes again."[45] The effect of all this was, as a former soldier stated, that Martin "sat together with the masters of Novogrudok" and "acted more as a liaison and had . . . taken on many of the suggestions of the civil administrators."[46] While the relatively passive and apathetic Artmann himself may not have wanted to engage this way, he did not or could not prevent the more active and ambitious Martin from doing so.

It seems clear that Martin was both ideologically and practically aligned with the Gebietskommissariat and as a result often acted in the furtherance of its goals. Captain Artmann accused Martin, who conveniently did not survive the war, of having acted independently in cooperation with the civilian authorities, saying that he believed Martin could have issued orders behind his back for the participation of the company in "Jewish Actions."[47] He claimed further that he had no knowledge of his soldiers' participation in the cordon of the Novogrudok killing site and that he had not ordered such actions.[48] There is both truth and obfuscation in Artmann's statements. It is highly unlikely that Lieutenant Martin acted against orders or without his commander's approval. This is both a common postwar defense tactic and, given the draconian discipline of the army described by the same witnesses, an extraordinarily improbable event. However, the preponderance of evidence indicates the following: Captain Artmann was an indecisive and lethargic commander who delegated the day-to-day running of the company to the much younger and much more active Lieutenant Martin. Indeed, Artmann appears content to have remained in the background both physically and as a leader. He did not *want* to know that his men were supporting genocide, but this does not mean that he was not well aware of their activities. Willful ignorance is, after all, conscious. Martin was *given* the authority to employ the company as a tool of genocidal policy by Artmann; he did not usurp it. Finally, given Martin's close ties, both ideologically and socially, with the civil administration, he was more than willing to help his new friends fulfill their missions and used his de facto authority as commander to do so.

The German policy of extermination in the East was, as elsewhere, accompanied by the expropriation and collection of Jewish property. Financial gain did not drive anti-Jewish actions here but was rather institutionalized from the beginning in the Reich.[49] While the process in Germany and western Europe followed a "more circumscribed and 'rational' path," in the East the almost complete power exercised by local authorities made systematic looting (and corruption) an ever-present facet of racial policy.[50] Given the morally and professionally questionable quality of many of the civilian administrators in the East, it is perhaps not surprising that the occupied Soviet Union played host to widespread theft, embezzlement, and other forms of corruption. These forms of "wild" plundering were a "mass phenomenon"; they were also widely tolerated, as long as the theft was not from the party itself and remained within reason.[51] Lohse, the civilian head of the RKO, apparently was already experiencing trouble controlling the "systematic" looting his office was to oversee. He was so worried that he sent a strongly worded memo to the HSSPF for the RKO on 25 September 1941 stating that he allowed no access to Jewish property and expected that SS and police units would hand over all Jewish property to the Gebietskommissariats.[52]

In Slonim, the theft of property was not a privilege reserved for men of rank; soldiers, too, were able to profit. While often the image these men attempted to portray of their participation after the war was one of isolated incidents and compulsory obedience, their relationship with

Jewish property reflects a different relationship with the Holocaust. Much of the debate over the relative guilt of the Wehrmacht in the crimes of the Third Reich has revolved around direct participation in killing and the relative amount of support for genocidal policies. However, looking at how soldiers voluntarily helped themselves to the spoils of murder can perhaps tell us much about the institutional and individual position of the German army in a way that a binary focus on killing or not killing fails to do. Looting of Jewish property by German soldiers certainly does not paint an image of a military fastidiously avoiding dirtying its hands with genocide.

For some men, this personal enrichment began immediately after the shooting. Franz L. recalled that, on the truck ride back from the Czepilov Forest the morning after the shooting, he observed that several fellow soldiers had "acted as grave robbers. They had taken 10–15 rings, watches, valuable pieces of clothing." He had then seen them send these things home to Germany, from the post office in Slonim.[53] First Lieutenant Glück himself set the example for his men. According to one private, Glück sent a *train car* full of Jewish possessions to his hometown of Rosenheim in Bavaria, along with a detachment of soldiers to escort it.[54] News of Glück's self-enrichment was widely known. A blacksmith from the 7th Company in Novogrudok noted that Glück had taken "confiscated Jewish property, particularly fur coats."[55] There appears to have been little reluctance to loot the bodies of the dead by some, though others certainly viewed such behavior with distaste. This very intimate form of enrichment weakens perpetrator claims of neutrality or passivity toward the killings, as it was completely voluntary.

The expropriation of property went beyond opportunistic looting. Several large garages near the 6th Company barracks in Slonim warehoused clothing from the shootings. The visiting 7th Company blacksmith recalled "huge mountains of 'good as new' clothes" that were guarded by 6th Company soldiers.[56] The Slonim synagogue was also used to store appropriated Jewish property. One Jewish worker received a written order from Dietrich Hick to remove the bathtub and sink from the apartment of a Jewish dentist and install them in a German official's house.[57] It is probable that soldiers, too, availed themselves of this kind of opportunity. Some of these goods were also destined for a special store set up in Slonim, where they were sold to the soldiers. One private recalled that the company would shop there for items to send home to their families. "I wanted to buy a watch," he testified, "but I didn't because there wasn't anything good left to buy."[58] Another soldier knew a Jewish woman named Nina who worked in the shop sorting the clothing of murdered Jews. He said that one day she told him, "Buy something for your wife and child before those brown scoundrels [meaning German civil administrators] sell it all."[59] The routine commoditization of murdered Jews' property was a particularly disturbing development and one that became more possible given a long-term association with the murder of the Jews.

In contrast, testimonies from Krupki and Krucha do not mention this kind of personal enrichment from killing, though it is possible it still took place. The men of these units had less experience with the intentional expropriation of Jewish property (as they did with these mass killings themselves). The tempo and newness of these operations likely meant that the opportunity for personal enrichment was perhaps not as apparent and certainly more fleeting, though still possible. We must remember that soldiers from the 354th in Krupki knowingly wore the clothes of murdered Jews during anti-partisan operations. In Slonim and Novogrudok, however, soldiers had plenty of time to realize that the murder of Jews offered the chance for personal gain, and they also began to see how they could take advantage.

Indeed, in Slonim, administrator Gerhard Erren exemplified this systematic looting, demanding a payment of two million rubles from the Jewish council or Judenrat. This and other extortions were publicized on posters throughout Slonim. After delivery of this sum at the end of September or beginning of October, Erren had the entire Jewish council murdered. A new council was assembled and again forced to deliver a high ransom in return for the release of three members of the Jewish community. After the payment of this sum, this second Jewish council was murdered, just one week before the mass executions.[60] In this environment, many soldiers asked why they too could not profit. The looting of the property of murdered Jews also suggests a growing desensitization to the brutality of Jewish policy. In short, this intimate connection to property is both an indicator *and* a result of prolonged daily exposure to Nazi policy, one not seen to this extent in earlier cases. Soldiers were not the only Germans who saw an opportunity here; German railway civilian workers in Slonim also helped themselves to the property of murdered Jews.

As soldiers seized Jewish property, they also began to seize Jewish bodies, in particular female bodies. By its very nature, group breaches of accepted conduct beget further breaches. In this instance, the legalized theft of property was intimately connected with what seems to have been an acceptance of sexual violence. Soldiers entered in a variety of non-consensual relationships that are important in expanding our picture of what military occupation looked like. Only recently has scholarly work begun to focus on sexual relationships and sexual violence during the Holocaust. Much of it has been centered on western Europe and on non-Jews.[61] When focusing specifically on Jews, the concentration camp experience has been predominant. With a few notable suggestions, little scholarship has examined these interactions on the eastern front.[62]

Much of this neglect is understandable. From a perpetrator or prosecution perspective, these crimes were not the most important. Indeed, crimes of the army itself were not pressing. German society refused to accept its soldiers as warriors in a genocidal war: it certainly did not want to consider their sexual behavior, even in the best light, let alone participation in sexual exploitation. In addition, from a legal perspective, rape and sexual exploitation were very difficult to prosecute without a complaining witness and were almost always beyond the statute of limitations for prosecutors in any case.

For survivors of both the Holocaust and sexualized violence, bearing witness to these events was doubly difficult. Survivors in many countries (for different reasons) were encouraged not to talk about their experiences during the war. Women were especially reticent to discuss sexual suffering. First, these survivors were of a generation for whom all issues of sexuality were intensely private and not for public consumption. Second, many of these women, who had been forced to trade sex for favors like food or safety, may have felt ashamed of their behavior and feared condemnation. Indeed, some women who did claim to have been raped had their claims discounted as fabrication. For these reasons (and others), discussion of sexualized violence has remained off-limits for some time.

One of the defining characteristics of this period of routinization was the frequency with which these German soldiers came into contact with Jews (of both sexes) as part of their daily duties. Jewish women cooked and cleaned for soldiers. Sixth Company men supervised Jewish laborers on a daily basis. For example, Jewish women were employed in the ammunition dump in Slonim, working on the captured weapons there.[63] Some Germans remembered them by name twenty years later. Sixth Company men retrieved Jews from the ghetto and returned them after work. They were aware of the restrictions and privations of the Jewish inhabitants of Slonim, for their workers talked about them. German soldiers were also treated by Jewish doctors in the local hospital, until Erren had them all shot.[64] One soldier recalled that he often brought bread and potatoes to a Jewish family in return for laundry service; the family disappeared during the November killing.[65] In Novogrudok, the 7th Company also "employed" Jews as laborers, craftsman, and assistants in its kitchen. This familiarity inevitably brought German soldiers into closer contact with the intended victims of Nazi policy, and it bred both contempt and attraction.

Throughout these cases, when German soldiers recall their interactions with Jews in the course of occupation, they overwhelmingly remember women: as workers or as beautiful victims (recall the Krupki killing and the Minsk opera singer). It is not, perhaps, surprising that gender is one lens through which soldiers both made sense of and took advantage of their power as occupiers. By September 1942, interactions between women in the East and German soldiers had apparently become sufficiently problematic that Wehrmacht chief Keitel issued a memorandum forbidding such relations.[66] Those stationed in rear areas (and most exposed to the Nazi genocidal project in action) encountered, for a variety of reasons, a population that was often disproportionately female. First, men between eighteen and fifty years of age rapidly became an endangered species in the East after 1941. Many were already fighting with the Red Army or perhaps had fled to the partisans. The first wave of mass killings by the Einsatzgruppen explicitly targeted Jewish men, which resulted in their deaths or another wave of flight. Escape was, by and large, unavailable to many women, who were often burdened with young children and unable to flee. Thus, the Jewish populations that these men encountered in the Soviet Union were often made up largely of women. As a subset of the populace, Jewish women were particularly vulnerable. These circumstances appear to have led to increased sexual interactions, the vast majority of which were exploitative.

Exploitation took a variety of forms. Sometimes Germans physically and violently forced Jewish women into sexual acts.[67] Jack Kagan, a survivor interviewed in Novogrudok, recalled that a German doctor passing through had been a "specialist" in entering homes and raping women, presumably Jewish women.[68] Ghettoization and the yellow star made the identification and targeting of Jewish women, in particular, easier. In Slonim, for example, a survivor recalled an ethnic German functionary and translator from Riga named Rolf Herz.[69] He was nicknamed "Kiloherz" by the Germans because he was very "slender and wiry."[70] Herz would "pretend to be a friend to the Jews, win their trust and get different information out of them. He would lure young Jewish girls into his apartment where he would prey upon them sadistically. Afterward, any trace of them would disappear behind them."[71] This kind of rape seems one that intentionally took advantage of the vulnerable position that Jews were placed in and appears to have been frequent during the Holocaust. Also typical of this particularly depraved behavior was the murder of the victims afterward. A recent study of secret recordings from rank-and-file German soldiers confirms that this sexual violence against both Jewish and non-Jewish women, combined with forced prostitution, was relatively common.[72]

Not all sexual interactions were as physically violent as these. Consider the more ambiguous case of Xavier H. During his testimony, investigators asked him to describe his actions on the day of the Slonim massacre. He replied, "In the course of the morning [November 14], I went into the town to see about my Jewish girlfriend, Ida, because I was afraid she had been caught up in the *Aktion*. This was, however, not the case."[73] Unfortunately, the police did not follow up on this astounding statement, and so the details of this relationship remain unclear. For two other men in 6th Company, intimate relationships with Jewish women are better documented.

It must be stated from the outset that the German word *Freundin* used in all these testimonies is ambiguous. It can mean "female friend" or "girlfriend" in a romantic sense. Even if meant in the latter sense, when used by German soldiers the word is still quite problematic. Without a great deal of additional corroborating evidence, it would be difficult to term these relationships in any way normal or consensual.[74] The power dynamics alone suggest that any relationship between a Jewish woman and an occupying soldier was at least partially exploitative. At best, these relationships involved instrumental sex in which the woman expected and received some kind of compensation for her participation. At worst, they constituted sexual slavery. The choice of the term *Freundin* could perhaps indicate wishful thinking or self-deception (or both) on the part of German soldiers about the nature of these interactions. These men perhaps found themselves at once attracted and conflicted about their desire for a Jewish woman. Others likely paid this no mind at all. Whether they believed the official Nazi line or not, they certainly knew how the party regarded such relationships. The euphemistic term "girlfriend" could serve to legitimize this coupling, at least in their own eyes. This is not without precedent. In a study of slavery in America, Edward Baptist notes that attractive, light-skinned black women were often purchased as "fancy maids" when in reality they were intended as sexual partners for their master."[75] As elsewhere in the Nazi linguistic world of euphemism, language here can perhaps provide some insight into the mind-sets of the perpetrators. Describing sexually coerced Jewish women as "girlfriends" perhaps allowed soldiers to normalize in their own minds what were clearly abnormal situations.

Intimate relationships existed in at least two verifiable instances in this study. The most bizarre includes First Lieutenant Glück himself. Though he was described by his soldiers as a "Jew-hater," was alleged to have shot two Jews in a drunken rage, and was the man who personally led several killing actions, two of his soldiers explicitly testified that Glück also had a Jewish "girlfriend." One soldier stated "Glück had a Jew as his lover, who lived with him in the *kaserne*. As the company was transferred by rail from Slonim, she was also at the train station. I can still see before my eyes," he continued, "as Glück went back and forth with the Jewish woman at the station. He took her by the shoulders and kissed her goodbye, right in front of our eyes."[76] Another former soldier,

Otto S., testified that while Glück was an "old fighter [*alter Kämpfer*] and a Nazi Blood Order wearer," because of his Jewish "girlfriend" he was "tolerant" toward the Jews.[77] Glück was most clearly *not* tolerant toward Jews; yet how did a man like this come to have a sexual relationship with one Jew while he was actively exterminating others in large numbers?

The nature of this relationship is very difficult to understand, yet similar interactions appear to have been quite common. Given Glück's willing and even zealous participation in the murder of Jews, his party background, and general reputation, it is hard to see this as much more than a sexual relationship from which the Jewish woman perhaps benefited materially. Yet the description of his behavior at the train station and the general awareness by the men of this liaison complicate matters. It would appear that the most likely explanation is that, for Glück, this was simply an extortion of sex and did not, Otto S.'s testimony notwithstanding, in any way affect how he carried out genocidal policy. Perhaps his "girlfriend" was also receiving preferential treatment or improved rations. In any case, it appears that Glück was able to separate his professional hatreds and tasks from his personal needs.

Another case of Jewish women living with German soldiers is more instructive. Here we arrive at the interesting story of Sergeant Major Erich Aichinger. He was thirty-seven, and a low-level municipal employee after the war.[78] Aichinger served as a platoon leader and also worked in the Ortskommandantur or military administration of Slonim. In his postwar testimony, Aichinger never mentions his relationships with Jewish women but does admit escorting Jews to the killing site and lingering to observe the murders.[79] In what is certainly a remarkable situation, most of what we know about Aichinger comes from a Jewish survivor who remembered him by name twenty-three years later.

The survivor was Abraham Orlinski, a thirty-eight-year-old engineer who had been born in Slonim. He had kept his occupation secret in order to avoid the first mass killings of intelligentsia. It is likely that he and his wife were permitted to retain their house because his wife was a doctor and merited some special consideration (at least temporarily) as a skilled professional. Abraham remembered Aichinger as a lanky man with dark blond hair and bright blue eyes.[80] The Jewish couple and this

German sergeant major came to share the kitchen in the same house; immediately upon their arrival, the Wehrmacht had seized a room with a separate entrance in the Orlinski house at number 4, Kosciusko Street. Aichinger occupied this room beginning in September 1941. In his deposition, Orlinski devotes much of his time to the behavior of his unlikely housemate.[81] Aichinger apparently had at least two "girlfriends" while living on Kosciusko Street. Both women were Jewish, and both lived with him in his room. His first companion is never named but apparently fell ill sometime in October and was taken away. Aichinger then entered into a relationship with her friend, Regina, who had frequently visited him with his first companion and also performed domestic duties. Regina then also lived in the room with him. It is never made explicit what kind of arrangement was made between these women and Aichinger, but at a minimum they received protection, shelter outside the ghetto, and likely more food, all which improved their chances for survival. It seems clear that these were also sexual relationships.

Aichinger frequently held get-togethers for members of the civil administration from the Gebietskommissariat with whom he worked within the Ortskommandantur. Regina served alcohol at these gatherings and overheard discussions of the upcoming November massacre of nonworking Jews. She then warned Orlinski, who initially suspected that she was trying to scare him out of the house so that she and Aichinger could have the whole place. (Regardless, he procured a work permit anyway and survived.) Aichinger arose early on November 14 and left the apartment at 4 a.m.

He returned around 6 p.m., drunk and distraught. As Orlinski remembered, "He looked agitated and even cried."[82] Aichinger had drunk so much at the massacre that he had been cautioned to stop and had replied that it was the only way he could watch.[83] In what must have been a surreal conversation, he went on to tell his Jewish housemate, Orlinski, that he had wanted to save his first girlfriend. She had asked that he save her mother as well. Aichinger said that he was unable to do this and then had watched her killed in the pits along with between eight and ten thousand others. Orlinski remained silent while Aichinger unburdened himself, and then finally asked why the Germans had done this. Aichinger replied that he believed there would not be enough food for all the Slonim

Jews and that Hitler had explained that no Jews could remain alive in Europe and only those behind the Urals had a chance of surviving.[84] It appears that Regina survived the November killing. One can only guess what must have been going through Orlinksi's mind as he listened to Aichinger describe the methodical murder of Orlinski's fellow Jews.

What are we to make of Aichinger's two sexual relationships with captive Jews in Slonim? His behavior appears shockingly callous. It is almost certain that he offered protection and better living conditions to Regina and her friend in exchange for sex and domestic service. He appears to have "dismissed" his first girlfriend when she became ill and was unable to fulfill those requirements. However, he had developed enough feeling for this first girlfriend to offer to rescue her. Yet this feeling did not extend to her mother, and his refusal to save them both is a clear indication that Aichinger was not about to go out of his way to interfere in the killing process. While perhaps others could look the other way for a high-ranking soldier who was sparing his sex partner, perhaps the rescue of her mother would have raised too many questions. Clearly, though, Aichinger was in no way concerned about the racial "dangers" of his behavior.

Explanations for why Germans extorted sex from captive Jews are likely varied. First, for the Germans, sex could be a form of release. It likely joined alcohol as a method of escape from the war in general and from the violence of the Nazi genocidal project specifically. At a deeper level, the illusion of a "normal" sexual relationship with a woman, as Doris Bergen notes, could act as a "normalizer," granting these men some form of a familiar life in what was certainly a strange world.[85] Of course, these relationships also reflect to some extent a sexual hierarchy among Germans in the East regarding choice of sexual partners, with civil administrators often pairing off with more desirable German secretaries, leaving non-Jewish locals and Jewish women to those of lesser rank. British recordings of captured German soldiers often indicate that female German employees of the Wehrmacht were very promiscuous.[86] Recall that Artmann and Martin in Novogrudok were allegedly in conflict over a German secretary in the Gebietskommissariat.

Some Germans may have deceived themselves that these relationships were real, while others certainly were consciously extorting sex. Some were *already* sexual sadists. Some perhaps *became* sadistic. Yet, a tiny minority of Germans appears also to have developed real feelings, which very rarely led to rescue. Consider the strange case of Willi Schulz, an army captain who fell in love with Ilse Stein, a Jew in the Minsk ghetto. He fled to the partisans with her and a truck filled with twenty-four Jews.[87]

When Jewish women had the chance to make decisions regarding these relationships, the motivation was almost assuredly survival, the options simpler, but the choices certainly far more agonizing. The question of agency or choice is therefore complex and highly charged in this context. The literature on sexual exploitation under slavery can be helpful in this regard. One historian has argued that while "no law or moral scruple prevented white men from forcing themselves on black females . . . some women negotiated this predicament by subjecting themselves to patrons, yielding to some white men who could protect them from the rest."[88] As one historian of American slavery has written, "The stark imbalance of power meant that women . . . chose, at best between negotiated surrender on the one hand and severe punishment and possible death on the other."[89] Such analysis seems equally apt in the context of the Holocaust for both men and women. The varying nature of sexual interaction bears this out, showing that some Jews at times had some ability to negotiate the terms of their abuse in ways that benefited them. Regardless, the overall environment was one in which the Germans held all the real power, as the frequency of violent rape proves. In more instrumental sexual relations, to the degree they were able, these women were making extremely difficult if not "choiceless" choices to use all means at their disposal.

How do we explain these varied and complex kinds of sexual interaction between Jews and Germans? There is, likely, no broad explanation for each type. However, while rape will always accompany war, there is no evidence that Germans had any plan or intention to systematically use rape as a weapon against Soviets and/or Jews in ways that we have seen in Bosnia or Rwanda. However, studies of Wehrmacht justice have also shown that the army declined to punish rape and sexual assault in most situations, provided it did not negatively affect discipline or the war effort, particularly against the partisans. Of course, most rapes were not reported, and the vast majority never made it to a court-martial. As more than one study has shown, "sex was part of a soldiers' everyday existence."[90]

The larger carte blanche given to Germans in the East created the environment for the behavior we have seen. The set of "Criminal Orders" issued before the invasion suspended the prosecution of most crimes committed by German soldiers. That immunity, combined with an anti-Slavic perspective that viewed the peoples of the East as subhuman and deserving of subjugation, meant that the occupied Soviet Union became something of a free-fire zone for all manner of immoral behavior. Willi Reese gave words to the amoral environment on the eastern front when he described in a letter home how he and his men had forced a Russian woman prisoner to "dance naked for us" and had "greased her tits with boot polish."[91] It is telling that Reese, who would not survive the war, titled his autobiographical manuscript "Confession."

This impact of this legal impunity must have been even more influential when applied to Jews, a subject population that was even more devalued and even more prostrate before German occupation than other civilians. Though some might contend that Nazi legal prohibitions against sexual contact between Germans and Jews made the sexual exploitation of Jews unlikely, many Germans clearly had little concern for charges of "race defilement" or *Rassenschande*. The SS men of Einsatzgruppe Sonderkommando 10a "habitually raped Jewish women to the point where they fell unconscious."[92] If soldiers did not broadcast this behavior, they did not avoid it either. Indeed, German military authorities rarely prosecuted "race defilement" and gave most men the legal benefit of the doubt, recognizing their "need" for sexual release.

At the local level, sexuality in the East seems to have operated under a moral code different from that observed in western Europe. German civil authorities (as well as military men) frequently abused alcohol to excess and participated in depraved sexual acts outside the pale of acceptability in the West, where "fraternization" with racially equal and more familiar partners was easier and more widespread. In his postwar suicide note, Polenz, the former civil administrator in Slonim, wrote that the sexual behavior of the German secretaries in the Gebietskommissariat (and also of Erren and his men) was "starkly criticized" by local women.[93] Indeed, there were at least three female secretaries working in

Erren's office whom Polenz appeared to be accusing.[94] Such behavior, which did not go unnoticed by the rank and file, reinforced the "official" immorality of the place. Indeed, Glück, the brutal Wehrmacht commander in Slonim, behaved in a similar manner. The connection between killing and sex is one already apparent in the earlier T-4 "euthanasia" program, which appears to have prefigured the Final Solution in almost every way. That killing operation had also been characterized by alcohol abuse and sexual promiscuity, often as diversions from the horrors of the workday.

This climate of sexualized violence was enhanced by the concurrent economic exploitation of the Jews. In the "Wild East," there was a greater freedom for all manner of behavior that was illegal or immoral at home, including widespread thievery and plunder. Germans (soldiers and civilians) systematically preyed upon the property of Jews throughout the Soviet Union. The ability of Germans to steal from Jews at will further reinforced that "normal" rules of behavior did not apply to Jews. Indeed, it made them in some ways a preferred source to be plundered. Perhaps it is not at all surprising that this plunder quickly extended from possessions to the body. One soldier in Slonim recalled that a Jewish woman had told him how she was robbed of a golden ring by a German with whom she had "dealings." The soldier further noted that this woman disappeared during the *Aktion*.[95] The connection between theft, sexual violence, and murder in the context of genocide remains of critical importance and merits further investigation.

One of the benefits of studying the Holocaust at the local level is that it is precisely here that the artificially clear lines drawn between victim and perpetrator begin to fray. Only hints of these complex interactions appear, yet they add texture to the experience of genocide on the ground. Not all of this familiarity bred contempt. Sometimes close interaction with Jews led to friendships. In 1941, Robert Ness, a twelve-year-old Jewish refugee from Augustov, lived outside of Slonim in the village of Petralevich (which would later become the scene of mass killings in 1942). He and his family took shelter in a hole they had dug in the backyard during the fighting for the town but returned to their home shortly after the Germans arrived. Robert's hobby was stamp collecting, which he continued even after fleeing with his family to Slonim. Because he did not "look Jewish," he would frequently move around the town, where he met Master Sergeant Ranger, a German soldier.[96] Apparently, the two shared an interest in stamps and began exchanging them with each other.

This friendship bore fruit on 14 November and led to rescue when Robert found himself caught out alone in Slonim during the pre-massacre roundup. The German police stopped the young boy, who, thinking quickly, told them he was seeking out Ranger about stamps. Fortunately, an army sergeant hustled the boy into a building, saying, "Today is not a day for stamp collecting." Robert was concealed behind a cabinet and overheard a lieutenant being asked by the police for more men, presumably for the killing operation. He remembered the officer replying, "I have no men for such things." Later, Robert's friend Ranger arrived and asked him what he was doing there. The German must have guessed the situation, as he asked Robert if he was a Jew. When Robert confirmed this, Ranger took the Jewish boy to his own house and pushed him into a washroom, saying, "Man, hide yourself." Ness found himself hiding with another boy. Sometime around five in the afternoon, Ranger returned. "The lieutenant says the shooting is over," he told Robert, and then pushed him out the back way to avoid the killers who were returning from Czepilov.[97] In this way, Ness survived the 14 November massacre. Robert remembered that this sergeant would later visit him in the ghetto to trade stamps and that he brought food to his family. A friendship of sorts between a Jewish boy and a German soldier both saved the boy's life and gives us a glimpse into how a small group of men aided Jews in Slonim.

There were other examples of genuine aid given to Jews and of helping Jews to escape. Survivor Szymon Goldberg testified that on the way to the killing site "many were able to flee from the column. The soldiers and policemen acted as though they hadn't seen, or they shot without aiming. Of those fleeing, no one was shot or wounded."[98] In his history, *The Destruction of Slonim Jewry,* Slonim resident Nachum Alpert related several similar examples of Germans (including soldiers) allowing Jews to escape or actively rescuing them:

Twenty Jewish barbers, who had been cutting the hair of German soldiers in their barracks, were rounded up and taken to the ditch. The soldiers ran after them, released them and started back toward town. A spark of hope arose in the hearts of the barbers, but on the way, Hick and his squad appeared and ordered them taken back to their executioners.[99]

A German guard, on duty at a post near the corner of Ruzany and Jurdzitka Street, used the roundup as a "cover" to chase a score of Jews into the cellar of a yeshiva in the Shulgass. When the roundup was over, he let them out one by one.

In one Jewish home a German found a Jew hiding under a bed, but did not report this to the local police. When they found the Jew under the bed, the German blamed his "nearsightedness" and under his breath swore at the *"verfluchte Schwein"* [damn swine].

Several German soldiers, "escorting" Jews into the forest in a truck, not only let the Jews "escape" but also showed them where to hide until the massacre was over.[100]

Another survivor, Leon Small, noted that the "medics who were temporarily stationed in Slonim showed themselves to be very helpful and behaved favorably [toward us]."[101] An eyewitness and survivor of the Slonim massacre interviewed by Daniel Fligelman, one of Emanuel Ringelblum's partners, reported in 1941 that Germans had helped Jews escape. The eyewitness added that "several Germans had refused to participate and were forced, as punishment, to groom and clean horses for two weeks."[102] It seems that more than a few soldiers took it upon themselves to help Jews when possible.

That these examples do not appear in postwar testimonies can be explained in several ways. Perhaps the men involved either had not survived the war, did not mention these actions to the police in order not to become involved as witnesses against their former comrades, or the police simply did not deem these statements to be relevant to the investigation. As is seen elsewhere, some men may have been ashamed of their own behavior even long after the war, viewing it perhaps as disloyal to their comrades. Others may have feared the reactions of their neighbors if the truth was told.

Similar incidents of aid also occurred in Novogrudok. A 7th Company soldier stood with a comrade on a railroad bridge, as part of the cordon. An elderly Jewish man approached and asked if he could pass to get his wife and child. He was allowed through and returned shortly with his family.[103] Another private was on guard duty outside Novogrudok when several Jews approached. He recalled, "We let them by unmolested. . . . I remembered the words of our captain that we shouldn't take it so seriously."[104] It seems that, for this soldier, Artmann's desire to remain uninvolved provided a positive example.

The routinization in Slonim also proved decisive for those who sought within the limits of their abilities to aid Jews. By recognizing how the system operated, those sympathetic to the plight of the Jews could find ways of helping. One area in which there seems to have been a larger amount of helping behavior, either self-interested or altruistic, was in the distribution of work permits. Approximately three weeks before the November killing in Slonim, Gebietskommissar Erren decided to identify necessary workers among the local population. A list of names was drawn up. The Gebietskommissar was seeking to eliminate what he termed "unnecessary eaters." According to one survivor, Erren himself crossed names off this list, effectively condemning those people to death.[105] The Nazi authorities issued special work permits printed on yellow cardboard to selected workers. The cards also listed the names of the worker's family. "Family," however, was limited only to a wife and two children. For eighteen-year-old Rachel Klenicki, this meant that one of her brothers did not receive a permit, and the family had to scrounge for a third card.[106] Survivors such as Zvi Szepetynski said that, for the Jewish inhabitants of Slonim, the yellow cards were literally "tickets to life."[107] Memory of these work permits that spared the holder from execution is ubiquitous among survivors from the occupied Soviet Union. For soldiers, the distribution of these cards presented a relatively easy and unobtrusive way to help Jews. It was also an opportunity for the less scrupulous among them to sell these cards to Jews for personal profit.

For Jewish laborers, the yellow cards (and their meaning) were no secret. Regina, Sergeant Aichinger's Jewish "girlfriend," had learned from him of the impending *Aktion* and tried to warn her flatmate, Orlinski. According to him, she said that he should try to obtain a work permit because there was a "plan to liquidate 10,000 non-working Jews and children."[108] Some soldiers used these permits as a way to help Jews they knew. Company Cook Alexander L. recalled that a Jew named Jakob who had built their baking oven came to him asking for a work permit. Alexander then went to the company first sergeant and requested a card for him. The first sergeant replied that many men had already come to get additional permits, and this would cause him difficulties, but he would see. According to the cook, Jakob did receive permits for him and his family, which he told L. with "tears of joy."[109] The procurement of these documents seems to have been a common method of aiding Jews employed by soldiers. Another Wehrmacht member, identified as Karl Ritter, supplied a pass to Dr. Leon Small. Small testified after the war that "I personally owe him my life," but that "the contradictions in this man were inexplicable."[110]

Sergeant Willy K. worked in the Ortskommandantur and was assigned two Jews, one for manual labor and another for clerical work. In November, one of these men came to him asking for a work permit that would show he worked for the Wehrmacht. At Sergeant K.'s request, a permit was issued, not by the Gebietskommissariat but instead by the Ortskommandant—that is, by the German army itself.[111] This is an interesting statement for two reasons. First, it shows how deeply 6th Company (particularly those manning the Ortskommandantur) was occupied with the day-to-day administration of Jewish policy. But second, it demonstrates how easy it was to aid Jews through the issuing of these yellow cards. For those who wished, this was the least challenging and least confrontational way to obstruct implementation of the Final Solution, because German economic interests on behalf of the war effort rather than opposition to Nazi racial policy could be invoked as the justification. The statement by the 6th Company first sergeant that many men had already come to get permits for their laborers perhaps indicates that others took this route. Yet, as in all instances of Wehrmacht aid to Jews, soldiers who aided or rescued Jews constituted a tiny minority of those involved. These actions seem limited as well to Jews the men knew personally. Finally, while they saved their bearers from the November execution, they did not rescue them from danger entirely.

It is important to address here the veracity of the sources themselves. None of the men questioned were on trial or charged with a crime. Moreover, they were testifying against Gerhard Erren and only rarely against a fellow Wehrmacht veteran. These men had little reason to fabricate stories of supplying work permits to Jews. The fact that these men supplied "their" Jews with lifesaving work permits does not on its face prove a moral justification and could indicate nothing more than a desire to retain a skilled worker. Sometimes this was the case. However, the evidence does not support such a conclusion for many of the instances of helping in Slonim. The fact, for example, that Alexander L. remembered Jakob's name probably indicates at least some personal concern. Much soldier testimony indicates that they knew the Jews who worked for them, to such an extent that the Jews felt comfortable to share their concerns with them. The bureaucratic nature of the permits, the ease with which they could be obtained, and the relatively low level at which they were issued likely made this a very attractive option for those wishing to ameliorate the condition of Jewish workers they had become familiar without attracting too much attention. On the other hand, those who cynically exploited Jewish desperation by selling work permits for self-enrichment—a practice often noted by Jewish survivors—were not likely to testify to such behavior after the war.

One of the clearest examples of altruistic rescue comes from a soldier in the same regiment as the 6th and 7th Companies, who was stationed in the town of Lida, fifty-five miles north of Slonim. Lida's experience in the Holocaust was very similar to that of Slonim, as was the participation of the German army there. The town had been occupied in June 1941. It had already witnessed the murder of 92 Jewish intelligentsia and 120 psychiatric patients.[112] The 3rd Battalion of the 727th (Glück and Artmann's sister battalion) occupied the town in 1941. The 12th Company of this battalion would be occupied with its own killings in the nearby town of Szczuczyn. Thirty-one-year-old Joachim Lochbihler from the 10th Company had been a brewery engineer in Nürnberg before he was called up. Because of this experience, he was assigned in August 1941 to manage and run the two local breweries in Lida. One of the breweries was almost totally destroyed, and Lochbihler therefore concentrated his efforts on the other.[113] This brewery had been owned by two Jewish brothers, Marc and Simon Pupko, and had produced award-winning beer since its founding in 1876.[114] The Pupko brothers stayed on to work in the brewery, along with other Jewish workers. One female survivor remembered that Lochbihler had allowed her husband to choose whomever he wanted from the ghetto to work and live there.[115] Lochbihler had arranged with Leopold Windisch, the official in charge of Jewish affairs in Lida, that these families could live in the brewery outside of the ghetto. Other Jewish workers, such as the carpenters, lived in the ghetto and came to work in the brewery during the day.[116]

Windisch was the deputy of the Gebietskommissar in Lida and the official in charge of Jewish affairs. He was energetic in his duties. Simon Remigolski, a Jew who had fled Lithuania after the murder of his family, acted as Windisch's interpreter, passing as a Pole. He recalled that Windisch often spoke of his duties regarding genocide. Windisch "stressed repeatedly that the Jews must be exterminated . . . and it was his task in the area of the *Gebietskommissariat* Lida to carry out the extermination of the Jews without mercy."[117] He was, in short, not a man to be manipulated lightly.

Still, Lochbihler risked deceiving him. As he recalled, "at the request of the Jews and also for technical reasons, I called on *Stabsleiter* Windisch and requested that the Jews be allowed to live in the brewery. I advised him that the Jews were necessary also at night and that the operation of the brewery depended on it. He allowed this." There was, however, a stipulation. Windisch told Lochbihler, "You are responsible to me in this to see that no one escapes."[118] Lochbihler was taking some personal and professional risk in assuming responsibility for the behavior of all the Jews in the brewery. Regardless, he arranged safe refuge in his establishment not only for his workers but their families, including nonworkers such as the elderly and children, who were given cover jobs within the operation.

Often, Germans protecting Jews did so for their own self-interest, to ensure that operations that they oversaw (and thus, they themselves) were successful. In this case, however, it is clear that Lochbihler protected the Jews of the Lida brewery because of his opposition to Nazi genocidal policy, or at least out of a genuine concern for the welfare of the Jews he could help. Lochbihler was described as a "very liberal, very decent man."[119] His humane and generous behavior toward the Jews in his care, which Lochbihler himself does not mention in much detail, even though it would have been in his best interest, was noted by several survivors in their testimony. Simon Pupko himself called the brewery "an oasis." Jews were allowed to celebrate the Seder and to live as normally as possible.[120]

In 1942, Lochbihler learned from a German railway worker that Lida's ghetto and its six thousand inhabitants were to be liquidated on May 8.[121] He informed his comrade, another soldier, named Lorenz Fischer, who also ran the brewery with him, that "they were going to snatch up our Jews and we had to prevent this."[122] At the same time, the Jews working in the brewery came to Lochbihler asking for help. He stated that "the Jews were understandably frightened and implored me to protect them from the execution. . . . There were terrible scenes. I still remember how a Jewish person fell on his knees and beseeched me to protect them."[123] Lochbihler promised that he would protect them and that he would devote his "whole person" to it. He further told them that he would "simulate a Wehrmacht operation" and that no one would enter the brewery. Michael Stoll, who was fourteen and worked in the brewery as an electrician's assistant, remembered Lochbihler telling him, "Michael, go into the house and wake everybody up and tell them to hide. Tonight we are killing off the ghetto. But don't worry, they are not going to touch you." Lochbihler added, "I am standing guard. They can't come into the brewery."[124] Beginning that night, at Lochbihler's insistence, the two German soldiers put on their helmets, shouldered their rifles, and stood guard outside the door.[125] Lochbihler heard shots later around dawn, and bullets landed in his vicinity, leading him to believe that shooting had already begun during the roundup. No one entered the brewery, and the Jews there avoided the execution. It was a particularly brutal one, with the children thrown into a separate trench and killed with hand grenades.[126]

Shura Pupko, a Jewish woman living in the brewery, remembered that this was not the first time Lochbihler had done such a thing. In March 1942, she testified, there was a "rehearsal" of a roundup. "For us," she continued, "Lochbihler stood outside the business and said these are my Jews and you aren't going to enter, they work for me and I don't need this rehearsal. This was his first step to save us."[127] Given that there was actually a real roundup in March 1942, which resulted in the murder of at least 235 Jews, it is conceivable that Lochbihler protected Jews here as well.[128]

He could not, however, save the Jews who lived in the ghetto. They did not arrive for work and were likely killed.[129] According to Shura Pupko, Lochbihler returned from the front near Minsk in 1943 to pick up beer and again warned the Jews in the brewery of an impending action. As she recalled, "He said there are many people in the woods, go, because they are going to kill you. It was a good warning."[130] This is more evidence of his altruistic motives and genuine concern. By February 1943 (and perhaps even before), the Pupko brewery became a place of respite for partisans such as the Bielski brothers before they sneaked into the Lida ghetto to recruit more fighters.[131] Though there does not appear to be any evidence connecting Lochbihler and partisans, the possibility that he turned a blind eye to potential partisan activity in his brewery is intriguing. After the war, Mr. and Mrs. Pupko testified on Lochbihler's behalf, and he was freed from an American POW camp where he was being held as a suspected war criminal.[132]

What does this episode tell us about rescue in Slonim? The Lida brewery case is the clearest example in this study of German soldiers attempting to aid Jews. The concurrence between survivor and soldier testimony shows that this was truly a case of a soldier wishing to help Jews. Lochbihler in his conversations with Windisch couched his arguments in terms of military necessity, but his subsequent treatment of the Pupko family and others, allowing them to practice their religion and live as comfortably as possible, indicates a concern for these people beyond simple economics. Lochbihler clearly took the initiative in saving Jews he had come to know within the limited opportunity and space that enabled him to do so. His exact reasons, however, remain a mystery, as do those of his partner, Fischer, who clearly also knew about the rescue of the brewery Jews.

As positive as this story may be, it is, like most examples of Wehrmacht rescue, both rare and limited. Lochbihler saved those Jews whom he knew personally. He was unable or unwilling to save even those Jews he knew who lived in the ghetto. Moreover, Lochbihler and the soldiers with him were in a relatively unique position, independent and isolated from their superiors. This allowed them to manage their laborers as they chose. In addition, being the expert in charge of an important Wehrmacht economic operation allowed Lochbihler to negotiate the terms of its operation, including those regarding his workers. These circumstances unfortunately were not easily translatable to more commonly experienced encounters between Jews and German soldiers.

The helping and rescue behavior of German soldiers must be defined by its rarity. Most soldiers for a variety of reasons did not make any efforts to help Jews. Indeed, most nonconformist behavior of these men is best termed evasion or noncompliance. They were most likely to refuse participation in killing when in closest proximity to the actual carrying out of violence. In contrast, soldiers seemed most likely to aid Jews when at a distance from violence. That is, they did not often save Jews at the last moment from shooting, but preferred to do so in more surreptitious ways that were much less visible to their comrades and superiors. Such situations allowed them to potentially act on their consciences without openly challenging the system. In terms of the process of increasing complicity, the routinization seen in both Slonim and Novogrudok also demonstrates perhaps a greater potential for rescue as well. As the tempo of killing operations slowed, those soldiers so inclined were able to work within a daily routine and a predictable system to help Jews. Unfortunately, few soldiers attempted or were interested in such aid.

Wehrmacht collusion in the Holocaust in Slonim and Novogrudok demonstrates a progression from improvised cooperation to routinized participation in Nazi genocidal policy. Most importantly, a triangular relationship between the SS, the Wehrmacht, and the civil administration developed that led to greater complicity for several reasons. First, army units stationed in these towns were viewed by civilian authorities specifically with their participation in mass murders in mind. Second, apart from the closer structural and operational relationships, these cases illustrate also the importance of cooperation between Wehrmacht officers and civil authorities on a personal level. In each town, administrators found willing collaborators in key army leaders who facilitated the greater involvement of the military in all aspects of the Nazi racial project. Additionally, the prolonged proximity to aspects of anti-Jewish policy not encountered in earlier killings like Krupki and Krucha led, in turn, to greater involvement of the soldiers. Put another way, the tempo and newness of participation in mass killings such as those in Krupki and Krucha likely made opportunities for both self-enrichment and rescue less apparent or more difficult for soldiers there. The involvement in ghettoization, forced labor, and appropriation of Jewish property that appears in the Slonim and Novogrudok cases and not earlier supports this argument. On another level, the permanence of units being stationed in towns also led to more complex relationships between Jews and soldiers. While these relationships often produce more questions than answers, they do indicate that prolonged contact with Jews resulted in connections that complicate our understanding of German soldiers' mentalities. This prolonged contact could also, as we have seen, lead to opportunities for rescue and assistance that were perhaps not as available or apparent earlier in the process.

Unfortunately, the trend toward greater complicity led army units, on the whole, to become more, not less, involved in genocide. Close cooperation between army units, the SS, and civilian authorities in anti-Jewish actions did not breed resistance to the racial project. Instead, most soldiers and units appear to have internalized the necessity of their role in assisting in the murder of Jews in the Soviet Union. This internalization reveals itself in more frequent smaller and decentralized killings. As the frozen ground delayed large-scale massacres until the spring, soldiers in the Generalbezirk Weissruthenien repeatedly conducted "Jew hunts" aimed specifically at Jews in smaller villages who had escaped previous roundups, and continued to kill Jews in smaller-scale executions.

CHAPTER EIGHT

Hunting Jews in Szczuczyn

Our company was required to complete activity reports for the battalion and for this reason conducted patrols in the area seizing Jews and shooting them. In these activity reports, these people were portrayed as having been shot while trying to escape. These reports were also compiled when Lieutenant Kiefer was present.

Former 12th Company clerk Alois H., 12 February 1965

A German Wehrmacht unit was stationed in Szczuczyn which would amuse itself every Saturday with "Jew games." They tortured and shot Jews indiscriminately and for no reason. I still remember how three soldiers demanded that a woman show them to the courtyard. Suddenly, one took his rifle and shot her on the spot.

Survivor Chaja Kirszenbaum, 25 February 1965

SOMETIME IN THE FALL OF 1941, twenty-four-year-old Lieutenant Oskar Ritterbusch led a patrol out of the town of Szczuczyn, forty-five miles (72 km) northwest of Slonim and forty-five miles east of Novogrudok. He commanded the 1st Platoon of the 12th Company, 727th Infantry Regiment. The patrol rode in two army trucks through the snow-covered countryside, rounding up Jews. Ritterbusch stopped in a small village, and his men got out. As they searched the village, they discovered a Jewish shoemaker and his family, which included an adult son, a hunchback. One soldier noticed the family also kept bees and had honey. Before confiscating two pails of honey, the Germans made the son taste it to ensure that it was not poisoned. Another soldier then ripped the pails out of the man's hands. Not understanding, perhaps, the hunchback resisted, and Lieutenant Ritterbusch ordered him thrown into the back of the truck with others who had been rounded up.[1] When one of his men explained that this man was a resident of the town and had just given them honey, the lieutenant replied, "I don't give a damn! He is a hindrance to his parents."[2] Paul B. recalled the lieutenant saying, "Away with him. It's no big deal."[3] B. also testified that he personally prevented another soldier from shooting the hunchback's mother. Ritterbusch's decision to kill him appears especially gratuitous and unwarranted by even the most brutal interpretation of policy.

In any case, the soldiers threw the hunchbacked Jewish man into the back of the truck, and the patrol continued. After a short distance, Lieutenant Ritterbusch stopped the truck, got out, and his soldiers forced the Jews to climb down. Ritterbusch explained what would happen next. The Jews would be told to run toward the forest, and the soldiers would then shoot them from behind. Before Ritterbusch himself gave the order, the hunchbacked man clung to Ernst N.'s arm and began to cry, for he had understood the officer's instructions in German. N. told him that he could do nothing to help him: "Orders were orders." However, he testified that he told the man to fall when the shooting started and not to move, and that he and an Austrian soldier had agreed to shoot over his head.[4] As we have already seen, such a statement is particularly suspect. After all the Jews were shot, the men of Ritterbusch's patrol returned to their base in Szczuczyn.

The actions of the 12th Company represent an end stage in the evolution of deepening Wehrmacht complicity in the Holocaust, one in which the tactical and ideological have rather seamlessly merged. Unlike previous instances, there was no large-scale massacre (at least not one uncovered in the course of the investigation). Indeed, most of the murders committed in Szczuczyn appear to have taken place after August 1941, under the jurisdiction of the 12th Company.[5] Instead, the face of complicity in Szczuczyn was characterized by repeated small-scale killings committed during normal operations over a long period of time, with little or no contact with civil authorities. Such influence does not seem to have been necessary, for this unit had already internalized the need to kill Jews and was doing it on a daily basis. The "Jew hunts" conducted by the 12th Company epitomized the ultimate fulfillment of the Jew-Bolshevik-partisan calculus, and the sadistic "Jew games" its soldiers played on Saturdays were the end result of prolonged exposure to genocidal killing and the internalization of the necessity to kill Jews. They also prefigured the incredibly brutal "large actions" against "partisans" and civilians that would come in 1942–1943.

The town of Szczuczyn (pronounced SHOO-CHIN) lies in western Belarus, seventy miles (113 km) east of Bialystok near the 1941 Soviet border.[6] It takes its name from the nearby river Shtushinka. The town itself began as the estate of a local noble family, the Scipions.[7] Jews had first begun settling in the region in large numbers at the end of the sixteenth century. In the nineteenth century, like Novogrudok, Szczuczyn was a center of the Mussar movement, which stressed the incorporation of an ethical dimension in traditional Orthodox Judaism. It had developed into a major regional center by 1936. Around twenty-five hundred Jews lived in the town or in the surrounding villages.[8]

The 12th Company, 727th Infantry Regiment, from Bechtolsheim's 707th Infantry Division arrived there in mid-August 1941, leaving a detachment behind in Ostryna, eleven miles to the northeast. The 3rd Battalion and the 10th Company with Joachim Lochbihler were headquartered in nearby Lida. The 11th Company was stationed in Grodno, thirty-five miles to the west. Upon arrival in Szczuczyn, Lieutenant Josef Kiefer quartered his company in what all the soldiers remembered as a "palace." This was evidently the former estate of Count Drucki-Lubecki on the northern edge of town.

In Szczuczyn, the character of the company-level leadership was decisive, for the company officers appear to have driven most of the decision making. They were relatively isolated (as Sibille was) and thus could essentially do what they pleased. Though the leaders in the 12th Company disagreed on methods, unfortunately they all agreed on the desired outcome—that is, the murder of the Jews. The company commander, Josef Kiefer, was a thirty-two-year-old active duty officer from Munich. With no high school diploma, he had begun a sales apprenticeship but was unable to complete it because his employer went out of business in the turbulent post–World War I German economy. After working briefly in his father's bakery, the nineteen-year-old Kiefer entered the Bavarian State Police in October 1928.[9] After seven years as a policeman in Munich, he was absorbed into the army in July 1935 as this branch of the police was militarized.[10] Kiefer served as an infantry noncommissioned officer during the occupation of Austria and the Sudetenland and then fought as a heavy machine gun section leader in Poland before being commissioned from the ranks as a lieutenant in 1940.[11]

His evaluations described him as a man who had proven himself in battle. He was a handsome man, "slender and wiry," with "flawless etiquette"; he wears a slightly smug expression in his military personnel file photo. His superiors noted his "exemplary service as a platoon leader" and declared him fully qualified to be an officer.[12] In his company commander training course, however, he was rated as only qualified to take command after further training.[13] He perhaps was a man promoted past his capabilities, but seems to have been reasonably competent and motivated.

As a military commander, Kiefer appears to have been strict but fair to his soldiers. He was a "hard and disciplined soldier" but one valued by his men for "knowing his job."[14] Kiefer was also "reserved and unapproachable."[15] In short, he appears to have been tactically competent and not disliked by his men. It is perhaps telling that these men also characterized him as a political extremist, and that this did not diminish their views of him. While some men claimed that their commander held no particularly racist beliefs, the bulk of the evidence suggests otherwise, beginning with two important decorations that he held.

Kiefer's personnel file indicates that he was awarded the prestigious Nazi Party Badge of Honor of 1923. Kiefer explained in his police interviews that as a fourteen-year-old boy he had merely served as a messenger during the Beer Hall Putsch and had later applied for the award during his police training. His three older brothers were all SA men as well.[16] Regardless of Kiefer's attempts to minimize its importance, this medal was not one awarded frivolously. At least one man also remembered that he wore the Gold Party Badge awarded to the first one hundred thousand party members.[17] That Kiefer chose to wear this optional party insignia on his Wehrmacht uniform indicates his pride in this distinction.

Kiefer's elite party status is powerfully suggestive of his ideological position. His soldiers testified to his attitude toward Jews. Though one man stated he was "not hostile to Jews and opposed atrocities," the majority of the men characterized him somewhat differently.[18] One soldier declared Kiefer a "convinced National Socialist [who] shared the National Socialist perspective on the Jewish Question."[19] Another observed that there were "already disputes between Kiefer and the Jews when they did not obey his ordinances."[20] A noncommissioned officer shed light on what kinds of regulations were meant here. Kiefer had yelled at him for allowing some Jews to walk on the sidewalk rather than in the street as required. He further recalled that Kiefer took note of two Jewish women who cooked for the company and required that they be dismissed.[21] This was in keeping with Wehrmacht guidelines forbidding Jews to work for the army, though clearly many other units ignored the rules and continued to exploit Jewish labor. Yet Kiefer was apparently "no brutal guy" and allegedly a man who believed that the "military should not dirty its hands in such things"—meaning actions against Jews.[22] Instead, he appears to have been a believer and an antisemite but with a professional approach that did not countenance "unnecessary" violence. He was, however, perfectly willing to murder Jews in the course of operations.

The two other officers in the company were Lieutenants Ernst Schaffitz and Oskar Ritterbusch. Schaffitz, who led the 2nd Platoon, was a former SA man and an "outspoken Jew-hater."[23] He was described as "callous" and "harsh," with a high-pitched voice.[24] He confessed to Polish authorities that he was a "fanatic Nazi."[25] Indeed, in 1935, he had written the local Nazi Party office to ask if he could be simultaneously a member of the Nazi Party and another German racist party.[26] Former soldiers consistently described Schaffitz as a brutal man deeply implicated in the murders of Jews. The characterization that he was "generally disliked" is probably representative.[27] One soldier went so far as to claim that several of his soldiers committed suicide as a result of his harassment.[28] However, we must not overlook the postwar interrogation context and the tendency of witnesses to often vilify those who were dead or otherwise immune from prosecution.[29] Still, Schaffitz apparently "had it in for the Jews." When approached by a Jewish panhandler, he responded, "You damned dirty Jews, go home! You have no business here."[30] The strongest condemnation of Schaffitz was that he "particularly wanted to break the spirit of the Jews."[31] Schaffitz's men portrayed him as particularly vulgar and cruel in his antisemitism.

Oskar Ritterbusch, on the other hand, appears to have been a more enigmatic character, somewhere between Kiefer and Schaffitz. At twenty-four, he had taken four semesters of exercise and biology at university toward his goal of becoming an athletic trainer.[32] Drafted in 1938, he served in the Polish campaign as a private and was promoted to lieutenant in September 1940. Ritterbusch served in a training unit before being transferred to the 727th Infantry Regiment shortly before the invasion of Russia.[33] The lanky, dark-haired officer was viewed as correct and strict. Others described him as "spirited," "self-confident," and a "Hitler Youth leader type."[34] Regarding his racial beliefs, former soldiers remembered that he "did not speak well of the Jews" and was also "harshly positioned against the Jews."[35] Yet, another noted that "as a rule, Ritterbusch did not go after Jews. . . . [He] only arrested them when ordered."[36] As we have seen, however, even this characterization is flatly contradicted by other accounts. It is interesting to note that of all the men accused in the five cases examined in this work, only Ritterbusch refused to testify at all regarding his actions in the war and remained silent regarding all questions about this period.

These officers were the important leaders of 12th Company, and their actions greatly affected the Jews in the local area. None was sympathetic toward Jews, but their various forms of antisemitism directly impacted the manner in which they inserted themselves and their soldiers into anti-Jewish policy.

The 12th Company in Szczuczyn killed Jews much more routinely in the course of its daily operations than the units in the other cases. These killings took a variety of different forms but for the most part were all carried out at the company level and below, without much involvement from any other organization. They indicate an acceptance and internalization of the necessity of anti-Jewish policy, as well as a certain vigor not previously seen. The killings in and around Szczuczyn were intrinsically motivated, decentralized, and repetitive.

With its smaller Jewish population and location away from significant supply routes, Szczuczyn did not receive the attention from the Einsatzgruppen that other towns in the area did. The Germans entered the town on 26 June 1941 and took the town's leaders hostage but released them after three days.[37] In July, a Judenrat (Jewish council responsible to the German authorities) was established, but more draconian measures were not imposed. William Moll fled to Szczuczyn from Lida with his family after their home in Lida had been destroyed. He remembered that there were cases of individual killings but nothing like mass murder.[38] EG B commander Nebe remarked with dissatisfaction on 13 July that "only 96 Jews were executed in Grodno and Lida during the first days. I gave orders to intensify these activities."[39] Though at least one Einsatzgruppen killing had taken place in Szczuczyn, the inhabitants of Szczuczyn had been left relatively unmolested by German forces before the arrival of the 12th Company.[40] This changed shortly after Kiefer's men came to town. Sometime in mid-August, a ghetto was established. Taking only what they could carry, twenty-five hundred Jews were confined to a small area of the town. The ghetto was not walled in but was apparently surrounded by a barbed-wire fence.[41] It is unclear who presided over this action, but it was likely the 12th Company, as German military maps do not indicate an external administrative unit being stationed there; the nearest was OK I/849 in Lida, thirty miles to the northeast.[42] During this period, a local police force was raised. The Yizkor (or Jewish community memory book) for Szczuczyn states that this police force was made up of ethnic Poles who collaborated "willingly and whole-heartedly."[43] Overall, with the exception of this force, it appears that the company was relatively isolated in the town and that Kiefer and the men of the unit wielded a great deal of power. This is not to say that larger killings did not take place—just not on the scale of Slonim or Novogrudok. William Moll's parents were killed in a shooting of prominent Jewish residents in December 1941.[44] German records and testimonies remain silent on the role Kiefer's men played in this action, though it is likely they were involved. Leopold Windisch, the *Referent* for Jewish affairs in Lida, was also responsible for ordering the murder of three thousand Jews in Szczuczyn, according to one survivor.[45]

Regardless, of all the cases examined, Szczuczyn demonstrates most explicitly the prevalence of "Jew hunting" as a pastime for German soldiers.[46] Soldiers and officers broke the monotony of duty in a small rural town by conducting patrols into the countryside, ostensibly aimed at rounding up partisans and suspected sympathizers. Usually conducted in platoon strength, these outings rarely if ever encountered partisans. One sergeant stated categorically, "during my time in Szczuczyn I never came into contact with partisans."[47] A company medic recalled that while "the mission of our unit was anti-partisan fighting, I myself encountered no partisans."[48] Many other former soldiers corroborate the general absence of partisans or combat. The battalion surgeon of the 3rd Battalion in Lida went even further, remarking that "no anti-partisan operations were carried out during our presence in Lida because partisan activity was very low. Partisan activity first started *after* the large Jewish action, *after* [emphasis mine] Jews fled to the forests."[49] Again, we see a partisan "threat" marshaled to support the killing of Jews, even when such a threat did not exist.

Most former soldiers agree that these patrols were generally made up of volunteers, and that while many different soldiers participated in these "Jew hunts," they were usually drawn from the same group. One man noted that these soldiers were "always the same people who Schaffitz sought out; however, I don't remember there being any direct orders."[50] Another noticed the special nature of these Jew hunts, saying "that these hunting patrols [*Jagdkommandos*] were usually created from the first platoon."[51] The 1st Platoon belonged to Ritterbusch, who led the operation discussed at the opening of the chapter.

Usually led by a squad leader but sometimes by a platoon leader, these patrols appear to have been mainly conducted in captured Soviet trucks. A soldier from the first platoon testified, "The patrol leader would then dismount in the village and talk with the mayor. We ourselves often never left the truck."[52] As Schrade's report had recommended several months earlier, this was *not* how one would go about fighting actual partisans. The fact that the men drove from village to village in trucks also indicates the low threat level, as this was not how actual anti-partisan operations were conducted.[53] Groups of men from the company would scour the countryside for Jews and either kill them where they were found or bring them back to the Drucki Palace where the unit was quartered and execute them there. One sergeant described the operations: "It is correct that we would repeatedly drive into towns, load Jews onto a truck and drive them to a gravel pit [a mile or so behind the palace] where we had to shoot them."[54] He noted that the patrols were mostly led by Lieutenant Schaffitz. Indeed, one can easily surmise that discussions with village officials involved asking if there were Jews in the village. Mayors were responsible for any "enemies" or even strangers in their village. As in previous cases, the men also took advantage of anti-Jewish operations to enrich themselves; robbery again accompanied murder. A 12th Company soldier remembered that during "searches of Jewish houses a few comrades took what they found."[55] Another soldier took shoes off dead Jews and sent them home.[56] Schaffitz, too, was accused of personally appropriating Jewish property.[57]

Moreover, the objectives and results of these "Jew hunts" were no secret to anyone in the company. Captain Kiefer himself testified that "as a result of a standing regimental order Jews were generally seen as partisans when found outside their place of residence." He clarified that these arrested Jews were only shot if they attempted to escape.[58] Kiefer's explanation reflects both the formulaic but conscious phraseology used during the war to describe the murders of Jews ("shot while trying to escape"), as well as his postwar attempt at self-exculpation. Clearly, all Jews were targets, wherever they were found. A company clerk, Georg L., confirmed this. "I contend," he said, "that Schaffitz actually issued orders to shoot Jews because I saw myself that *kommandos* were assembled by him in our office with the purpose of conducting raids against the Jews." He added that "people from these raids returned and told that they had again shot Jews."[59] The 12th Company had moved far beyond assisting in executions when asked, to independently and actively targeting Jews for murder.

Kiefer's unit also intentionally reported murdered Jews as partisan casualties. Clerk Georg L. described the process. "When [Schaffitz] returned, he would report to the company clerk that several partisans were shot to death in the operation. In actuality, it was generally known throughout the company that these were Jews who were in no way partisans."[60] L. also had been present in the command post as various company outposts also reported Jews killed.[61] The other company clerk corroborated these statements, adding, "There was an order by which all people without identification were to be shot."[62] Finally, the former company first sergeant explicitly described the misleading reporting process and suggested another reason for the company's "Jew hunts." He recalled that "our company was required to complete activity reports for the battalion and for this reason conducted patrols in the area seizing Jews and shooting them. In these activity reports, these people were portrayed as having been shot while trying to escape. These reports were also compiled when Lieutenant Kiefer was present."[63] Perhaps the commander hoped to impress his superiors with results and encouraged the murder of Jews to pad his body counts. In any case, it was an open secret within the company that Jews were being killed because they were Jews. This was intentionally disguised in official reports with the use of the term "partisans" and the description "shot while trying to escape."

The significance of these "Jew hunts" and their subsequent reporting should not be underestimated. They indicate how deeply this Wehrmacht unit had accepted its role in killing Jews and how fully it dedicated itself to the fulfillment of the goals of the Mogilev Conference. First, the 12th Company took the initiative in and around Szczuczyn to hunt down Jews and kill them. It acted unilaterally, without the influence from civilian authorities that was felt by the 6th and 7th Companies in Slonim and Novogrudok. Indeed, it appears that SS, SD, or police units were rarely, if ever, involved in the 12th Company's activities. Second, the reporting process and widespread knowledge of the real aim of these patrols demonstrate that no pretense was necessary to motivate soldiers to kill. The participation of the men in actual killing seems far greater and more transparent in Szczuczyn than elsewhere. Third, the company's reporting practices indicate that its superiors were also well aware of the killings and condoned them. If the entire company knew of Kiefer's problematic bookkeeping, it is a good bet his commander, Major Mayr, did as well. Finally, the focus on the killing of Jews in the small villages and countryside surrounding Szczuczyn (while a sizable ghetto was maintained in the town itself) is powerful evidence again of the impact of the organizational climate and command directives in the 707th.

As noted, the commander of the 707th Infantry Division, General Bechtolsheim, was a rabid antisemite. This might explain his eagerness to develop a "division of labor" between the army and the SS in which the army would consolidate and kill Jews in the countryside while the SS and Einsatzgruppen would murder Jews in established ghettos and larger towns. As we have seen, he published orders in November 1941 clearly stating that "where larger or smaller groups of Jews are encountered in the countryside, they may either be executed [by army units themselves] or consolidated in ghettos in designated places where they will then be given over to the civil administration, that is, the SD."[64] In a letter to Gebietskommissar Erren in nearby Slonim, First Lieutenant Glück alludes to a 29 November order from the 727th Infantry Regiment that the "flat lands are to be cleared and kept free of Jews."[65] The "Jew hunts" around Szczuczyn are definitive evidence of the execution of this policy on the ground and must make us wonder whether the 6th and 7th Companies also were following this guidance.[66] The prevalence of these "Jew hunts" and the early ghettoization in Szczuczyn suggests that such activities had been well under way *before* this order was written. Kiefer's leadership must also be seen, then, in the context of this higher-level division and regimental guidance, which appears to have established a standard operating procedure for participation in genocide. Jew hunting in and around Szczuczyn was a direct result of Bechtolsheim's agreement with the SS.

The 12th Company was not the only German army unit to engage in this type of activity. Again, Serbia is exemplary, as it, too, saw similar hunts for Jews, prior to the German invasion of the Soviet Union. Walter Manoschek explains that the "Polish ghettoization phase" was skipped there as German forces "developed a regional model" as a solution.[67] In Serbia, battalions created *Jagdkommandos* that also included members of the SD. For Manoschek, these mixed patrols "marked the transition from a division of labor to direct cooperation between the Wehrmacht and police apparatus."[68] This is exactly the kind of cooperation seen in the 707th. These hunts were conducted in Poland as well. Christopher

Serbia — 12th

not mopping up but an extension of anti-Jewish policy

Browning, for example, has found that similar types of "Jew hunts" were carried out by police battalions. These hunters sought Jews who had escaped from the ghetto or from previous roundups.[69] He, too, notes these were low-level, decentralized operations (and thus difficult to study). Yet, while similar to the "Jew hunts" around Szczuczyn, these operations were much more, as Browning wrote, an "end phase of the Final Solution." Twelfth Company directed its operations, however, at a different population. Rather than escapees from ghettos or from previous roundups, the victims of these hunts seemed to be simply Jews living in more remote areas yet to be reached by German troops or death squads. In this sense, then, these operations were less a mopping up and more an *active* extension of anti-Jewish policy into the hinterlands. These operations did not seek to round up remnants, but to capture new populations of Jews. Moreover, they demanded initiative to be successful. It would have been very easy to *not* capture and kill Jews in this way, had that been the desire. The 12th Company could simply have gone about its business and its patrolling *without* murdering Jews.

The palace where the 12th Company was quartered served not only as the starting point for its "Jew hunts" but also the end point for other killings. According to the Yizkor book for Szczuczyn, forty Jews were shot on the palace grounds by German soldiers in mid-August, which would have been around the time of the unit's arrival. The Szczuczyn ghetto was created shortly after this killing, housing over two thousand people. Two weeks later, the local police, on German orders, assembled the Jewish intelligentsia, including the rabbi and teachers, whom the Germans then shot outside of the town.[70] This could very well be the same killing that claimed William Moll's parents, though the timing does not match up between the two sources. Kiefer and his men likely played a role in this as well.[71]

Beyond this action, the palace played host to regular shootings. A noncommissioned officer stated, "I believe it was a few hundred meters behind the palace where the shootings took place. These shootings must have been carried out by members of the company because only the 12th company was located in this palace."[72] Kiefer himself described a shooting that took place there. A patrol arrested a Jewish family (mother, father, and son) and brought them to Kiefer. He personally questioned them, recalling after the war that they had come from the Baltic. Then, according to him, he ordered them taken to the jail. He heard shots shortly thereafter and learned from his men that the Jews had been "shot while trying to escape."[73] Of course, this is postwar dishonesty. The Jewish *family* was not shot while trying to escape, but had been executed on his orders. Several men of the company recalled the killing because various kinds of paper money had fluttered through the air when the victims were killed. One soldier explained more honestly that "they were shot because they were Jews and because they had no identification [*Ausweis*]."[74] This is a very revealing comment, as it *directly* relates to guidance regarding *Zivilisten ohne Ausweis*—civilians without identification—which was mentioned at both the Mogilev Conference and in reports of "enemies" killed. This shooting in Szczuczyn again shows that many of the "enemies" reported killed in this period were indeed Jews. While the first sergeant attempted after the war to argue that there was simply a firing range behind the palace, which explained the shooting, the men of the company clearly killed literally in their own backyard. The shooting pit appears to have been the site of multiple killings over an extended period.

One of these killings appears to have taken place in December 1941 while Captain Kiefer was away.[75] Lieutenant Schaffitz, as senior ranking officer, took over acting command of the company. First Sergeant H. (who himself was deeply implicated in the crimes of 12th Company) alleged that Schaffitz then rounded up twenty-five to thirty Jewish laborers and demanded their deaths.[76] It is unclear exactly how this shooting took place, but the company clerk testified it happened in the park behind the palace. Moreover, he personally remembered seeing the "money, gold, jewelry, and valuables" from these Jews that were delivered to the company office and later sent on to the battalion headquarters in Lida.[77] Thus, we see that even in decentralized killing operations, expropriated property was collected and passed on to higher headquarters, who certainly knew where such things were coming from. In Szczuczyn, the Wehrmacht itself collected these valuables.

Schaffitz's period of temporary command became an important point of contention in postwar legal proceedings, where Kiefer (and others) attempted to place all the blame for 12th Company's atrocities on Schaffitz.

He was painted as a virulent antisemite and as having carried out his killings unilaterally, without sanction or orders, and apparently without the approval of the vast majority of the company. Given that Schaffitz died in a Polish prison in 1956, this was no doubt a useful defense tactic. However, like much postwar testimony, it tells half truths. Kiefer *was* often gone and often represented by Schaffitz. Upon his return to the unit, Kiefer testified, he was informed of Schaffitz's excesses by First Sergeant H. Further, he stated that he reported Schaffitz to his superiors and requested his transfer.[78] The commander claimed that he had harshly reprimanded the lieutenant for his actions. According to Kiefer, Schaffitz was disciplined by the battalion commander and was relieved for "*independently* carrying out shootings of Jews."[79] 707th Division records indicate that by April Schaffitz was indeed transferred to the 9th Company in the same battalion.[80] However, there is no evidence of any further "punishment."

It was well known in the battalion that the relationship between Kiefer and Schaffitz was "hostile."[81] This conflict tells us much about the nature of the killings in which the 12th Company was active. Perhaps Schaffitz had the company's work Jews executed as a way to deliberately antagonize his commander. What these personal enmities do *not* tell us is that Schaffitz was censured for killing Jews or that Kiefer and his superiors at the battalion level disapproved of the murder of Jews in principle. It appears that Kiefer *was* angry at his lieutenant's undisciplined and somewhat insubordinate behavior. However, Kiefer was certainly well aware of the "Jew hunts" taking place in his command and that these were being reported to the battalion. The battalion, in turn, knew that Jews were being killed and would not have punished Schaffitz simply for this. Indeed, by all indications, this was standard operating procedure.

However, Schaffitz's zeal to kill Jews constituted a challenge to Kiefer's authority in several cases. Kiefer apparently had been meeting with a young Jewish woman who was teaching him Russian and translating a book on the Russian Revolution.[82] This woman was among those allegedly killed on Schaffitz's orders. Also among the laborers rounded up for execution was a glassworker. When told there were no other similar craftsmen left, Schaffitz ordered the men to determine whether no one else was capable of this work. Though the answer was no, Schaffitz stubbornly

12th Company — excessive brutality

ordered the only glassworker in town to be killed along with the rest.[83] Kiefer may well have been angered at the killing of his personal tutor, as well as of the skilled Jewish workers who supported the company. Killing Jews on patrol was one thing, but rounding up and killing Jews from Szczuczyn, or those "employed" by the company, may have been actions in which Kiefer felt Schaffitz was overreaching. In any case, beyond being transferred to a new unit, Schaffitz apparently did not suffer any significant negative repercussions. He continued his "patrolling" with the 9th Company.

The killings committed by the 12th Company in and around Szczuczyn demonstrate an important stage in the evolution of Wehrmacht complicity. In a small town under little or no outside influence by SS or civil authorities, Kiefer and his company carried out killings of Jews on their own as a natural component of their day-to-day operations. They seemed to fully embody the message of the sample operations from the Mogilev Conference. Moreover, the 12th Company reported these killings to its superiors either plainly or in euphemistic language that did not conceal the truth from anyone. This was a departure from earlier killings that were as a rule either isolated or mass events. Execution of genocide without top-down direction emphasizes that, by this point, killing Jews in the countryside had become policy and that the unit had internalized the necessity of anti-Jewish actions. Participation in killing had become normalized and was no longer an extraordinary event but a daily element of duty in the East. In the case of Szczuczyn, with no close supervision, leaders were able to act with as much (or as little) zeal and initiative as they wished. Here, the leaders of 12th Company chose to carry out the "spirit of the order" to its maximum extent rather than in a perfunctory manner. In his murder of working Jews, Schaffitz appears to have exceeded even this mandate. Indeed, beyond the shift in German tactics, what *further* distinguished the behavior of the 12th Company was its excessive brutality. In these acts, we have arrived at the end result of prolonged participation in murder.

While the behavior of German soldiers toward Jews was certainly cruel from Krupki to Novogrudok, Kiefer's men exhibited especially gratu-

itous brutality and sadistic behavior, which appears to have resulted
from the independent nature of the operations, prolonged contact with
genocide, and/or a deeper belief in the necessity of killing Jews, or at
least a desire to do so. Individuals in previous cases may have carried out
their duties with excessive violence, but in Szczuczyn such behavior became commonplace as German soldiers sought additional opportunities
gratuitously to brutalize Jews.

Israel Zlocowski was a forty-eight-year-old father of four who had fled
to Szczuczyn from the nearby town of Bilitsa. In the ghetto, he would go
from door to door to give the children food.[84] One morning in the fall of
1941 he was standing in line by the Judenrat, waiting for work. "Suddenly I heard a shout," Israel remembered. " 'They are coming.' I hid
myself in a nearby courtyard and watched as an officer and sergeant
from the *infantry regiment* [emphasis mine] stationed in Szczuczyn approached. At the same time, I saw an acquaintance of mine from Bilitsa
named Dwora Kaplan walk out of her door. The sergeant drew his pistol
and shot her on the spot for no reason."[85] This kind of gratuitously unnecessary killing was a new development.

A few months later, in February 1942, this random violence struck
closer to home for Israel. He and his son Jakob had worked especially
hard the day before and spent the morning at home. A neighbor appeared and warned that "the Germans were coming." "My son Jakob and
I immediately leapt over the wire and hid outside the ghetto," he said.
"When we returned to the ghetto a few hours later, we found my son David and my mother-in-law shot to death." His wife had hidden under the
bed and told Israel what had happened. The German *"infantry soldiers"*
[emphasis mine] came into the living room, forced their son and her
mother into the street, and shot them to death.[86] Given that survivors are
often understandably unable to distinguish between SS, Wehrmacht,
police, and other German units, the fact that Israel and his wife twice
specifically identify the perpetrators as German infantry soldiers is remarkable and means that, in this case, they must be referring to the men
of the 12th Company. In addition, the size of the town and the apparent
lack of other German SS or police units also makes it almost certain that
Kiefer's unit is described in these testimonies. Belarusian metalworker
Viktor Schtemplewski recalled that "it very often happened that Jews

were shot in the ghetto for the slightest sign of insubordination."[87] In the
nearby town of Ostryna, Schaffitz allegedly had a Jewish family shot
when he saw them looking out the window.[88] Here, unlike in previous
instances of complicity, Wehrmacht soldiers entered an existing ghetto
and apparently shot Jews at random, taking Jewish lives without even the
slightest pretense of military rationale or connection to any organized
action.

However, the brutality of the company did not stop with random killings. Some German soldiers apparently found the ghetto a ready place to
torment Jews. Saturdays were special for the men of the 12th Company
and terror-filled for the Jews of Szczuczyn. The ghetto became the scene
of so-called "Jew games" in which soldiers would torment and kill Jews.
Chaja Kirszenbaum was twenty when the Germans arrived. She remembered, "A German Wehrmacht unit was stationed in Szczuczyn which
would amuse itself every Saturday with 'Jew games.' They tortured and
shot Jews indiscriminately and for no reason. I still remember how three
soldiers demanded that a woman show them to the courtyard. Suddenly,
one took his rifle and shot her on the spot."[89] Other Jewish survivors
confirmed these actions by 12th Company soldiers. Azriel Weinstein
had been deported to the Szczuczyn ghetto from his native Rozanka. He
too remembered a Wehrmacht unit that often amused itself with "Jew
games" and that many Jews were shot as a result.[90] Golda Schwartz
moved with her family to Szczuczyn from Ostryna when she was twelve.
She remembered that "the Germans came mostly on Shabbat to see if
the Jews were clean. They killed those they found on the street."[91] This
German accusation that Jews were unclean was almost certainly an antisemitic slur and not some misplaced concern for public health. Liber
Losh elaborated, describing a similar incident that occurred in February 1942. During an inspection of sanitary conditions, German soldiers
killed nine men and nine women.[92] Sometimes the killings had frivolous
justifications. Jewish survivor Azriel Weinstein recalled one such incident. In the winter of 1941–42, thirteen to fifteen Jews were shot by German soldiers because "they had not pumped enough water."[93] Liber
Losh clarified that this killing resulted from a "brief water shortage in
the German quarters."[94]

The sadistic behavior of these Wehrmacht soldiers represents a qualitative change in the anti-Jewish violence, even when compared with other units in the 727th Infantry Regiment. The initiative-taking here transcended even the dubious explanation of duty, reaching the level of sport. German soldiers in Szczuczyn apparently not only acted brutally in the course of their assigned tasks, but also sought out opportunities to entertain themselves by murdering and abusing Jews. The "hygiene inspections," the intentional scheduling of "Jew games" on the Sabbath, and indiscriminate brutality indicate a significant sadistic and antisemitic turn that constituted a new and sinister development. There is little testimony in other, earlier cases exhibiting a similar volume and tenor of sadistic behavior. Soldiers were no longer simply carrying out orders, even if coldly or harshly; they were deriving pleasure from tormenting their victims. How do we explain this shift to brutality?

First, it appears that the leadership condoned it. Earlier, a meeting had taken place at the battalion headquarters in Lida where the battalion commander, Captain Rudolf Mayr, had passed on orders that all Jews were to be treated as partisans. There was no ambiguity as to what this meant. Again, the echoes of the Mogilev Conference reverberate. Kiefer himself admitted during questioning that "this order meant in practice that we should kill all Jews."[95] At the small unit level, Jews were repeatedly killed at close quarters. The "official" reporting of these killings by the company sent a clear message that the murder of Jews was a nonevent and part of normal military routine. The decentralized nature of these operations (such as the one commanded by Ritterbusch) allowed men who were so inclined to take liberties that they may not have taken under closer supervision. Still, what led to the Saturday "Jew games"? While Kiefer was certainly supportive of killing Jews during operations, he does not seem to have instigated gratuitous brutality and sadism.

It is more probable that Schaffitz, with his more rabid and brutal antisemitism, readily encouraged such "excesses" when he commanded the company. The acting commander was, after all, "a beast who bullied his own men when there were no Jews left to shoot."[96] However, given that these activities seem to have been ongoing, we must assume that Kiefer himself was at least indifferent. First Sergeant H. admitted that although "close contact with Jews was forbidden for soldiers, if a soldier was occasionally caught in the ghetto, he would not have expected any special punishment from Kiefer."[97] If soldiers were "caught in the ghetto," what were they doing there in the first place? The first sergeant's remark further seems to indicate that soldiers entering the ghetto for unauthorized activities was not infrequent. Indeed, H.'s attitude seems to indicate that the company leadership adopted a permissive attitude toward this kind of behavior; there certainly is no evidence of any punishment, even in postwar testimony where such testimony, even if fabricated, would be to Kiefer's advantage.

Another explanation could be a certain level of boredom or desire for excitement. Over five hundred miles from the front, with no real insurgent activity to speak of, perhaps soldiers sought to relieve the tedium by preying upon the local Jewish population. The soldiers themselves do not even mention these more gratuitous atrocities, much less offer any explanation in their postwar statements, given the legal context of these interviews. "Sensation seeking" as an explanation for increased tendency to violence has support within the social psychological scholarship. One study "described the seductive appeal of risky behavior as an escape from boredom."[98] This search for excitement can, for some, "lead to evil acts in certain circumstances."[99] Psychologists conducting work in this area, then, characterize this mode of violent behavior as one affecting "groups of individuals who are characterized by high sensation seeking and low self-control" and who "are prone to feeling bored," seeking to "escape this aversive state by engaging in arousing activities."[100] This social-psychological perspective has particular value here in explaining the behavior of a small number of soldiers in Szczuczyn: bored, seeking thrills, and provided with a supply of helpless victims. It seems that here, as in other atrocities in similar contexts, the deliberate dehumanization and targeting of civilians led inexorably to progressively more vicious behavior above and beyond that "required" of the military situation.

An increasingly virulent antisemitism among the men could also be a factor. The fact that these "Jew games" took place on Saturdays, the Jewish Sabbath, cannot simply be a coincidence. The men of the 12th Company deliberately chose to attack Jews on their holy day. The use of "hygiene" and cleanliness as the justification seems to indicate an intentional effort by the soldiers to mock the Jews' own religious tenets in seeking to be ritually clean on the Sabbath. The cynical justifications for this brutality indicate a motivation to torment and kill beyond cold and clinical, if specious, "military" calculations or even abstract scientific racism. These Germans designed uniquely antisemitic torments to add insult to injury. This indicates another level of premeditation: soldiers not only planned to victimize Jews, but also did so in a manner calculated to be particularly humiliating. Certainly the brutal behavior of Schaffitz and the extreme racist views he shared with Kiefer could have spread among the men. At a minimum, this would have encouraged similar behavior from those predisposed to act sadistically. In Szczuczyn, killing became a pastime.

Another powerful explanation for the more violent behavior of the 12th Company is socialization. People are changed by what they do. This is not just true in a numbing, brutalizing sort of way, though that kind of acclimatization happens. The social/psychological theory of cognitive dissonance, first espoused by Leon Festinger in 1957, is instructive in this regard.[101] The theory argues that when our actions and our beliefs are conflicting, we are thrown into a progressively more uncomfortable mental state. This "dissonance arousal" is, in essence, a threat to our conception of self.[102] The effect on our self-image is vital because "people experience dissonance after engaging in an action that leaves them feeling stupid, immoral, or confused. Moreover, the greater the personal commitment or self-involvement implied by the action and the smaller external justification for that action, the greater the dissonance and, therefore, the more powerful the need for self-justification."[103] In order to escape this threat to our mental well-being, we seek to change either our beliefs or our actions to bring our mental and physical states into congruence. In many situations, it is easier to change beliefs than acts. Often, individuals overcorrect, becoming *more* violent. This theory is borne out by the Holocaust. Most men found it more difficult to physically stop participating than to rationalize their behavior. We have these mental gymnastics in every case.

By this model, the brutality we see in the 12th Company (and by other units with long-term exposure to the Nazi genocidal project) can be explained as a function of a mental change attempting to justify actions that

Local
Moral
Universe

had already been committed. In this sense, increasingly brutal action could be used to convince a soldier of his own virulent antisemitism, which then justified his brutal actions. If participation in murder began incrementally, as we see beginning in Krupki, then perhaps Szczuczyn represents the natural result of all these small steps. As Fred Katz notes, "through this type of localized incremental decision-making the individual can readily become involved in profound evil."[104] Perhaps the killers in Szczuczyn found themselves in Katz's "Local Moral Universe" that "dictated behavior totally at variance with the ideals in which participants had been brought up to believe."[105] This kind of transformation appears elsewhere in Holocaust perpetrator statements. Walter Mattner was on the staff of the HSSPF in Mogilev in October 1941. He participated in the shooting of 2,273 Jews there and described his reactions in a letter to his wife: "My hand was shaking a bit with the first cars. By the tenth car, I was aiming calmly and shooting dependably at the many women, children and babies. Bearing in mind that I have two babies at home, I knew that they would suffer exactly the same treatment, if not ten times as bad, at the hands of these hordes."[106] This killer began attempting to resolve his own cognitive dissonance in a matter of hours. We can, then, imagine the potential outcomes of contact with murder over months for some German soldiers.

Of relevance here as well is Katz's concept of "Cultures of Cruelty." He noted during the trials of Auschwitz guards that some men chose to behave with excessive and imaginative cruelty beyond the already structurally cruel task to which they were bent. Certainly, antisemitism played a role. However, Katz also identifies similar behavior in the murders at My Lai, which arguably lacked a similarly powerful ideological underpinning; racism surely existed but was not as fundamental a factor in army behavior. It appears that a similar "culture of cruelty" developed at least for some soldiers in Szczuczyn and found its expression in increasingly creative and brutal degradations against its captive Jewish population.

And so the progressively deeper involvement of the German army in the Holocaust culminates in soldiers murdering Jews for sport in the ghetto of a small town. The "Jew hunts" and "games" conducted by the 12th Company in Szczuczyn stand out as qualitatively different from the actions of German units in Krupki, Krucha, Slonim, and Novogru-dok. Unlike previous killings, the behavior of Kiefer's men, which extends into early 1942, is characterized not only by a general acceptance of a specious military rationale for killing Jews whenever they were encoun-tered as part of normal operations, but also by a greater dehumanization leading to ever more sadistic atrocities against Jews committed *outside* of military operations. This turn shows in stark relief that these soldiers could not live in proximity to genocide and remain untouched. The be-havior of the 12th Company demonstrates the increasingly violent poten-tial unleashed by prolonged contact with Nazi genocidal policy and, more importantly, the depths to which some appear to have internalized agreement with this policy.

Concept of cruelty

CHAPTER NINE

Endgame

It has been shown to me that in the trial against Erren it has been
made clear that the 6th Company, 727th Infantry under the command of First Lieutenant Glück participated in the transport of the
Jews in Slonim with trucks to the killing site and in the cordoning
off of the town during the Action of 14 November 1941. To this I
declare that this occurred without my knowledge and against my
order that units in my regiment could in no way participate in
Jewish actions.

Statement of Josef Pausinger, former commander, 727th Infantry
Regiment, 4 May 1961

THE SUMMER OF 1941 represented for the Germans the high-water
mark in the invasion of the Soviet Union. Victories were frequent,
huge numbers of prisoners were taken, and vast amounts of land were
captured. The men in the German army must have been optimistic that
Hitler's great gamble would soon pay off with a complete collapse of the
Soviet Union. In early October, the Wehrmacht began the assault on
Moscow, Operation Typhoon, an offensive it believed would bring about
Stalin's final defeat. It failed. Already by the end of October, "the Wehrmacht and the Red Army resembled two punch-drunk boxers, staying
precariously on their feet but rapidly losing the power to hurt each
other."[1] By the end of November, it became clear that Moscow would not
fall and that the Red Army was very much alive. A bitter Soviet counteroffensive beginning on 5 December put an exclamation point on that realization. The war diary of one panzer group recorded the results in de-

pressing detail: "Discipline is breaking down. More and more soldiers are heading west on foot without weapons, leading a calf on a rope or pulling a sled loaded with potatoes. The road is under constant air attack. Those killed by bombs are no longer being buried. All the hangers-on (cargo troops, Luftwaffe, supply train) are pouring back to the rear in full flight."[2]

These deteriorating conditions at the front in 1941 had serious implications for the units in this study. German setbacks rapidly became an emergency that required immediate reinforcement. This meant a scouring of the rear areas for forces not yet committed to battle. The 354th Infantry Regiment, along with the other infantry regiments in the security divisions, quickly received orders to join the very real war against the Red Army. By 16 December, the 354th found itself in actual combat. The 339th Division also was called to battle by January 1942. Despite protestations of a dangerous anti-partisan war, these soldiers must have found fighting the Red Army a shocking change from rear-area duty. These Soviet enemies shot back. By 25 January 1942, the 2nd Battalion of the 354th had been consolidated into one company under a lieutenant; in less than two months, the 5th and 7th Companies had lost forty-three men killed or missing, forty-six wounded, and thirty-six men evacuated for frostbite or sickness. The battalion's supply trains had been "shot to pieces," one infantry artillery piece destroyed by a direct hit, and one antitank gun "crushed by a tank."[3] The rHGM complained of the loss of its only real combat power, and the fighting formations at the front complained of the poor quality of the units they received from the rHGM.

The 707th Infantry Division marched down a slightly different path. As the rear areas were robbed of anyone capable of fighting, Bechtolsheim's division became one of the only units capable of any offensive action there. He also became the military commander of Generalbezirk Weissruthenien, which now stretched all the way to Minsk. As such, he became partly responsible for carrying out the anti-partisan war in Belarus.[4] The 707th played a leading role in at least two major anti-partisan operations in the summer of 1942, Operations Bamberg and Dreieck-Viereck. However, in keeping with previous experience, these operations often found and killed more civilians than actual partisans. After Bamberg, the division reported 3,423 partisans and "helpers" killed.

During this massive operation, the 707th lost seven dead and eight wounded (489 dead "partisans" for every German killed).[5] In the course of Operation Dreieck-Viereck, the 6th Company, 727th Infantry Regiment, having left Slonim, drove fifteen to twenty civilians into a barn and burned it to the ground while gunning down anyone who attempted to escape.[6] Though purportedly fighting partisans, Bechtolsheim's men seemed up to their old tricks. They also demonstrated the evolution of an increasingly indiscriminate and lethal brand of "anti-partisan" operations. During Operation Cottbus in the spring of 1943, forty-five hundred "enemy casualties" were reported, along with 492 rifles.[7] Either the partisans were adept at some kind of exceptional weapon-sharing tactic, or the vast majority of these dead were civilians.

The 707th may have avoided the front through its anti-partisan operations initially, but eventually it was consumed along with much of the German army in savage fighting. Encircled near Bobruisk along with seventy thousand men of the Ninth Army, it simply disappeared in July 1944, part of the catastrophic collapse of Army Group Center during the Soviet counteroffensive Operation Bagration.[8] The 286th Security Division met its death near Orscha, sixty-two miles east of Krupki.[9] Army Group Center suffered staggering casualties, with twenty-five divisions and over three hundred thousand men gone in less than two weeks.[10] The 339th Infantry Division (along with Nöll and Sibille's 691st Infantry Regiment) had already been largely destroyed in November 1943.[11] The 354th Infantry Regiment suffered heavy losses as well throughout 1943.

The wholesale destructions of these units, as well as their preceding general employment as conventional units, had important repercussions for this study. First, most of them left behind the rear-area duties in which they were engaged with Jewish policy, never to return. To be sure, they encountered new areas of Nazi state violence, such as POW treatment and the creation of "desert zones" behind the lines, which required the comprehensive deportation of entire civilian populations, but for the most part their role in the murder of the Jews had ended. This means that any longer-term study of these particular men and their participation in the Holocaust becomes increasingly more difficult past the spring of 1942 as they were replaced by other units.

Post war process.
legal process.
Incomprehensible
inactivity

Second, the physical destruction of these organizations at the front often meant that much of their documentation, especially at lower levels, was also destroyed, burned, or scattered across Russian battlefields. This limits the source material for 1941, but particularly for later periods. Moreover, the kinds of materials created by units engaged in combat tell us much less about the unit's relationship with Nazi genocidal policy—generally they were too busy trying to stay alive to pontificate about Judeo-Bolshevism. The destruction wrought by the catastrophic war in the Soviet Union extended beyond the material. It also killed potential witnesses and suspects. The turnover of personnel scattered men who had seen and participated in the mass killings of 1941 across a vast and increasingly more lethal battlefield. In addition, the ability to blame all excesses on fallen comrades would complicate the process of trying these men after the war.

Unfortunately, few of the perpetrators identified in this study ever went to trial, let alone paid for their crimes. In 1970, a Dutch newspaper characterized the entire postwar German legal process as one of "incomprehensible inactivity."[12] For a variety of reasons, legal, political, and cultural, Wehrmacht crimes in the East tended not to be pursued. The Nuremberg Tribunals and subsequent Nuremberg Military Tribunals (NMT) focused, for the most part, on high-level political and SS players in the Nazi regime, as well as on more sensational perpetrators such as the German medical establishment.[13] The Einsatzgruppen received a great deal of attention in subsequent trials, but these again focused on leadership, and the army did not figure prominently at all. Even the trials of the most guilty perpetrators ended with light sentences and quick clemencies.[14] One important exception to the focus on higher leaders was the Ulm Einsatzgruppen Trial of 1958, which did focus on lower-lever perpetrators and caused outrage among the defendants, as their superiors were already out of jail by that time.[15]

The German military high command received its own trials, which focused mainly on aggressive war, mistreatment of POWs, and violations of the prohibitions against harming civilians. Though most were convicted, none were sentenced to death. Military reprisals and crimes

Hostages/ — Balkan — Yugo/ Greece

against civilians in Yugoslavia and Greece warranted their own proceeding, which came to be known as the "Hostages Trial" or "Balkan generals trial." In general, however, Allied prosecution of military war criminals confined itself to higher-level commanders and those responsible for crimes committed against Allied prisoners, particularly American and British POWs. Even then, prosecutors "had to overcome the widely held and frequently cited belief that atrocities occur in all wars, on all sides, and that there was nothing ideologically or qualitatively distinct about the German military's conduct."[16] While the SS was among those organizations officially termed "criminal," the military escaped this pronouncement.[17] In addition, the sheer number of Wehrmacht prisoners and the ignorance of Allied military counterintelligence teams of the regime's crimes in the East allowed many war criminals to escape detection and successfully become denazified. The struggle over the criminality of the military certainly "went to the heart of German postwar national identity."[18]

As West Germany regained its sovereignty in 1949, it also assumed responsibility for the prosecution of Nazi crimes. Unfortunately, the political climate of the 1950s did not support energetic prosecution of lower-level perpetrators, in either Germany. In the West, the Allies themselves had already begun pardoning or commuting the sentences of the same criminals they had convicted at Nuremberg. This new leniency also coincided with the end of denazification, which allowed many former Nazis to return to their prewar occupations and often the same positions they had left. The growing Cold War impressed upon the Allies the need for military experts who had fought the Red Army, and a focus on prosecuting Wehrmacht veterans was counterproductive in this regard. As Donald Bloxham writes, "The leaders of the liberal democracies lost concern for examining the war record of their new ally, and their counterparts in the BRD [Bundesrepublik Deutschland, or West Germany] proved adept at exploiting the situation to whitewash the record of German soldiery. The process was consummated symbolically when in 1951 Dwight Eisenhower publicly withdrew any general accusation against the Wehrmacht."[19] In East Germany, any continued prosecution of Nazis threw an uncomfortable light on the deep complicity of Germans in the Third Reich at a time when the Communist government was seeking to unite all East Germans as socialist victims of Nazi oppression. The GDR would increasingly confine itself to outing prominent West Germans with Nazi pasts for political purposes, pointing out the speck in its neighbor's eyes and ignoring the log in its own.

Domestically, the crimes of the Third Reich were overshadowed by the return of Wehrmacht POWs from Soviet captivity in the 1950s. These men were seen as heroes, "courageous men who had fought and won the battle against Communist brutality."[20] They were installed in the triad of German suffering along with ethnic German expellees from the East and bombing victims. This inward focus left no room to consider Germans as perpetrators, at least individually. Konrad Adenauer's 1955 visit to Moscow and his recognition of Germany's obligation to pay reparations to the Jewish people seemed for many to close the book on both national and individual discussions of culpability in Nazi genocide. In Moscow, Adenauer himself pointed out to the Soviets, for example, that "in exceptional cases, German soldiers may have committed excesses, but even the western Allies had been willing to overturn sentences for war crimes, issued immediately after the war in an 'atmosphere burdened by emotional feelings.'"[21] Indeed, for Adenauer, a focus on restitution allowed him to "reassure conservative voters that it was not the first step toward a more extensive judicial, political, and social confrontation with crimes of the Nazi era."[22] One prominent historian has argued that the "delay and thus denial of justice was the greatest single failing of Adenauer's approach to building a democracy after Nazism."[23]

The German legal apparatus itself was not particularly interested in prosecuting military defendants. Indeed, it often seemed eager to justify crimes committed in the East. The fact that practically all Wehrmacht proceedings failed to come to trial is one reflection of this tendency. Many jurists seemed to legitimize the crimes committed in the war of annihilation. One 1972 trial ruled that the destruction of twenty-five Greek villages and murder of at least 690 civilians as a reprisal measure was "necessary" because the partisans "violated the basic rules of the international law."[24] At other times, courts consciously used a legal element from the Military Criminal Code that stated "if the guilt of the subordinate is small, then a sentence may be dispensed with" to absolve both military and nonmilitary defendants alike, such as police or Einsatzgruppen members.[25]

Despite such institutional obstacles, the Central Office for the Investigation of National Socialist Crime began operation in the small baroque town of Ludwigsburg near Stuttgart in December 1958. The Central Office would serve from then on as a clearinghouse for all information regarding the investigation of Nazi criminals, assisting local prosecutors and referring cases to the appropriate authorities. Headquartered in a former women's prison, these men of the Central Office must have felt that in the German legal system the inmates were running the asylum. Conscientious investigators and prosecutors in Ludwigsburg and elsewhere in West Germany often found the deck stacked against them, for they faced a variety of challenges.

The first was the law itself. Generally, all crimes committed during the Nazi era had various statutes of limitations based on the potential sentence, all beginning at the end of the war. If an investigation was opened against an individual, this clock would stop. Otherwise, it would continue to run and, eventually, grant the suspect immunity from prosecution. Initially, for example, crimes subject to life imprisonment had a statute of limitations of twenty years; those subject to imprisonment for more than ten years, fifteen years; and other criminal acts, ten years.[26] Investigators scrambled to at least open investigations against Nazi criminals even when suspects remained at large or unknown, and thereby to interrupt the statute of limitations clock, allowing more time to investigate. The potential length of sentence due to the definition of the crime and its accompanying statute of limitations thus had a great impact on the course of postwar justice.

Those definitions of various categories of crimes further constrained legal action. The statute of limitations on first-degree murder was eventually abolished, thus allowing it to remain one of the only crimes within the reach of prosecutors. It was, however, defined in the following particularly unhelpful way: "A murderer is a person who kills another person from thirst for blood, satisfaction of his sexual desires, avarice, or other base motives in a malicious or brutal manner or one dangerous to public safety or in order to permit the commission or concealment of another criminal act."[27] Thus, it was motive that defined murder. The legal requirement to prove "base motives" or a "malicious or brutal manner" often made it impossible to charge suspects with murder, as they rarely admitted to racial hatred, and because routinized methods of killing in the East, when not accompanied by individual "excesses," were not deemed "malicious or brutal." German law required that murderers be proven to have been initiative takers.[28] This meant that most of these men fell into the category of "aiding and abetting" or accessories/accomplices to murder, which constituted a lesser charge with lighter sentences.[29] The statute of limitations on manslaughter, a more easily tried offense covering many of the actions of these Wehrmacht soldiers, had run out in 1960.[30] A sleeper amendment to the legal code added in 1968 further hamstrung prosecution of all but the worst Nazi killers. It required that in order to sentence a convicted accomplice to life in prison, the burden of base motives must now be met.[31] If base motives could not be proven, then the maximum sentence was capped at fifteen years. Now, given that all crimes that carried a maximum sentence of fifteen years had a statute of limitations of fifteen years, this meant that the overwhelming majority of "accomplices"—if they had not already been tried—could no longer be indicted for their crimes after this amendment.[32] By 1971, one justice official had been predicting a coming "landslide" of new investigations that needed to be opened based on the statute of limitations imposed.[33]

These legal loopholes were particularly convenient, given the reluctance of West German courts to convict anyone not at Nuremberg of being a main perpetrator *(Haupttäter)*. Indeed, many judges deemed Hitler, Himmler, and Heydrich to be the *Haupttäters*, lumping everyone else into the category of accomplices or accessories. For the West German legal system and many judges, this was evidence of a belief that Hitler, Himmler, and Heydrich "bore sole responsibility for the regime's murderous actions."[34] The case against Otto Bradfisch was illustrative of this. Bradfisch was Schönemann's superior, in charge of Einsatzkommando 8 in Belarus. The court ruled that he had not shown any "desire to kill independent of the order" or to have had a "hostile attitude" toward Jews.[35] This was by no means exceptional. Indeed, in 1971 *Der Spiegel* published a damning piece accusing the Hamburg prosecutor's office of gross negligence. It noted that the case against Gerhard Erren, the Gebietskommissar in Slonim, had been "pending" for twelve years without result.[36] This apparent lack of effort in prosecuting war criminals was perhaps even more widespread when the accused were soldiers. In the case of the massacre of forty-three hundred Italian soldiers at Cephalonia, a German court weakly wrote that "no living Wehrmacht soldiers could be found" who were "responsible or participated" in the shootings. In addition, officers who were deposed did not "'come into question as suspects' either due to lack of evidence or because the elements of the crime of manslaughter had fallen under the statute of limitations."[37]

One can add to these difficulties that, because of the at best incomplete nature of denazification, the judges and police investigators had often been Nazis themselves and were less than unbiased. In 1949, for example, 81 percent of judges in Bavaria were former Nazis.[38] The overall body of jurisprudence created by West German judges indicated that their former Nazi affiliation was not benign. They often used the law to convict as few as possible and to sentence that few as leniently as possible. Certainly one reason for these rulings was the desire of some judges to avoid scrutiny of their own behavior during the Third Reich. Ties to the former regime were not limited to the judiciary. Like the judges, more than a few policemen were reticent to put much effort into investigating war criminals. Many police investigators and other personnel had served in the Nazi police and sometimes even in the SD or Einsatzgruppen, and sometimes they helped their comrades. One former Einsatzgruppen killer became a senior police official after the war. In this position, he clearly benefited from both his knowledge of the criminal system and his familiarity with those tasked with investigating him.[39] When German police officials served a search warrant on the former commander of the SD in Warsaw, Ludwig Hahn, they were astonished to find that he already had "not just ten binders of photocopied witness statements [in the case against him] but also photocopies of the most recent notes of the States Attorney's office [in the case against him] from which he could learn the names and addresses of witnesses who had not yet been interviewed."[40] High-ranking SS man Werner Best often appeared as defense witness in the 1960s and was a "central figure" in the self-help network for accused Nazi war criminals. One investigator characterized him as a "spider in a web."[41]

Finally, prosecutors and investigators did not possess the vast knowledge of the contours of the Holocaust that we have today. They were often scrambling to beat the statute of limitations and were unable to unearth many perpetrators. Because of the Cold War, much of the information concerning crimes in the East remained locked behind the Iron Curtain and often unavailable. Jewish witnesses were hard to locate. Many police investigators seemed less than interested in uncovering the truth; often, for example, they would uncritically accept a suspect's statement that he knew nothing, without further questioning. Moreover, while many of the prosecutors in Ludwigsburg were young and energetic in their preliminary investigations, local prosecutors to whom the cases were subsequently assigned for trial were often not excited about taking on cases that offered little chance of success and would be unpopular in the public eye, if not in their own. The German news magazine *Der Spiegel* reported that the Hamburg prosecutor left the files on the Erren case sealed in their shipping boxes in his office for a whole year.[42] The head of the Central Office himself predicted pessimistically in 1972 that "in a few years the point would be reached where 'convictions of those perpetrators still alive will fail due to the almost insurmountable difficulties of the burden of proof.'"[43]

The legal outcomes of the cases in this study illustrate the impact of many of these obstacles. In the case of the 354th Infantry Regiment and the murder of the Jews of Krupki, most of those investigated were not charged, owing to lack of evidence. These were mainly enlisted soldiers. The court was remarkably sensitive to the defendants, stating: "The fact that countless suspects could give no explanation for why they were not engaged does not rule out that such circumstances could have presented themselves. It is well within the realm of possibility that as a result of the long passage of time or due to difficult experiences in the course of the war that the suspects have forgotten. In any case, concrete evidence of their participation has not been found."[44] Even the main perpetrators avoided any prosecution. The court dismissed regimental commander von Rekowski's case because it could not be proven that he knowingly supported the action. Lieutenant Nick and the commander of the 10th Company escaped prosecution because it could not be proven that they were not in personal danger had they disobeyed orders. The battalion adjutant, Lieutenant Speth, was found guilty of being an accessory. However, because of the statute of limitations, he was released as well. Charges against the first sergeant of 12th Company, Hans H., were dismissed owing to lack of evidence. The court found that Major Waldow, the battalion commander, had not acted out of his "own base motives," but as a result of his age and education should have known better. His actions were described by the court in ways indicating that an indictment would follow, but the proceedings went no further as a result of his heart condition and inability to stand trial.[45] Werner Schönemann, who had led his own unit in Einsatzkommando 8 that killed tens of thousands of Jews, was found guilty of aiding and abetting murder on twelve counts of a total of 2,170 people and sentenced to only six years in prison.[46]

Friedrich Nöll, commander of the 3rd Company, 691st Infantry Regiment, had returned to Germany after the war and by December 1945 had resumed his prewar occupation as an elementary school teacher in his hometown of Griesheim.[47] However, he and his first sergeant, Emil Zimber, went to trial and were actually convicted for their actions in Krucha. The battalion commander, Commichau, who issued the order, did not survive the war. The 691st regimental commander declined responsibility, replying to questioning with the self-exculpatory platitude that "these things can only be judged in light of the situation at the time, where the troops had to live in the worst conditions for weeks on end and were exposed to constant treacherous partisan attacks."[48] Of course, as we have seen, this type of partisan warfare was hardly present at the time of the murders. In the end, the court found Friedrich Nöll guilty of knowingly overseeing a minimum of sixty cases of manslaughter, noting that he could not have "feared for life and limb as a result of his refusal" and was "merely afraid that his avoidance of the order would be uncomfortably noted."[49] When Nöll weakly told the court that his personal intervention in the killings was "superfluous" because his "people were so well behaved," the presiding judge acidly replied, "'Behaved' is a fully tasteless expression here. As we will hear from witnesses, thank God that not all people are 'so well behaved.'"[50] Emil Zimber, Nöll's right-hand man, had returned to work as a policeman after the war. He was given three years' probation by the denazification court.[51] When he was tried in 1953, Zimber was found guilty as an accessory to the sixty cases of manslaughter; the court concluded "that the achievement of the battalion commander's desires would have been unthinkable without Zimber's supporting activities."[52] He remained indignant to the end. In a letter seeking an appeal, he wrote, "It is inconceivable that one could now describe us old soldiers as murderers. . . . I am also of the opinion that a civilian court cannot pass judgment on a wartime event."[53] If the court's judgment appeared at least somewhat stern, its sentences were not. Nöll and Zimber were initially sentenced to four and three years in prison respectively, but these were both reduced by a year on appeal in 1956.

Nöll's prison time paints him as a conflicted man in much the same way that his behavior in Krucha does. According to supervisors, he "conscientiously" worked as an orderly in the prison hospital. The prison doctor described this man who had ordered the murder of women and children as working "tirelessly" and treating patients with a "touching diligence."[54] The warden characterized him as having served his sentence as a form of "atonement," which he "as a believing Christian unconditionally accepted." He further noted that "in many conversations with him, it [was] apparent that he had been tormented with his guilt for many years" and that he "recognized without condition" that his actions were a "grave injustice." Nöll had lacked the "moral courage and manliness" to refuse. His jailer concluded his assessment of the former army officer by judging that his crimes had "at least subjectively been atoned for."[55] Public outcry in his village of Griesheim had ended Friedrich Nöll's teaching duties by 1956.[56] His only son was missing and presumed dead on the eastern front. Nöll appears in the end to be a sad, broken man, yet this outcome should not distract from his fateful decisions in October 1941 and certainly provides no succor to the innocent men, women, and children of Krucha murdered on his orders.

Finally, the cases of Slonim and Novogrudok also failed to provide any substantive punishment for Wehrmacht crimes. In the Slonim case, only a private and a sergeant were tried, and not for the murder of the Jews but for a hanging that took place shortly before. The charges were dismissed for lack of evidence.[57] The vast majority of soldiers who testified to their participation in the November killing operation in Slonim were, in fact, testifying against Gerhard Erren, the Gebietskommissar, and were not themselves charged with anything. The "Golden Pheasant" of Slonim had returned to Germany and, like Nöll, resumed duties as a teacher.[58] Erren himself was convicted of conspiracy to commit murder and sentenced to life in prison. Unfortunately, the conviction was overturned on appeal owing to a technicality, and Erren was then conveniently unable to stand trial for health reasons.[59] The Hamburg justice minister, Ernst Heinsen, a Social Democrat, lamented in 1971 that "no Gebietskommissar has yet been convicted in any case in West Germany."[60] Leopold Windisch, the Gebietskommissar in Lida, also benefited from legal malfeasance. After a yearlong trial, he got a mistrial because a regional court judge had been secretly taping the proceedings.[61] He was finally sentenced to life in prison in 1969.[62]

Johann Artmann, whose 7th Company assisted in the killings in Novogrudok, stuck to the fantastically unlikely story that "if members of my company stood sentry duty at the execution site, then someone must have ordered them to do so. I was certainly not that person. I ordered nothing of the kind and had no knowledge of it. . . . I am aware of no guilt. I have done nothing that would justify the charges leveled against me."[63] Amazingly, he was spared prosecution because the court reasoned that "it could not expect a conviction on the charges"; it had determined that Lieutenant Martin had acted alone.[64]

For the 12th Company in Szczuczyn, charges against Captain Kiefer were dropped for lack of evidence. Charges against Lieutenant Ritterbusch were dropped because "he appeared after investigation . . . not sufficiently suspect" and because "countless witnesses based on their knowledge of the accused found it out of the question [that he could have committed the acts]."[65] Lieutenant Schaffitz, however, was turned over to a Polish court and sentenced to death in 1948 (though this was later commuted to a life sentence).[66] He died in a Warsaw prison.

How well do the units in this study represent the German army's participation in the Holocaust as a whole? Consider a 25 July 1941 order from the 102nd Infantry Division, also stationed in rHGM. It reported that "until further notice, an Advance Group . . . under the leadership of SS-Obersturmführer Schulz-Isenbeck is detached from Group III of Einsatzkommando 9 (currently in Vileyka) and is attached to the division staff. Tasks of the Advance Group: Support and advising of the Division in all political and state-security affairs . . . Supervision of political and criminal affairs in the division area."[67] This fragmented mention of cooperation with the Einsatzgruppen in the daily orders of a Wehrmacht unit is typical. In the absence of a court case or other detailed investigation into a specific act, the meaning of such references appears frustratingly vague. However, we know that "political and criminal affairs" almost always included anti-Jewish policy. We also know that SS-Obersturmführer Schulz-Isenbeck had led an action that murdered eighty Jews in Lida on 5 July 1941 and that in the first half of August, EK 9 "in Vileyka shot at least 320 Jews in various 'operations,' including women and children."[68] While we may not know exactly what kind of interaction Schulz-Isenbeck had with the 102nd Division, this relationship is highly suggestive of this unit's complicity in the Holocaust. What was the SD advising the Wehrmacht about, and what were they supervising? The Mogilev Conference offered some plausible answers. Yet as this one piece of fragmentary evidence shows, in the absence of further documentation it is difficult to conclusively prove complicity.

Yet, in order to better weigh the significance of this study, we must consider the issue of representativeness. How characteristic were the actions of the military units, as well as the actions of the individuals and leaders involved? Indeed, how typical were these units themselves? We have already seen that the security divisions such as the 286th were second- or third-rate at best. They were underequipped, undermanned, undertrained, and overage. After the winter crisis of 1941–42, these divisions lost their best-trained infantry regiments to frontline duty; these losses, if they were made good at all, were filled by even more unsuitable units such as *Landesschützen* battalions.[69] In regard to its antisemitic orders and complicity, the 286th is certainly in line with its fellow security divisions in rHGM, the 221st and 403rd. The 707th and 339th Infantry Divisions were also not so far removed from other frontline divisions fighting in rHGM. Both these units were of higher quality and ended up fighting at the front. In any case, all the units investigated here are far

more typical of the Wehrmacht as a whole than the SS or police formations that have provided material for several excellent prior studies.[70]

Situational factors played an important role in determining both
whether and how units would become involved in genocide. These can
be temporal, spatial, and mental. How do we sort all these in an attempt
to determine how far the findings of this study apply? In this endeavor,
the legal concepts of means, motive, and opportunity provide a useful
framework. Assuming that most units possessed the ability to murder
Jews by shooting, what about motive? Did other units possess similar
organizational climates and mentalities that would allow them to kill,
given the chance?

A brief survey of thirteen other divisions in rHGM helps address
these questions.[71] These "control" divisions, first- and second-line infantry divisions, as well as two security divisions, passed through central Belarus in the same areas as the case study units. Some were fighting
in conventional combat, and others were temporarily involved in occupation or rear-area duties. Between June 21 and November/December
1941, these divisions followed a roughly northeasterly trajectory from
Warsaw through Minsk toward Smolensk before becoming ensnared in
the struggle for Moscow. Looking at the documentary record of these
other divisions can help us better situate the units described in this book.

First, several of these divisions also exhibited antisemitic climates in
their orders and reports. The division commander of the 252nd Infantry
Division, General der Kavallerie Diether von Böhm-Bezing, told his
men at the end of September: "As your division commander and comrade for two long years, I know that each of you has worked through this
war that was forced upon us by international Jewry and freemasonry toward the greatest victory our history has ever known even as this can
only be achieved through difficult battle on Russian soil."[72] Three
months later, his Christmas message exuded a similar antisemitic, anti-
Bolshevik tone: "In these days of Christmas, the sacrifice of our fallen
and wounded comrades finds its transfiguration. Entrenched in this
Russian ground that we have freed from Bolshevism and the Jews, we
want to prepare ourselves to go forward to the final victory in firm confi-
dence in our strength, in unerring belief in the future of our Fatherland,
and with a tenacious will. Comrades of the 252nd Division, not for us,

but all for our homeland, our people, our Führer."[73] In both messages distributed to his entire command, the general identifies Jews and Bolsheviks as the main enemy. The 258th Division, like other units in the East, chose the phrase "Beat the Jew Kommissar" as its password for Russian soldiers to use when deserting.[74] In the 221st Security Division, one regimental commander reported to the division that "the Jewish question must be more radically solved."[75] The 87th Division reported that "it can be observed that, compared to Jews in the formerly Polish regions, the Jews [in Minsk] give off a very self-confident and insolent impression."[76]

Other units did not perhaps display their antisemitism so prominently, but at least some of them were already dealing with issues of Nazi racial policy. Feldkommandantur 184 in Brest presided over the mass arrest of the male population there on 7 July 1941 in which the 162nd Division was involved; the next day Police Battalion 307 and the SD shot four thousand Jews and four hundred non-Jews.[77] Less than a week later, the war diary for the 102nd Infantry Division reported on Lithuanian militias operating in its area: "For the first time, questions have surfaced whose solution, because of their half-political character, is particularly delicate. A decision from the Army is not forthcoming despite multiple requests. . . . As they so far proved quite useful and also emphasize antisemitism and convey an anti-Bolshevik character, the division has ordered that militias [*Hilfspolizeitruppen*] be recognized as legal, and be treated favorably, but that all political discussions be refused."[78] At this time, the 102nd was stationed just east of Vilnius, Lithuania. Clearly, here the division's leadership was willing to accept (or even encourage) a violent solution to certain "questions," as long as it was not directly involved in approving it. Again, passivity by the command allowed the unit to follow an inertial path to ever-deeper complicity.

Antisemitic rhetoric found expression in concrete policies as well. The 78th Infantry Division expressly forbade the use of Jews as interpreters and in any other capacity.[79] The 252nd Infantry Division (whose commander already demonstrated his adherence to Nazi racial beliefs) ordered on 26 July 1941 that "requests or complaints from the Jewish population are to be rejected by all units. The complainant is to be referred to the responsible police office."[80] Such referrals would have had predictably negative results. These control divisions also routinely used Jews as slave labor. The 87th Division noted on 16 July that "Jews, which are heavily represented in the White Russian Soviet republic, were subjected to coercive measures through a general order by Army Group Center (Rear)."[81] The report went on to describe the imposition of the yellow star and the creation of Jewish councils and ghettos, all presumably under the auspices of the army. The 221st Security Division likewise reported conducting repair work on roads and bridges using "all available Jews."[82] The 102nd Division assigned its civil affairs staff section the task of "acquisition of Jewish-administered assets."[83] The rHGM noted that "200 suspect civilians, mainly Jews, were caught as a result of street checkpoints."[84] Thus, the documentation suggests that these units were acting on the antisemitic rhetoric they were preaching.

Jews were not only abused, subjected to forced labor, and robbed of their property, but also physically targeted and specifically identified as casualties, most notably by the 252nd and 102nd Divisions. In July, the 232nd Infantry Regiment of the 102nd Infantry Division was reporting Jews killed in the course of its security operations. On 20 July, it claimed two Communist functionaries, three Jews, and five Poles had been executed "because they were still active as communists after the occupation of the area . . . and in particular had incited the population against the Wehrmacht."[85] Two days later, the same regiment reported four Jews shot for "continuing terrorism of the local population, sabotage of Wehrmacht efforts, plundering, etc."[86] The 162nd Infantry Division ominously reproached its own troops, saying: "The notion that it is only the police but not the army who should shoot partisans, armed people, and suspicious persons is completely false. It is completely vital that we demonstrate our will to take drastic measures . . . on the spot in a timely manner."[87] Such an order is also interesting in that it suggests that some soldiers needed additional convincing in order to carry out this policy. As we have seen, a blurring of the lines between the anti-partisan effort and racial policy was also a recurring theme in the cases treated here.

Another way in which these formations abetted the Holocaust was through their close collaboration with the SS, Einsatzgruppen, and other Nazi organizations, as seen in the case of Schulz-Isenbeck. Evidence from other divisions suggests that they, too, were not unaware of the actions of these killing units and in many cases supported them. Organizationally, several units made their relationship with the Einsatzgruppen clear. In a memorandum explaining its duties for rear security, the 102nd Division explicitly stated that under the jurisdiction of Section VII (an *army* staff section) were "general administrative affairs of the land and civil population . . . *collection of assets managed by Jews* [emphasis mine] . . . Police affairs . . . Liaison with Order Police, Security Police, and SD."[88] The executive officer of the 87th Infantry Division returned from a meeting at rHGM headquarters and noted in the unit war diary: "Jews are to be collected together in ghettos. . . . Cooperation with the police [including] Einsatzkommando Major Dr. Bratfisch [*sic*]."[89] The 252nd Division informed its soldiers on 16 July that "Einsatzkommando 8 of the SD, with its headquarters in Baranovichi [*sic*] . . . and a branch office in Slonim and Novogrudok is dependent on the cooperation of the Division. This command primarily handles all political issues and defensive affairs, but also advises the *Feldkommandanturen* in the selection of trusted persons as mayors and economic leaders. Captured communists (civilians) are to be handed over to the SD."[90] The next day it was clear that this cooperation was already taking place, as the division reported the "execution of a police roundup in Slonim in the course of the day during which a large number of communists and unsafe elements were arrested."[91] This was most likely one of the first Einsatzgruppen actions against Jews in Slonim.

Recognition of structural relationships led to actual collaboration in other control divisions as well. The 102nd Division informed its units that a ten-man advance party from Einsatzkommando 9 had been attached to the division. Likewise, the 87th Division reminded its men that "suspect persons and those who are not caught in the act are to be handed over with the proper documentation to Einsatzkommando 8 of the security police and the SD in Minsk."[92] The 162nd Division went so far as to request that elements of Einsatzgruppe B conduct an action against "former Communist party members" near Bialystok; seventeen individuals were arrested and "liquidated."[93] Four of these divisions also had working relationships with both SS infantry and cavalry brigades, which as we have seen were deeply involved in carrying out the Final Solution in the East.[94] Being assigned control of these SS units did not always mean direct complicity in acts of genocide. At times, they were assigned as actual combat units. This was likely the case for two squadrons of the 1st SS Cavalry Regiment that formed the so-called Vorausabteilung (advance section) and were attached to the 162nd Infantry Division to help combat a Soviet counterattack.[95] However, when the Vorausabteilung was transferred to the 252nd Infantry Division on 17 August, it had already been very busy murdering at least eleven thousand Jewish men, women, and children in the northern reaches of the Pripet Marshes.[96] The documentary evidence of collaboration between army units and Einsatzgruppen certainly needs more investigation but indicates a high degree of active cooperation in genocide.

If there was one area in which almost complete agreement existed between these units and those highlighted in the previous cases, it was in the necessity of harshness against all civilians encountered during antipartisan operations. In September, the 258th Infantry Division forwarded a typical declaration from its corps headquarters: "Ruthlessly fight the partisan with the harshest measures. Any charity and lenience is wrong and indicates weakness which ultimately costs us our own blood."[97] The 162nd Division ordered one regiment to round up and shoot all "suspect men" in three towns.[98] The 87th Division exhibited a particularly anti-Polish attitude in a memorandum from 8 July 1941: "The basic principle regarding personal behavior toward the population is that the Pole is not to be seen as our friend, but as our enemy. German soldiers are met with happiness by the Polish population only as a result of the repression and expropriation of the bolshevik ruler. This should, however, not conceal that the Poles are ruled by a strong nationalism and that they wait for the moment to fall upon the German army from behind as they did in 1918."[99] Certainly in these actions we can see the same brutal policy toward civilians as was suggested at the Mogilev Conference. The 162nd Division went so far as to order that "every civilian on the battlefield is to be shot at."[100] These kinds of guidance, though not necessarily always directed at Jews, certainly reflected an expansive definition of "enemy" and encouraged ruthless elimination of those termed so. Such a unit culture could then ease the way for Jews to be treated similarly.

If many of these control divisions held similar antisemitic beliefs and also exhibited similarly harsh and brutal attitudes toward civilians, why, then, did these units not participate in the mass killings of Jews that the 707th, 339th, and 286th did? The first possibility may be that some did, but that no records exist to prove participation, or at least there were no trials involved that brought to light the details of such involvement. Certainly, many more units participated in the Nazi genocidal project than were uncovered in investigations after the war. As the Wehrmacht evaded most judicial attention, however, we lack the specificity and corroboration that such investigations provide.

When army units had the opportunity to participate or were assigned such duties, it seems that they did. Yet not all of these divisions had the opportunity. At least some of these divisions were mainly occupied with fighting and mopping up surrounded pockets of Red Army soldiers before being thrown into the destructive battles for Smolensk and Moscow. Very simply, this meant that by their position on the battlefield these units were often too busy with combat to be involved in genocidal policy, though they could certainly have been involved in carrying out the Commissar Order and with anti-partisan-related atrocities against civilians.

An example of the importance of opportunity (and its combination with motive) comes from two of the units that appear most prominently in conjunction with anti-Jewish actions among the control divisions. The 102nd and the 252nd both spent a large amount of time in rear areas, conducting security operations. It is perhaps not surprising then that they became more deeply embroiled in carrying out genocide, for this is where, by and large, it was taking place. Rear-area duty was not something these units looked forward to. Neither the 102nd nor the 252nd was happy with its assignment. Trying to put a positive spin on his mission, the commander of the 252nd termed this duty "quiet but not to be undervalued detail work."[101] The 102nd Division, however, expressed its feelings more honestly in its war diary. After learning that the division would again be relegated to rear-area duty, the officer in charge of the war diary recorded: "That this wish [for frontline duty] was once again not fulfilled raises in the best of us a feeling of bitterness."[102] The experience of these divisions before they, too, were sent to the front supports some of the conclusions of this study. The longer a unit was involved on a daily basis and at close proximity to genocidal policy, the deeper it grew complicit and the more extreme its actions became.

This is not to say that all divisions behaved equally. The 28th Infantry Division told its men that "poor treatment by our own troops drives the population into the arms of the partisans."[103] The 78th Division likewise instructed its soldiers that they were to "refrain from violent reprisals against towns where communist cells were found or in whose vicinity attacks on [German soldiers] have taken place when it cannot be without a doubt proven that the inhabitants were the perpetrators or were in contact with them."[104] The division commander, General Curt Gallenkamp, personally warned his soldiers against the thefts of property and livestock that were increasing in the division area. "I will leave no doubt that I will have every complaint investigated by the military police and will sentence the offenders by court-martial."[105] German units, however, were often much harsher in their punishments of theft than of murders.

In Army Group North (Rear), the 207th Security Division did publish an order in July 1941 in which the division commander termed the Einsatzgruppen actions "fully separate from those of the troops" and then "once again forbid expressly that members of the division take part in, supervise, authorize, or supply troops to such actions."[106] An infantry regiment commander in Army Group South remarked, "If we considered them [Soviet POWs] as proper soldiers and told them we were taking them prisoner and sending them to Germany to show them the social conditions [there], then their resistance would be less."[107] The 112th Division in Belarus reported that the population had been "thankful" that the division had "avoided unnecessary harshness in the acquisition of provisions and feed and had punished violations by individual soldiers. In this way," the staff summarized, "we won their trust and received alerts of unsafe elements."[108]

An understanding of the necessity of winning hearts and minds, while perhaps a rare insight in the German army, does not simultaneously prove any disagreement with racial policy. It does indicate that units could have different interpretations of what behavior was to be accepted, depending on the context, and that divisional commanders could foster different unit climates. In the end, however, the actions of the majority made any winning of hearts and minds impossible. A propaganda specialist sent in 1943 to assist German forces reported frankly that he "saw no way of carrying out his job, 'since there is nothing favorable to us that I can say to the people.' "[109]

The 102nd Infantry Division in Belarus provides an excellent example of this bipolarity in operation, in the context of the anti-partisan war. The division received the following order from its parent headquarters, the 40th Army Corps, on 13 August 1941. Recognizing that it would be difficult to catch partisans in the act, the order, which was passed on to all units, stated: "All suspects are to be immediately shot at the order of a company or other commander. Communist party members, members of a communist organization, or Jews are particularly suspicious if they are found near the scene of a crime and cannot prove that they are inhabitants of the nearest village or contradict themselves under questioning."[110] Such an order clearly demanded both a very loose definition of suspect and particularly ruthless treatment of those cursorily deemed suspicious. However, two weeks later, the division appeared to publish more-nuanced guidelines that distinguished between cut-off enemy soldiers and real partisan resistance. In a division order, under the heading "Behavior upon Capture," the 102nd told its units: "Prisoner statements in the last couple days have revealed that it is only the fear of being shot that has kept the greater part of bypassed soldiers from giving themselves up to captivity. It is strictly forbidden to shoot prisoners. . . . Earlier regulations for partisans, snipers, etc. are not affected."[111] Even this slightly more lenient verbiage still draws a distinction between "prisoners" and "partisans," with the latter clearly still subject to summary execution.

In the end, however, these statements are more indicative of a disconnect in military leadership: orders advocating a more nuanced treatment of the population were often overshadowed by those demanding ever more brutal behavior. Perhaps individual officers or even staff sections were willing to be more circumspect in dealing with civilians, but the larger organizational mentality tended to drown out their voices.

In other regions of the Soviet Union as well, the German army also placed itself at the disposal of the Nazi murder machine. The most atrocious example occurred in Kiev. On 24 September 1941, while the Mogilev Conference was in full swing, explosives left behind by NKVD operatives killed an army artillery commander and his chief of staff.[112] In retaliation, Wehrmacht commander Major General Friedrich Eberhard,

Babi Yar

in close coordination with the SS and the Einsatzgruppen, ordered a massive reprisal that culminated in the killing of over thirty-three thousand Ukrainian Jews. The German army did not simply spur this killing, but again actively assisted the Einsatzgruppen in the now infamous massacre of Jews at Babi Yar. It was the largest mass shooting on Soviet soil.

Much larger portions of the German army participated in some degree in the mass starvation and murder of Soviet POWs throughout the occupied territories. One general taped in captivity in 1944 recalled a camp of twenty thousand POWs who "at night howled like wild beasts" from starvation. "Then," he continued, "we marched down the road and a column of 6,000 tottering figures went past, completely emaciated, helping each other along. . . . Soldiers of ours on bicycles rode alongside with pistols; everyone who collapsed was shot and thrown into the ditch."[113] Experiences like these were probably more frequent for German soldiers than those involving Jews; however, they, too, contributed to an organizational environment that encouraged brutality.

German soldiers also operated in a climate in which knowledge of the Nazi genocidal project was not hard to come by. In fact, there were many reports *from* German soldiers about all facets of the Holocaust from a variety of perspectives. One German soldier, Hubert Pfoch, spent a good deal of time near a Jewish transport when his troop train stopped at Treblinka station in August 1942. Even at that relatively early stage in the Final Solution, he wrote in his diary, "Every day ten to fifteen thousand are gassed and burned."[114] Another soldier learned of mass executions from his father, who was an engineer in East Galicia.[115] Many more men observed firsthand killings in the Soviet Union, so that very quickly the intent and execution of genocide were no mysteries to the men, but an ever-present and (at least institutionally) acceptable condition of war in the East.

The important point here is that the overall culture in the Wehrmacht was not a neutral one. Rather, the environment advocated and rewarded escalating violence and participation in Nazi genocidal plans that purportedly lay outside the realm of military affairs. A survey of similar kinds of units in the same region at the same time suggests that they have much in common with the units in this study. Expressions of blatant antisemitism were not isolated, though there were varying levels of virulence among different divisions. What was certainly prevalent was a proclivity to violence against civilians and a willingness to knowingly collude with the SS, SD, and police battalions. Moreover, in units such as the 252nd and 102nd that were employed as occupation troops, we see glimpses of the same progression toward a normalization of complicity in genocide. It would appear that many units were as *capable* of similar genocidal behavior as the ones investigated for this study. The deciding factor appears to have been, to a large extent, whether or not the unit was put into a situation of extended contact with Jews and occupation policy— that is, whether or not it had the opportunity to participate. More often than not, those that did have the opportunity ended up becoming more and more complicit. However, some units, but more often individuals, did refuse to comply, managed to evade participation, or, more rarely, attempted to aid Jews.

Determining the frequency of noncompliance or refusal to obey orders (and the motivations for such choices) in the Wehrmacht is extraordinarily difficult. The case of FK 551 in Belarus is a good introduction to the complexities of analyzing noncompliance. On 22 July, the commander of FK 551 wrote a heated memorandum to the 252nd Infantry Division (one of the control divisions in rHGM), to which FK 551 was attached. He complained that the previous day a German police battalion from Baranovichi had swooped down upon various factories and slave labor details, arresting Jews. He further argued that this raid had deprived him of irreplaceable laborers and impeded operations that supported the Wehrmacht. The police had torn up and trashed special identification cards that the FK itself had issued to its Jewish slave laborers. The lieutenant colonel closed by angrily terming the entire operation a "great injury to my office in front of the Jews, that I cannot accept." He ended by requesting that "the police regiment be given orders which will prevent such behavior in the future."[116]

The 252nd acted quickly, forwarding the report to rHGM the next day. It requested that the HSSPF ensure that identification papers issued by the Wehrmacht would be honored in order to both keep important operations running and to recognize the authority of the *Feldkommandanturen*.

Additionally, the division requested that in the future if there were "political or police" concerns about individuals under the authority of the FK that it be notified before any action was taken. It was noted in the file that the matter was "satisfactorily settled"; in the future the HSSPF would recognize army-issued identification.[117]

This small exchange illustrates the complex task of identifying both evasion and motivations for behavior. In this case, it appears that the conflict was far more jurisdictional than moral and that it was the interests of the army rather than those of the victims that predominated. However, in other cases, similar objections may have been attempts at expressing some form of moral outrage in a manner that would be both less challenging and also more convincing if couched in military terms. Yet some men objected out of pure utilitarian reasons: two German soldiers recorded in captivity in Britain agreed, for example, that it was a mistake, from a diplomatic perspective, to kill the Jews when they did, with one man arguing that "we should have put it off until later."[118] Such objections clearly hold absolutely no moral outrage, camouflaged or otherwise.

A more well known, but no less problematic example is that of the military chaplain in the 295th Infantry Division in the Ukraine. After the Jewish adults of Byelaya Tserkov had been murdered, the young children of the town were locked in a house without food, water, or any kind of care. The military chaplain, Dr. Reuss, who had been called to the house by Wehrmacht soldiers, filed a lengthy report to his superiors in which he described in detail the inhumane conditions and how the soldiers were "shaken" and had "expressed their outrage." Reuss then alluded to the risk of disease and the fact that German soldiers were able to enter the house at their leisure, which had resulted in "a reaction of indignation and criticism."[119] Successive reports also remarked upon the negative impact of this scene on soldier morale. Eventually, the children were executed as a solution. What was the chaplain's motivation in this instance? Was he truly only concerned about morale and disease, or was that how he chose to word his complaint in order to receive the most attention? The answer is unclear; however, the length at which he describes the plight of the children suggests at least a modicum of concern for their welfare. Even Josef Sibille, who refused outright to murder the Jews in his area, remarked after the war that he would not "expect upstanding German soldiers to soil their hands with such things."[120] This consideration of honor may have been his primary motivation, or he may have simply been unwilling to openly condemn the immorality of the army out of some feeling of loyalty, even years after the fact. Regardless, the examples of Sibille and Lochbihler are vital in demonstrating that agency *did* exist and that soldiers could choose, without penalty, to refuse participation.

Cases of Wehrmacht refusal, rescue, or helping were statistically uncommon; most men went along. In addition, those men who had acted to help Jews returned to a postwar Germany that did not want to recall Nazi crimes and was at best ambivalent about the ethical correctness of resistance, demonstrated by the reaction to the July 20 plot against Hitler; many Germans viewed this attempt by some military officers to kill Hitler and take power as treason rather than legitimate opposition to the Nazi state. Thus, men like Lochbihler and Sibille did not speak of their actions, even to family. Despite these silences, recent scholarship has uncovered several cases of Wehrmacht soldiers refusing to participate in killing or even acting as rescuers, though not specifically in Belarus.[121]

Major Karl Plagge, commander of a Wehrmacht vehicle repair facility in Vilnius, acted in much the same vein as Lochbihler, though to such an extent that he was named a "Righteous among the Nations" by Yad Vashem. Plagge took on more Jews than necessary, treated them exceptionally well, and even attempted to rescue some of them from immediate execution. In the end, he persuaded the SS to create a separate work camp for "his" Jews that saved them at least temporarily.[122] Writing after the war, Plagge explained his behavior, saying that "if on earth there should only be 'Scourges and Victims,' then it is an obligation to stand, not on the side of the castigator but to espouse the cause of the victim."[123]

Some examples of rescue are even more extraordinary, such as the case of Sergeant Anton Schmid, a Viennese soldier who smuggled Jews out of the Vilnius ghetto across the Lithuanian border into Belarus, releasing them in Lida (among other places). One of the Jews Schmid saved was Szymon Goldberg, who escaped the killings in Novogrudok and Slonim and later testified against Gerhard Erren.[124] When a ghetto in Lida was established, the Gestapo noted the presence of many Jews from Vilnius who, under torture, revealed how they came to be there.

Schmid was arrested, tried, and executed.[125] In his last letter to his wife and daughter, he wrote, "my dearest Steffi and Gerta, it is a terrible blow for us, but please, please forgive me. I acted only as a human being and did not want to hurt anyone."[126] A friend described Schmid in the following way: "He was a simple, frank, and unreligious man, consistent in thought and speech and socially awkward. He was no philosopher, didn't read the newspaper let alone books. He was not a very intellectual person. His one outstanding characteristic was his humanity."[127]

Cases such as these are made extraordinary by their rarity. Most German soldiers did not react this way, as indeed most Europeans did not. However, this study has shown that some men, like Joachim Lochbihler, *did* find the courage and opportunity to aid those Jews they came into contact with. Unfortunately, the vast majority did not object to Nazi genocidal policy or, if they did, did not take any action on that objection.

Even rarer still were soldiers who spoke out against the killing and sought to encourage others to disobey. Such behavior, much more than individual refusal, put soldiers in real danger of being executed. Lieutenant Reinhold Lothy was one such individual. In April 1944, he was ordered to lead a raid behind the lines, capture Red Army soldiers, and then, as a "birthday present to the Führer," behead them with entrenching spades.[128] He refused to do this and also reportedly informed his men about the concentration camps and the murder of the Jews, leaving no doubt what he thought of them. He was shortly thereafter denounced and sentenced to a punishment battalion, whose extraordinarily dangerous missions he barely survived. Another young officer whose actions fall into this rarest category of attempting to persuade others to resist was Lieutenant Michael Kitzelmann, who was assigned to the 262nd Infantry Division in the Soviet Union. His own soldiers denounced him for expressing his opposition to the war and the brutal German occupation. Unlike Lothy, he was sentenced to death and executed.[129] The dating of these acts to the later years of the war, when Germany's inevitable defeat was clear enough to all but the most fanatical, also suggests that the catastrophic situation in which these men found themselves was perhaps a contributing factor to their decisions. With the exception of these last two cases, acts of Wehrmacht resistance or rescue tended to be highly individual in nature. Soldiers could often get away with refusing to kill, but encouraging their peers to also disobey crossed into the dangerous territory of defeatism or mutiny: acts such as these merited executions from Nazi courts. The charge was usually the subversion of morale or disruption of the war effort. With that being said, every Lochbihler or Schmid was surrounded by comrades who looked the other way or assisted rescue efforts in some small way.

While these cases of refusal and assistance are not statistically significant, we dismiss them at our peril. The fact that some men chose to actively refuse participation in genocide (and that most of these did so without any consequences) restores agency to a debate often overpowered by protests of duress, threats of execution, and helplessness. That Lochbihler, Sibille, and men like them found the courage and the ability to follow their conscience forces us to view the actions of the majority who chose to be complicit in a much different light. Indeed, the fact that it was participation in killing itself that sparked the most outrage but that playing other roles in killing operations met little opposition must also call into question the general position of soldiers with regards to Nazi genocidal policy. Given the clear knowledge that they could refuse to participate without fear of any real repercussions, let alone execution, we must turn to other explanations for the relative lack of noncompliance. Absent the threat of death, we must conclude that these men were motivated by some combination of agreement with the policy, deference to authority, and fear of the social consequences of refusal in their peer group. Because such motivations are much more mundane than fear of death, they are perhaps much more disturbing.

Conclusion

IN MARCH 1943, German soldier Friedrich Koch wrote in a letter home: "I have known, up to now, no unspoilt men, but only such who have forgotten their natures and those who have won their natures back, or are in the process of winning them back."[1] The German army never won back its nature on the eastern front; in fact, it was being true to its nature, at least as intended by the Nazis. Many have viewed the war on the eastern front as an aberration and have either unconsciously or intentionally sought to explain why the war in the Soviet Union was so violent, so vicious, and why both the actual and intended treatments of the civilian population were so murderous. Nazi behavior in the East is generally compared unfavorably to its conduct and occupation of western Europe. This dichotomy is correctly noted, but often falsely explained. Indeed, the policies and behaviors of the Third Reich in the East were *not* the exception, but the standard. It is in the East that we see the true face of Nazi imperialism, through its racial, colonial, economic, and, ultimately, genocidal aims.[2] In short, there was nothing anomalous about Nazism's grand and lethal plans for expansion eastward.

Only there could Hitler realize his own Manifest Destiny, unhampered by the longer historical relationships and common backgrounds present in western Europe; in the Nazi view, Germans had much more in common racially and culturally with western Europeans. As one historian wryly put it, "No Pole could have imagined conditions in the [occupied] Channel Islands, where NCOs [noncommissioned officers] lined German troops up in front of flower beds, barking at them: 'You can look at the flowers, you can smell the flowers, but in no circumstances are you to pick the flowers.'"[3] Eastern lands were always the goal of German territorial expansion. Nazi racist ideology justified this expansion and saw Slavs and Jews as subhumans who could be removed from these new territories by deportation, forced starvation, and extermination. In addition, the vast resources of the East offered the possibility for a self-sustaining German empire, invulnerable to economic threats that had previously helped limit its hegemony in Europe. The Second World War must, then, also be seen as the extension of Nazi imperial policy by military means. The explicit connection between the prosecution of the war and the Holocaust rarely is highlighted but is clear when observing the actions of the Wehrmacht on and behind the eastern front.

We should, then, perhaps, not be surprised at all that the German army, which had played an important role in government policy since Frederick the Great, should become one of the tools the Nazis used to carry out their colonial and genocidal project in the East. Yet it is in this light that we must look at Wehrmacht complicity in the Holocaust. The military itself was harnessed at all levels to enable the realization of the Nazi dream, whether by destroying the Soviet ability to resist at the front, by systematic economic plunder, or by maintaining the control necessary for the total eradication of racially inferior inhabitants of future Nazi lands. The conquest and plunder of the East was premeditated, but the role of the army in genocide evolved.

The Wehrmacht, as an organization, did not require much coercion to become a part of Hitler's lethal vision of the future. This is certainly not to say that most German soldiers were rabid antisemites or sadistic killers, but merely that the long- and short-term culture throughout the military *predisposed* it to furthering Nazi goals. Senior leadership, too, yearned for a crusade to the east. Generals and enlisted men alike, many of them shocked and horrified by the anarchic Weimar years and the associated Bolshevik terror, saw the Soviet Union as a very real threat to Germany's survival. After examining thousands of secret recordings of German POWs, historian Sönke Neitzel and social psychologist Harald Welzer contended that "far more important than ideology for soldiers' perceptions and interpretations, and thus for their concrete decisions and actions, was their military value system."[4] It is this organizational culture, shaped by the situation on the eastern front and by long- and short-term historical trends, that enabled the Wehrmacht to be shaped into a tool of Nazi genocide.

The question of ideological penetration of Nazi values as an explanation for perpetrator behavior remains a contested one for historians of the Wehrmacht and the Holocaust in general. Certainly, the propagandistic education of the troops became a matter of increasing importance over time. By mid-1942, the Wehrmacht propaganda branch had grown to division strength, approximately fifteen thousand troops.[5] Later still, the army would create actual propaganda officers for the education of the soldiers, even though such officers in the Red Army had been the object of particular derision and had been executed for this behavior. German soldiers received and watched antisemitic and anti-Bolshevist films. A monthly for Nazi Party propagandists stated with pride (and no small amount of exaggeration) that in 1941 about thirty million soldiers had attended films arranged by the district film offices for the military.[6] Of course, it is difficult to measure reception. How much did such training change minds, build upon preexisting prejudice, or simply pass without effect? Certainly, some soldiers absorbed Nazi racist values. One can find anecdotal evidence of this in its linguistic transmission. For example, the virulent Nazi propaganda publication *Der Stürmer* frequently called for the "extermination" of Jews "root and branch." The secret recordings of German POWs indicate that this message filtered down at least to the lowest levels. One soldier was recorded saying that the SS had "burned the village down root and branch."[7] Another soldier on the eastern front wrote home that "this time no quarter will be given" and that the Jews "must be exterminated, root and branch, or we do not achieve our goal."[8] The common use of stock Nazi phraseology is not without importance. As an organization, the Wehrmacht certainly leaned heavily toward antisemitism, but one should not as easily ascribe such beliefs to all its members.

The descent into ever-deeper complicity simply cannot be attributed solely to racial thinking. Neitzel and Welzer argued that "we cannot say that the majority felt they were waging an 'eliminatory' or a 'racial war'" and that "ideology played only a subordinate role" in their mentality.[9] Perhaps this swings the argument too far away from the importance of ideology. The real question of importance, of course, is what constitutes "ideology"? While racial doctrine may not have *driven* soldiers to participate, underlying prejudices that it legitimized certainly eased the process. Moreover, if we consider the imagined "threat" Jews posed to the military and its role as a moral fig leaf for collaboration in genocide, there appears to have been perhaps a bit more ideology driving participation. Neitzel and Welzer are likely disturbingly correct when they concluded that "to perpetrate atrocities . . . soldiers did not need to be either racist or antisemitic."[10] However, they were certainly not without beliefs. Their worldview was informed by elements of racial theory, anti-Communism, brutalization in combat, anti-Slavic prejudice, and many other factors.

For many of these same men, some conception of honorable ways of fighting made them hesitant to approach genocide too closely. Yet while they may have been politely antisemitic or have agreed in principle on the necessity of a solution to the "Jewish question," some were also reticent to physically carry out the extermination of the Jews. As they had done before, Nazi leaders successfully translated their message into a form that would resonate with the intended audience. The connection of Jews with Bolshevism and then with the fledgling partisan movement served this purpose very well. Jews ceased to become noncombatants and became, at least on paper, potential military targets. Women and children were transformed into scouts and messengers, and men became fighters. This convenient formulation also had the additional benefit of easily merging with the structure of more legitimate operations against actual insurgents, providing both psychological and tactical cover. Of course, some leaders and men were sufficiently ideologically motivated that they did not require any pretext. Others, as we have seen, were troubled by the real effects this ideological war had on the loyalties and cooperation of the local populations. Finally, a tiny minority acted to aid, protect, or rescue those victimized by the Nazi state. By and large, however, German military occupation policy erred on the side of security and a racial hierarchy that resulted in a ruthless attitude toward civilians, both Jews and non-Jews, and a brutal and lethal treatment of both, often for similar reasons. This, of course, made the Wehrmacht an attractive partner for Nazi planners.

That this transformation of the army into an arm of Nazi genocidal policy took place during the first year of the war is also vitally important. Some have sought to place Wehrmacht brutality in the context of a brutalizing war that was increasingly not going in Germany's favor or was a response to equally tenacious combat by the Red Army. In reality, the key steps of this evolving complicity took place in the halcyon days when it appeared that the war would end quickly with a Nazi victory. While it may be true that "antisemitic sentiments among the troops increased as conditions at the front worsened and as soldiers were no longer merely exposed to racist propaganda but also observed and in some cases participated in mass murder of Jews," such conditions were clearly not required for army participation in genocide.[11] The Red Army was disintegrating in front of these units, and the rear remained a relatively peaceful place. Thus, if pressure toward greater violence resulted from a downturn in German military fortunes, that appeared at a later date.

If all politics is local, then all genocide must be as well, or perhaps even personal. The Wehrmacht did not simply agree in principle with Nazi genocidal policy in some vague or theoretical sense. German soldiers dragged Jews from their homes, prevented them from escaping, marched them to their deaths, and sometimes personally killed them. They looked their victims in the eyes. When not engaged in killing operations, these men used Jews as slave labor, stole their property, and sometimes extorted sexual favors from them. Not every soldier, of course, approached his role in the same way, and certainly not every soldier was a willing participant.

The trajectories of the units in this book along an increasingly more complicit path demonstrate the complexity inherent in explaining how and why some men killed while others did not. One cannot draw a direct line from the larger institutional culture and ideological climate discussed above to acts of murder on the ground, though the former certainly played an important role in promulgating the latter. While the initially bitter and polarized debate over a monocausal explanation for perpetrator behavior (ideological, situational, or psychological) played an important role in posing questions, gathering evidence, and weighing answers, such an approach is no longer sufficient in addressing why some people murder others.[12] In fact, the more difficult historical challenge is to understand the complex interplay *between* different factors, which occurred on a variety of scales in both time and space. German soldiers did not adhere to values in a vacuum disconnected from their daily lives, nor did they interact with their environment in purely rational ways. Instead, their beliefs influenced how they viewed certain situations, while at the same time long-term physical participation in the Nazi genocidal project could change or modify those belief systems.

The result was the creation of a world whose moral boundaries had become dangerously warped. A world in which an officer could aggressively challenge his superior's anti-Catholic views while remaining silent on the order to murder forty Jewish civilians. A world in which a soldier could execute an old man as a suspected partisan while refusing to execute a Jewish woman. A world in which a soldier could look down on his comrade for looting dead bodies after a night spent preventing survivors from escaping the pits. And a world in which a soldier could say "I merely once had to serve in the cordon as Jews were shot," while claiming to have never participated in the shooting of civilians.[13]

This study has also demonstrated the decisive impact of a unit culture that encouraged complicity. Murderous leaders led murderous units. In every instance of complicity in the murder of the Jews of Belarus examined here, a key leader led, encouraged, or permitted this behavior. Personalities such as Captain Kiefer, Lieutenant Glück, Lieutenant Martin, Lieutenant Schaffitz, and others actively inserted themselves (and their men) into the killing process. At the opposite extreme stood Josef Sibille, who refused any participation and, through this refusal, eliminated the participation of any of his men as well. In the middle of this spectrum and likely representing the majority of leadership were men such as Major Waldow, Captain Nöll, and Captain Artmann, who, while not driving participation themselves, permitted it, enabled it, and supported it. Artmann was too ineffectual to stop it, and Nöll, who likely recognized the immorality of what he was doing, was simply too weak to say no. The role of leadership in Wehrmacht complicity places the "obedience to orders" defense in an entirely different light. The arguments of Omer Bartov (and others) regarding the draconian discipline in the German army and the statistics of Nazi military justice also must highlight the importance of leadership in *not* committing atrocities. If the threat (real or perceived) of swift punishment for a refusal to obey orders drove some men to kill, certainly an order to the contrary (like Sibille's) would have prohibited such killing. That it took explicit and repeated refusals to prevent complicity illuminates the power of an institutional climate predisposed to participation.

Yet leadership is only one important factor. The behavior of these units in carrying out the Final Solution in Belarus suggests that if leadership must be seen along a spectrum of varied participation, so too must the soldiers. This is a spectrum of behavior based on choice, for it must be recognized that, concerning the murder of Jews, the admittedly severe system of military discipline offered a surprising degree of individual agency. It seems every unit had a core group of men who could be counted on to murder. As one soldier who refused to shoot during the Krucha killing told his first sergeant, "I told him that wasn't my thing, and besides, there would certainly be enough people who would do this voluntarily."[14] But many units also had small groups of men who evaded or refused participation. The majority, however, fell into the larger group who neither sought out nor refused involvement. They carried out orders given to them.[15] One of the participants in the Krupki killing, for example, explained his actions escorting Jews to their deaths this way: "I never committed these acts independently but always under orders."[16] Moreover, as the choices presented became less stark, these men tended toward greater complicity. For example, while this study has yielded examples of men refusing to shoot, it has not uncovered a single soldier refusing to guard Jews prior to their execution or refusing to participate in any aspect of an action beyond killing. This suggests that it was actually easier for men to refuse the direct act of killing than to refuse supporting (but equally lethal) roles. Commanders were more willing to respect the emotional sensitivity of a good German soldier when it came to shooting than when it was related to guarding Jews at a killing site, though both acts inevitably led to murder.

For some men, expressions of masculinity played a role in their behavior.[17] The desire to show one's strength and virility through unflinching violence and cold murder certainly drove some of the more active killers. For others, playing the role of a soldier, obeying orders even in the face of difficult tasks, fit their conception of manhood. It is obviously not always clear what gendered approaches to these situations the men had. However, how they refused *can* tell us much about the normative view of masculinity in these units.

Soldiers always seemed to express their inability to participate from a position of weakness. Even years after the war, this was how these men explained their refusal to commit murder. Wilhelm Magel, who refused to shoot at Krucha, said that he had been thinking of his children whose mother had recently died and "didn't want to see that."[18] He did not challenge the legality of the killing. Yet in a letter he sent to his brother that same day, he indicated that he was not in agreement with the action.[19] By claiming weakness or sentimentality as their reason for nonparticipation, soldiers like Magel and others avoided directly challenging the actions of their comrades. This allowed them to remain within the community of their peers. Conversely, taking a moral position and openly identifying the actions of one's comrades as wrong risked exclusion from that community and "social death."[20]

Though statistically rare, those men who did choose to refuse participation or even to take action to help Jews represent vital counterbalances to a common vision of the futility of nonconformity, dissent, and resistance in the Third Reich. The actions of men like Lochbihler and Sibille demonstrate a degree of agency that necessarily complicates our conception of the power of duress. Historian Nechama Tec has done an extensive study examining the collective biographies of rescuers, specifically in Poland. She found that though rescuers were "a very heterogeneous group," one characteristic they had in common was "individuality or separateness."[21]

Tec's analysis probably holds for Wehrmacht soldiers as well, though most would not fall into the category of rescue but rather of evading or refusing participation. Josef Sibille certainly at least acted as an individual in the face of the Nazi monolith by refusing to allow his children to join the Hitler Youth, until the pressure on him at work became unbearable. His religious convictions may have also been influential in the position he took. We know less about Lochbihler. He was thirty-two and from Nürnberg, a city that had certainly earned its Nazi credentials. Even in his testimony after the war, he did not go into great detail regarding his aid to the Jews in the Pupko brewery. Yet he had kept in touch with the Pupkos after the war, telling investigators that he had their address in Mexico.[22] He appears to have been a man, much like Anton Schmid, who simply acted out of human kindness toward a group of people who were being unfairly persecuted. Sadly, the majority of men were unable or unwilling to take such a stand.

Indeed, more than a few chose the opposite approach, extorting sex and property alike from a desperate, captive Jewish population, for example. In some ways, these behaviors are more disturbing than those more lethal actions associated with actual killing of Jews, because such conduct was always entirely voluntary. Men who may have felt coerced into participating in anti-Jewish actions felt no such official compulsion to demand sex, loot bodies, or profit from Jewish property. Explaining how a German soldier could buy the clothing of a murdered Jewish child and then send it home to his own children seems far more difficult than explaining how that same man became involved in the massacre of that Jewish child.

Actions like these are the greatest evidence of the progressive nature of Wehrmacht complicity in the East. German soldiers observed these opportunities over time and learned these behaviors. Prolonged contact with the Nazi genocidal project led to a greater acceptance of the warped world in which it took place and of the distorted morality by which it functioned. Moreover, these men found themselves in an organization whose climate made them more, not less, likely to accept such perversions. However, men like Sibille demonstrate that this was not an inevitable process, but one that could be interrupted by a leader focused on setting a positive example.

War and genocide are inextricably linked. All genocides in the modern era (and most throughout history) have occurred in the context of war or armed conflict. Moreover, in each of these, militaries have played a key supporting and/or active role in the mass killing of civilians. The addition of a military to a genocidal (or pre-genocidal) situation can often be the spark required to ignite a full-fledged genocide. The behavior of the German army during the Holocaust in the Soviet Union shows how deeply and rapidly a supposedly professional organization can become involved in the murder of women and children, given extended exposure to genocidal policy. The deputy for Jewish affairs in Lida, the rabid Leopold Windisch, himself recognized this connection early on. During a selection, he told his interpreter, "The fate of the Jews is dependent on the movement of the front."[23]

The fact that institutional and unit cultures were decisive for the participation of German soldiers, even in an openly racist and violent regime such as the Third Reich, highlights for us the real impact of organizational structures and attitudes in influencing behavior. The experiences of German soldiers in killing in the East also allow us the rare opportunity to connect the more general elements of a dysfunctional organization with the very real and specific impacts they have at the ground level, on the lives of real people.

In an era whose wars continue to be less clearly defined and are increasingly fought in the midst of civilian populations, the lessons we can learn from these Wehrmacht units regarding the critical impact of leadership and unit culture become even more important. The actions of a few American units in Iraq and Afghanistan reinforce that this lesson has not been fully learned and that maintaining an ethical environment in a complex war is very difficult, even in an ethically upright force. At least five members of the U.S. Army's 5th Stryker Brigade have been accused of war crimes, including forming a "kill team" that targeted unarmed Afghan civilians and took body parts as trophies. Investigators have focused on the command climate created by the brigade commander. An official who observed the unit in training noted, "When you feel violent intent coming down from the command and into the culture of the brigade, that's when you end up with things like the rogue platoon. He [the brigade commander] established a culture that allowed that kind of mindset to percolate. And there are second- and third-order effects that come with that. Clearly, the guys who were pulling the trigger

are the proximate cause of the crime, but the culture itself is the en-
abler."[24] This commander had openly "sneered" at the army's counterinsurgency policy and "told shocked U.S. and NATO officials that he
was uninterested in winning the trust of the Afghan people."[25]

By pointing out the importance of leadership and unit climate, I am
not comparing this one unit's aberrant behavior to that of Wehrmacht
units systematically supporting and implementing the policies of a racist
and genocidal regime. Indeed, it is the rarity of such crimes in the U.S.
military that makes them so shocking. Moreover, it is the lack of a larger
societal and institutional culture bent on genocide that limits atrocity to
isolated incidents. At the same time, this incident starkly demonstrates
that, despite advances in technology, the benefits of an all-volunteer force,
and the overall ethical climate of a military, dysfunctional unit cultures
originating from upper leadership can still result in crimes that would
not seem out of place in the Wehrmacht.

What this study of units and individuals at ground level has conclusively demonstrated is that an unspecified notion of "complicity" does not
do adequate justice to Wehrmacht participation in the Holocaust. German
soldier Willi Reese himself struggled with his membership in an organization so deeply compromised and his relative guilt. In 1943, he wrote:

> We are war. Because we are soldiers.
> I have burned all the cities,
> Strangled all the women,
> Brained all the children,
> Plundered all the land.
> I have shot a million enemies,
> Laid waste the fields, destroyed the churches,
> Ravaged the souls of the inhabitants,
> Spilled the blood and tears of all the mothers.
>
> I did it, all me—I did
> Nothing. But I was a soldier.[26]

Indeed, while at the higher levels generals could agree on general support and compliance with Nazi genocidal policy, in the cities, towns,

and villages throughout the Soviet Union, it was often ordinary soldiers who helped turn these paper promises into action. Not all participated directly in the killing, but most were exposed to the murderous nature of Nazi war in some form or another. However, these men were simply the last in a chain of individuals whose involvement in their own dysfunctional communities made them a step on the road to genocide. The speed and extremity with which most modern organizations and most individuals can be bent toward evil is one lesson from the faraway forests of Belarus that we ignore at our own peril. Conversely, we see that even in the darkest of times, there were a few who stood against the storm of violence. In the context of modern genocide, the experience of the Holocaust in Belarus should caution us against ever becoming too comfortable with the righteousness of our own behavior.

> I did it, all me—I did
> Nothing.

Abbreviations

BA-L	Bundesarchiv Berlin Lichterfelde (Berlin, Germany)
BA-MA	Bundesarchiv Militärarchiv (Freiburg, Germany)
BA-ZS	Bundesarchiv Zentrale Stelle zur Aufklärung nationalsocialistischer Verbrechen (Ludwigsburg, Germany)
BStA	Minsk: Belarussian State Archive (Minsk, Belarus)
HSA-D	Hessisches Staatsarchiv Darmstadt (Darmstadt, Germany)
LA-NRW-Münster	Landesarchiv Nordrhein-Westfalen (Münster, Germany)
StA-Freiburg	Stadtarchiv Freiburg (Freiburg, Germany)
USC	Shoah Foundation Institute, Visual History Archive
USHMM	United States Holocaust Memorial Museum (Washington, D.C.)

Notes

Introduction

1. "Lisa Nussbaum," United States Holocaust Memorial Museum, http://www.ushmm
   .org/wlc/en/idcard.php?ModuleId=10006336 (accessed May 2013).
2. "Derman (neé Nussbaum), Lisa," USC Shoah Foundation Institute: Interview no.
   23224, Visual History Archive, 2009.
3. For individuals who appear only in German judicial archives, I have used only first
   name and last initial to comply with the requisite archival privacy regulations. For
   individuals whose names or personal information appears in other sources, I have
   used full names.
4. "N., Anton Statement, 7 February 1961" (BA-ZS: B162/1550), 145–146.
5. Carolyn Starks and Lynette Kalsnes, "Holocaust Survivor Tells Story a Final
   Time," *Chicago Tribune*, 30 July 2002, http://articles.chicagotribune.com/2002-07
   -30/news/0207300220_1_holocaust-remembrance-day-nazis-holocaust-memorial
   -museum (accessed May 21, 2013).
6. Hannes Heer, "Killing Fields: The Wehrmacht and the Holocaust in Belorussia,
   1941–1942," *Holocaust and Genocide Studies* 11, no. 1 (1997): 97. The term "Wehrmacht" technically refers to all fighting arms of the German military during World
   War II. When discussing complicity in this book, especially from a historiographical

standpoint, in atrocities committed during the war, I will use the term "Wehrmacht" to generally mean the German army *(das Heere)*.

7. Einsatzkommando 8 was a subordinate killing squad from Einsatzgruppe B, operating predominantly in what is now Belarus. Specifically, the 354th assisted Teilkommando Schönemann, which was subordinated to Einsatzkommando 8.

8. Klaus Wiegrefe, "Abrechnung mit Hitlers Generälen," *Der Spiegel,* 11 November 2001, 89.

9. On the difficulties of selecting collaborators in Belarus, see, for example, Martin Dean, *Collaboration in the Holocaust: Crimes of the Local Police in Belorussia and Ukraine, 1941–44* (New York: St. Martin's Press, 2000), 42.

10. "Nazi War Crimes Show Bombed—Police Suspect Extremists," *Deutsche Presse-Agentur,* 9 March 1999.

11. Jan Phillipp Reemtsma, Ulrike Jureit, and Hans Mommsen, eds., *Verbrechen der Wehrmacht: Dimensionen des Vernichtungskrieges 1941–1944: Ausstellungskatalog* (Hamburg: Hamburger, 2002), 697.

12. Steve Crawshaw, "Germans Own Up to Horrors Committed on Eastern Front," *Independent,* 17 April 1995, 8.

13. Franz Wilhelm Seidler, *Verbrechen an der Wehrmacht: Kriegsgreuel der Roten Armee 1941/42* (Selent: Pour le Mérite, 1998).

14. Reemtsma, Jureit, and Mommsen, *Verbrechen der Wehrmacht,* 687.

15. Hannes Heer, *Vom Verschwinden der Täter: Der Vernichtungskrieg fand statt, aber Keiner war dabei* (Berlin: Aufbau-Verlag, 2004), 36.

16. For more on the Wehrmacht exhibition and associated debates, see Helmut Donat and Arn Strohmeyer, eds., *Befreiung von der Wehrmacht? Dokumentation der Auseinandersetzung über die Ausstellung "Vernichtungskrieg-Verbrechen der Wehrmacht 1941 bis 1944" in Bremen 1996/97* (Bremen: Donat, 1997).

17. Valerie Hébert, "From Clean Hands to *Vernichtungskrieg:* How the High Command Case Shaped the Image of the Wehrmacht," in *Reassessing the Nuremburg Military Tribunals: Transitional Justice, Trial Narratives, and Historiography,* ed. Kim C. Priemel and Alexa Stiller (New York: Berghahn Books, 2012), 200.

18. Ibid., 201.

19. Donald Bloxham, *Genocide on Trial: The War Crimes Trials and the Formation of Holocaust History and Memory* (Oxford: Oxford University Press, 2001), 11–12.

20. David Clay Large, "Reckoning without the Past: The HIAG of the Waffen-SS and the Politics of Rehabilitation in the Bonn Republic, 1950–1961," *Journal of Modern History* 59, no. 1 (1987): 111.

21. Maria Hohn, *GIs and Fräuleins: The German-American Encounter in 1950s West Germany* (Chapel Hill: University of North Carolina Press, 2002), 59–60.

22. Hébert, "From Clean Hands to *Vernichtungskrieg,*" 208.

23. Eighteen percent replied that they did not know. Elisabeth Noelle-Neumann and Erich Peter Neumann, *The Germans: Public Opinion Polls, 1947–1966* (Allensbach: Bonn, Verlag für Demoskopie, 1967), 202.

24. For an excellent discussion of this postwar construction of collective memory, see Robert G. Moeller, *War Stories: The Search for a Usable Past in the Federal Republic of Germany* (Berkeley: University of California Press, 2001).

25. See, for example, Erich von Manstein, *Lost Victories* (Chicago: H. Regnery, 1958); Günther Blumentritt, *My Military Career* (Karlsruhe, Germany: Historical Division, Headquarters, United States Army, Europe [Foreign Military Studies Branch], 1946); Heinz Guderian, *Panzer Leader* (Washington: Zenger, 1979); Wilhelm Keitel and Walter Görlitz, *The Memoirs of Field-Marshal Wilhelm Keitel* (New York: Cooper Square Press, 2000).

26. For a fascinating study of this phenomenon, see Ronald M. Smelser and Edward J. Davies II, *The Myth of the Eastern Front: The Nazi-Soviet War in American Popular Culture* (New York: Cambridge University Press, 2008).

27. Famed historian of Germany Gordon Craig briefly covers genocidal plans in his seminal work on Germany, 1866–1945. In his work on the army's political history, however, he does not treat it at all, choosing instead to focus on historical junctures where the military failed to resist Hitler. While he was certainly critical of the German army and its relationship with the Nazis and covered very briefly the Nazi genocidal project, he was—like others—more interested in the military's role in the failure of democracy in Germany and in furthering Hitler's expansionist policies. These shortcomings aside, Craig still deservedly stands as a giant of German history. Gordon Alexander Craig, *The Politics of the Prussian Army, 1640–1945* (Oxford: Clarendon Press, 1955); Gordon Alexander Craig, *Germany, 1866–1945* (New York: Oxford University Press, 1978).

28. See Raul Hilberg, *The Destruction of the European Jews* (Chicago: Quadrangle Books, 1961); Hans Buchheim, Martin Broszat, and Hans-Adolf Jacobsen, *Anatomie des SS-Staates*, 2 vols. (München: Deutschen Taschenbuch Verlag, 1967); Christian Streit, *Keine Kameraden: Die Wehrmacht und die sowjetischen Kriegsgefangenen, 1941–1945* (Stuttgart: Deutsche Verlags-Anstalt, 1978).

29. Manfred Messerschmidt, *Die Wehrmacht im NS-Staat: Zeit der Indoktrination* (Hamburg: R. v. Decker, 1969).

30. Omer Bartov, *The Eastern Front, 1941–45: German Troops and the Barbarisation of Warfare* (New York: St. Martin's Press, 1986).

31. Apart from John Demjanjuk (accused of being a prison guard at Sobibor), other cases have come to light. Former Waffen-SS trooper Adolf Storms has been charged with the execution of Jewish slave-laborers in 1945. Another Waffen-SS member, Heinrich Boere, a Dutch volunteer, was convicted of the murder of three Dutch civilians in 1944 and sentenced to life in prison. For Demjanjuk, see Nicholas Kulish, "Man Tied to Death Camp Goes on Trial in Germany," *New York Times*, 1 December 2009. For Storms, see Roger Boyes, "Ex–SS Trooper Adolf Storms Charged over Mass Shooting of Jews," http://www.timesonline.co.uk/tol/news/world/europe/article6920433.ece. For Boere, see Roger Boyes, "Laughing SS Hitman Finally Faces Court for Murders," *Times* (London), 29 October 2009; Victor Homoloa and Alan Cowell, "Ex-Nazi Guilty in Wartime Murders," *New York Times*, 24 March 2010.

32. See Judy Dempsey, "Former Nazi Officer Convicted of Murdering Italian Civilians," *New York Times*, 12 August 2009; Nicholas Kulish, "In Germany, Whispers of 'Enough' at a War-Crimes Trial," *New York Times*, 8 February 2009.

33. Cottrell, Chris. Nearly 70 Years Later, a New Round of Auschwitz Prosecutions" *New York Times*, 10 April 2013.

34. For an excellent study of this phenomenon in Germany, see Harald Welzer, Sabine Moller, and Karoline Tschuggnall, *Opa war kein Nazi: Nationalsozialismus und Holocaust im Familiengedächtnis* (Frankfurt am Main: Fischer Taschenbuch Verlag, 2002).

35. See, for example, Theo J. Schulte, *The German Army and Nazi Policies in Occupied Russia* (New York: St. Martin's Press, 1989); Walter Manoschek, *"Serbien Ist Judenfrei": Militärische Besatzungspolitik und Judenvernichtung in Serbien 1941/42* (München: R. Oldenbourg, 1993); Karel C. Berkhoff, *Harvest of Despair: Life and Death in Ukraine under Nazi Rule* (Cambridge, Mass.: Belknap Press of Harvard University Press, 2004); Bernhard Chiari, *Alltag hinter der Front: Besatzung, Kollaboration und Widerstand in Weissrussland, 1941–1944* (Düsseldorf: Droste Verlag, 1998); Wendy Lower, *Nazi Empire-Building and the Holocaust in Ukraine* (Chapel Hill: University of North Carolina Press, 2005); Mark Mazower, *Inside Hitler's Greece: The Experience of Occupation, 1941–1944* (New Haven, Conn.: Yale University Press, 1993).

36. See Raffael Scheck, *Hitler's African Victims: The German Army Massacres of Black French Soldiers in 1940* (Cambridge: Cambridge University Press, 2006); Sarah Bennett Farmer, *Martyred Village: Commemorating the 1944 Massacre at Oradour-Sur-Glane* (Berkeley: University of California Press, 1999); Jochen Böhler, *Auftakt zum Vernichtungskrieg: Die Wehrmacht in Polen 1939* (Frankfurt am Main: Fischer Taschenbuch Verlag, 2006); Alexander B. Rossino, *Hitler Strikes Poland: Blitzkrieg, Ideology, and Atrocity* (Lawrence: University Press of Kansas, 2003).

37. For the notable exceptions see H. F. Meyer, *Von Wien nach Kalavryta: Die blutige Spur der 117. Jäger-Division durch Serbien und Griechenland* (Mannheim: Bibliopolis, 2002); Ben Shepherd, *War in the Wild East: The German Army and Soviet Partisans* (Cambridge, Mass.: Harvard University Press, 2004); Ben Shepherd, "Wehrmacht Security Regiments in the Soviet Partisan War, 1943," *European History Quarterly* 33, no. 4 (2003); Truman Anderson, "Incident at Baranivka: German Reprisals and the Soviet Partisan Movement in Ukraine, October–December 1941," *Journal of Modern History* 71, no. 3 (1999). In addition, scholar David Wildermuth is researching the path of one division through Belarus and its involvement in atrocities against Jews. David Wildermuth, "Who Killed Lida's Jewish Intelligentsia? A Case Study of Wehrmacht Involvement in the Holocaust's 'First Hour,'" *Holocaust and Genocide Studies* 27, no. 1 (2013, forthcoming).

38. Christian Hartmann, *Wehrmacht im Ostkrieg: Front und militärisches Hinterland 1941–42* (München: R. Oldenbourg, 2009).

39. Omer Bartov, *Hitler's Army: Soldiers, Nazis, and War in the Third Reich* (New York: Oxford University Press, 1991); Omer Bartov, *Germany's War and the Holocaust: Disputed Histories* (Ithaca, N.Y.: Cornell University Press, 2003). Bartov would later mediate his own position, seeing a compromise explanation. "It is quite possible, of course, to stake out a third position, one which stresses a crucial factor neglected both by Browning's circumstantial interpretation and by Goldhagen's essentialist view, namely the powerful impact of ideology and indoctrination on the perpetrators."

40. Daniel Jonah Goldhagen, *Hitler's Willing Executioners: Ordinary Germans and the Holocaust,* 1st ed. (New York: Alfred A. Knopf, 1996).

41. Theodor W. Adorno, *The Authoritarian Personality* (New York: Harper, 1950). Most discussions of psychological explanations for perpetrator behavior have moved beyond Adorno's "personality profile" approach to become more situational in nature.

42. Edward A. Shils and Morris Janowitz, "Cohesion and Disintegration in the Wehrmacht in World War II," *Public Opinion Quarterly* 12, no. 2 (1948): 281.

43. See Stanley Milgram, *Obedience* (University Park: Pennsylvania State University Press, 1969), videocassette, 1 videocassette (45 min.): sd., b&w, 1/2 in.; Stanley Milgram, *The Individual in a Social World: Essays and Experiments,* Addison-Wesley Series in Social Psychology (Reading, Mass.: Addison-Wesley, 1977); Philip G. Zimbardo, Ken Musen, and John Polito, *Quiet Rage: The Stanford Prison Study* (Stanford, CA: Stanford Instructional Television Network, Stanford University, 1992), videorecording, 1 videocassette (50 min.): sd., col. with b&w sequences, 1/2 in.

44. Philip G. Zimbardo, Ebbe B. Ebbesen, and Christina Maslach, *Influencing Attitudes and Changing Behavior: An Introduction to Method, Theory, and Applications of Social Control and Personal Power* (New York: Random House, 1977), 42.

45. Christopher R. Browning, *Ordinary Men: Reserve Police Battalion 101 and the Final Solution in Poland* (New York: Harper Perennial, 1998), 73.

46. See Harald Welzer, *Täter: Wie aus ganz normalen Menschen Massenmörder werden* (Frankfurt am Main: S. Fischer, 2005).

47. See Browning, *Ordinary Men.*

48. Welzer, *Täter,* 22.

49. Thomas Kühne, *Kameradschaft: Die Soldaten des nationalsozialistischen Krieges und das 20. Jahrhundert* (Göttingen: Vandenhoeck & Ruprecht, 2006), 273.

50. For more, see Thomas Kühne, "Male Bonding and Shame Culture: Hitler's Soldiers and the Moral Basis of Genocidal Warfare," in *Ordinary People as Mass Murderers: Perpetrators in Comparative Perspectives,* ed. Olaf Szejnmann Claus-Christian W. Jensen (New York: Palgrave Macmillan, 2008).

51. See, for example, Sönke Neitzel and Harald Welzer, *Soldaten: The Secret World of Transcripts of German POWs* (New York: Alfred A. Knopf, 2012).

52. Christopher R. Browning, *Collected Memories: Holocaust History and Postwar Testimony* (Madison: University of Wisconsin Press, 2003), 11–12.

53. Robert Coles, *The Moral Life of Children* (Boston: Houghton Mifflin, 1986), 16.

1. The Deadliest Place on Earth

1. Timothy Snyder, "Holocaust: The Ignored Reality," *New York Review of Books* 56, no. 12 (2009).

2. Thomas C. Fox, "The Holocaust under Communism," in *The Historiography of the Holocaust,* ed. Dan Stone (New York: Palgrave Macmillan, 2005), 422.

3. Ibid., 421.

4. See Christian Gerlach, "German Economic Interests, Occupation Policy, and the Murder of the Jews in Belorussia, 1941/43," in *National Socialist Extermination Policies: Contemporary German Perspectives and Controversies,* ed. Ulrich Herbert (New York: Berghahn Books, 2000), 210.

5. "Kosenkova, Margarita Interview, 8 July 2009" (author's personal archive).

6. Andrew Savchenko, *Belarus: A Perpetual Borderland* (Boston: Brill, 2009).

7. Jan Zaprudnik, *Belarus: At a Crossroads in History* (Boulder, Colo.: Westview Press, 1993), 37.

8. Ibid., 62–63.

9. Zvi Y. Gitelman, "Soviet Jewry before the Holocaust," in *Bitter Legacy: Confronting the Holocaust in the USSR,* ed. Zvi Y. Gitelman (Bloomington: Indiana University Press, 1997), 1.

10. Mordechai Altshuler, *Soviet Jewry on the Eve of the Holocaust: A Social and Demographic Profile* (Jerusalem: Centre for Research of East European Jewry, Hebrew University of Jerusalem, 1998), 104.

11. Shalom Cholawsky, *The Jews of Bielorussia during World War II* (Amsterdam: Harwood Academic, 1998), xx.

12. American Jewish Committee, *The American Jewish Year Book 5681,* vol. 22 (Jewish Publication Society of America, 1921), 274.

13. Vejas G. Liulevicius, *War Land on the Eastern Front: Culture, National Identity and German Occupation in World War I* (Cambridge: Cambridge University Press, 2000), 121.

14. Daniel Romanovsky, "Nazi Occupation in Northeastern Belarus and Western Russia," in Gitelman, *Bitter Legacy,* 235.

15. Liulevicius, *War Land on the Eastern Front,* 132.

16. Zaprudnik, *Belarus,* 78.

17. Arkady Zeltser, "The Belorussian Shtetl in the 1920s and 1930s," in *Revolution, Repression, and Revival: The Soviet Jewish Experience,* ed. Zvi Y. Gitelman and Yaacov Ro'i (Lanham, Md.: Rowman & Littlefield, 2007), 105.

18. Zaprudnik, *Belarus,* 81.

19. John Kiler, "The Holocaust and the Soviet Union," in Stone, *Historiography of the Holocaust,* 277.

20. Hans-Heinrich Nolte, "Destruction and Resistance: The Jewish Shtetl of Slonim, 1941–44," in *The People's War: Responses to World War II in the Soviet Union,* ed. Bernd Bonwetsch and Robert W. Thurston (Urbana: University of Illinois Press, 2000), 31.

21. Jews made up 8.2 percent of the population but represented 49.3 percent of administrative posts. See ibid., 31 and 35n.

22. David R. Marples, "Kuropaty: The Investigation of a Stalinist Historical Controversy," *Slavic Review* 53, no. 2 (1994): 516n.

23. Ezra Mendelsohn, *The Jews of East Central Europe between the World Wars* (Bloomington: Indiana University Press, 1983), 16.

24. Zaprudnik, *Belarus,* 82.

25. Mendelsohn, *Jews of East Central Europe,* 69.

26. See ibid., 73.

27. Israel Gutman, "Do the Poor Poles Really Look at the Ghetto? Introduction to the Hebrew Edition of *Neighbors*," in *The Neighbors Respond: The Controversy over the Jedwabne Massacre in Poland*, ed. Joanna B. Michlic and Antony Polonsky (Princeton, N.J.: Princeton University Press, 2004), 419.

28. "Protocol of Interrogation of Lubov Israelevna Abramovich, 25 September 1995" (New Scotland Yard War Crimes Unit [WCU]: D7852), 3.

29. Zaprudnik, *Belarus*, 91.

30. Jan Tomasz Gross, *Revolution from Abroad: The Soviet Conquest of Poland's Western Ukraine and Western Belorussia* (Princeton, N.J.: Princeton University Press, 1988), 194.

31. For a study of some of the anti-Jewish violence in 1919 in Ukraine, see Henry Abramson, *A Prayer for the Government: Ukrainians and Jews in Revolutionary Times, 1917–1920* (Cambridge, Mass.: Harvard University Press, 1999). For more on the effects of Soviet policy on Holocaust collaboration, see Berkhoff, *Harvest of Despair*.

32. Abramson, *Prayer for the Government*, 112.

33. Barbara Leslie Epstein, *The Minsk Ghetto, 1941–1943: Jewish Resistance and Soviet Internationalism* (Berkeley: University of California Press, 2008), 12.

34. Ibid., 18.

35. See, for example, Martin Dean, *Collaboration in the Holocaust: Crimes of the Local Police in Belorussia and Ukraine, 1941–44* (New York: St. Martin's Press, 2000).

2. A Weapon of Mass Destruction

Epigraph: "Richtlinien für das Verhalten der Truppe in Russland, 29 May 1941" (BA-MA: RH 26–252–91), 33.

1. Hull devotes a small portion of her conclusion to the suggestion that the greatest gift of German army history to its Nazi descendants was in the realm of standards of behavior. Her argument concerning these norms and institutional memory is a powerful and convincing one. For two viewpoints on this debate see Isabel V. Hull, *Absolute Destruction: Military Culture and the Practices of War in Imperial Germany* (Ithaca, N.Y.: Cornell University Press, 2005); Robert Gerwarth and Stephan Malinowski, "Der Holocaust als 'Kolonialer Genozid'? Europäische Kolonialgewalt und nationalsozialistischer Vernichtungskrieg," *Geschichte und Gesellschaft* 33, no. 3 (2007). Birthe Kundrus confronts this same debate, concluding that a focus on continuing "mentalities" can provide useful comparisons. See Birthe Kundrus, "From the Herero to the Holocaust? Some Remarks on the Current Debate," *Africa Spectrum* 40, no. 2 (2005).

2. Hull, *Absolute Destruction*, 126.

3. Ibid., 107.

4. George Steinmetz, *The Devil's Handwriting: Precoloniality and the German Colonial State in Qingdao, Samoa, and Southwest Africa* (Chicago: University of Chicago Press, 2007), 199.

5. Ibid., 205.

6. Hull, *Absolute Destruction*, 64.

7. Steinmetz, *Devil's Handwriting,* 239.

8. John N. Horne and Alan Kramer, *German Atrocities, 1914: A History of Denial* (New Haven, Conn.: Yale University Press, 2001), 430.

9. Ibid., 138.

10. Omer Bartov, *Hitler's Army: Soldiers, Nazis, and War in the Third Reich* (New York: Oxford University Press, 1991), 59.

11. Many historians argue that the larger Wehrmacht, particularly in the officer corps, incorporated new class and social strata of society that had not been previously a part of the military.

12. For a very detailed study on this phenomenon, see Vejas G. Liulevicius, *War Land on the Eastern Front: Culture, National Identity and German Occupation in World War I* (Cambridge: Cambridge University Press, 2000).

13. Gordon Alexander Craig, *The Politics of the Prussian Army, 1640–1945* (Oxford: Clarendon Press, 1955), 377.

14. Some historians view this pact as a critical failing that doomed the Weimar Republic. While one could perhaps take this view in hindsight, Ebert had little choice at the time but to accept the support of the only viable military force around to prevent what he saw as a devastating Communist revolution. This presumes the Spartacists represented an imminent and real threat that was not vastly overblown in Ebert's fears and perceptions, an assessment that is at the heart of the controversy.

15. Craig, *Politics of the Prussian Army,* 362.

16. Jeremy Noakes and Geoffrey Pridham, eds., *Nazism, 1919–1945: A Documentary Reader,* vol. 3 (Exeter, UK: University of Exeter Press, 1995), 637.

17. Saul Friedländer, *Nazi Germany and the Jews: The Years of Persecution, 1933–1939,* vol. 1 (New York: HarperCollins, 1997), 75.

18. For more on antisemitism in the Reichswehr, see Jürgen Förster, "Aber für die Juden wird auch noch die Stunde schlagen, und dann wehe Ihnen!" Reichswehr und Antisemitismus, in *Deutsche, Juden, Völkermord: Der Holocaust als Geschichte und Gegenwart,* ed. Klaus-Michael Mallmann and Jürgen Matthäus (Darmstadt: Wissenschaftliche Buchgesellschaft, 2006).

19. Jochen Böhler, *Auftakt zum Vernichtungskrieg: Die Wehrmacht in Polen 1939* (Frankfurt am Main: Fischer Taschenbuch Verlag, 2006), 202.

20. Ibid.

21. Saul Friedländer, *The Years of Extermination: Nazi Germany and the Jews, 1939–1945* (New York: HarperCollins, 2007), 13.

22. Noakes and Pridham, *Nazism, 1919–1945,* 928.

23. Alexander B. Rossino, *Hitler Strikes Poland: Blitzkrieg, Ideology, and Atrocity* (Lawrence: University Press of Kansas, 2003), 16.

24. Noakes and Pridham, *Nazism, 1919–1945,* 939.

25. Ibid., 941.

26. Ernst Klee, Willi Dressen, and Volker Riess, *"The Good Old Days": The Holocaust as Seen by Its Perpetrators and Bystanders,* 1st U.S. ed. (New York: Free Press, 1991), 5.

27. Dieter Pohl, *Die Herrschaft der Wehrmacht: Deutsche Militärbesatzung und einheimische Bevölkerung in der Sowjetunion 1941–1944* (München: Oldenbourg, 2008), 53.

28. See Böhler, *Auftakt zum Vernichtungskrieg.*

29. In the last days of May 1940, Vinkt became the scene of the execution of between 86 and 140 civilians as hostages and reprisals.

30. Raffael Scheck, *Hitler's African Victims: The German Army Massacres of Black French Soldiers in 1940* (Cambridge: Cambridge University Press, 2006), 165.

31. Jürgen Förster, *Die Wehrmacht im NS-Staat: Eine strukturgeschichtliche Analyse* (München: R. Oldenbourg Verlag, 2007), 168–169.

32. Karel C. Berkhoff, "The 'Russian' Prisoners of War in Nazi-Ruled Ukraine as Victims of Genocidal Massacre," *Holocaust and Genocide Studies* 15, no. 1 (2001): 3. Indeed, therefore, they could not be rehabilitated or reeducated. Bolshevism and, by extension, Judaism were a part of their racial makeup that could not be removed.

33. Adolf Hitler, *Mein Kampf* (Boston: Houghton Mifflin, 1939), 950.

34. For a discussion of the earlier roots of the desire for eastern territory, see Michael Burleigh, *Germany Turns Eastwards: A Study of Ostforschung in the Third Reich* (Cambridge: Cambridge University Press, 1988); Liulevicius, *War Land on the Eastern Front.*

35. Ben Kiernan, *Blood and Soil: A World History of Genocide and Extermination from Sparta to Darfur* (New Haven, Conn.: Yale University Press, 2007), 418.

36. Ibid., 428.

37. Ibid., 422.

38. David Olusoga and Casper W. Erichsen, *The Kaiser's Holocaust: Germany's Forgotten Genocide and the Colonial Roots of Nazism* (London: Faber and Faber, 2010), 13.

39. Kiernan, *Blood and Soil,* 426.

40. Hitler, *Mein Kampf,* 950.

41. Ibid., 935.

42. Ibid., 961.

43. Kiernan, *Blood and Soil,* 445.

44. Christian Gerlach, *Kalkulierte Morde: Die deutsche Wirtschafts- und Vernichtungspolitik in Weissrussland 1941 bis 1944* (Hamburg: Hamburger Edition, 1999), 46.

45. Pohl, *Die Herrschaft der Wehrmacht,* 66.

46. "Decree for the Conduct of Courts-Martial in the District 'Barbarossa' and for Special Measures for the Troops, 13 May 1941," in *Nazi Conspiracy and Aggression,* vol. 3 (Washington, D.C., Government Printing Office, 1946), 637, Document 886-PS.

47. Ibid., 638.

48. Ibid., 637.

49. "Richtlinien für das Verhalten der Truppe in Russland, 29 May 1941," 33.

50. Ibid.

51. *Nazi Conspiracy and Aggression,* vol. Supplement A (1947), 352, Document 884-PS.

52. "Soldaten der Ostfront" (BA-MA: RH 26-102-7), Anl. 67.

53. Jan Phillipp Reemtsma, Ulrike Jureit, and Hans Mommsen, eds., *Verbrechen der Wehrmacht: Dimensionen des Vernichtungskrieges 1941–1944: Ausstellungskatalog* (Hamburg: Hamburger, 2002), 56.

54. Peter Witte, Michael Wildt, Martina Voigt, Dieter Pohl, Peter Klein, Christian Ger-
    lach, Christoph Dieckmann, and Andrej Angrick, eds., *Der Dienstkalender Hein-
    rich Himmlers 1941/42* (Hamburg: Christians, 1999), 139n.

55. Ibid., 150.

56. Reemtsma, Jureit, and Mommsen, *Verbrechen der Wehrmacht*, 58–60.

57. "Besondere Anordnungen für den Fall 'B' über Militärische Hoheitsrechte, Sicher-
    ung, und Verwaltung im Rückwärtigen Gebiet, Beute, Kriegsgefangene, 15 June
    1941" (BA-MA: RH 26–28–18).

58. "rHGM Korpsbefehl Nr. 18, 24 June 1941" (BA-MA: RH 26–221–12b), Anl. 193.

59. Meeting notes, 19 May 1941, taken by Major Schmidt von Altenstadt with General
    Wagner, in Reemtsma, Jureit, and Mommsen, *Verbrechen der Wehrmacht*, 61.

60. In a further illustration of the complexity of perpetrator personalities, Wagner
    would be forced to commit suicide in 1944 as part of the plot against Hitler.

61. "OKW Order No. 3058/41, 8 September 1941," in *Nazi Conspiracy and Aggression*,
    vol. 4 (1946), Document 1519-PS.

62. Christian Streit, *Keine Kameraden: Die Wehrmacht und die sowjetischen Kriegsge-
    fangenen, 1941–1945* (Stuttgart: Deutsche Verlags-Anstalt, 1978), 79.

63. See table ibid., 138–139.

64. Ibid., 72.

65. Konrad Jarausch, *Reluctant Accomplice: A Wehrmacht Soldier's Letters from the
    Eastern Front* (Princeton, N.J.: Princeton University Press, 2011), 259–261.

66. Mordechai Altshuler, *Soviet Jewry on the Eve of the Holocaust: A Social and Demo-
    graphic Profile* (Jerusalem: Centre for Research of East European Jewry, Hebrew
    University of Jerusalem, 1998), 17.

67. "Ereignismeldung UdSSR Nr. 73, 4 September 1941" (USHMM: 1999.A.0196 [Reel
    1]), 2–722180.

68. This calculus has been discussed previously by André Mineau. See Mineau, *Opera-
    tion Barbarossa: Ideology and Ethics against Human Dignity* (New York: Rodopi,
    2004), 116. His useful formulation is as follows:

    | "Commencement of Operation Barbarossa | Jew = Bolshevik |
    | A few months into the operation | Jew = Bolshevik = partisan |
    | After encounter with enemy / partisans | civilian = partisan." |

    This book fundamentally alters Mineau's position by contending that the
    Jew-partisan connection was made almost instantaneously and that no actual
    contact with the enemy was required to justify crimes against civilians (Jews or
    non-Jews).

69. "rHGM Order: Creation of Game Preserve, 18 June 1941" (BA-MA: RH 26–221–12a),
    Anl. 387.

70. "221 SD Div. Befehl: Versprengte Truppen, 8 July 1941" (BA-MA: RH 26–221–12a),
    Anl. 309.

71. "rHGM Memo: Wichtigkeit der Strassenzüge und Ausbesserung der Strassen, 19
    July 1941" (BA-MA: RH 22–224), Anl. 156.

72. "221 SD Memo, 11 August 1941" (BA-MA: RH 26–221–13b), Anl. 488.

73. "403 Ic Tkb, Juli 1941" (BA-MA: RH 26-403-4a).

74. "Judgment against Leopold Windisch, Lg Mainz, 17 July 1969" (Yad Vashem: TR. 10/665).

75. Gerlach, *Kalkulierte Morde,* 537.

76. See Felix Römer, *Der Kommissarbefehl: Wehrmacht und NS-Verbrechen an der Ostfront 1941/42* (Paderborn: Schöningh, 2008.).

77. Christian Hartmann, *Wehrmacht im Ostkrieg: Front und militärisches Hinterland 1941–42* (München: R. Oldenbourg, 2009), 487.

78. Christian Streit, *Keine Kameraden: Die Wehrmacht und die sowjetischen Kriegsgefangenen 1941–1945* (Bonn: Verlag J. H. W. Dietz Nachf., 1991), 91.

79. Jörn Hasenclever, *Wehrmacht und Besatzungspolitik in der Sowjetunion: Die Befehlshaber der rückwärtigen Heeresgebiete 1941–1943* (Paderborn: Schöningh, 2010), 69.

80. Konrad Jarausch's edited collection of his father's wartime letters provides a glimpse into the mind-set of a man attempting to care for POWs with hopelessly insufficient support. Konrad Jarausch, Klaus Jochen Arnold, and Konrad Hugo Jarausch, *Das stille Sterben . . . : Feldpostbriefe von Konrad Jarausch aus Polen und Russland 1939–1942* (Paderborn: Schöningh, 2008). See also Klaus Jochen Arnold, *Die Wehrmacht und die Besatzungspolitik in den besetzten Gebieten der Sowjetunion: Kriegführung und Radikalisierung im "Unternehmen Barbarossa"* (Berlin: Duncker & Humblot, 2005), 397–404; Christian Hartmann, "Massensterben oder Massenvernichtung? Sowjetische Kriegsgefangene im 'Unternehmen Barbarossa' aus dem Tagebuch eines deutschen Lagerkommandanten," in *Der Deutsche Krieg im Osten 1941–1944,* ed. Christian Hartmann et al. (München: R. Oldenbourg Verlag, 2009).

81. Christian Streit, "Das Schicksal der Verwundeten Sowjetischen Kriegsgefangenen," in *Vernichtungskrieg: Verbrechen der Wehrmacht 1941–1944,* ed. Hannes Heer and Klaus Naumann (Hamburg: Hamburger Edition, 1995), 79.

82. Interestingly, in the First World War, the death rate was only 5.4 percent. Heer and Naumann, *Vernichtungskrieg,* 188.

83. Niall Ferguson, "Prisoner Taking and Prisoner Killing in the Age of Total War: Towards a Political Economy of Military Defeat," *War in History* 11, no. 2 (2004): 186. For additional contrast, 33 percent of American and 24.8 percent of British POWs died in Japanese captivity.

84. It is in this way that non-Russians like the Ukrainian John Demjanjuk and many others like him were able to escape death in POW camps by volunteering to serve as guards at concentration and extermination camps.

85. Arnold, *Die Wehrmacht und die Besatzungspolitik,* 500.

86. For more on the German army as occupier and collaborator in anti-Jewish policy, see Theo J. Schulte, *The German Army and Nazi Policies in Occupied Russia* (New York: St. Martin's Press, 1989); Wolfgang Curilla, *Die deutsche Ordnungspolizei und der Holocaust im Baltikum und in Weissrussland, 1941–1944* (Paderborn: Schöningh, 2006).

87. Shalom Cholawsky, *The Jews of Bielorussia during World War II* (Amsterdam: Harwood Academic, 1998), 47.

88. Ben Shepherd, *War in the Wild East: The German Army and Soviet Partisans* (Cambridge, Mass.: Harvard University Press, 2004), 73.

89. Christopher R. Browning, "The Nazi Decision to Commit Mass Murder: Three Interpretations; The Euphoria of Victory and the Final Solution; Summer–Fall 1941," *German Studies Review* 17, no. 3 (1994): 474.

90. Olusoga and Erichsen, *Kaiser's Holocaust,* 105.

91. "OKW Order No. 02041/41, 12 September 1941," in *Nazi Conspiracy and Aggression,* vol. 3 (1946), 636, Document 878-PS.

92. "OKW Order No. 02061/41, 16 September 1941," in *Nazi Conspiracy and Aggression,* vol. 6 (1946), Document C-148.

93. "rHGM Befehl: Partisanenabt. Der Sowjets, 26 July 1941" (BA-MA: RH 22–224), 177.

94. "rHGM Befehl: Kollektive Gewaltmassnahmen, 12 August 1941" (BA-MA: RH 22–224), Anl. 502.

95. Yaacov Lozowick, "Rollbahn Mord: The Early Activities of Einsatzgruppe C," *Holocaust Genocide Studies* 2, no. 2 (1987): 234.

96. Richard Rhodes, *Masters of Death: The SS-Einsatzgruppen and the Invention of the Holocaust* (New York: Vintage Books, 2003), 17.

97. Christopher Browning has laid out in detail how this may have occurred and how the changes in killing patterns in the summer of 1941 reflect a change in policy. See Christopher R. Browning, "Beyond 'Intentionalism' and 'Functionalism': The Decision for the Final Solution Reconsidered," in *The Path to Genocide: Essays on Launching the Final Solution,* ed. Christopher R. Browning (Cambridge: Cambridge University Press, 1992). See also Christopher R. Browning, *Ordinary Men: Reserve Police Battalion 101 and the Final Solution in Poland* (New York: Harper Perennial, 1998), 11.

98. Ibid., 105.

99. Martin Cüppers, *Wegbereiter der Shoah: Die Waffen-SS, der Kommandostab Reichsführer-SS und die Judenvernichtung 1939–1945* (Darmstadt: Wissenschaftliche Buchgesellschaft, 2005), 139.

100. Christopher R. Browning and Jürgen Matthäus, *The Origins of the Final Solution: The Evolution of Nazi Jewish Policy, September 1939–March 1942* (Lincoln: University of Nebraska Press, 2004), 281. The order was passed on 1 August.

101. Ibid.

102. Philip W. Blood, *Hitler's Bandit Hunters: The SS and the Nazi Occupation of Europe* (Washington, D.C.: Potomac Books, 2006), 58.

103. Browning and Matthäus, *Origins of the Final Solution,* 320.

104. Ibid., 312.

105. Ibid., 325.

106. Christian Gerlach, however, argues that these deportations did not necessarily mean a decision to kill German Jews, that this decision was not made until December 1941. See Christian Gerlach, "The Wannsee Conference, the Fate of German Jews, and Hitler's Decision in Principle to Exterminate All European Jews," *Journal of Modern History* 70, no. 4 (1998).

3. Improvised Murder in Krupki

Epigraph: "S., Erich Statement, 14 April 1965" (BA-ZS: B162/3876), 447.

1. "Krupka" is the German transliteration of "Krupki." "Krupki" will be used throughout, except in places where German documents or speakers are being directly quoted.

2. "M., Bruno Statement, 24 May 1966" (BA-ZS: B162/3876), 102; "R., Georg Statement, 25 January 1967" (LA-NRW: Münster: Q124/3548).

3. "K., Walter Statement, 9 May 1966" (BA-ZS: B162/3876), 534.

4. Other sources put the total number of dead at nineteen hundred. See "Soviet Extraordinary State Commission Report, 26 Sep 1944," in *Krupki Rayon,* ed. Henadz Pashkou (Minsk: Belaruskaia Entsyklapedyia, 1999), 184.

5. Martin Dean and Geoffrey P. Megargee, eds., *Encyclopedia of Camps and Ghettos II: Ghettos in German-Occupied Eastern Europe,* vol. B (Bloomington: Indiana University Press, 2012), 1692.

6. "The Untold Stories: The Murder Sites of the Jews in the Occupied Territories of the Former USSR," Yad Vashem the Holocaust Martyrs' and Heroes' Remembrance Authority, http://www1.yadvashem.org/untoldstories/krupki/Krupki.html.

7. "Kosenkova, Margarita Interview, 8 July 2009" (conducted by author; in author's personal archive). Interpreter: Vadim Ovsyanik.

8. "Dranitsa, Nadezhda Vladimirovna Interview, 24 July 2011" (interview conducted and translated by Yauheniya Spallino-Mironava).

9. Michael Mann, *The Dark Side of Democracy: Explaining Ethnic Cleansing* (New York: Cambridge University Press, 2005), 195–196.

10. See Wolf Gruner and Jörg Osterloh, eds., *Das "Grossdeutsche Reich" und die Juden: Nationalsozialistische Verfolgung in den "angegliederten" Gebieten,* Wissenschaftliche Reihe des Fritz Bauer Instituts (Frankfurt am Main: Campus Verlag, 2010).

11. See Ben Shepherd, *Terror in the Balkans: German Armies and Partisan Warfare* (Cambridge, Mass.: Harvard University Press, 2012).

12. This average age is based on a 10th Company personnel roster of 215 soldiers from 1939. "10th Company Personnel Roster, 27 August 1939" (LA-NRW: Münster: Q124/3541), 61–74.

13. These averages are derived from the demographic data of thirty-four NCOs and officers from the 354th interviewed after the war. This is admittedly not a large sample, but these numbers are not out of proportion to similar units in this study and are thus likely a useful approximation.

14. "10th Company Personnel Roster, 27 August 1939," 69.

15. Georg Tessin, *Verbände und Truppen der deutschen Wehrmacht und Waffen-SS im Zweiten Weltkrieg 1939–1945,* vol. 8 (Osnabrück: Biblio, 1979), 58–59.

16. "Richtlinien für die Ausbildung der Sicherungs-Divisionen und der dem Befehlshaber des rückwärtigen Heeres-Gebiets unterstehenden Kräfte, 21 March 1941" (BA-MA: RH 26–286–3), Anl. 12.

17. "Befehl für die Bereitstellung zum Vormarsch, 20 June 1941" (BA-MA: RH 26–286–3), Anl. 38.

18. "Waldow, J. Statement, 28 January 1964" (BA-ZS: B162/3875), 183.

19. See the following testimonies: "G., Konrad Statement, 11 May 1966" (BA-ZS: B162/3876), 519; "Gänsler, W. Statement, 3 August 1966" (BA-ZS: B162/3876), 563; "K., Werner Statement, 13 June 1966" (BA-ZS: B162/3876), 646.

20. "Korück 559 Kriegestagebuch, 8 July 1941" (BA-MA: RH 23–124), 7.

21. The most comprehensive work on German POW policy is that of Christian Streit. Christian Streit, *Keine Kameraden: Die Wehrmacht und die sowjetischen Kriegsgefangenen 1941–1945* (Bonn: Verlag J. H. W. Dietz Nachf., 1991).

22. Transcript of interview with Bruno Menzel, Ingo Helm, Christian Frey, Alexander Berkel, and Peter Hartl, "Die Wehrmacht—Eine Bilanz" (ZDF and Cinecentrum Berlin Film- und Fernsehproduktion, 2007).

23. "Erläuterungen zur Übergabe des Gefangenen-Durchgangslager 127 von Kdt. r.A.559 an A.O.K. 2/O.Q.2, 14 July 1941" (BA-MA: RH 23–124), Anl. 24.

24. "F., Gunther Statement, 10 May 1966" (BA-ZS: B162/3876), 524.

25. "R., Georg Statement, 25 January 1967," 47–48.

26. "H., Erhard Statement, 17 May 1966" (BA-ZS: B162/3876), 496.

27. Christian Gerlach, "German Economic Interests, Occupation Policy, and the Murder of the Jews in Belorussia, 1941/43," in *National Socialist Extermination Policies: Contemporary German Perspectives and Controversies,* ed. Ulrich Herbert (New York: Berghahn Books, 2000), 217.

28. Miriam Tokarski and Ron N. Levitan (trans.), "A Motherly Poem: Miriam Aygas' Story," in *Minsk, Ir Va-Em (Minsk, Jewish Mother-City, a Memorial Anthology),* ed. Shlomo Even-Shushan (Jerusalem: Association of Olim from Minsk and Its Surroundings in Israel, 1975–1985). Accessed online via JewishGen at http://www.jewishgen.org/yizkor/minsk/min2_357.html.

29. Nachum Alpert, *The Destruction of Slonim Jewry: The Story of the Jews of Slonim during the Holocaust* (New York: Holocaust Library, 1989), 24–25.

30. Tokarski and Levitan, "Motherly Poem."

31. The camp near Minsk is mentioned specifically in an Einsatzgruppen report from 13 July 1941 describing the selections, daily executions, and the murder of 1,050 Jews. See Yitzhak Arad, Schmuel Krakowski, and Shmuel Spector, eds., *The Einsatzgruppen Reports: Selections from the Dispatches of the Nazi Death Squads' Campaign against the Jews, July 1941–January 1943* (New York: Holocaust Library, 1989), 22.

32. Transcript of interview with Menzel, Helm, Frey, Berkel, and Hartl, "Die Wehrmacht—Eine Bilanz," I.

33. "Ereignismeldung UdSSR Nr. 73, 4 September 1941" (USHMM: 1999.A.0196 [Reel 1]), 2-722198–722199.

34. *True to Type: A Selection from Letters and Diaries of German Soldiers and Civilians Collected on the Soviet-German Front* (London: Hutchinson & Co., 1945), 29. The problematic nature of this source warrants a brief note. The diary alluded to belonged to a Private Heidenreich. The entries cited appear only in this book, which apparently originated in the Soviet Union and was a collection that sought to portray the crimes of the German army. It is not impossible that the entries were edited to that aim by Soviet authorities, as the original diary has apparently never surfaced.

German authorities interviewed Heidenreich's sister and widow, neither of whom knew of his keeping a diary. However, Heidenreich was a soldier in 12th Company (as stated in the book and confirmed by soldiers from the unit). He was captured in 1943, according to a member of the unit. Moreover, he writes that his battalion guarded a POW camp in Minsk in July 1941, which is correct. Many of the details he mentions (for example, the weather on the day of the mass execution in Krupki, a partisan action in which a soldier is shot in the leg, and the Christmas celebration that was canceled when the unit was forced to move to the front) are corroborated by other soldiers' testimony. While some dates appear to be inaccurate, in the final analysis it appears that, regardless of the circumstances under which this text was written, whether an actual diary or something Heidenreich himself wrote willingly (or perhaps unwillingly) in Soviet custody, the portions of the published entries that can be checked against other sources have proven to be accurate.

35. "M., Bruno Statement, 8 September 1961" (BA-ZS: B162/3876); Menzel, Helm, Frey, Berkel, and Hartl, "Die Wehrmacht—Eine Bilanz."

36. Yitzhak Arad, *The Holocaust in the Soviet Union* (Lincoln: University of Nebraska Press, 2009), 152.

37. "Map: Einsatz der Sich. Div. 286, 28 July 1941" (BA-MA: RH 26–286–3), Anl. 61.

38. "Tätigkeitsberichte Nr. 1 über den Einsatz der Eingreifgruppe vom 26.7–1.8.1941" (BA-MA: RH 26–286–4), Anl. 67.

39. "M., Richard Statement, 2 December 1963" (BA-ZS: B162/3875), 136.

40. "HGM Ib Report, 19 September 1941" (BStA Minsk: 655-1-1).

41. "Erfahrungsbericht über die bisherigen Unternehmungen mit Panje-Spähtrupps, 13 Oct. 1941" (BA-MA: RH 26–286–4/2), Anl. 117.

42. That such patrols took place was confirmed by soldier Willi B. "B., Willi Statement, 10 December 1963" (BA-ZS: B162/3875).

43. "H., Erhard Statement, 17 May 1966," 499–500.

44. EK 8 was commanded by Otto Bradfisch and assigned to Einsatzgruppe B, commanded by Arthur Nebe.

45. Irene Sagel-Grande, H. H. Fuchs, and C. F. Rüter, eds., *Justiz und NS-Verbrechen. Sammlung deutscher Strafurteile wegen nationalsozialistischer Tötungsverbrechen 1945–1966*, vol. 20 (Amsterdam: University Press Amsterdam, 1979), 165–166. Schönemann returned to Berlin in October 1941 and resumed his law studies. He then served with Einsatzkommando 13 in Slovakia and was involved in killings of civilians there in connection with the anti-partisan war. After the war, he was briefly punished by the Austrians before fleeing the continent. He lived in Lebanon, Egypt, Greece, Spain, and Switzerland before being arrested by the Germans in 1961.

46. "L., Robert Statement, 27 February 1963" (BA-ZS: B162/3290), 240.

47. "K., Kurt, Statement, 14 February 1963" (BA-ZS: B162/3290), 209.

48. "K., Willy Statement, 1 March 1963" (BA-ZS: B162/3291), 268.

49. "K., Kurt, Statement, 14 February 1963," 210.

50. Sagel-Grande, Fuchs, and Rüter, *Justiz und NS-Verbrechen*, 166.

51. "Einsatzkommando 8 Report, 5 August 1941" (BStA Minsk: 655-1-1).

52. "3/IR 354 Report, 29 August 1941" (BStA Minsk: 655-1-1), 118.

53. Both Speth and Waldow claimed that they were only asked to support a "resettling" of the Jews. However, this is clearly a postwar attempt at avoiding responsibility (and is itself contradicted by Speth's later remembrance of his conversation with Schönemann).

54. "Waldow, J. Statement, 28 January 1964," 186–187.

55. "S., Werner Statement, 11 March 1964" (BA-ZS: B162/3875), 221.

56. Much postwar testimony revolved around whether or not Meyer-Schöller was actually the regimental adjutant at the time. He claimed to have already been the commander of the 11th Company and that another officer had taken over. The documents and testimony are not conclusive, but given Waldow's and Speth's conviction that it was Meyer-Schöller, it is likely that he was the adjutant. In any case, contrary to von Rekowski's statements, the most important conclusion here is that the 3rd Battalion's support of the Einsatzgruppen in this massacre was both known and condoned by its higher headquarters.

57. "Waldow, J. Statement, 28 January 1964," 187.

58. "S., Werner Statement, 11 March 1964," 221. SS, SD, and Einsatzgruppen are meant here. Himmler's preinvasion agreement with the Wehrmacht specified logistic support, and in practice this seems to have been understood as manpower in addition to matériel.

59. One company commander claimed not to have been notified at this meeting that the goal of the action was the shooting of the Jews. However, this is a common attempt at self-exculpation.

60. That these were peat pits was also confirmed by the Extraordinary State Commission. See "Soviet Extraordinary State Commission Report, 26 Sep 1944," 184. In addition, a visit to the site confirms the geographical description of the killing site.

61. "M., Franz Statement, 25 May 1966" (BA-ZS: B162/3876), 480–481.

62. "K., Walter Statement, 11 December 1963" (BA-ZS: B162/3875), 165.

63. "M., Richard Statement, 10 March 1965" (BA-ZS: B162/3876), 420.

64. "L., Wilhelm Statement, 5 March 1965" (BA-ZS: B162/3876), 410.

65. "W., Paul Statement, 28 November 1963" (BA-ZS: B162/3875), 157.

66. "H., Hans Statement, 10 March 1964" (BA-ZS: B162/3875), 228–229.

67. "L., Robert Statement, 27 February 1963," 235.

68. "Schier, H. Statement, 1 May 1965" (BA-ZS: B162/3876), 351.

69. "N., Hermann Statement, 18 March 1964" (BA-ZS: B162/3875), 234.

70. See Dean and Megargee, *Encyclopedia of Camps and Ghettos II,* 1692; "Statement of Maria Tarasovna Shpunt before Extraordinary State Commission," in Pashkou, *Krupki Rayon,* 185.

71. "H., Bruno Statement, 1 November 1967" (LA-NRW: Münster: Q234/3548), 32; "K., Walter Statement, 9 May 1966," 532.

72. Transcript of interview with Menzel, Helm, Frey, Berkel, and Hartl, "Die Wehrmacht—Eine Bilanz."

73. "H., Bruno Statement, 1 November 1967," 32–33.

74. "M., Bruno Statement, 24 May 1966," 486.

75. "Kosenkova, Margarita Interview, 8 July 2009."

76. "K., Walter Statement, 11 December 1963," 165–166.

77. "Statement of Maria Tarasovna Shpunt before Extraordinary State Commission," 185.

78. "S., Erich Statement, 3 November 1966" (LA-NRW: Münster: Q124/3547), 105.

79. "R., Georg Statement, 25 January 1967," 103.

80. "From the Reminiscence of S. Ia. Shaloumova, a Resident of Krupki," in Pashkou, *Krupki Rayon*, 191. See also "Shpunt, M., 26 September 1944" (LA-NRW: Münster: Q234/3556), 51.

81. "S., Erich Statement, 3 November 1966," 105.

82. "Einstellungsverfügung Zst Dortmund 45 Js 9/64 Gg. Waldow U. A., 9 September 1969" (BA-ZS: B162/3911), 741.

83. Some testimonies indicate victims were forced to enter the pit, while others state that the victims were shot outside the pit. Schönemann testified that they entered the pit, so this is likely the most reliable explanation.

84. "K., Erwin Statement, 21 October 1964" (BA-ZS: B162/3875), 269.

85. Leonid Smilovitsky, "Draft of entry for 'Krupki' entry in USHMM Encyclopedia of Camps and Ghettos (Personal Correspondence)," 2008.

86. "Schönemann, W. Statement, 5 April 1963" (BA-ZS: B162/3291), 376–377. It is likely that this was a feeble effort to avoid the legal repercussions of having his actions deemed "cruel," namely that this would make him eligible for prosecution.

87. "S., Erich Statement, 3 November 1966," 106.

88. Dean and Megargee, *Encyclopedia of Camps and Ghettos II*, 1692–1693; "Shpunt, M., 26 September 1944."

89. "Dranitsa, Nadezhda Vladimirovna Interview, 24 July 2011."

90. *True to Type*, 31.

91. "C., Herbert Statement, 17 December 1963" (BA-ZS: B162/3875), 153. Some testimonies obscure the participation of Schrade's platoon by claiming that the "volunteers" were actually for an anti-partisan operation and that Schrade's platoon was on such a mission the day of the execution. It is true that Schrade took only volunteers on his anti-partisan patrols, but his platoon was in Krupki the day of the shooting, as confirmed by several men. Another potential explanation is that this photo was taken at Drozdy. It is also possible that the photograph (which is missing) does not depict Schrade at all.

92. "H., Bruno Statement, 15 January 1965" (BA-ZS: B162/3876), 378.

93. "L., Reinhold Statement, 22 February 1967" (LA-NRW: Münster: Q124/3548), 92.

94. Sönke Neitzel and Harald Welzer, *Soldaten: The Secret World of Transcripts of German POWs* (New York: Alfred A. Knopf, 2012), 139.

95. "L., Wilhelm Statement, 5 March 1965," 410; "S., Gustav Statement, 2 March 1965" (BA-ZS: B162/3876), 398; "G., Konrad Statement, 11 May 1966," 518–519.

96. "Schönemann, W. Statement, 9 March 1962" (BA-ZS: B162/3277), 618.

97. A soldier in the 9th Company, Friedrich Scholz, described the weather for the period as *Sauwetter*, with strong wind and heavy rain. Scholz was related to a soldier in 10th Company as well. He was killed on 27 December 1941. See "Friedrich Scholz Diary" (author's personal collection). This diary, which ends in December 1941, was supplied to me by a family member.

98. "L., Robert Statement, 27 February 1963," 235.

99. "G., Konrad Statement, 11 May 1966," 519.
100. "K., Willy Statement, 1 March 1963," 266.
101. "Krukowskij, A. Statement, 26 September 1944" (LA-NRW: Münster: Q234/3556), 58.
102. "K., Erwin Statement, 21 October 1964," 269; "Waldow, J. Statement, 28 January 1964," 187.
103. "Testimony of A. V. Kriuchkoskii, a Resident of Krupki," in Pashkou, *Krupki Rayon*, 185. See also "Krukowskij, A. Statement, 26 September 1944," 57–58.
104. Martin Dean, *Collaboration in the Holocaust: Crimes of the Local Police in Belorussia and Ukraine, 1941–44* (New York: St. Martin's Press, 2000).
105. "S., Helmut Statement, 1 May 1965" (BA-ZS: B162/3876), 351.
106. "Dranitsa, Nadezhda Vladimirovna Interview, 24 July 2011."
107. Ibid.
108. Dean and Megargee, *Encyclopedia of Camps and Ghettos II*, 1693.
109. "Dranitsa, Nadezhda Vladimirovna Interview, 24 July 2011."
110. "Kosenkova, Margarita Interview, 8 July 2009."
111. "Ereignismeldung UdSSR Nr. 124, 25 October 1941" (USHMM: 1999.A.0196 [Reel 2]), 2–723043. The nearby town of Kholoponichi was also the site of a large mass shooting that was, again, supported by soldiers from the 3rd Battalion.
112. The Kholoponichi killings are less well documented than the killings in Krupki. However, the 1st and 3rd Platoons of the 10th Company appear to have assisted TK Schönemann's killers here as well. See, for example, "S., Martin Statement, 9 January 1965" (BA-ZS: B162/3876), 365–366; "Nier, E. Statement, 23 May 1966" (BA-ZS: B162/3876), 494.
113. "Tätigkeitsberichte Nr. 10 über den Einsatz des verst. IR 354 in der Zeit vom 4.9.–14.9.41, 19 September 1941" (BA-MA: RH 26-286-4), Anl. 95.
114. "Von Rekowski, S. Statement, 30 March 1967" (LA-NRW: Münster: Q234/3548), 119.
115. "Merkblatt über Zuständigkeit, Unterstellung, und Aufgaben, 2 November 1941" (BA-MA: RH 26-339-5), Anl. 13.
116. "rHGM Korpsbefehl 55, 29 September 1941" (BA-MA: RH 22-225), 95.
117. "286 SD Ic Tätigskeitbericht, Sep-Dec 1941" (BA-MA: RH 26-286-5). Neumann assumed command of EG B from Nebe in November 1941.
118. "221 SD order to FK 549, 18 July 1941" (BA-MA: RH 26-221-12a), Anl. 381.
119. "286 SD Memo: Vorgänge in Boguschewskoje, 7 September 1941" (BA-MA: RH 26-286-4), Anl. 88.
120. "286 SD Personnel Report" (BA-MA: RH 26-286-5).
121. "M., Richard Statement, 2 December 1963," 136.
122. "Waldow, J. Statement, 10 February 1969" (LA-NRW: Münster: Q124/3549), 65.
123. "J., Erich Statement, 26 May 1966" (BA-ZS: B162/3876), 475.
124. "S., Martin Statement, 9 January 1965," 364.
125. "D., Paul Statement, 23 October 1964" (BA-ZS: B162/3875), 274–275.
126. "S., Martin Statement, 29 March 1967" (LA-NRW: Münster: Q124/3548), 113.
127. The 10th Company commander also reported calling Major Waldow and requesting to be released from the order to support the execution. It is possible that this occurred. However, as a commander, First Lieutenant B. was much more vulnerable to a legal

charge himself and therefore more likely to invent some form of reluctance or resistance. In addition, Waldow does not corroborate this phone call. Finally, Lieutenant B.'s presence at the execution site does not support his discomfort with the mission. "B., Paul Statement, 17 September 1968" (LA-NRW: Münster: Q124/3548), 37.

128. "L., Paul Statement, 18 April 1967" (LA-NRW: Münster: Q124/3548), 146–147.

129. "S., Erich Statement, 3 November 1966," 106.

130. "H., Bruno Statement, 1 November 1967," 34.

131. Neitzel and Welzer, *Soldaten*, 239.

132. Transcript of interview with Menzel, Helm, Frey, Berkel, and Hartl, "Die Wehrmacht—Eine Bilanz."

133. "K., Erwin Statement, 21 October 1964," 269.

134. "M., Bruno Statement, 8 September 1961," 49.

135. "N., Hermann Statement, 18 March 1964," 237.

136. "L., Paul Statement, 18 April 1967," 145–146.

137. Daniel Bar-On, "The Bystander in Relation to the Victim and the Perpetrator: Today and during the Holocaust," *Social Justice Research* 14, no. 2 (June 2001): 129.

138. "L., Reinhold Statement, 26 October 1964" (BA-ZS: B162/3875), 284.

139. "C., Herbert Statement, 17 December 1963," 154.

140. "S., Walter Statement, 24 November 1964" (BA-ZS: B162/3876), 317.

141. Schrade did not survive the war, so no testimony from him exists.

142. "S., Fritz Statement, 5 August 1966" (BA-ZS: B162/3876), 569.

143. "L., Richard Statement, 9 December 1963" (BA-ZS: B162/3875), 131. It is worthwhile noting that even under the already harsh guidelines for the treatment of civilians, reprisals could only be ordered by battalion commanders.

144. "K., Erwin Statement, 10 November 1966" (LA-NRW: Münster: Q234-3547), 124.

145. Ibid., 125.

146. "S., Fritz Statement, 5 August 1966," 569.

147. Leonid Smilovitsky, "Draft of entry for 'Krupki' entry in *USHMM Encyclopedia of Camps and Ghettos* (Personal Correspondence)," 2008.

148. "F., Gunther Statement, 10 May 1966," 526.

149. Very few Jews survived the September 18 action. Thus, practically the entirety of what we know of their experiences comes from German soldier postwar testimony.

150. "J., Erich Statement, 26 May 1966," 476.

151. "L., Helmut Statement, 25 July 1966" (BA-ZS: B162/3876), 591.

152. "Koschwitz, W. Statement, 13 June 1966" (BA-ZS: B162/3876), 641.

153. "M., Richard Statement, 12 January 1967" (LA-NRW: Münster: Q124/3548), 44; "M., Richard Statement, 10 March 1965," 420.

154. "L., Reinhold Statement, 26 October 1964," 284.

155. "Friedrich Scholz Diary."

156. "Dranitsa, Nadezhda Vladimirovna Interview, 24 July 2011."

157. "K., Erwin Statement, 21 October 1964," 507.

158. "J., Erich Statement, 26 May 1966," 476.

159. "K., Kurt, Statement, 14 February 1963," 214; "K., Willy Statement, 1 March 1963," 266.

160. Neitzel and Welzer, *Soldaten,* 115–117.

161. Schmuel Spector, "Aktion 1005—Effacing the Murder of Millions," *Holocaust Genocide Studies* 5, no. 2 (1990): 164.

162. "Baranchik, V. Statement, 28 December 1945" (BStA Minsk: 1363-1-1919), 23b.

163. "Kosenkova, Margarita Interview, 8 July 2009."

164. "The Untold Stories: The Murder Sites of the Jews in the Occupied Territories of the Former USSR."

165. Dean and Megargee, *Encyclopedia of Camps and Ghettos II,* 1693.

166. John Kiler, "The Holocaust and the Soviet Union," in *The Historiography of the Holocaust,* ed. Dan Stone (New York: Palgrave Macmillan, 2006), 282.

167. "Dranitsa, Nadezhda Vladimirovna Interview, 24 July 2011."

4. Mogilev and the Deliberate Targeting of Jews

Epigraph: "W., Leopold Statement, 29 July 1953" (HSA-D: H-13 Darmstadt, Nr. 919 I, Bd. II), 326.

1. The 691st Infantry Regiment was part of the 339th Infantry Division, a regular infantry unit.

2. "Magel, Wilhelm Statement, 8 August 1951" (HSA-D: H-13 Darmstadt, Nr. 979 I, Bd. II), 172.

3. This area encompassed most of modern-day Belarus.

4. For an excellent summary of recent historiography in this area, see Ben Shepherd, "The Clean Wehrmacht: The War of Extermination and Beyond," *Historical Journal* 52, no. 2 (2009). For more on the anti-partisan connection and killings of Jews, see Truman Anderson, "Incident at Baranivka: German Reprisals and the Soviet Partisan Movement in Ukraine, October–December 1941," *Journal of Modern History* 71, no. 3 (1999); Ben Shepherd, *War in the Wild East: The German Army and Soviet Partisans* (Cambridge, Mass.: Harvard University Press, 2004); Dieter Pohl, *Die Herrschaft der Wehrmacht: Deutsche Militärbesatzung und einheimische Bevölkerung in der Sowjetunion 1941–1944* (München: Oldenbourg, 2008).

5. This conference is not unknown to historians. Indeed, it has often been mentioned in passing or briefly summarized. However, a detailed analysis and discussion of the consequences of this meeting have not yet been conducted. For some (but certainly not all) previous citations of this conference, see Christopher R. Browning and Jürgen Matthäus, *The Origins of the Final Solution: The Evolution of Nazi Jewish Policy, September 1939–March 1942* (Lincoln: University of Nebraska Press, 2004); Jan Phillipp Reemtsma, Ulrike Jureit, and Hans Mommsen, eds., *Verbrechen der Wehrmacht: Dimensionen des Vernichtungskrieges 1941–1944: Ausstellungskatalog* (Hamburg: Hamburger, 2002).

6. Jan Zaprudnik, *Historical Dictionary of Belarus* (Lanham, Md.: Scarecrow Press, 1998), 152.

7. "rHGM Stabsbefehl 56, 6 September 1941" (BA-MA: RH 22-225), 29–30.

8. These individuals are referred to as *versprengte* in contemporary military reports.

9. Leonid D. Grenkevich and David M. Glantz, *The Soviet Partisan Movement, 1941–1944: A Critical Historiographical Analysis* (Portland, Ore.: Frank Cass Publishers, 1999), 323. Grenkevich argues that almost 10 percent of German forces were arrayed against the partisans, even in 1941. Notwithstanding that all units stationed behind the front were not fighting partisans, the dubious quality of security divisions and police units in fighting a conventional war likely minimizes the overall effects of their absence from the front. From the summer of 1942 onward, however, the partisan units in Belarus became far more deadly, controlled large amounts of territory, and certainly had a negative effect on the German war effort.

10. Mark Mazower, *Hitler's Empire: How the Nazis Ruled Europe* (New York: Penguin Press, 2008), 144.

11. Timothy P. Mulligan, "Reckoning the Cost of People's War: The German Experience in the Central USSR," *Russian History* 9 (1982): 31.

12. Grenkevich and Glantz, *Soviet Partisan Movement*, 71.

13. Hannes Heer, "The Logic of the War of Extermination: The Wehrmacht and the Anti-Partisan War," in *War of Extermination: The German Military in World War II, 1941–1944*, ed. Hannes Heer and Klaus Naumann (New York: Berghahn Books, 2000), 97.

14. "rHGM Memo: Partisanenabt. Der Sowjets, 26 July 1941" (BA-MA: RH 22–224).

15. "OKH Memo: Behandlung Feindlicher Zivilpersonen, 25 July 1941" (BStA Minsk: 655–1–1), 34.

16. Mulligan, "Reckoning the Cost of People's War," 32.

17. "286 SD Personnel Reports, 22 June–31 December 1941" (BA-MA: RH 26–286–5). This is out of an average strength of 5,700 men. Compare this, for example, with the 78th Infantry Division, which suffered 255 killed in action on July 22 alone in the battle for Mogilev. See "78 ID Casualty Charts, June–December 1941" (BA-MA: RH 26–78–27).

18. For a more extreme case, consider the 707th Infantry Division in western Belarus, which reported 10,940 prisoners shot while losing two Germans killed and five wounded in October 1941. Jürgen Förster, "The Wehrmacht and the War of Extermination against the Soviet Union," *Yad Vashem Studies* 14 (1981): 32. In addition, these ratios skyrocket when one adds all reported enemy casualties to all reported German casualties. For a nicely detailed discussion of these issues, see Mulligan, "Reckoning the Cost of People's War."

19. Henry Abramson, *A Prayer for the Government: Ukrainians and Jews in Revolutionary Times, 1917–1920* (Cambridge, Mass.: Harvard University Press, 1999), 112.

20. Martin Cüppers, *Wegbereiter der Shoah: Die Waffen-SS, der Kommandostab Reichsführer-SS und die Judenvernichtung 1939–1945* (Darmstadt: Wissenschaftliche Buchgesellschaft, 2005), OCLC Number: 59080200. 201.

21. Christian Gerlach, "German Economic Interests, Occupation Policy, and the Murder of the Jews in Belorussia, 1941/43," in *National Socialist Extermination Policies: Contemporary German Perspectives and Controversies*, ed. Ulrich Herbert (New York: Berghahn Books, 2000), 217.

22. "rHGM Korpsbefehl 53, 16 Sept. 1941" (BA-MA: RH 22–225).

23. These were officers in command positions (23/60).

24. "350 IR Bericht, 19.8.1941" (BA-MA: RH 22–221), 295.

25. Michael Wildt, *Generation of the Unbound: The Leadership Corps of the Reich Security Main Office* (Jerusalem: Yad Vashem, 2002), 19.

26. Peter Black, "Arthur Nebe: Nationalsozialist im Zwielicht," in *Die SS: Elite unter dem Totenkopf: 30 Lebensläufe,* ed. Ronald M. Smelser and Enrico Syring (Paderborn: Schöningh, 2000), 371–372. Nebe was executed for his participation in the July 20 plot. Some have argued that he deliberately inflated the numbers of Jews he reported killed. Yet all evidence indicates that he was quite content to play his role in Nazi genocide and that his subsequent displeasure with the regime may have stemmed from the imminent Nazi defeat but not opposition to the Holocaust.

27. Guenter Lewy, *The Nazi Persecution of the Gypsies* (Oxford: Oxford University Press, 2000), 206.

28. Browning and Matthäus, *Origins of the Final Solution,* 289.

29. Philip W. Blood, *Hitler's Bandit Hunters: The SS and the Nazi Occupation of Europe* (Washington, D.C.: Potomac Books, 2006), 57.

30. Andrej Angrick, "Erich von dem Bach-Zelewski: Himmlers Mann für alle Fälle," in Smelser and Syring, *Die SS,* 36–37.

31. His physician Ernst Grawitz noted that Bach-Zelewski "suffers from flashbacks connected with the shootings of Jews which he himself conducted." Richard Rhodes, *Masters of Death: The SS-Einsatzgruppen and the Invention of the Holocaust* (New York: Vintage Books, 2003), 226.

32. Christopher R. Browning, *Ordinary Men: Reserve Police Battalion 101 and the Final Solution in Poland* (New York: Harper Perennial, 1998), 15.

33. While Magill's regiment did kill women and children in Pinsk, his reports indicate that he interpreted his orders more narrowly and generally killed only men. Cüppers, *Wegbereiter der Shoah,* 177; Martin Cüppers, "Vorreiter der Shoah: Ein Vergleich der Einsätze der beiden SS-Kavallerieregimenter im August 1941," in *Krieg und Verbrechen: Situation und Intention: Fallbeispiele,* ed. Timm C. Richter (München: Meidenbauer, 2006).

34. See Cüppers, "Vorreiter der Shoah," 92; Henning Herbert Pieper, "The SS Cavalry Brigade and Its Operations in the Soviet Union, 1941–1942" (University of Sheffield, 2012).

35. Browning and Matthäus, *Origins of the Final Solution,* 312.

36. Ibid., 281.

37. Ibid.

38. Blood, *Hitler's Bandit Hunters,* 58.

39. "Teilnehmer-Verzeichnis am Partisanen-Lehrgang vom 24.9.1941, 23 Sep 1941" (BA-MA: RH 22–225), 76–77. Max Montua was the commander of Police Regiment Mitte, which was made up of Police Battalions 307, 316, and 322. For more on Montua and Police Battalion 322, see Christopher R. Browning, *Ordinary Men: Reserve Police Battalion 101 and the Final Solution in Poland* (New York: Harper Perennial, 1998), 13–14; Klaus-Michael Mallmann, Wolfram Pyta, and Volker Riess, eds.,

Deutscher Osten 1939–1945: Der Weltanschauungskrieg in Photos und Texten (Darmstadt: Wissenschaftliche Buchgesellschaft, 2003), 136–142. For the actions of the 307th and 316th, see Peter Longerich, *Holocaust: The Nazi Persecution and Murder of the Jews* (Oxford: Oxford University Press, 2010), 203–205.

40. The agendas for the conference remain in the archives. Unfortunately, minutes (if any were taken) do not appear to have survived the war.

41. "Einleitungsworte zum Partisanenbekämpfungs Lehrgang, 24 Sep. 1941" (BA-MA: RH 22–225), 81.

42. Ibid., 79–80.

43. "rHGM Tagesordnung für den Kursus 'Bekämpfung von Partisanen' v. 24–26.9.41, 23 Sep. 1941" (BA-MA: RH 22–225), 72.

44. Ibid., 70.

45. Christopher R. Browning, *The Path to Genocide: Essays on Launching the Final Solution* (Cambridge: Cambridge University Press, 1992), 104.

46. Christian Gerlach, *Kalkulierte Morde: Die deutsche Wirtschafts- und Vernichtungspolitik in Weissrussland 1941 bis 1944* (Hamburg: Hamburger Edition, 1999), 587.

47. "rHGM Tagesordnung für den Kursus 'Bekämpfung von Partisanen' " v. 24–26.9.41, 23 Sep. 1941," 70.

48. Ibid.

49. "Vortragsfolge für den Kursus" (BA-MA: RH 22–225), 74.

50. "Aktennotiz über Kursus 'Bekämpfung von Partisanen' beim Bef.rückw.H.Geb. Mitte (25. u.26.9.1941), 2 October 1941" (BStA Minsk: 655–1–1), 279.

51. "Pol. Rgt. Mitte Befehl für Partisanenlehrgang, 24 Sep. 1941" (BA-MA: RH 22–225), 88. This was most likely from EG B, Nebe's command.

52. "Kriegstagebuch Nr. 1: Polizei Bataillon 322" (BA-ZS: Dok. Sammlung CSSR 396).

53. "rHGM Tagesordnung für den Kursus 'Bekämpfung von Partisanen' v. 24–26.9.41, 23 Sep. 1941," 73.

54. "SR 2 Befehl für das Unternehmen 'Kussikowitschi,' 26 Sep. 1941" (BA-MA: RH 22–225), 92.

55. Ibid., 93.

56. "rHGM Entwurf-Der Partisan seine Organisation und seine Bekämpfung, 12 Oct. 1941" (BA-MA: RH 22–225), 122.

57. Ibid., 124.

58. Ibid., 125.

59. Ibid., 122.

60. Edward B. Westermann, "Partners in Genocide: The German Police and the Wehrmacht in the Soviet Union," *Journal of Strategic Studies* 31, no. 5 (2008): 787.

61. Irene Sagel-Grande, H. H. Fuchs, and C. F. Rüter, eds., *Justiz und NS-Verbrechen. Sammlung deutscher Strafurteile wegen nationalsozialistischer Tötungsverbrechen 1945–1966*, vol. 20 (Amsterdam: University Press Amsterdam, 1979), 630.

62. "Nöll u.a. Urteil, 8 May 1954" (BA-ZS: B162/14058), 543.

63. "Sibille Letter, 2.2.1953" (HSA-D: H-13 Darmstadt, Nr. 979 I, Bd. III), 599a.

64. "Teilnehmer-Verzeichnis am Partisanen-Lehrgang vom 24.9.1941, 23 Sep. 1941."

65. Friedrich Hoffman, *Die Verfolgung der nationalsozialistischen Gewaltbrechen in Hessen* (Baden-Baden: Nomos Verlagsgesellschaft, 2001), 103.

66. "354 IR Meldung, 30 Oct. 1941" (BA-MA: RH 26–286–4, Anl. 130

67. "Wehrmacht Propaganda Leaflet (Undated)" (BStA Minsk: 655–1–1), 298.

68. See, for example, "350 IR Bericht, 16 October 1941" (BA-MA: RH 26–221–22b), Anl. 483; "350 IR Bericht, 18 October 1941" (BA-MA: RH 26–221–22b), Anl. 486; "350 IR Bericht, 22 October 1941" (BA-MA: RH 26–221–22b), Anl. 499.

69. "221 SD Bericht, V-A IR 350, 14 Oct. 1941" (BA-MA: RH 26–221–22b, Anl. 475).

70. Westermann, "Partners in Genocide," 788–789.

71. "rHGM Korpsbefehl 55, 29 September 1941" (BA-MA: RH 22–225), 95.

72. "rHGM Besprechung mit den Generalstabsoffizieren der Divisionen, 30.9.1941" (BA-MA: RH 22–225), 98.

73. "286 SD Ic Tätigskeitbericht, Sep–Dec 1941" (BA-MA: RH 26–286–5). This was the killing unit at Krupki and Kholoponichi.

74. "Merkblatt über Zuständigkeit, Unterstellung, und Aufgaben, 2 November 1941" (BA-MA: RH 26–339–5), Anl. 13.

75. "Kdt. in Weissruthenien, Befehl Nr. 24, 24 Nov. 1941" (BStA Minsk: 378–1–698).

76. Christopher R. Browning, *Nazi Policy, Jewish Workers, German Killers* (Cambridge: Cambridge University Press, 2000), 120–121.

77. Browning and Matthäus, *Origins of the Final Solution*, 506, ff. 239.

78. Ibid., 410.

79. Isabel V. Hull, *Absolute Destruction: Military Culture and the Practices of War in Imperial Germany* (Ithaca, N.Y.: Cornell University Press, 2005), 126.

80. See Chapter 1 and John Horne, "Civilian Populations and Wartime Violence: Towards an Historical Analysis," *International Social Science Journal* 54, no. 174 (2002); Alan Kramer and John Horne, "German 'Atrocities' and Franco-German Opinion, 1914: The Evidence of German Soldiers' Diaries," *Journal of Modern History* 66, no. 1 (1994).

81. H. R. Trevor-Roper, ed. *Hitler's Table Talk, 1941–1944: His Private Conversations* (New York: Enigma Books, 2000), 25.

82. Karl Fuchs, Horst Fuchs Richardson, and Dennis E. Showalter, *Sieg Heil! War Letters of Tank Gunner Karl Fuchs, 1937–1941* (Hamden, Conn.: Archon Books, 1987), 145.

83. Walter Bähr and Hans Walter Bähr, *Kriegsbriefe Gefallener Studenten, 1939–1945* (Tübingen: R. Wunderlich, 1952), 241.

84. Raul Hilberg, *The Destruction of the European Jews,* 3 vols. (New York: Holmes & Meier, 1985), 1:301.

85. "Memo from Armament Inspector, Ukraine to Chief of Industrial Armament Department (Gen. Georg Thomas), 2 December 1941," in *Nazi Conspiracy and Aggression,* vol. 5 (Washington, D.C.: Government Printing Office, 1946), Document 3257-PS, 995.

86. "V., Adam Statement, 7 July 1953" (HSA-D: H-13 Darmstadt, Nr. 979 I, Bd. II), 271.

87. "W., Hans Statement, 26 August 1953" (HSA-D: H-13 Darmstadt, Nr. 919 I, Bd. II), 341.

88. "rHGM Casualty Reports" (BA-MA: RH 22–228), 61.

89. Some examples from letters are instructive of some soldiers' beliefs, including anti-semitism, though these letter collections do not include letters from the soldiers in this study. See, for example, Walter Manoschek, *Es gibt nur eines für das Juden-tum: Vernichtung- das Judenbild in deutschen Soldatenbriefen 1939–1944* (Hamburg: Hamburger, 1995); Anatoly Golovchansky, *"Ich Will Raus Aus Diesem Wahnsinn": Deutsche Briefe von der Ostfront 1941–1945 aus sowjetischen Archiven* (Wuppertal: P. Hammer, 1991); Fuchs, Richardson, and Showalter, *Sieg Heil!;* Ortwin Buchbender and Reinhold Sterz, *Das andere Gesicht des Krieges: Deutsche Feldpostbriefe, 1939–1945* (München: Beck, 1983); Bähr and Bähr, *Kriegsbriefe Gefallener Studenten.*

90. One of the limitations of postwar testimony as a source is that soldiers are most re-luctant to discuss antisemitism, either their own or that of their comrades. Because of legal definitions of the time, these men were often very careful to avoid any impli-cation of racism or acknowledgment of Nazi genocidal ideals. Even so, there is suf-ficient evidence from these sources (as well as from survivors) to indicate that these types of leaders and men were prevalent. One must also recognize the tendency of some soldiers to demonize a few rather than cast blame more widely.

91. "B., Josef Statement, 29 June 1953" (HSA-D: H-13 Darmstadt, Nr. 979 I, Bd. II), 310.

92. "rHGM Entwurf-Der Partisan seine Organisation und seine Bekämpfung, 12 Oct. 1941," 124–126. "Strangers to the village" were reported as *Ortsfremde.*

93. "Magel, Wilhelm Statement, 8 August 1951," 173.

94. Christopher R. Browning, *Ordinary Men: Reserve Police Battalion 101 and the Final Solution in Poland* (New York: Harper Perennial, 1998), 14.

95. "Meeting Notes (Hitler, Rosenberg, Lammers, Keitel, Göring) 16 July 1941" (Trial of the Major War Criminals before the International Military Tribunal, 1949, vol. 38: Document 221-L), 88. This took place after Stalin's 3 July 1941 radio broadcast urging all Soviet people to resist.

96. Given a choice between a 50:1 and 100:1 ratio of hostages per German soldier, some army commanders routinely chose the 100:1 number.

97. Christopher R. Browning, "The Wehrmacht in Serbia Revisited," in *Crimes of War: Guilt and Denial in the Twentieth Century,* ed. Omer Bartov, Atina Grossmann, and Mary Nolan (New York: New Press, 2002), 36.

98. Ibid., 37.

99. Ben Shepherd, *Terror in the Balkans: German Armies and Partisan Warfare* (Cambridge, Mass.: Harvard University Press, 2012), 328.

100. Ibid., 243.

101. Browning, "Wehrmacht in Serbia Revisited," 40.

102. "Judgment in the Hostage Case (*United States of America vs. Wilhelm List, et al.*)," in *Nazi Conspiracy and Aggression,* vol. 11 (Washington, D.C.: Government Print-ing Office, 1950), 1240.

103. For more on the Wehrmacht in Serbia, see Walter Manoschek, *"Serbien ist Juden-frei": Militärische Besatzungspolitik und Judenvernichtung in Serbien 1941/42* (München: R. Oldenbourg, 1993); Christopher R. Browning, "Wehrmacht Reprisal Policy and the Murder of the Male Jews in Serbia," in *Fateful Months: Essays on the*

Emergence of the Final Solution (New York: Holmes & Meier, 1991); H. F. Meyer, *Von Wien nach Kalavryta: Die blutige Spur der 117. Jäger-Division durch Serbien und Griechenland* (Mannheim: Bibliopolis, 2002).

104. Blood, *Hitler's Bandit Hunters,* 276. Blood correctly distinguishes between *Partisanenbekämpfung* (anti-partisan war) and *Bandenbekämpfung* (bandit fighting, the term that quickly replaced *Partisanenbekämpfung*). While the former could be considered a traditional counterinsurgency between armed combatants, the latter encompassed mass killing of civilians, including Jews.

105. Ben Kiernan, *Blood and Soil: A World History of Genocide and Extermination from Sparta to Darfur* (New Haven, Conn.: Yale University Press, 2007), 386.

106. Laurent Dubois, *Haiti: The Aftershocks of History* (New York: Metropolitan Books, 2012), 232.

107. "Judgment in the Hostage Case (*United States of America vs. Wilhelm List, et al.*)," 529.

108. Wolfgang Kahl, "Vom Mythos der 'Bandenbekampfung': Polizeiverbande im zweiten Weltkrieg," *Die Polizei: Fachzeitschrift fur das Polizeiwesen,* no. 2 (1998): 53.

109. Joanna Bourke notes that many men at My Lai were veterans of real combat and that for them the role of the actual guerrilla war in Vietnam was very significant in their behavior. Dave Grossman describes some characteristics that German units had in common with the U.S. unit at My Lai. However, he adds that the very important ingredients relating to actual casualties and frustration caused by the insurgency were vital in this atrocity. For the distinction, see Joanna Bourke, *An Intimate History of Killing: Face-to-Face Killing in Twentieth-Century Warfare* (New York: Basic Books, 1999), 171–214; Dave Grossman, *On Killing: The Psychological Cost of Learning to Kill in War and Society* (New York: Back Bay Books, 2009), 190–191.

110. "Befehl Nr. 1 für Unternehmen 'Dreieck,' 11 September 1942" (BA-MA: RH 23–25), 63.

111. "Gefechtsbericht über Unternehmen 'Dreieck' und 'Viereck' vom 17.9–2.10.1942, 19 October 1942" (BA-MA: RH 23–25), 25.

112. Westermann, "Partners in Genocide," 774.

113. Hans Joachim Schröder, "German Soldiers' Experiences during the Initial Phase of the Russian Campaign," in *From Peace to War: Germany, Soviet Russia, and the World, 1939–1941,* ed. Bernd Wegner (Providence, R.I.: Berghahn Books, 1997), 322.

5. An Evil Seed Is Sown

Epigraphs: "V., Karl Letter, 22 September 1953" (HSA-D: H-13 Darmstadt, Nr. 979 I, Bd. II), 354. "Magel, Wilhelm Statement, 24 June 1951" (HSA-D: H-13 Darmstadt, Nr. 979 I, Bd. I), 161.

1. "Magel, Wilhelm Statement, 16 June 1951" (HSA-D: H-13 Darmstadt, Nr. 979 I, Bd. I), 162–163.

2. Georg Tessin, *Verbände und Truppen der deutschen Wehrmacht und Waffen-SS im Zweiten Weltkrieg 1939–1945,* vol. 1 (Osnabrück: Biblio, 1979).

3. See Horst Müller and Hans-Dieter Kluge, *Der Kyffhäuser* (Leipzig: Edition Leipzig, 2002).

4. See "Map: 339 ID Dispositions in France" (BA-MA: RH 26–339–3).

5. Klaus-Jürgen Thies, *Der Ostfeldzug: Heeresgruppe Mitte, 21.6.1941–6.12.1941- ein Lageatlas der Operationsabteilung des Generalstabs des Heeres* (Bissendorf: Biblio-Verlag, 2001), 75; "rHGM Korpsbefehl 54, 19 Sept. 1941" (BA-MA: RH 22–225), 68. The unit had first arrived in Kovno, Lithuania, in August, and one can only speculate what elements of anti-Jewish policy it observed there.

6. "Map: rHGM, 9 October 1941" (BA-MA: RH 26–221–14b), Anl. 885.

7. "B., Emil Statement, 26 March 1953" (HSA-D: H-13 Darmstadt, Nr. 979 I, Bd. I), 246.

8. Martin Dean and Geoffrey P. Megargee, eds., *Encyclopedia of Camps and Ghettos II: Ghettos in German-Occupied Eastern Europe,* vol. B (Bloomington: Indiana University Press, 2012), 1690.

9. "M., Erwin Statement, 16 February 1953" (HSA-D: H-13 Darmstadt, Nr. 979 I, Bd. I), 235.

10. "S., Willi Statement, 9 August 1951" (HSA-D: H-13 Darmstadt, Nr. 979 I, Bd. I), 178; Dean and Megargee, *Encyclopedia of Camps and Ghettos II,* 1690.

11. "W., Hans Statement, 26 August 1953" (HSA-D: H-13 Darmstadt, Nr. 919 I, Bd. II), 335.

12. "Nöll, F. Statement, 11 February 1952" (HSA-D: H-13 Darmstadt, Nr. 979 I, Bd. I), 11.

13. "Nöll, F. Statement, 25 April 1951" (HSA-D: H-13 Darmstadt, Nr. 979 I, Bd. I), 32; "Nöll, F. Statement, 11 February 1952," 11.

14. "H., Josef Statement, 7 May 1952" (HSA-D: H-13 Darmstadt, Nr. 979 I, Bd. I), 44.

15. "V., Adam Statement, 7 July 1953" (HSA-D: H-13 Darmstadt, Nr. 979 I, Bd. II), 271.

16. "Nöll, F. Statement, 25 April 1951," 32.

17. "Zimber, E. Statement, 19 June 1953" (HSA-D: H-13 Darmstadt, Nr. 979 I, Bd. II), 258.

18. "Magel, Wilhelm Statement, 16 June 1951," 163.

19. "S., Willi Statement, 9 August 1951," 178.

20. Dean and Megargee, *Encyclopedia of Camps and Ghettos II,* 1690.

21. "S., Karl Statement, 5 December 1953" (HSA-D: H-13 Darmstadt, Nr. 979 I, Bd. II), 382; Dean and Megargee, *Encyclopedia of Camps and Ghettos II,* 1690.

22. "S., Karl Statement, 16 December 1953" (HSA-D: H-13 Darmstadt, Nr. 979 I, Bd. II), 390.

23. "F., Mathias Statement, 29 June 1953" (HSA-D: H-13 Darmstadt, Nr. 979 I, Bd. II), 304.

24. "Z., Adolf Statement, 24 September 1953" (HSA-D: H-13 Darmstadt, Nr. 979 I, Bd. II), 360.

25. "S., Willi Statement, 9 August 1951," 178.

26. "V., Adam Statement, 7 July 1953," 272.

27. This is partially a trope in postwar German testimony. There was a tendency to highlight the behavior of the locals as especially brutal and gratuitous as compared to the professional behavior of German soldiers. This tendency, however, does not mean that locals did not actively collaborate.

28. "B., Josef Statement, 29 June 1953" (HSA-D: H-13 Darmstadt, Nr. 979 I, Bd. II), 310. It is worth noting that former German soldiers were far more willing to discuss atrocities committed by local populations than by their own comrades.

29. "Z., Adolf Statement, 24 September 1953," 359.

30. "S., Karl Statement, 16 December 1953," 390.

31. "W., Hans Statement, 26 August 1953," 336.

32. "S., Karl Statement, 5 December 1953," 383.

33. "S., Willi Statement, 9 August 1951," 178–179.

34. "B., Karl Statement, 5 December 1953" (HSA-D: H-13 Darmstadt, Nr. 979 I, Bd. II), 379.

35. Christopher R. Browning and Jürgen Matthäus, *The Origins of the Final Solution: The Evolution of Nazi Jewish Policy, September 1939–March 1942* (Lincoln: University of Nebraska Press, 2004), 391.

36. "Schäfer, W. Statement, 29 December 1953" (HSA-D: H-13 Darmstadt, Nr. 979 I, Bd. II), 392.

37. "S., Willi Statement, 9 August 1951," 178.

38. "Magel, Wilhelm Statement, 8 August 1951" (HSA-D: H-13 Darmstadt, Nr. 979 I, Bd. II), 173.

39. "W., Hans Statement, 26 August 1953," 337. Similar reactions were seen among other German units unused to the act of killing at close quarters. See Christopher R. Browning, *Ordinary Men: Reserve Police Battalion 101 and the Final Solution in Poland* (New York: Harper Perennial, 1998), 62–63.

40. "L., Wilhelm Statement, 5 February 1953" (HSA-D: H-13 Darmstadt, Nr. 979 I, Bd. I), 215. The trauma and distress relating to first-time participations in killing are not uncommon and can be seen in other killing units, even those tasked explicitly with murder, such as Police Battalion 101.

41. "Magel, Wilhelm Statement, 8 August 1951," 172.

42. Postwar reporting of the trial in newspapers confirms that this was the testimony given in court, and it does not appear that Magel's story was disproven.

43. "1941 in Russland: Befehl zu Erschiessungen verweigert," *Abendpost,* 3 May 1954, 6.

44. "W., Leopold Statement, 29 July 1953" (HSA-D: H-13 Darmstadt, Nr. 919 I, Bd. II), 326.

45. C. F. Rüter, H. H. Fuchs, and Adelheid L. Rüter-Ehlermann, eds., *Justiz und NS-Verbrechen. Sammlung deutscher Strafurteile wegen nationalsozialistischer Tötungsverbrechen 1945–1966,* vol. 12 (Amsterdam: University Press Amsterdam, 1974), 374; Ulrike Jureit, Michael Wildt, and Birgit Otte, *Crimes of the German Wehrmacht: Dimensions of a War of Annihilation, 1941–1944; An Outline of the Exhibition,* trans. Paula Bradish (Hamburg: Hamburger Edition HIS Verlag. mbH, 2004), 29; Rüter, Fuchs, and Rüter-Ehlermann, *Justiz und NS-Verbrechen,* 377. For a characterization of Kuhls, see "B., Josef Statement, 29 June 1953," 310.

46. "Bataillonskommandeur gab Erschiessungsbefehl," *Darmstädter Tagblatt,* 3 May 1954. Josef Sibille kept a series of newspaper clippings from the trial. His family was kind enough to share them with me.

47. "Sibille Letter, 2.2.1953" (HSA-D: H-13 Darmstadt, Nr. 979 I, Bd. III), 599a. Grosskopp's name does not appear on the surviving list of participants at the conference.

However, as this list was compiled *before* the conference, it is quite possible that there were late additions and subtractions.

48. Ibid., 207–209.
49. Rüter, Fuchs, and Rüter-Ehlermann, *Justiz und NS-Verbrechen*, 377.
50. "Sibille Letter, 2.2.1953," 208.
51. Rüter, Fuchs, and Rüter-Ehlermann, *Justiz und NS-Verbrechen*, 377.
52. Some dissent against Nazi crimes was framed in terms that might be more acceptable to authorities, with crimes described as bad for morale or against the interests of military necessity rather than as morally wrong.
53. "Correspondence with Christiane Sibille, 3 October 2010" (author's personal collection).
54. "Correspondence with Dr. Wolfgang Nöll, 23 August 2010" (author's personal collection).
55. "Nöll Denazification Questionnaire, 1948" (HSA-D: H-13 Darmstadt, Nr. 979 I, Bd. I). This organization was a collection of previous post–World War I groups advocating for a return of German colonies.
56. "F., Mathias Statement, 29 June 1953," 303.
57. "B., Karl Statement, 5 December 1953," 379.
58. "W., Hans Statement, 26 August 1953," 330–331.
59. "F., Mathias Statement, 29 June 1953," 304.
60. "Nöll, F. Statement, 25 April 1951," 33. This behavior is identical to that of Major Trapp, the commander of Reserve Police Battalion 101, who also remained at his headquarters during a mass killing. See Browning, *Ordinary Men*, 57.
61. "K., Helmuth Statement, 28 July 1953" (HSA-D: H-13 Darmstadt, Nr. 979 I, Bd. II), 318.
62. "Bataillonskommandeur Gab Erschiessungsbefehl."
63. "Als Kompaniechef brauchte ich das nicht zu wissen," *Darmstädter Echo*, 2 March 1956.
64. "Wehrmacht- Härter als üblich," *Der Spiegel*, 12 Aug 1969, 50.
65. "Zimber, E. Statement, 9 January 1952" (HSA-D: H-13 Darmstadt, Nr. 979 I, Bd. I), 8.
66. "Zimber Entnazifierungsakte" (StA Freiburg: D180.2, No. 16878). Zimber actually presented a signed statement of his neighbors "proving" that he had never uttered such a statement. His accuser did not sign.
67. "V., Adam Statement, 7 July 1953," 271.
68. "W., Hans Statement, 26 August 1953," 331.
69. "V., Adam Statement, 7 July 1953," 272.
70. "Bataillonskommandeur Gab Erschiessungsbefehl."
71. "Zimber, E. Statement, 7 May 1952" (HSA-D: H-13 Darmstadt, Nr. 979 I, Bd. I), 49.
72. "Major Alfred Commichau Personnel File" (BA-MA: PERS 6-11125).
73. Verantwortung Stiftung: Erinnerung, Zukunft, "Aussenkommando des Frauenzuchthaus Cottbus auf dem Rittergut Straupitz," Bundesarchiv (Germany), http://www.bundesarchiv.de/zwangsarbeit/haftstaetten/index.php.en?action=2.2&id=100000699.
74. "Commichau Letter to Wehrbezirkskommando Cottbus, 5 July 1940" (BA-MA: PERS 6-11125).

75. "M., Erich Statement, 19 September 1952" (HSA-D: H-13 Darmstadt, Nr. 979 I, Bd. I), 74.

76. Ibid.

77. "Major Alfred Commichau Evaluation, 26 February 1942" (BA-MA: PERS 6–11125).

78. "Ereignismeldung UdSSR Nr. 133, 14 November 1941" (USHMM: 1999.A.0196 [Reel 2]), 2–723188.

79. *"Ordnungsdienst"* here is a term that likely means local auxiliaries or militia. Often, these were volunteer forces from the Baltic states or local militias. "339 ID Lagebericht, Abt. Vii, 15 November 1941" (BA-MA: RH 26–339-7), Anl. 6.

80. "339 ID Tätigkeitsbericht für November 1941, 3 December 1941" (BA-MA: RH 26–339-7), Anl. I/10.

6. Making Genocide Routine

Epigraph: "L., Franz Statement, 20 March 1961" (BA-ZS: B162/1550), 130–131.

1. Ibid., 131–132.

2. "M., Karl Statement, 7 July 1962" (BA-ZS: B162/5088), 2741.

3. Georg Tessin, *Verbände und Truppen der deutschen Wehrmacht und Waffen-SS im Zweiten Weltkrieg 1939–1945,* vol. 12 (Osnabrück: Biblio, 1975), 156.

4. Hannes Heer, "Extreme Normalität: Generalmajor Gustav Freiherr von Mauchenheim Gen. Bechtolsheim- Umfeld, Motive und Entschlussbildung eines Holocaust-Täters," *Zeitschrift für Geschichtswissenschaft* 51, no. 8 (2003): 731.

5. "Generalmajor Gustav Freiherr von Mauchenheim Gen. Bechtolsheim Personal Nachweis" (BA-MA: PERS 6–1616).

6. Ibid.

7. "Generalmajor Gustav Freiherr von Mauchenheim Gen. Bechtolsheim Officer Evaluation, 15 April 1939" (BA-MA: PERS 6–1616).

8. "Generalmajor Gustav Freiherr von Mauchenheim Gen. Bechtolsheim Officer Evaluation, 26 February 1943" (BA-MA: PERS 6–1616).

9. Ibid.

10. "rHGM Tagesmeldung, 14 August 1941" (BA-MA: RH 22–226), 36.

11. The 8th Company also murdered Jews in Stolpce and Baranovichi. See Martin Dean, *Collaboration in the Holocaust: Crimes of the Local Police in Belorussia and Ukraine, 1941–44* (New York: St. Martin's Press, 2000), 46.

12. Christopher R. Browning, *Ordinary Men: Reserve Police Battalion 101 and the Final Solution in Poland* (New York: Harper Perennial, 1998), 18.

13. Christian Gerlach, "German Economic Interests, Occupation Policy, and the Murder of the Jews in Belorussia, 1941/43," in *National Socialist Extermination Policies: Contemporary German Perspectives and Controversies,* ed. Ulrich Herbert (New York: Berghahn Books, 2000), 223.

14. H. D. Handrack, *Das Reichskommissariat Ostland: Die Kulturpolitik Der deutschen Verwaltung zwischen Autonomie und Gleichschaltung 1941–1944* (Hannover-Münden: Gauke, 1981), 83.

15. Christian Gerlach, *Kalkulierte Morde: Die deutsche Wirtschafts- und Vernichtungs-spolitik in Weissrussland 1941 bis 1944* (Hamburg: Hamburger Edition, 1999), 161.

16. Ibid., 162.

17. Christopher R. Browning and Jürgen Matthäus, *The Origins of the Final Solution: The Evolution of Nazi Jewish Policy, September 1939–March 1942* (Lincoln: University of Nebraska Press, 2004), 394.

18. Ernst Klee, Willi Dressen, and Volker Riess, *"The Good Old Days": The Holocaust as Seen by Its Perpetrators and Bystanders,* 1st U.S. ed. (New York: Free Press, 1991), 181.

19. "Map: Vorläufiger Einsatzraum 707 ID, 21 August 1941" (BA-MA: RH 26-221-13b), Anl. 570.

20. Nachum Alpert, *The Destruction of Slonim Jewry: The Story of the Jews of Slonim during the Holocaust* (New York: Holocaust Library, 1989), 3.

21. Zvi Shefet, *Ha-Adamat'meah Toldot Kehilat Slonim (Hell on Earth: The History of Slonim's Jewish Community), 1992* (Givataim, Israel: Slonim Jewish Association, 1992).

22. *The Jewish Encyclopedia: A Descriptive Record of the History, Religion, Literature, and Customs of the Jewish People from the Earliest Times to the Present Day* (New York: Funk & Wagnalls, 1907), s.v. "Slonim" (by Herman Rosenthal and J. G. Lipman), 408.

23. Ibid., 409.

24. Klee, Dressen, and Riess, *"Good Old Days,"* 178. The USHMM estimates 20,000, while a book written by a survivor cites an official census number of 14,461. See Martin Dean and Geoffrey P. Megargee, eds., *Encyclopedia of Camps and Ghettos II: Ghettos in German-Occupied Eastern Europe,* vol. B (Bloomington: Indiana University Press, 2012), 1274.

25. *Jewish Encyclopedia,* s.v. "Slonim," 409.

26. Hans-Heinrich Nolte and Ljuba Israeljewna Abramowitsch, *Die Leere in Slonim* (Dortmund: Internationales Bildungs- und Begegnungswerk GmbH, 2005), 29.

27. "AHC Interview with Luba Abramovich, 19 Jan 2008 (transcript)" (Leo Baeck Institute: AHC 840), 14.

28. "Protocol of Interrogation of Lubov Israelevna Abramovich, 25 September 1995" (New Scotland Yard War Crimes Unit [WCU]: D7852), 2.

29. "Wolkowyski, S. Statement, 17 July 1964" (BA-ZS: B162/5092), 5663; Klaus-Jürgen Thies, *Der Ostfeldzug: Heeresgruppe Mitte, 21.6.1941-6.12.1941- ein Lageatlas der Op-erationsabteilung des Generalstabs des Heeres* (Bissendorf: Biblio-Verlag, 2001), 7.

30. "Protocol of Interrogation of Lubov Israelevna Abramovich, 25 September 1995," 4.

31. EM 11—3 July 1941, in *The Einsatzgruppen Reports: Selections from the Dispatches of the Nazi Death Squads' Campaign against the Jews, July 1941-January 1943,* ed. Yitzhak Arad, Schmuel Krakowski, and Shmuel Spector (New York: Holocaust Library, 1989), 5.

32. "252 ID Kriegestagebuch, 17 July 1941" (BA-MA: RH 26-252-73), 56.

33. "AHC Interview with Luba Abramovich, 19 Jan 2008 (transcript)," 2.

34. "Protocol of Interrogation of Lubov Israelevna Abramovich, 25 September 1995," 5.

35. Nolte and Abramowitsch, *Die Leere in Slonim,* 47; Dean and Megargee, *Encyclopedia of Camps and Ghettos II,* 1274.

36. EM 32—24 July 1941, and EM 50—12 August 1941, in Arad, Krakowski, and Spector, *Einsatzgruppen Reports,* 45, 83.

37. Raul Hilberg, *The Destruction of the European Jews* (3 vols.), vol. 1 (New York: Holmes & Meier, 1985).

38. "E., Kurt Statement, 15 May 1962" (BA-ZS: B162/5088), 2754.

39. "L., Franz Statement, 1 February 1960" (BA-ZS: B162/5088), 108; "S., Otto Einstellung, 2 February 1961" (BA-ZS: B162/1506), 12.

40. John R. Angolia, *For Führer and Fatherland: Political and Civil Awards of the Third Reich* (San Jose, Calif.: R. James Bender, 1978), 186–192.

41. "H., Johannes Statement, 6 February 1960" (BA-ZS: B162/5088), 128.

42. "S., Otto Einstellung, 2 February 1961," 12.

43. "Voruntersuchung gegen Erren u.a., 6 October 1965" (Yad Vashem: TR.10/1170).

44. "M., Michael Statement, 9 August 1960" (BA-ZS: B162/5088), 1154.

45. "Robert R. Letter to Ludwigsburg, 22 October 1959" (BA-ZS: B162/5088), 28–29.

46. "F., Johann Statement, 22 March 1960" (BA-ZS: B162/5102), 75–76.

47. "S., Otto Statement, 2 February 1960" (BA-ZS: B162/5088), 114.

48. "N., Anton Statement, 7 February 1961" (BA-ZS: B162/1550), 144.

49. It is unclear from the statements exactly what kind of formation this was, but likely it consisted of a volunteer unit. It is also possible, given the distance and direction from Zyrowice, that this was the same killing site later used during the Slonim massacre.

50. "Metzner, Alfred Statement, 18 September 1947" (BA-ZS: B162/5088), 77.

51. "L., Franz Statement, 1 February 1960," 107.

52. "Metzner, Alfred Statement, 18 September 1947," 77.

53. "L., Franz Statement, 1 February 1960," 106–107.

54. "Erren, G. Statement, 2 November 1960" (BA-ZS: B162/5102), 13.

55. Ibid.

56. Wolfgang Curilla, *Die deutsche Ordnungspolizei und der Holocaust im Baltikum und in Weissrussland, 1941–1944* (Paderborn: Schöningh, 2006), 613.

57. Hermann H. was the head of a *Schutzpolizei* detachment in Slonim of six to eight Germans and twenty to thirty local police. "H., Hermann Statement, 10 January 1962" (BA-ZS: B162/5088), 2346–2347.

58. "M., Karl Statement, 7 July 1962," 2737–2738.

59. "S., Georg Statement, 24 March 1960" (BA-ZS: B162/5102), 66.

60. "Eilender, K. Statement, 11 February 1961" (BA-ZS: B162/5088), 2205.

61. Shefet, *Ha-Adamat'meah Toldot Kehilat Slonim (Hell on Earth: The History of Slonim's Jewish Community), 1992.*

62. "AHC Interview with Luba Abramovich, 19 Jan 2008 (transcript)," 2.

63. "A., Erich Statement, 16 March 1960" (BA-ZS: B162/5102), 92; "F., Johannes Statement, 23 March 1960" (BA-ZS: B162/5102), 69–70.

64. "M., Ivo Statement, 30 May 1960" (BA-ZS: B162/5088), 803.

65. "L., Alexander Statement, 6 December 1961" (BA-ZS: B162/5088), 2666–2667.

66. See "R., Hubert Statement, 28 June 1960" (BA-ZS: B162/1551), 82; "G., Ludwig Statement, 31 May 1960" (BA-ZS: B162/5102), 198; "H., Xavier Statement, 30 May 1960" (BA-ZS: B162/5102), 194–195; "O., Ernst Statement, 22 March 1960" (BA-ZS: B162/5102), 80.

67. See "R., Hubert Statement, 28 June 1960," 82; "R., Hubert Statement, 6 January 1960" (BA-ZS: B162/5102), 204; "N., Anton Statement, 28 November 1961" (BA-ZS: B162/5088), 2115.

68. "Szepetynski, Z. Statement, 24 June 1965" (BA-ZS: B162/5092), 5714.

69. "N., Anton Statement, 7 February 1961," 143.

70. "Abschrift: Der Anteil der Juden an der Partisanenbewegung Sowjetrusslands— von Moshe Kaganovich, 25 August 1961," (BA-ZS: B162/3409), 413.

71. "Protocol of Interrogation of Lubov Israelevna Abramovich, 25 September 1995," 5.

72. "AHC Interview with Luba Abramovich, 19 Jan 2008 (transcript)," 3.

73. "Klenicki, R. Statement, 5 February 1962" (BA-ZS: B162/5088), 2473.

74. Alpert, *Destruction of Slonim Jewry,* 372.

75. Ibid., 90.

76. David Meltser and Vladimir Levin, *The Black Book with Red Pages: Tragedy and Heroism of Belorussian Jews,* trans. Kevin Mulloney (Cockeysville, Md.: VIA Press, 2005), 216.

77. "P., Friedrich Statement, 18 March 1960" (BA-ZS: B162/5102), 121.

78. It is unclear from the testimony who exactly these Lithuanians were. It is likely that they were volunteers from Lithuania, brought in to serve as auxiliary military units.

79. "L., Alexander Statement, 6 December 1961," 2677.

80. "F., Johannes Statement, 23 March 1960," 71. This claim of not having aimed is also a frequent trope in these statements, and its veracity must be approached with caution.

81. "L., Franz Statement, 1 February 1960," 107–108.

82. "R., Hubert Statement, 6 January 1960," 202.

83. "N., Anton Statement, 7 February 1961," 142.

84. "P., Friedrich Statement, 18 March 1960," 121.

85. "D., Ferdinand Statement, 21 March 1960" (BA-ZS: B162/5102), 84.

86. "Metzner, Alfred Statement, 18 September 1947," 78.

87. "M., Karl Statement, 7 July 1962," 2740.

88. "A., Gabriel Statement, 8 May 1961" (BA-ZS: B162/5088), 1469.

89. Alpert, *Destruction of Slonim Jewry,* 93.

90. "Eilender, K. Statement, 11 February 1961," 2205–2206.

91. "N., Anton Statement, 7 February 1961," 144–145.

92. "Goldberg, S. Statement, 16 August 1961" (BA-ZS: B162/5088), 2437.

93. Gerlach, *Kalkulierte Morde,* 623.

94. Samuel D. Kassow, *Who Will Write Our History? Emanuel Ringelblum, the Warsaw Ghetto, and the Oyneg Shabes Archive* (Bloomington: Indiana University Press, 2007), 285, 297.

95. Joseph Kermish, "Emmanuel Ringelblum's Notes Hitherto Unpublished," *Yad Vashem Studies* 7 (1968): 179.

96. "Protocol of Interrogation of Lubov Israelevna Abramovich, 25 September 1995," 5–6.

97. The primary focus of this chapter is Slonim. However, the case of the 7th Company in Novogrudok, though less well documented, demonstrates similar qualities and supports most of the contentions made about Slonim.

98. Yehuda Bauer, "Nowogrodek—the Story of a *Shtetl*," *Yad Vashem Studies* 35, no. 2 (2007): 48.

99. Ibid., 47. Traub would die in a Yugoslav POW camp in 1946.

100. "K., Alois Statement, 17 September 1963" (BA-ZS: B162/3453), 270–271.

101. "W., Anton Statement, 21 August 1963" (BA-ZS: B162/3454), 395.

102. Chaim Leibovich, "Schokdey Melocho' Ort School," in *Novogrudok: The History of a Jewish Shtetl,* ed. Jack Kagan (London: Vallentine Mitchell, 2006), 62.

103. "H., Anton Statement, 11 November 1963" (BA-ZS: B162/3453), 311.

104. "H., Anton Statement, 4 November 1963" (BA-ZS: B162/3454), 525.

105. "K., Joseph Statement, 2 August 1963" (BA-ZS: B162/3454), 373.

106. "W., Anton Statement, 21 August 1963," 396.

107. "K., Alois Statement, (Undated)" (BA-ZS: B162/3454), 536–537.

108. "A., Johann Statement, 22 September 1964" (BA-ZS: B162/3454), 542.

7. The Golden Pheasant and the Brewer

Epigraphs: "Orlinski, A. Statement, 14 July 1964" (BA-ZS: B162/5092), 5659. "L., Franz Statement, 20 March 1961" (BA-ZS: B162/1550), 130–131.

1. Dieter Pohl, *Die Herrschaft der Wehrmacht: Deutsche Militärbesatzung und einheimische Bevölkerung in der Sowjetunion 1941–1944* (München: Oldenbourg, 2008), 107.

2. The *Reichswasserschutz* was responsible for patrolling and policing German waterways. See Friedrich Wilhelm, *Die Polizei im Ns-Staat: Die Geschichte ihrer Organisation im Überblick* (Paderborn: Schöning, 1999), 96–97.

3. C. F. Rüter and D. W. De Mildt, eds., *Justiz und NS-Verbrechen. Sammlung deutscher Strafurteile wegen nationalsozialistischer Tötungsverbrechen 1945–1999.* vol. 39 (Amsterdam: Amsterdam University Press, 2008), 678–679.

4. "R., Gerda Statement 14 March 1960" (BA-ZS: B162/5102), 100.

5. "Polenz Suicide Note, 10 May 1961" (BA-ZS: B162/5088), 1477.

6. "Metzner, Alfred Statement, 18 September 1947" (BA-ZS: B162/5088), 78.

7. "Polenz Suicide Note, 10 May 1961," 1477.

8. "Klenicki, R. Statement, 5 February 1962" (BA-ZS: B162/5088), 2475.

9. "Goldberg, S. Statement, 16 August 1961" (BA-ZS: B162/5088), 2438.

10. Yehuda Bauer, "Nowogrodek—the Story of a *Shtetl*," *Yad Vashem Studies* 35, no. 2 (2007): 48.

11. "Führer Erlass über Die Ernennung von Wehrmachtsbefehlshabern in den neu besetzten Ostgebieten, 25 June 1941" (BStA Minsk: 370-1-49), 5.

12. "Wehrmachtbefehlshaber Ostland Memo, 2 August 1941" (BStA Minsk: 370-1-49), 14–15.

13. Gerhard Schoenberner and Mira Schoenberner, *Zeugen sagen aus: Berichte und Dokumente über die Judenverfolgung im "Dritten Reich"* (Berlin: Union Verlag, 1988), 133.

14. Martin Dean and Geoffrey P. Megargee, eds., *Encyclopedia of Camps and Ghettos II: Ghettos in German-Occupied Eastern Europe,* vol. B (Bloomington: Indiana University Press, 2012), 1274.

15. "B., Ernst Statement, 1 June 1960" (BA-ZS: B162/5102), 205–206.

16. "Erren, G. Statement, 2 November 1960" (BA-ZS: B162/5102), 17.

17. "O., Ernst Statement, 22 March 1960" (BA-ZS: B162/5102), 80–81.

18. Ibid.

19. "D., Ferdinand Statement, 21 March 1960" (BA-ZS: B162/5102), 84.

20. Jonathan Steinberg, "The Third Reich Reflected: German Civil Administration in the Occupied Soviet Union, 1941–4," *English Historical Review* 110, no. 437 (1995): 621.

21. Mark Mazower, *Hitler's Empire: How the Nazis Ruled Europe* (New York: Penguin Press, 2008), 152.

22. "Letter from Oblt. Glück to Geb. Komm. Erren, 4 December 1941" (BStA Minsk: 1450-2-38), 563.

23. "Letter from Geb. Komm. Erren to Oblt. Glück, 4 December 1941" (BStA Minsk: 1450-2-38), 564.

24. "Kdt. in Weissruthenien, Befehl Nr. 24, 24 Nov. 1941" (BStA Minsk: 378-1-698).

25. "N., Arthur Statement, 21 May 1965" (BA-ZS: B162/3454), 581. The Gebietskommissar for Novogrudok was Wilhelm Traub.

26. Ibid., 579.

27. "B., Georg Statement, 3 November 1963" (BA-ZS: B162/3454), 519; "D., Ludwig Statement, 16 September 1963" (BA-ZS: B162/3453), 256; "E., Lorenz Statement, 19 May 1965" (BA-ZS: B162/3453), 561.

28. "L., Xaver Statement, 15 November 1963" (BA-ZS: B162/3453), 316.

29. "Kagan, Jack Interview, 4 July 2009" (author's personal archive).

30. "B., Georg Statement, 3 November 1963," 519.

31. "K., Alois Statement, (Undated)" (BA-ZS: B162/3454), 536.

32. "B., Georg Statement, 3 November 1963," 519.

33. "K., Alois Statement (Undated)," 536–537.

34. "N., Arthur Statement, 21 May 1965," 579.

35. "M., Kaspar Statement, 5 November 1964" (BA-ZS: B162/3454), 527.

36. Ibid.

37. Ibid.

38. "K., Alois Statement (Undated)," 536–537.

39. "A., Johann Statement, 22 September 1964" (BA-ZS: B162/3454), 541.

40. "M., Kaspar Statement, 5 November 1964," 527.

41. "E., Lorenz Statement, 19 May 1965," 562.

42. "N., Arthur Statement, 21 May 1965," 579.

43. "B., Georg Statement, 3 November 1963," 520.

44. "N., Arthur Statement, 21 May 1965," 579.

45. "M., Kaspar Statement, 5 November 1964," 528.

46. "B., Georg Statement, 3 November 1963," 520.

47. "A., Johann Statement, 22 September 1964," 545.

48. Ibid., 543–544.

49. Götz Aly takes a much more extreme view of the financial element of the Holocaust, granting it perhaps excessive significance as a cause of anti-Jewish policy. However, his work is important in its frank depiction of the myriad ways in which the murder

of Jews and financial questions came together in the Third Reich. See Götz Aly, *Hitler's Beneficiaries: Plunder, Racial War, and the Nazi Welfare State* (New York: Metropolitan, 2007).

50. Martin Dean, "Seizure of Jewish Property and Inter-Agency Rivalry in the Reich and in the Occupied Soviet Territories," in *Networks of Nazi Persecution: Bureaucracy, Business, and the Organization of the Holocaust,* ed. Gerald D. Feldman and Wolfgang Seibel (New York: Berghahn Books, 2005), 89.

51. Frank Bajohr, "The Holocaust and Corruption," ibid., 132–134. For more on this, see Frank Bajohr, *Parvenüs und Profiteure: Korruption in der NS-Zeit* (Frankfurt: S. Fischer, 2001).

52. "RKO Memo to HSSPF, RKO: Polizeiliche Massnahmen und Behandlung jüdischen Vermögens, 25 September 1941" (BStA Minsk: 1450-2-38), 653.

53. "L., Franz Statement, 20 March 1961" (BA-ZS: B162/1550), 133.

54. "E., Kurt Statement, 15 May 1962" (BA-ZS: B162/5088), 2753–2754.

55. "K., Joseph Statement, 2 August 1963" (BA-ZS: B162/3454), 372.

56. "K., Joseph Statement, 13 May 1965" (BA-ZS: B162/3454), 549.

57. "Rotstein, I. Statement, 26 September 1962" (BA-ZS: B162/5102), 295.

58. "N., Anton Statement, 7 February 1961" (BA-ZS: B162/1550), 144.

59. "N, Wilhelm Statement, 4 December 1961" (BA-ZS: B162/5088), 2159.

60. "Holc, Johann Statement, 13 October 1965" (BA-ZS: B162/5092), 5663.

61. See, for example, Jeffrey Burds, "Sexual Violence in Europe in World War II, 1939–1945," *Politics & Society* 37, no. 1 (2009); David Raub Snyder, *Sex Crimes under the Wehrmacht,* Studies in War, Society and the Military (Lincoln: University of Nebraska Press, 2007), Internet Resource Date of Entry: 20061003; Ebba D. Drolshagen, *Der freundliche Feind: Wehrmachtssoldaten im besetzten Europa* (München: Droemer Knaur, 2009); Birgit Beck, *Wehrmacht und sexuelle Gewalt: Sexualverbrechen vor deutschen Militärgerichten 1939–1945* (Paderborn: Schöningh, 2004); Kundrus Birthe, "Forbidden Company: Romantic Relationships between Germans and Foreigners, 1939 to 1945," *Journal of the History of Sexuality* 11, no. 1/2 (2002).

62. These excellent works have begun the discussion but still are often unable to focus specifically on the Jewish experience. Nonsexual and homosexual relationships remain almost completely unexplored. See the following works, for example: Regina Mühlhäuser, "Rasse, Blut und Männlichkeit: Politiken sexueller Regulierung in den besetzten Gebieten der Sowjetunion (1941–1945)," *Feministische Studien* 25, no. 1 (2007); Regina Mühlhäuser, *Eroberungen: Sexuelle Gewalttaten und intime Beziehungen deutscher Soldaten in der Sowjetunion 1941–1945* (Hamburg: Hamburger Edition, 2010); Wendy Jo Gertjejanssen, "Victims, Heroes, Survivors: Sexual Violence on the Eastern Front during World War II" (dissertation, University of Minnesota, 2004); Sonja M. Hedgepeth and Rochelle G. Saidel, eds., *Sexual Violence against Jewish Women during the Holocaust* (Waltham, Mass.: Brandeis University Press, 2010); Doris Bergen, "Sexual Violence in the Holocaust: Unique and Typical?" in *Lessons and Legacies: The Holocaust in International Perspective,* ed. Dagmar Herzog (Evanston, Ill.: Northwestern University Press, 2006).

63. "T., Heinrich Statement, 2 October 1959" (BA-ZS: B162/25532), 8. One explanation for the prevalence of women in armaments work was that they were perceived by the Nazis as less of a threat.

64. "S., Otto Statement, 2 February 1960" (BA-ZS: B162/5088), 114.

65. "E., Kurt Statement, 15 May 1962," 2756.

66. "OKW Memo: Unerwünschte Verkehr deutscher Soldaten mit Einwohnern in den besetzten Ostgebieten, 15 September 1942" (BA-ZS: UdSSR 404 III. Teil Bild Nr. 418–814), 69.

67. It is not unlikely that some German soldiers also forced men into sex, but no evidence of such behavior was uncovered in this study. Men so assaulted would also be the least likely to be left alive by their attackers.

68. "Kagan, Jack Interview, 4 July 2009."

69. "Voruntersuchung gegen Erren u.a., 6 October 1965" (Yad Vashem: TR.10/1170).

70. "Erren, G. Statement, 2 November 1960," 7.

71. "H., Johann Statement, 13 October 1965," 5663.

72. Sönke Neitzel and Harald Welzer, *Soldaten: The Secret World of Transcripts of German POWs* (New York: Alfred A. Knopf, 2012), 164–175.

73. "H., Xavier Statement, 30 May 1960" (BA-ZS: B162/5102), 194 [suchte dort meine jüdische Freundin mit Vornamen Ida auf].

74. Because of the ambiguity of the term and to avoid the implication of a fully consensual relationship, "girlfriend" will be placed in quotation marks.

75. See Edward E. Baptist, " 'Cuffy,' 'Fancy Maids,' and 'One-Eyed Men': Rape, Commodification, and the Domestic Slave Trade in the United States," *American Historical Review* 106, no. 5 (2001).

76. "L., Franz Statement, 20 March 1961," 134. A second soldier, Otto Stocker, also testified to Glück's relationship.

77. "S., Otto Statement, 2 February 1960," 12.

78. "A., Erich Statement, 30 April 1960" (BA-ZS: B162/1550), 46.

79. Aichinger was also accused of leading the hanging action in which Stocker was involved.

80. "Orlinski, A. Statement, 14 July 1964," 5658.

81. Ibid.

82. Ibid., 5660.

83. Ibid.

84. Ibid., 5659–5560.

85. Bergen, "Sexual Violence in the Holocaust," 187.

86. Neitzel and Welzer, *Soldaten,* 172.

87. Johannes Winter, "Hauptmann Willi Schulz: Judenretter und Deserteur," in *Retter in Uniform: Handlungsspielräume im Vernichtungskrieg der Wehrmacht,* ed. Norbert Haase and Wolfram Wette (Frankfurt am Main: Fischer Taschenbuch Verlag, 2002), 131.

88. Vincent Brown, *The Reaper's Garden: Death and Power in the World of Atlantic Slavery* (Cambridge, Mass.: Harvard University Press, 2008), 107.

89. Baptist, " 'Cuffy,' 'Fancy Maids,' and 'One-Eyed Men,' " 1644.

90. Neitzel and Welzer, *Soldaten,* 169.

91. Willy Peter Reese and Stefan Schmitz, *A Stranger to Myself: The Inhumanity of War; Russia, 1941–1944,* trans. Michael Hoffmann (New York: Farrar, Straus and Giroux, 2005), 148. Reese was killed in 1944.

92. Neitzel and Welzer, *Soldaten,* 166.

93. "Polenz Suicide Note, 10 May 1961," 14781.

94. "R., Gerda Statement 14 March 1960," 97.

95. "R., Robert Statement, 30 December 1959" (BA-ZS: B162/5088), 55.

96. It is unclear whether Ranger belonged to the 6th Company.

97. "Ness, Robert" (USC Shoah Foundation Institute: Interview no. 5388, Visual History Archive, 2009).

98. "Goldberg, S. Statement, 16 August 1961," 2436.

99. Nachum Alpert, *The Destruction of Slonim Jewry: The Story of the Jews of Slonim during the Holocaust* (New York: Holocaust Library, 1989), 89–90.

100. Ibid., 92.

101. "Small, L. Statement, 9 February 1962" (BA-ZS: B162/5088), 2481.

102. Samuel D. Kassow, *Who Will Write Our History? Emanuel Ringelblum, the Warsaw Ghetto, and the Oyneg Shabes Archive* (Bloomington: Indiana University Press, 2007), 458, 439n.

103. "S., Peter Statement, 5 October 1963" (BA-ZS: B162/3453), 294.

104. "W., Anton Statement, 21 August 1963" (BA-ZS: B162/3454), 394.

105. "Rotstein, I. Statement, 26 September 1962," 293.

106. "Klenicki, R. Statement, 5 February 1962," 2473.

107. "Szepetynski, Z. Statement, 24 June 1965" (BA-ZS: B162/5092), 5711.

108. "Orlinski, A. Statement, 14 July 1964," 5659.

109. "L., Alexander Statement, 6 December 1961" (BA-ZS: B162/5088), 2676.

110. "Small, L. Statement, 9 February 1962," 2480.

111. "K., Willy Statement, 5 December" (BA-ZS: B162/5088), 2168.

112. Dean and Megargee, *Encyclopedia of Camps and Ghettos II,* 1224.

113. An Einsatzgruppen report from 18 August blames a Pole for burning down the brewery in Lida. See Yitzhak Arad, Schmuel Krakowski, and Shmuel Spector, eds., *The Einsatzgruppen Reports: Selections from the Dispatches of the Nazi Death Squads' Campaign against the Jews, July 1941–January 1943* (New York: Holocaust Library, 1989), 92.

114. "L., Joachim Statement, 5 July 1965," 1807; Leon Lauresh and Irene Newhouse, "Pupko Brewery," JewishGen, http://www.shtetlinks.jewishgen.org/Lida-District/lida-city/beer.htm.

115. "Pupko, Shura" (USC Shoah Foundation Institute: Interview no. 37107, Visual History Archive, 2009). Translated by Lindsay MacNeill.

116. "F., Lorenz Statement, 6 July 1965" (BA-ZS: B162/3440), 1811.

117. "Remigolski, S. Statement, 16 October 1947" (Yad Vashem: RG M.21, File 184 [General Committee of the Liberated Jews in the American Occupation Zone-Munich]).

118. "L., Joachim Statement, 5 July 1965," 1808.

119. "Goldfischer, Bella" (USC Shoah Foundation Institute: Interview no. 24412, Visual History Archive, 2009).

120. Sioma Pupko and Sheldon Clare (trans.), "The Story Told by Sioma and Mrs. Pupko," in *Sefer Lida (Book of Lida)*, ed. Alexander Manor, Itzchak Ganusovitch, and Aba Lando (Tel Aviv: Former residents of Lida in Israel and the Committee of Lida Jews in USA, 1970), 311–313.

121. Dean and Megargee, *Encyclopedia of Camps and Ghettos II*, 1227.

122. "F., Lorenz Statement, 6 July 1965," 1811–1812.

123. "L., Joachim Statement, 5 July 1965," 1809.

124. "Stoll [Stolowicki], Michael" (USC Shoah Foundation Institute: Interview no. 23405, Visual History Archive, 2009).

125. Both Lochbihler and Lorenz F. verify this.

126. Dean and Megargee, *Encyclopedia of Camps and Ghettos II*, 1227.

127. "Pupko, Shura." Translation and transcription by Lindsay MacNeill, USHMM.

128. Dean and Megargee, *Encyclopedia of Camps and Ghettos II*, 1226.

129. "L., Joachim Statement, 5 July 1965," 1809–1810.

130. "Pupko, Shura." Translation and transcription by Lindsay MacNeill, USHMM.

131. Peter Duffy, *The Bielski Brothers: The True Story of Three Men Who Defied the Nazis, Saved 1,200 Jews, and Built a Village in the Forest* (New York: HarperCollins, 2003), 149.

132. Pupko and Clare, "Story Told by Sioma and Mrs. Pupko," 311–313.

8. Hunting Jews in Szczuczyn

Epigraphs: "H., Alois Statement, 12 February 1965" (BA-ZS: B162/3438), 1354. "Kirszenbaum, C. Statement, 25 February 1965" (BA-ZS: B162/3438), 1438.

1. "B., Paul Statement, 31 May 1970" (BA-ZS: B162/26286), 185.

2. "N., Ernst Statement, 3 March 1971" (BA-ZS: B162/25111), 91.

3. "B., Paul Statement, 16 September 1971" (BA-ZS: B162/25111), 143.

4. "N., Ernst Statement, 3 March 1971," 91–92. Such an exculpatory detail as shooting over the victim's head likely allowed this man to relate details of a killing in which he had been involved while remaining (in his mind) immune from prosecution.

5. Forty Jews were shot in mid-August at the Drucki-Lubecki palace. Another massacre, this time of the Jewish "intelligentsia" and leadership, was carried out at around the same time. It is quite likely that the 12th Company carried out or assisted in these killings. See Martin Dean and Geoffrey P. Megargee, eds., *Encyclopedia of Camps and Ghettos II: Ghettos in German-Occupied Eastern Europe*, vol. B (Bloomington: Indiana University Press, 2012), 1291.

6. This is not to be confused with the town in Poland of the same name.

7. L. Losh, ed., *Sefer Zikaron Le-Kehilot Szczuczyn Wasiliszki Ostryna Nowy-Dwor Rozanka (Book of Remembrance for the Communities of Shtutshin, Vasilishki, Ostrina, Novi Dvor, and Rozanka)*, trans. Chaim Charutz (Tel Aviv, 1966), 12. Accessed online at http://www.jewishgen.org/Yizkor/szczuczyn-belarus/Szczuczyn.html.

8. Ibid., 89.

9. "Kiefer, J. Statement, 13 August 1970" (BA-ZS: B162/26286), 198.

10. "Kiefer, J. Personalnachweis" (BA-L: DS A 116), 2213.

11. Ibid., 2214, 2220.

12. "Beurteilung für den Oberfeldwebel Kiefer, Josef, 12 July 1940" (BA-L: DS A 116), 2262; "Beurteilung des Leutnant Kiefer, 18 January 1941" (BA-L: DS A 116), 2256.

13. "Beurteilungsnotizen über Leutnant Kiefer, 25 February 1941" (BA-L: DS A 116), 2252.

14. "H., Alois Statement, 2 April 1970" (BA-ZS: B162/26286), 144.

15. "B., Heinrich Statement, 17 February 1970" (BA-ZS: B162/26286), 112.

16. "Kiefer, J. Statement, 13 August 1970," 201.

17. "G., Friedrich Statement, 2 March 1970" (BA-ZS: B162/26286), 118.

18. "H., Ernst Statement, 3 March 1970" (BA-ZS: B162/26286), 122.

19. "H., Alois Statement, 2 April 1970," 147.

20. "L., Franz Statement, 25 May 1970" (BA-ZS: B162/26286), 168.

21. "F., Wilhelm Statement, 15 April 1970" (BA-ZS: B162/26286), 159. This was likely in response to an order from OKW (Keitel) on 13 September 1941. See Christian Gerlach, "German Economic Interests, Occupation Policy, and the Murder of the Jews in Belorussia, 1941/43," in *National Socialist Extermination Policies: Contemporary German Perspectives and Controversies*, ed. Ulrich Herbert (New York: Berghahn Books, 2000), 221.

22. "L., Georg Statement, 16 February 1970" (BA-ZS: B162/26286), 98; "H., Alois Statement, 2 April 1970," 147.

23. "H., Alois Statement, 12 February 1965," 1354.

24. "F., Wilhelm Statement, 15 April 1970," 161.

25. "Schaffitz, E. Statement (Undated)" (BA-ZS: B162/3436), 1175a. The language of this confession indicates that it was perhaps coerced or at least edited by Communist officials. However, Schaffitz's actual behavior in Szczuczyn corroborates in any case the veracity of a statement such as this.

26. "Schaffitz Letter, 26 August 1935" (BA-L: PK K0203), 123.

27. "H., Alois Statement, 2 April 1970," 148–149.

28. "L., Georg Statement, 9 April 1946" (BA-ZS: B162/3436), 1182.

29. Schaffitz died in a Polish prison in 1956, a fate likely not lost upon his former comrades.

30. "M., Johann Statement, 17 March 1970" (BA-ZS: B162/26286), 139.

31. "S., Ludwig Statement, 9 February 1965" (BA-ZS: B162/3438), 1351.

32. "Ritterbusch, O. Statement, 30 September 1970" (BA-ZS: B162/25111), 157.

33. He claimed this was a result of having overstayed a leave. Ibid.

34. "H., Alois Statement, 2 April 1970," 148.

35. "B., Heinrich Statement, 17 February 1970," 113; "L., Franz Statement, 25 May 1970," 169.

36. "B., Paul Statement, 16 September 1971," 145.

37. These were likely elements of the 35th Infantry Division, based on its location on 29 June. See Klaus-Jürgen Thies, *Der Ostfeldzug: Heeresgruppe Mitte, 21.6.1941–*

6.12.1941—ein Lageatlas der Operationsabteilung des Generalstabs des Heeres (Bissendorf: Biblio-Verlag, 2001), 10; Losh, *Sefer Zikaron*, 83.

38. "Moll [Molczadski], William" (USC Shoah Foundation Institute: Interview no. 13573, Visual History Archive, 2009).

39. Szczuczyn does not appear in the Einsatzgruppen reports explicitly. Nearby Lida is frequently mentioned and likely served as a base of operations for an Einsatzkommando. It is highly likely that some of the smaller, earlier killings in Szczuczyn were carried out by this unit. However, on the whole, there were no major killings there. Yitzhak Arad, Schmuel Krakowski, and Shmuel Spector, eds., *The Einsatzgruppen Reports: Selections from the Dispatches of the Nazi Death Squads' Campaign against the Jews, July 1941–January 1943* (New York: Holocaust Library, 1989), 23.

40. "P., Emil Statement 18 October 1961" (BA-ZS: B162/3411), 1115.

41. Dean and Megargee, *Encyclopedia of Camps and Ghettos II*, 1291.

42. "Map: rHGM, 25 July 1941" (BA-MA: RH 26–224), 175.

43. Losh, *Sefer Zikaron*, 84.

44. "Moll [Molczadski], William."

45. "Bakscht, C. Statement, 3 December 1947" (Yad Vashem: RG M.21, File 184 [General Committee of the Liberated Jews in the American Occupation Zone–Munich]).

46. Similar types of hunts took place in Poland, some of them even closely approximating actual sport hunting, with Jews driven by the "hunters" who then shot at them. See Sönke Neitzel and Harald Welzer, *Soldaten: The Secret World of Transcripts of German Pows* (New York: Alfred A. Knopf, 2012), 140–141.

47. "F., Wilhelm Statement, 15 April 1970," 160.

48. "W., Rupert Statement, 26 May 1971" (BA-ZS: B162/25111), 121.

49. "S., Willibald Statement, 8 December 1964" (BA-ZS: B162/3436), 1165–1166.

50. "L., Georg Statement, 28 February 1950" (BA-ZS: B162/3436), 1185.

51. "M., Jakob Statement, 24 May 1971" (BA-ZS: B162/25111), 106.

52. "B., Quirin Statement, 14 April 1970" (BA-ZS: B162/26286), 157.

53. Recall Sergeant Schrade's (12th Company, 354th Infantry) recommendations that reconnaissance for anti-partisan operations be conducted by a small group of native speakers while disguised in civilian clothes.

54. "H., Maximilian Statement, 2 March 1971" (BA-ZS: B162/25111), 85.

55. "M., Johann Statement, 17 March 1970," 139.

56. "B., Franz Statement, 15 April 1970" (BA-ZS: B162/26286).

57. "L., Georg Statement, 9 April 1946," 1182.

58. "Kiefer, J. Statement, 9 December 1964" (BA-ZS: B162/3436), 1172.

59. "L., Georg Statement, 28 February 1950," 1184.

60. "L., Georg Statement, 10 December 1964" (BA-ZS: B162/3436), 1178.

61. "L., Georg Statement, 9 April 1946," 1182. In his 1950 and 1964 testimonies, L. claimed that his 1946 statement had been coerced by American counterintelligence officers and that it had been written for him. It is far more likely that he later regretted his condemnation of former comrades and sought to nullify his own testimony. Despite his protestations, testimony from soldiers and other historical evidence corroborates his statements.

62. "S., Ludwig Statement, 9 February 1965," 1358.

63. "H., Alois Statement, 12 February 1965," 1354.

64. "Kdt. in Weissruthenien, Befehl Nr. 24, 24 Nov. 1941" (BStA Minsk: 378-1-698).

65. "Letter from Oblt. Glück to Geb. Komm. Erren, 4 December 1941" (BStA Minsk: 1450-2-38), 563.

66. Thus, one could make the argument that the November order is a codification of existing policy rather than a directed change.

67. Walter Manoschek, " 'Gehst mit Juden Erschiessen?' Die Vernichtung der Juden in Serbien," in *Vernichtungskrieg: Verbrechen der Wehrmacht 1941–1944*, ed. Hannes Heer and Klaus Naumann (Hamburg: Hamburger Edition, 1995), 39.

68. Ibid., 41.

69. Christopher R. Browning, " 'Judenjagd' Die Schlussphase der 'Endlösung' in Polen," in *Deutsche, Juden, Völkermord: Der Holocaust als Geschichte und Gegenwart*, ed. Klaus-Michael Mallmann and Jürgen Matthäus (Darmstadt: Wissenschaftliche Buchgesellschaft, 2006). Browning also addresses the relative dearth of sources that mention "Jew hunts" *(Judenjagd)*. It seems that, at least in the Wehrmacht case, this can be explained by the fact that such actions were clearly reported as "anti-partisan patrols," though everyone knew their actual meaning.

70. Losh, *Sefer Zikaron*, 84.

71. If they did participate, they likely assisted an element from the Einsatzkommando 9 from Lida.

72. "G., Friedrich Statement, 25 May 1971" (BA-ZS: B162/25111), 110.

73. "Kiefer, J. Statement, 13 August 1970," 206.

74. "M., Johann Statement, 17 March 1970," 137.

75. Kiefer was often gone as acting battalion commander as well as an instructor for officer training courses. It appears he was gone especially during the period of December 1941–February 1942.

76. "H., Alois Statement, 1 March 1971" (BA-ZS: B162/25111), 74. H., as senior ranking NCO, was deeply complicit in the atrocities committed by his company. As such, he, of course, placed all blame on Schaffitz and claimed these killings were for the men "a very uncomfortable thing."

77. "L., Georg Statement, 28 February 1950," 1184.

78. "Kiefer, J. Statement, 13 August 1970," 205.

79. "Kiefer, J. Statement, 9 February 1970" (BA-ZS: B162/25111), 46.

80. "707 ID Officer Personnel List, 15 April 1942" (BA-MA: RH 26-707-5), 60–62.

81. "S., Willibald Statement, 8 December 1964," 1165.

82. "Kiefer, J. Statement, 13 August 1970," 205. It is unclear but likely that she was Jewish.

83. "L., Georg Statement, 28 February 1950," 1185.

84. "Schwartz, G. Statement, 25 July 1993" (Yad Vashem: Document 03/6922). Translated by Shoshana Stiftel. Accessed online at: http://www.shtetlinks.jewishgen.org/Lida-District/yv-shwarz.htm.

85. "Zlocowski, I. Statement, 22 February 1962" (BA-ZS: B162/3426), 642.

86. Ibid.

87. "Schtemplewski, V. Statement, 7 February 1968" (BA-ZS: B162/3427), 988.

88. "L., Georg Statement, 28 February 1950," 1184.

89. "Kirszenbaum, C. Statement, 25 February 1965," 1438.

90. "Weinstein, A. Statement, 25 February 1965" (BA-ZS: B162/3438), 1440.

91. "Schwartz, G. Statement, 25 July 1993."

92. "Losh, L. Statement" (Yad Vashem: Document 03/4378, O33C). Translated by Shoshana Stiftel. Accessed online at http://www.shtetlinks.jewishgen.org/Lida -District/yv-losh.htm.

93. "Weinstein, A. Statement, 25 February 1965," 1440.

94. "Losh, L. Statement."

95. "Kiefer, J. Statement, 9 February 1970," 41–42.

96. "L., Georg Statement, 9 April 1946," 1182.

97. "H., Alois Statement, 2 April 1970," 145.

98. Roy F. Baumeister and W. Keith Campbell, "The Intrinsic Appeal of Evil: Sadism, Sensational Thrills, and Threatened Egotism," *Personality & Social Psychology Review* (Lawrence Erlbaum Associates) 3, no. 3 (1999): 215.

99. Ibid., 216.

100. Ibid., 217.

101. See Leon Festinger, *A Theory of Cognitive Dissonance* (Stanford, CA: Stanford University Press, 1962).

102. Ziva Kunda, *Social Cognition: Making Sense of People* (Cambridge, Mass.: MIT Press, 1999), 217.

103. Elliot Aronson, "Dissonance, Hypocrisy, and the Self-Concept," in *Cognitive Dissonance: Progress on a Pivotal Theory in Social Psychology,* ed. Eddie Harmon-Jones and Judson Mills (Washington, D.C.: American Psychological Association, 1999), 111–112.

104. Fred E. Katz, *Ordinary People and Extraordinary Evil: A Report on the Beguilings of Evil* (Albany: SUNY Press, 1993), 37.

105. Fred E. Katz, *Confronting Evil: Two Journeys* (Albany: SUNY Press, 2004), 75.

106. Klaus Wiegrefe and George Bönich, "Nazi Atrocities, Committed by Ordinary People," *Der Spiegel Online,* 18 March 2008.

9. Endgame

Epigraph: "Pausinger, Josef Statement, 4 May 1961" (BA-ZS: B162/5088), 1447.

1. David M. Glantz and Jonathan M. House, *When Titans Clashed: How the Red Army Stopped Hitler* (Lawrence: University Press of Kansas, 1995), 81.

2. J. Adam Tooze, *The Wages of Destruction: The Making and Breaking of the Nazi Economy* (London: Allen Lane, 2006), 500.

3. "286 SD Memo, 25 January 1942" (BA-MA: RH 26–286–5).

4. One indication, however, of the quality of the 707th Division was that it supplied a sizable number of soldiers to a new elite Ski-Battalion Schlebrügge in January 1942. See "707 ID Tagesbefehl 3/42, 16 January 1942" (BStA Minsk: 378–1–445), 2.

5. Jan Phillipp Reemtsma, Ulrike Jureit, and Hans Mommsen, eds., *Verbrechen der Wehrmacht: Dimensionen des Vernichtungskrieges 1941–1944: Ausstellungskatalog* (Hamburg: Hamburger, 2002), 482.

6. This atrocity is known primarily because an investigation was opened into it after the war. See BA-ZS B162/1550 and B162/1551.

7. Ruth Bettina Birn, "Two Kinds of Reality? Case Studies on Anti-Partisan Warfare during the Eastern Campaign," in *From Peace to War: Germany, Soviet Russia, and the World, 1939–1941,* ed. Bernd Wegner (Providence, R.I.: Berghahn Books, 1997), 290.

8. Georg Tessin, *Verbände und Truppen der deutschen Wehrmacht und Waffen-SS im Zweiten Weltkrieg 1939–1945,* vol. 12 (Osnabrück: Biblio, 1975), 156; Glantz and House, *When Titans Clashed,* 208.

9. Georg Tessin, *Verbände und Truppen der deutschen Wehrmacht und Waffen-SS im Zweiten Weltkrieg 1939–1945,* vol. 9 (Osnabrück: Biblio, 1974), 16.

10. Glantz and House, *When Titans Clashed,* 209.

11. Tessin, *Verbände und Truppen der deutschen Wehrmacht und Waffen-SS im Zweiten Weltkrieg 1939–1945,* 9:214–215.

12. "NS-Verfahren: Bombe los," *Der Spiegel,* 5 April 1971, 100.

13. See Donald Bloxham, *Genocide on Trial: The War Crimes Trials and the Formation of Holocaust History and Memory* (Oxford: Oxford University Press, 2001); Paul Weindling, *Nazi Medicine and the Nuremberg Trials: From Medical War Crimes to Informed Consent* (New York: Palgrave Macmillan, 2004).

14. See Hilary Earl, *The Nuremberg SS-Einsatzgruppen Trial, 1945–1958* (New York: Cambridge University Press, 2009).

15. For some of the latest research on the Ulm trial, see Patrick Tobin, "No Time for 'Old Fighters': Postwar West Germany and the Origins of the 1958 Ulm Einsatzkommando Trial," *Central European History,* no. 44 (2011).

16. Valerie Hebert, *Hitler's Generals on Trial: The Last War Crimes Tribunal at Nuremberg* (Lawrence: University Press of Kansas, 2010), 2.

17. The tribunal did single out the highest commanders in the military. Though it termed the "General Staff and High Command of the German Armed Forces" criminal, the court specifically delineated which individuals comprised this group, ignoring the military as a whole. While membership itself in the SS was a criminal offense, it was not for Wehrmacht veterans. For the text of this statement, see "Nuremberg Trial Proceedings Vol. 1, Indictment: Appendix B," Lillian Goldman Law Library, http://avalon.law.yale.edu/imt/countb.asp.

18. Hebert, *Hitler's Generals on Trial,* 4.

19. Bloxham, *Genocide on Trial,* 131.

20. Robert G. Moeller, *War Stories: The Search for a Usable Past in the Federal Republic of Germany* (Berkeley: University of California Press, 2001), 89.

21. Ibid., 101.

22. Jeffrey Herf, *Divided Memory: The Nazi Past in the Two Germanys* (Cambridge, Mass.: Harvard University Press, 1997), 283.

23. Ibid., 288.

24. Joachim Perels, "Perceptions and Suppression of Nazi Crimes by the Postwar German Judiciary," in *Nazi Crimes and the Law,* ed. Henry Friedlander and Nathan Stoltzfus (New York: Cambridge University Press, 2008), 89.

25. Ingo Müller, *Hitler's Justice: The Courts of the Third Reich,* trans. Deborah Lucas Schneider (Cambridge, Mass.: Harvard University Press, 1991), 257.

26. Adalbert Rückerl, *The Investigation of Nazi Crimes, 1945–1978: A Documentation* (Hamden, Conn.: Archon Books, 1980), 52.

27. Ibid., 43.

28. See Rebecca Elizabeth Wittmann, "The Wheels of Justice Turn Slowly: The Pretrial Investigations of the Frankfurt Auschwitz Trial, 1963–65," *Central European History* 35, no. 3 (2002): 351.

29. The German Supreme Court ruled that the main consideration in distinguishing between murder and lesser charges was the "interest shown in the accomplishment of the deed." This meant that subordinates carrying out orders to murder but without showing "interest in the accomplishment of the crime" were to be charged with the lesser crime of accessory to murder. See Rückerl, *Investigation of Nazi Crimes,* 43.

30. Müller, *Hitler's Justice,* 245.

31. Rebecca Wittmann, "Tainted Law: The West German Judiciary and the Prosecution of Nazi War Criminals," in *Atrocities on Trial: Historical Perspectives on the Politics of Prosecuting War Crimes,* ed. Patricia Heberer and Jürgen Matthäus (Lincoln: University of Nebraska Press, 2008), 220.

32. This small amendment was responsible for catastrophically ending a massive investigation of the perpetrators in the Reich Security Main Office, the bureaucratic organ responsible for planning the Final Solution. The burden of proving base motives for these "desk murderers" was simply too much and gave the prosecution no chance of success. See ibid., 221. For a more detailed discussion of the intricacies of the postwar legal world, see Rebecca Wittmann, *Beyond Justice: The Auschwitz Trial* (Cambridge, Mass.: Harvard University Press, 2005), 36–49.

33. "Recht/NS-Verfahren: Seift und Seift," *Der Spiegel,* 15 February 1971, 79.

34. Perels, "Perceptions and Suppression of Nazi Crimes by the Postwar German Judiciary," 98.

35. Ibid., 96–97.

36. "NS-Verfahren: Bombe los," 100.

37. "Wehrmacht—Härter als üblich," *Der Spiegel,* 12 Aug 1969, 50. For more on the Cephalonia massacre see Richard Lamb, *War in Italy, 1943–1945: A Brutal Story* (New York: St. Martin's Press, 1994), 133.

38. Wittmann, "Tainted Law," 212.

39. This was Georg Heuser of Sonderkommando 1b of Einsatzgruppe B. He went on to command an SD section in Minsk. For a detailed discussion of his postwar career and trial, see Jürgen Matthäus, "'No Ordinary Criminal': Georg Heuser, Other Mass Murderers, and West German Justice," ibid.

40. "NS-Verfahren: Bombe los," 102.

41. "Alte Kameraden," *Der Spiegel,* 28 June 1982, 68.

42. "NS-Verfahren: Bombe los," 100. The prosecutor's office retorted that the DA in question had been working from copies.

43. "Kriegs Verbrechen-Sichergestellte Eier," *Der Spiegel*, 8 May 1972.

44. "Einstellungsverfügung Zst Dortmund 45 Js 9/64 Gg. Waldow U. A., 9 September 1969" (BA-ZS: B162/3911), 717.

45. See ibid.

46. See Irene Sagel-Grande, H. H. Fuchs, and C. F. Rüter, eds., *Justiz und NS-Verbrechen. Sammlung deutscher Strafurteile wegen nationalsozialistischer Tötungsverbrechen 1945–1966*, vol. 20 (Amsterdam: University Press Amsterdam, 1979), 164–184.

47. "Gefangenenpersonalakte Friedrich Nöll 1957–1960" (HSA-D: H 18 Dieburg Nr. 1539).

48. "M., Erich Statement, 19 September 1952" (HSA-D: H 13 Darmstadt, Nr. 979 I, Bd. I), 74.

49. C. F. Rüter, H. H. Fuchs, and Adelheid L. Rüter-Ehlermann, eds., *Justiz und NS-Verbrechen. Sammlung deutscher Strafurteile wegen nationalsozialistischer Tötungsverbrechen 1945–1966*, vol. 12 (Amsterdam: University Press Amsterdam, 1974), 383.

50. "Als Kompaniechef brauchte ich das nicht zu wissen," *Darmstädter Echo*, 2 March 1956.

51. "Zimber Entnazifierungsakte" (StA Freiburg: D180.2, No. 16878).

52. Rüter, Fuchs, and Rüter-Ehlermann, *Justiz und NS-Verbrechen*, 384. In his denazification proceedings, Zimber was given three years' probation. Of course, this court did not know of his activities in the Soviet Union. "Zimber Entnazifierungsakte."

53. "Zimber, E. Letter to the Office of the Delegate for Security, 10 March 1954" (HSA-D: H-13 Darmstadt, Nr. 979 I, Bd. II), 495–496.

54. "Beurteilungsbogen III (Werkdienstbeamter), 23 December 1957" (HSA-D: H-18 Dieburg Nr. 1539); "Gefangenenpersonalakte Friedrich Nöll 1957–1960."

55. "Dieburg Prison Warden Memo to Oberstaatsanwalt Darmstadt, 6 January 1958" (HSA-D: H 18-Dieburg Nr. 1539).

56. "Memo to Hessische Minister für Erziehung U. Volksbildung, 13 June 1953" (HSA-D: H-1, No, 3010), 15; "Memo to Regierungspräsidenten Darmstadt, 2 Nov 1957" (HSA-D: H-1, No, 3010), 52; "Dieburg Prison Warden Memo to Oberstaatsanwalt Darmstadt, 6 January 1958."

57. See "S., Otto Einstellung, 2 February 1961" (BA-ZS: B162/1506). Stocker was also accused of shooting two Jews "while trying to escape," on Glück's orders. The hanging was ruled legal. Moreover, the court ruled that Private S. was following orders, and so the charges against him were dismissed.

58. Ernst Klee, Willi Dressen, and Volker Riess, *"The Good Old Days": The Holocaust as Seen by Its Perpetrators and Bystanders*, 1st U.S. ed. (New York: Free Press, 1991), 291.

59. C. F. Rüter and D. W. De Mildt, eds., *Justiz und NS-Verbrechen. Sammlung deutscher Strafurteile wegen nationalsozialistischer Tötungsverbrechen 1945–1999*, vol. 39 (Amsterdam: Amsterdam University Press, 2008), 672–763. Apparently, the jury had been called for one fiscal year and the trial occurred in the next, invalidating its judgment.

60. "NS-Verfahren: Bombe los," 100.

61. "Diziplinarverfahren—Laute Leitung," *Der Spiegel,* 2 June 1969, 62.

62. Martin Dean and Geoffrey P. Megargee, eds., *Encyclopedia of Camps and Ghettos II: Ghettos in German-Occupied Eastern Europe,* vol. B (Bloomington: Indiana University Press, 2012), 1227.

63. "A., Johann Statement, 22 September 1964" (BA-ZS: B162/3454), 544–545.

64. "Beschluss der 2. Strafkammer des Landgerichts Traunstein gg. Artmann, 11 January 1966" (BA-ZS: B162/3456).

65. "Beschluss der 3. Strafkammer des Landgerichts Tübingen gg. Ritterbusch, 15 September 1972" (BA-ZS: B162/25111).

66. "Urteilsspruch- Bezirksgericht Warschau, 9 December 1948" (BA-ZS: B162/3436), 1191a.

67. "102 ID Div. Befehl, 25 July 1941" (BA-MA: RH 26–102–9), Anl. 348.

68. Peter Longerich, *Holocaust: The Nazi Persecution and Murder of the Jews* (Oxford: Oxford University Press), 221. See BA-ZS B162/3921, B162/3922.

69. These units were poorly equipped, poorly trained reservists incapable of any real military operations.

70. See, for example, Edward B. Westermann, "'Ordinary Men' or 'Ideological Soldiers'? Police Battalion 310 in Russia, 1942," *German Studies Review* 21, no. 1 (1998); Harald Welzer, *Täter: Wie aus ganz normalen Menschen Massenmörder werden* (Frankfurt am Main: S. Fischer, 2005); Christopher R. Browning, *Ordinary Men: Reserve Police Battalion 101 and the Final Solution in Poland,* 1st ed. (New York: HarperCollins, 1992); Christopher R. Browning, "'Judenjagd' die Schlussphase der 'Endlösung' in Polen," in *Deutsche, Juden, Völkermord: Der Holocaust als Geschichte und Gegenwart,* ed. Klaus-Michael Mallmann and Jürgen Matthäus (Darmstadt: Wissenschaftliche Buchgesellschaft, 2006); Jürgen Matthäus, "What about the 'Ordinary Men'? The German Order Police and the Holocaust in the Occupied Soviet Union," *Holocaust and Genocide Studies* 10, no. 2 (1996); Daniel Jonah Goldhagen, *Hitler's Willing Executioners: Ordinary Germans and the Holocaust,* 1st ed. (New York: Alfred A. Knopf, 1996); Wendy Lower, "'Anticipatory Obedience' and the Nazi Implementation of the Holocaust in the Ukraine: A Case Study of Central and Peripheral Forces in the Generalbezirk Zhytomyr, 1941–1944," *Holocaust and Genocide Studies* 16, no. 1 (2002); Edward B. Westermann, "'Friend and Helper': German Uniformed Police Operations in Poland and the General Government, 1939–1941," *Journal of Military History* 58, no. 4 (1994); Helmut Krausnick and Hans-Heinrich Wilhelm, *Die Truppe des Weltanschauungskrieges: Die Einsatzgruppen der Sicherheitspolizei und des SD, 1938–1942* (Stuttgart: Deutsche Verlags-Anstalt, 1981); Martin Cüppers, *Wegbereiter der Shoah: Die Waffen-SS, der Kommandostab Reichsführer-SS und die Judenvernichtung 1939–1945* (Darmstadt: Wissenschaftliche Buchgesellschaft, 2005), OCLC Number: 59080200; Andrej Angrick and Ulrich Prehn, *Besatzungspolitik und Massenmord: Die Einsatzgruppe D in der südlichen Sowjetunion 1941–1943* (Hamburg: Hamburger Edition, 2003).

71. These were the 7th ID, 28th ID, 78th ID, 252nd ID, 102nd ID, 112th ID, 87th ID, 258th ID, 206th ID, 162nd ID, and 197th ID, 221st SD, and 403rd SD.

72. "252 ID Message from Division Commander, 29 September 1941" (BA-MA: RH 26-252-77).

73. "252 ID Message from Division Commander, 12 December 1941" (BA-MA: RH 26-252-79).

74. "258 ID Ic Report, 15 August 1941" (BA-MA: RH 26-258-45).

75. "350 IR Bericht, 19.8.1941" (BA-MA: RH 22-221), 295.

76. "87 ID Minsk Situation Report, 25 July 1941" (BA-MA: RH 26-87-25).

77. Christian Gerlach, "German Economic Interests, Occupation Policy, and the Murder of the Jews in Belorussia, 1941/43," in *National Socialist Extermination Policies: Contemporary German Perspectives and Controversies*, ed. Ulrich Herbert (New York: Berghahn Books, 2000), 217.

78. "102 ID, Kriegstagebuch, 13 July 1941" (BA-MA: RH 26-102-5).

79. "78 ID Div. Befehl, 3 November 1941" (BA-MA: RH 26-78-29).

80. "252 ID Div. Befehl, 26 July 1941" (BA-MA: RH 26-252-75), 67.

81. "87 ID Minsk Situation Report, 25 July 1941."

82. "221 SD Memo: Strassen- und Brückenerkundung, 21 September 1941" (BA-MA: RH 26-221-14b), 727.

83. "102 ID Anl. 3, Merkblatt für die Versorgung beim Einsatz als Sich. Div., 19 July 1941" (BA-MA: RH 26-102-9), Anl. 320.

84. "rHGM Tagesmeldung, 15 July 1941" (BA-MA: RH 22-226), 6.

85. "232 IR Report to 102 ID, 20 July 1941" (BA-MA: RH 26-102-9), Anl. 318.

86. "232 IR Report to 102 ID, 22 July 1941" (BA-MA: RH 26-102-9), Anl. 323.

87. "162 ID Gefärhdung der Versorgung, 17 August 1941" (BA-MA: RH 26-162-10).

88. "102 ID Anl. 3, Merkblatt für die Versorgung beim Einsatz als Sich. Div., 19 July 1941," Anl. 320.

89. "87 ID Kriegestagebuch, 20 July 1941" (BA-MA: RH 26-87-22).

90. "252 ID Div. Befehl 10, 16 July 1941" (BA-MA: RH 26-252-75).

91. "252 ID Kriegestagebuch, 17 July 1941" (BA-MA: RH 26-252-73).

92. "87 ID Div. Befehl, 6 August 1941" (BA-MA: RH 26-87-25), 3.

93. EM 43, 5 August 1941, in *The Einsatzgruppen Reports: Selections from the Dispatches of the Nazi Death Squads' Campaign against the Jews, July 1941–January 1943*, ed. Yitzhak Arad, Schmuel Krakowski, and Shmuel Spector, eds. (New York: Holocaust Library, 1989), 67.

94. These were the 87th ID, 102nd ID, 162nd ID, and 252nd ID. See, for example, 6/23, 6/27, 7/19, and 7/28 in "Kommandostab Rfss Kriegestagebuch" (USHMM: RG-48.004M, 1993.A.0019), Reel 1.

95. See ibid.; Cüppers, *Wegbereiter der Shoah*, 138.

96. Cüppers, *Wegbereiter der Shoah*, 150.

97. "258 ID XII Armeekorps Befehl, 27 September 1941" (BA-MA: RH 26-258-46).

98. "162 ID Div. Befehl, 14 August 1941" (BA-MA: RH 26-162-10), Anl. 74.

99. "87 ID Div. Memorandum, 8 July 1941" (BA-MA: RH 26-87-25).

100. "Div. Befehl für die Vorbereitung der vorgesehenen Operationen, 25 September 1941" (BA-MA: RH 26-162-10), 102.

101. "252 ID Div. Commander Message, 23 August 1941" (BA-MA: RH 26-252-75), 33.

102. "102 ID Kriegestagebuch, 7 July 1941" (BA-MA: RH 26-102-5).

103. "28 ID Memo Partisanenbekämpfung, 16 September 1941" (BA-MA: RH 26-28-20).

104. "78 ID Besondere Anordnungen zum Div. Befehl 38/41, 20 August 1941" (BA-MA: RH 26-78-29).

105. "78 ID Div. Befehl 34/41, 12 August 1941" (BA-MA: RH 26-78-29).

106. "207 SD Memo: Regelung des Einsatzes der Sicherheitspolizei und des SD im Verbande des Heeres, 22 July 1941" (BA-ZS: B162/3300), 792.

107. Sönke Neitzel, *Tapping Hitler's Generals: Transcripts of Secret Conversations, 1942–45,* trans. Geoffrey Brooks (Barnsley, UK: Frontline, 2007), 195, Document 111, 11–12 Oct. 1944.

108. "112 ID, Ic Tätigskeitberichte, 25 May–31 December 1941" (BA-MA: RH 26-112-74), 32.

109. Birn, "Two Kinds of Reality?" 291.

110. "102 ID Div. Befehl Nr. 23, 13 August 1941" (BA-MA: RH 26-102-61), Anl. 7.

111. "102 ID Div. Befehl Nr. 27, 25 August 1941" (BA-MA: RH 26-102-61), Anl. 30.

112. Yitzhak Arad, *The Holocaust in the Soviet Union* (Lincoln: University of Nebraska Press, 2009), 174.

113. Neitzel, *Tapping Hitler's Generals,* 189, Document 103, 27 July–8 Aug. 1944.

114. Gitta Sereny, *Into That Darkness: An Examination of Conscience* (New York: Vintage Books, 1983), 158–159.

115. Sönke Neitzel and Harald Welzer, *Soldaten: The Secret World of Transcripts of German POWs* (New York: Alfred A. Knopf, 2012), 121.

116. "Fk 551 Report to 252 ID, 22 July 1941" (BA-MA: RH 26-252-75), 53.

117. "252 ID to rHGM: Meldung der Feld-Kdtr. 551 V.22.7.1941, 23 July 1941" (BA-MA: RH 26-252-75), 54. Christopher Browning quotes at length a similar altercation between killing units and administrators that took place on 27 October 1941 in Slutsk. There, Order Police units murdered "indispensable" Jewish workers without prior coordination. Christopher R. Browning, *Ordinary Men: Reserve Police Battalion 101 and the Final Solution in Poland* (New York: Harper Perennial, 1998), 19–20.

118. Neitzel and Welzer, *Soldaten,* 126.

119. Klee, Dressen, and Riess, *"Good Old Days,"* 143.

120. "Sibille Letter, 2.2.1953" (HSA-D: H-13 Darmstadt, Nr. 979 I, Bd. III), 208.

121. See, for example, Detlef Bald and Wolfram Wette, *Zivilcourage: Empörte, Helfer und Retter aus Wehrmacht, Polizei und SS* (Frankfurt am Main: Fischer Taschenbuch, 2004); Norbert Haase and Wolfram Wette, eds., *Retter in Uniform: Handlungsspielräume im Vernichtungskrieg der Wehrmacht* (Frankfurt am Main: Fischer Taschenbuch, 2002).

122. For more on Plagge, see Michael Good, *The Search for Major Plagge: The Nazi Who Saved Jews* (New York: Fordham University Press, 2005); Karl-Heinz Schoeps, "Holocaust and Resistance in Vilnius: Rescuers in 'Wehrmacht' Uniforms," *German Studies Review* 31, no. 3 (2008).

123. Good, *Search for Major Plagge,* 223.

124. "Goldberg, S. Statement, 16 August 1961" (BA-ZS: B162/5088), 2434.

125. Arno Lustiger, "Feldwebel Anton Schmid—Judenretter in Wilna 1941–1942," in Haase and Wette, *Retter in Uniform*.
126. Ibid., 62–63.
127. Ibid., 48.
128. See Hermine Wüllner, "Leutnant Reinhold Lothy—Mordtaten Verweigert," ibid.
129. See Jakob Knab, "Empörung über den weltanschaulichen Vernichtungskrieg im Osten: Der katholische Leutnant Michael Kitzelmann," in Bald and Wette, *Zivilcourage*.

Conclusion

1. Walter Bähr and Hans Walter Bähr, *Kriegsbriefe Gefallener Studenten, 1939–1945* (Tübingen: R. Wunderlich, 1952), 244.
2. More recent scholarship has recognized the imperial and colonial nature of Nazi expansion. See, for example, Wendy Lower, *Nazi Empire-Building and the Holocaust in Ukraine* (Chapel Hill: University of North Carolina Press, 2005).
3. Michael Burleigh, *The Third Reich: A New History* (New York: Hill & Wang, 2000), 432–433.
4. Sönke Neitzel and Harald Welzer, *Soldaten: The Secret World of Transcripts of German POWs* (New York: Alfred A. Knopf, 2012), 238.
5. Daniel Uziel, "Wehrmacht Propaganda Troops and the Jews," Shoah Resource Center, the International School for Holocaust Studies, 2–3.
6. This number most likely exaggerates the actual number of soldier viewings, even when including the same soldier seeing multiple films. "Die Arbeit der Partei-Propaganda im Kriege," *Unser Wille und Weg*, 1941.
7. Neitzel and Welzer, *Soldaten*, 146.
8. Irene Guicking, Ernst Guicking, and Jürgen Kleindienst, *Sei Tausendmal Gegrüsst: Briefwechsel Irene und Ernst Guicking 1937–1945*, Reihe Zeitgut. Spezial; 1 (Berlin: JKL Publikationen, 2001), CD.
9. Neitzel and Welzer, *Soldaten*, 237.
10. Ibid.
11. See Omer Bartov, *Hitler's Army: Soldiers, Nazis, and War in the Third Reich* (New York: Oxford University Press, 1991). 159.
12. I refer here to the heated and often polemic debate beginning in the 1980s between intentionalism (the idea that Hitler and his followers knew and intended from the beginning that the objective of the Final Solution would be the physical extermination of the Jews) and functionalism (the belief that Nazi genocidal policy evolved over time through the many decisions of various actors and institutions, without a master plan). A second iteration of this debate occurred between Christopher Browning and Daniel Goldhagen. Their respective books *Ordinary Men* and *Hitler's Willing Executioners* drew wildly divergent conclusions from the same source base, with Browning highlighting situational and psychological factors and Goldhagen crediting ideology for killing. Most historians found Browning's interpretation convincing and Goldhagen's deeply flawed, both conceptually and historically.
13. "R., Georg Statement, 1 October 1963" (BA-ZS: B162/3453), 282.

14. "W., Leopold Statement, 29 July 1953" (HSA-D: H-13 Darmstadt, Nr. 919 I, Bd. II), 326.

15. For a more detailed discussion of individual responses to killing, see Waitman W. Beorn, "Negotiating Murder: A Panzer Signal Company and the Destruction of the Jews of Peregruznoe, 1942," *Holocaust and Genocide Studies* 23, no. 2 (2009).

16. "M., Richard Statement, 21 July 1966" (BA-ZS: B162/3876), 602.

17. See, for example, the work of Thomas Kühne: *Kameradschaft: Die Soldaten des nationalsozialistischen Krieges und das 20. Jahrhundert* (Göttingen: Vandenhoeck & Ruprecht, 2006), and "Male Bonding and Shame Culture: Hitler's Soldiers and the Moral Basis of Genocidal Warfare," in *Ordinary People as Mass Murderers: Perpetrators in Comparative Perspectives,* ed. Olaf Szejnmann Claus-Christian W. Jensen (New York: Palgrave Macmillan, 2008).

18. "Magel, Wilhelm Statement, 16 June 1951" (HSA-D: H-13 Darmstadt, Nr. 979 I, Bd. I), 163.

19. "L., Wilhelm Statement, 9 August 1951" (HSA-D: H-13 Darmstadt, Nr. 979 I, Bd. I), 175.

20. See again Kühne, *Kameradschaft.*

21. Nechama Tec, "Righteous Gentiles," in *The Holocaust: Problems and Perspectives of Interpretation,* ed. Donald L. Niewyk (Boston: Wadsworth, 2011), 217.

22. "L., Joachim Statement, 5 July 1965" (BA-ZS: B162/3440), 1807.

23. "Remigolski, S. Statement, 16 October 1947" (Yad Vashem: RG M.21, File 184 [General Committee of the Liberated Jews in the American Occupation Zone–Munich]).

24. Anna Mulrine, "Pentagon Had Red Flags about Command Climate in 'Kill Team' Stryker Brigade," *Christian Science Monitor,* 28 October 2010.

25. Craig Whitlock, "Brigade's Strategy: 'Strike and Destroy,'" *Washington Post,* 14 October 2010.

26. Willy Peter Reese and Stefan Schmitz, *A Stranger to Myself: The Inhumanity of War; Russia, 1941–1944,* trans. Michael Hoffmann (New York: Farrar, Straus and Giroux, 2005), xv.

Acknowledgments

This book is the culmination of six years of research and writing. Throughout, I have been the recipient of a great deal of support from a great many people who deserve to be recognized. First, I would like to thank my wife, Christina Frances Mobley, an excellent historian in her own right, who not only read draft after draft of this text and provided me with constructive criticism; she even contributed to the content by discovering and following up on stories she found compelling. Moreover, she accompanied me to Moscow in December; I cannot think of a truer indication of spousal dedication. In addition, I owe my love of history and of writing to my parents, Charles and Leanne Beorn, whose countless trips to museums and historical sites and endless gifts of books stoked my intellectual curiosity. We were (and remain) the family that methodically reads every line of every exhibit.

I owe an incredible debt to my other "father," my adviser at the University of North Carolina–Chapel Hill, Professor Christopher R. Browning. It is rare for a scholar of his stature to take the time and interest in his advisees that Chris does. His professional and scholarly mentorship and guidance have had an inestimable impact on my life. I would be remiss to not mention the personal and professional value of the fantastic dinners and conversations with Chris and his better half, Jenni, over glasses of always amazing wine and home-cooked meals. I owe a similar debt of gratitude to Konrad H. Jarausch at UNC for his always insightful and valuable criticism and encouragement. Joe Glatthaar, Karen Hagemann, and Donald Raleigh also represented the best that UNC has to offer as readers for my project in its most embryonic form. In addition, I am grateful for the support and advice of Professor Dr. Michael Mallmann, who served as my adviser in Germany. This manuscript further benefited from the feedback given by Hilary Earl and Edward Westermann, who read portions of it. Robert Citino also provided astute critiques and advice. The Holocaust Geographies group, which took me on when I was but a graduate student, has contributed to this final product in ways that they probably cannot imagine by helping me to reconceptualize and to broaden my intellectual boundaries; many thanks to my colleagues Tim Cole, Simone Gigliotti, Alberto Giordano, Anna Holian, Paul B. Jaskot, Anne Kelly Knowles, Marc Masurovsky, and Erik Steiner. I must single out Anne in particular for her amazing ability to help an author think through and verbalize difficult theoretical concepts over a cup of tea.

I have been incredibly fortunate to have had the support of three great museums dedicated to memorializing and researching the Holocaust. It is not possible for me to express enough my gratitude to the United States Holocaust Memorial Museum for its support and interest in my project. I am particularly indebted to Peter Black, Judy Cohen, Martin Dean, Geoff Megargee, Gretchen Skidmore, Jennifer Ciardelli, and Lindsay MacNeill for their guidance, interest, and helpful answers to seemingly infinite requests for more information. I also appreciate the research work of Andre Becker on their behalf. Likewise, I have been honored to both learn and teach with the Museum of Jewish Heritage in New York City, and for that I must thank David Marwell and Shiri Sandler for their tireless support. Lastly, I must thank Eliot Nidam, David Silberklang, and Arkadi Zeltser for their scholarly assistance and personal hospitality at Yad Vashem in Jerusalem.

I am also incredibly fortunate to have found a home both academic and physical at the University of Nebraska at Omaha and have already benefited greatly from the warm and generous welcome there. I very much appreciate the support of the History Department in the final stages of this project. I am also forever the better for having found a new friend in the indomitable Sam Fried, Auschwitz survivor and Omaha resident, and his wife, Frances, whose tireless dedication to educating future generations about the Holocaust and other genocides continues to inspire me.

Entering the archives and conducting primary historical research can often be like learning to swim. One simply has to jump in and start flailing around until someone throws you a line. I am eternally grateful to the following dedicated archival professionals without whom my discoveries might well have remained neatly filed away: Dr. Tobias Hermann and my Kurdish friend Sidar Toptanci at the Zentral Stelle in Ludwigsburg, Judy Cohen and the others mentioned above at the USHMM, the staff of the Bundesarchiv-Militärarchiv Freiburg, the Bundesarchiv-Lichterfelde, the Hessischesstaatsarchiv Darmsadt, the Landesarchiv Nordrhein-Westfalen Münster, the Belarussian State Archive Minsk, and Yad Vashem.

For my research in Belarus, I am eternally grateful for the logistical and professional assistance provided by Frank Swartz, director of the East European Jewish Heritage project, and Vadim Osvyanik, without whose skills as an interpreter my work would have been simply impossible. I am also incredibly thankful for the work of Yauheniya Spallino-Mironava, a fantastically talented UNC graduate student, whose family, in a spectacular stroke of luck, hails from Krupki. Not only did Jenya translate various documents for me from Belarusian, but she also undertook at her own expense a trip to visit her relatives and conduct oral interviews for me. These interviews have added a depth to this project that would have been impossible without her help.

While the intellectual and archival guidance I have received allowed this book to be imagined, it could not have been created without the generous financial support I have received from the following organizations: the Fulbright Foundation, the Harry Frank Guggenheim Foundation, the National Science Foundation, the Holocaust Education Foundation and the amazing Zev Weiss, the Conference on Jewish Material Claims against Germany, the Society for Military History, the American Historical Association, the German Historical Institute, the United States Holocaust Memorial Museum, the Museum of Jewish Heritage, and the University of North Carolina–Chapel Hill.

The subject of participation in the Holocaust can be a particularly sensitive one. I am incredibly fortunate to have found several relatives of German soldiers in this study willing to share their family's history with me. I would like to offer heartfelt thanks to the Bergers, Nölls, and Sibilles for their kindness and openness. I would also like to thank the family of Jenya Spallino for sharing their memories as well.

Finally, I would like to thank my editors, Kathleen McDermott and Andrew Kinney for expertly guiding me through every step of the process of publishing. I would also like to recognize copy editors Glenn Novak and Pamela Nelson and my indexer, Michael Grutchfield, for helping me to polish this final product. All errors remaining in the text are mine alone.

Index

Abramovich, Luba, 139, 140, 143, 144, 148
Abramson, Henry, 36
Adorno, Theodore, 17
Agency, 7–8, 231, 233, 240–242
Aichinger, Erich, 151, 168–170, 176–177
Alcohol, use of by perpetrators, 135, 173; by
  SS, 72, 75; by Glück, 140, 146; by
  Aichinger, 169–170
Alpert, Nachum, 145, 174–175
Amelung, Waldemar, 142, 146, 148–149, 154
Anti-partisan war, 8, 50, 56, 70, 225,
  269n9; interconnected with Holocaust,
  7, 56, 118; during invasion of Poland, 48;
  orders regarding, 60–61, 95, 227; and
  "tactical muscle memory," 85–86, 113;
  tactics of, 98–99, 101, 112–113, 191–192,
  207–208, 224; as "bandit fighting"
  (Bandenbekämpfung), 116–117, 274n104.
  See also Mogilev Conference; Partisan
  movement; names of specific formations

Antisemitism: under Stalin, 28, 33; in
  Russian empire, 31–32; in World War
  I German occupation, 32; in prewar
  Poland, 34–35; in Belarus, 36, 66, 78,
  139; in traditional German army, 45–46;
  and anti-Communism, 50, 51, 53;
  institutionalized by Wehrmacht, 57–59,
  93, 219–220, 235–237; in Wehrmacht
  soldiers, 86, 111, 224–225, 235, 237–238;
  in occupation officers, 140–141, 188–189,
  220–221; slurs, used by Wehrmacht
  soldiers, 200, 202–203; and concentration camp guards, 204
Army Group Center (Rear) (rückwärtige
  Heeresgebiet Mitte/rHGM), 67, 95, 120,
  137, 207, 208; collaboration with SS, 54,
  56–57, 80–81, 98, 107, 219; orders
  regarding Jewish laborers, 57, 222,
  229–230; organizational culture, 70, 81,
  86, 103, 220–229; headquarters, 92, 94,

CPSIA information can be obtained
at www.ICGtesting.com
Printed in the USA
BVHW041436200223
658107BV00007B/82/J

9 780674 725508